PARLIAMENTARY REPRESENTATION

by

J. F. S. ROSS

Second (Enlarged) Edition

London 1948

EYRE & SPOTTISWOODE

15 Bedford Street, W.C.2

First published November 1943
Second impression July 1944
Second (enlarged) edition 1948

*This book is produced in complete conformity
with the Authorized Economy Standards and
is made and printed in Great Britain for
Eyre and Spottiswoode (Publishers) Limited,
15 Bedford Street, London, W.C. 2, by
Billing and Sons Ltd., Guildford and Esher*
F8130

PREFACE TO THE SECOND EDITION

THE General Election of 1945 and other happenings since this book was first published have necessitated a substantial expansion in this new edition. It is hoped that the new matter, and its arrangement in a separate Part IV, will commend themselves to the reader. I regret that the appearance of the new edition has been so long delayed; but (apart from the many difficulties with which publishers and printers have in these days to contend) the labour entailed in making such an analysis is extremely heavy, and a writer who has to depend on his own unaided efforts cannot hope to bring it to as speedy a conclusion as he would wish—especially when the work has to be done in somewhat scanty leisure.

No pains have been spared to maintain a high standard of accuracy, and it is hoped that if any errors have crept in they will prove to be of a minor character.

I desire to acknowledge the kindness of the many members of parliament who were good enough to answer the questionnaire I sent them, and the help I received from Pilot Press Ltd. in sending it out.

Finally I should like to take this opportunity of expressing my warm appreciation of the generous reception accorded to the book by critics, members of parliament, and the general public. The many interesting letters and papers that I have received from correspondents all over the world have given me much pleasure and proved very helpful.

J. F. S. ROSS

SOUTHPORT,
July, 1947

PREFACE TO THE FIRST EDITION

THIS book, planned and commenced in March 1933, represents the results of nearly ten years of detailed investigation and thought. I believe that the method it employs of basing proposals for political change not on abstract theories but on the plain facts of the case closely studied is extremely valuable, if not essential, in the difficulties and complexities of modern civilization.

The subject of parliamentary representation occupies a key position in our scheme of democratic government, and I believe that it is vitally important to remedy the serious defects from which that representation now suffers. Nevertheless, I disclaim any intention of suggesting that the reforms I propose would bring about a political millennium or provide a panacea for all the ills of our democratic institutions. My aims and beliefs are far more modest but, I hope, not less worthy of consideration on that account.

I am under no illusion that the work is free from flaws and minor inaccuracies, but I have been at pains to verify my facts as closely as the means at my disposal have permitted, and I have tried to present them with exactness and candour.

I have acknowledged in an appendix the chief sources from which my data have been compiled. It only remains for me to thank the friends and correspondents who have been kind enough to answer my enquiries and to give me information on various points, including amongst others Lord Windlesham, Mr. W. R. Davies, Mr. J. S. Middleton, Mr. G. R. Shepherd, Mr. Ian Harvey, and Mr. J. H. Humphreys. My special thanks are due to Mr. Douglas Jerrold for salutary criticisms of the book in manuscript. It should hardly be necessary to add that none of these gentlemen has any responsibility whatever for the conclusions reached or the opinions expressed in the book. Finally, my thanks are due to the University of London for a grant from its Publication Fund in aid of publication.

J. F. S. ROSS

Southport,
February, 1943

CONTENTS

PART I

THE PERSONNEL OF PARLIAMENT

PART II

CAUSE AND EFFECT

PART III

A SCHEME OF REFORM

PART IV

THE NEW ERA

"The fact that the British Parliament is ceasing to be an efficient instrument for the government of a modern community has become . . . patent and painful to the more intelligent among politicians themselves. . . ."

H. G. WELLS: *The Work, Wealth, and Happiness of Mankind.*

"Unquestionably there are, in several quarters, indications of a feeling . . . that the House of Commons . . . no longer adequately represents the varied interests which go to make up the nation as a whole."

SIR J. A. R. MARRIOTT: *The Mechanism of the Modern State.*

"During the past fifty years the British Parliament has become progressively less efficient."

W. IVOR JENNINGS: *Parliamentary Reform.*

"There is every year less and less personal independence among members of Parliament: every year they are more and more disposed to vote strictly as their party whips direct."

LORD HUGH CECIL: *Conservatism.*

"In short, the action of the House of Commons has tended to become more and more party action. . . . The party cabal has become the Treasury Bench."

A. L. LOWELL: *The Government of England.*

"The thesis is universally admitted that the legislatures of the modern state are in an unsatisfactory condition; it is, indeed, some of the stoutest defenders of the parliamentary system who demand their reconstruction."

H. J. LASKI: *Democracy in Crisis.*

"Misgivings about the working of the parliamentary system of government have been spreading and deepening. . . . Can we not, in this crisis, rise above mere calculations of party advantage, and strive to turn our system into a just and efficient machine of government?"

RAMSAY MUIR: *How Britain is Governed.*

"Let us stop being subjective and traditional—let us discount our own ideas, our experience, our beliefs and set notions, and start out to *find out*, in the impersonal, detached, attitude of science."

For Top Executives Only (BUSINESS BOURSE, New York, 1936).

"The light of day thrusts between our eyelids, and the multitudinous sounds of morning clamour in our ears. A time will come when men will sit with history before them or with some old newspaper before them and ask incredulously 'Was there ever such a world?'"

H. G. WELLS: *What are We to do with Our Lives?*

CHAPTER I

INTRODUCTION

IN recent years dissatisfaction with the working of the parliamentary system has been widespread. It is unnecessary to instance the disasters the system has suffered in Italy, in Germany, and elsewhere. In Britain and in America, to go no farther afield, criticism of representative institutions has come from all sides, and has given evidence that it is based on deep-seated uneasiness and is not merely superficial or factitious. If, at the moment, the voice of the critic is less audible, that is rather because attention is directed elsewhere than because there is any real recovery of confidence in the system. The tense international situation —revolutions and dictatorships: wars and the fear of wars: rearmament and defence: one crisis succeeding another—these and other happenings have tended to divert attention from the defects of the parliamentary system, even though some of the happenings have thrown new light on those defects.

Temporary loss of interest in a problem, however, does not constitute a solution of it: and this problem is of far-reaching importance and essentially urgent. A case can, indeed, be made out for considering that the defects of our parliamentary system constitute a major cause of our most acute political troubles, international as well as national.* Be that as it may, we cannot afford to disregard the evidence that the system is not working well. With the adequacy of democratic institutions widely questioned and their efficiency unfavourably compared with that of the totalitarian dictatorships, it behoves upholders of representative government to see that it has a fair chance to function properly. Nay, more; we must see that government *is* representative, that we are not fobbed off with a spurious article, that we do not allow oligarchy to masquerade as democracy.

For the failure of parliament to conform to our ideals and fulfil our expectations many causes have been assigned, over a long period, and many remedies have been propounded. Restricted suffrage, open voting, the inequality of constituencies, plural voting, wrong methods of voting, the high cost of elections, the expense attendant on membership, the excessive size of the House of Commons, its antiquated and time-wasting procedure, its subordination to the executive government and to the party whips, the misconception of its functions, the existence of the second chamber, the absurd inadequacy and inconvenience of its accommodation at Westminster—all these, and other, causes have been blamed, not forgetting the enormous growth in the scope and complexity of the problems of government.

Some of these causes have been removed, in whole or part, by such reforms (or at any rate changes) as adult suffrage, voting by ballot, redistribution of seats, limitation of election expenses, payment of mem-

* See, for instance, S. R. Daniels, *The Case for Electoral Reform* (1938), section 1.

bers, and modifications of procedure, such as the closure. Good or bad, however, these changes have not sufficed to produce the desired efficiency, and many others have been advocated. New methods of voting, the abolition of the second chamber, the creation of two parliaments, political and social, side by side, the devolution of functions to regional or other bodies, the adoption of the standing-committee system, and the drastic reform of procedure, are amongst the proposals that have received publicity and been discussed widely, if not well. Much of the discussion, however, has been vitiated by the lack of either accurate knowledge or clear thinking.

Amidst all this welter of criticism and exhortation one aspect of the problem has received little attention. We discuss theories of representation and methods of voting, the arts of canvassing and electioneering, the intricacies of procedure that new members of parliament have to master, their functions as members, their relations to their constituents, to their parties, to the government: anything and everything about members—except the members themselves.

It is astonishing that so little regard should be paid to the *personnel* of parliament. What sort of people do we choose to represent us? What qualifications for their duties do our members possess? How are they selected as candidates in the first case? Why are these kinds of people chosen and not others? Taking the whole House together, what are its outstanding personal characteristics? There is little interest shown in these questions and little information available, beyond the potted biographies of individuals that the newspapers and books of reference give us; and these, as they stand, do not answer our questions.

Moreover, these questions suggest others. What sort of people *should* we have to represent us in parliament? Do we need people who are in some way specially qualified, people of special gifts, special attainments, or special experience? Or do we require, as Professor Laski asserts, nothing more than "an average sample of ordinary men"?* Do we, as a matter of fact, ever seriously consider what sort of people should be in parliament? Are we not, perhaps, content if we are represented by a member of our own party, satisfied to let it go at that without too close a scrutiny of the member's personal fitness?

No doubt, other things being equal, whoever chooses the candidates who appear before us will select those who are in their opinion the "best" available. No doubt, if other things were equal—which in practice they never are, the claims of party being so strong—electors would vote for the candidates who were in their opinions the "best" of those nominated. This, however, does not help us. By *what* standards are candidates selected? What is the criterion of "goodness" as a candidate?

May it not be that in this neglected question of the personnel of representation is to be found one of the root causes of the malaise and inefficiency that so obviously afflict democratic government and bring parliamentary institutions into disrepute? To suggest this is not to

* H. J. Laski, *Democracy in Crisis* (1933), chapter II.

imply that the better-known criticisms of parliament are unfounded. Some of them are plainly to the point: as, for instance, those of the gross inefficiency and waste of valuable time involved in a parliamentary "division"—an antiquated piece of procedure that is an astonishing example of cumbrous ineptitude.* Nor is it to suggest that the question of personnel can be treated in a vacuum, apart from other problems of representation. On the contrary, it is clear that this question is closely bound up with such problems as those of electoral method, election expenses, and payment of members, and (less directly) of procedure and constitutional practice.

I suggest, then, that the whole question of parliamentary representation requires reconsideration, and that it should be approached from a new angle—namely, that of a study of the actual personnel of the House of Commons. I suggest that we need first and foremost to ascertain the *facts* of representation. Instead of starting with philosophical theories we should first look, with our eyes open, at these 602† men and women who are elected to represent us. Who are they? What are they? Why are we represented by these kinds of people, and not by other kinds? Are these the people best fitted for the job?—and, if not, why do we give it to them?

When we have really found out the facts, when we know something definite of the hitherto neglected natural history of the genus M.P., we shall be in a better position to criticize the laws and customs that have evolved that genus and that now perpetuate it. When we know what *is* we can better determine what *ought to be*. In these days to evolve political theories out of our inner consciousness, disregarding the stubborn facts that stare us in the face, is to write ourselves off as the belated and ineffective survivors of the mediæval schoolmen. What is needed above all things in the initial approach to these, and most other, political problems of the day is not the rhetoric of the professional politician, or the flowing periods of the academic theorizer, but the objective analysis of the researcher.

This book is written, then, in the belief that a great part of the social, political, and economic unrest that disturbs us to-day and that offers so serious a menace to the development, and even to the survival, of civilization owes its existence to the neglect of scientific method: for that method, so astonishingly and overwhelmingly successful in the solution of material (technological) problems, has hardly been applied at all in the sphere of human relations.

It is, indeed, widely recognized that the exploitation of the material resources of the world has outstripped its moral and political development, so that we have bishops suggesting that scientists and inventors should cease their activities for a period of years. But such suggestions, apart from their obvious practical futility, miss the point altogether. The trouble is not that material progress has been too rapid, but that

* See, on this point, H. G. Wells, *The Work, Wealth, and Happiness of Mankind* (1932), pages 573-4.
† Excluding the "six counties" members.

social and political progress has been too slow. The remedy does not lie in Canutian injunctions to the rising tide of scientific knowledge and invention—that will not be stayed by ecclesiastical adjurations—but in the intensive development of modern methods in sociology and politics.

This has been said before; indeed, it has been said many times in recent years. But it has not received any general acceptance, and least of all from politicians. As a rule they ignore contentions of this kind altogether, but if they do notice them it is only to brush them aside contemptuously. Even serious and able writers on political and social questions seem all too often content with methods of approach that in physical science and in technology were discarded as obsolete a century or more ago. Some of them seem, indeed, unable to conceive that any other methods are possible.

There are, moreover, even to-day, all too many people who have no conception of what constitutes the scientific spirit, of what is meant by scientific method. For them science means physics and chemistry, and the scientific attitude, if it means anything at all, is taken to connote materialism and an indifference, or even hostility, to the finer but less tangible things of the mind and spirit.

For their benefit, and with apologies to better-informed readers, let it be said that the scientific spirit is the spirit of the man who believes that knowledge is better than ignorance, that exactness is better than vagueness, that clear thinking is better than muddle-headedness, that truth, however unpalatable, is better than falsehood, however agreeable.

The scientific worker is not necessarily opposed to tradition; he is certainly not, *qua* scientist, opposed to art or religion or the things of the spirit generally. If these things are true, if they are not based on ignorance, superstition, or muddle-headedness, they have nothing to fear from the scientific investigator. If it be objected that social and political questions are outside his purview, that the scientific approach is inapplicable to such things, then, again, it is clear that the objector misconceives the basis of the scientific attitude, that he has not yet perceived the inwardness of the scientific spirit, that he has failed to grasp the significance of the scientific method.

Scientific method consists, broadly, in the accurate and painstaking determination of facts, the elimination of bias from measurement and record, the basing of judgement on knowledge and not on prejudice. It involves both a desire for the truth and a willingness to accept it when found: it requires its followers to be prepared to sacrifice their oldest beliefs, their most cherished ideas, if its operations prove those beliefs to be ill-founded, those ideas to be chimerical.

What is there in all this hostile to, or inconsistent with, the things of the spirit, the ideals and hopes that are the inspiration of life? To say that a scientific approach is detrimental to the consideration of human affairs, injurious to the study of human needs and aspirations, inimical to the best interests of mankind, is either to misapprehend that approach or to take a very cynical view of the human spirit.

Magna est veritas et prevalebit: but if truth is to prevail it must first be discovered, and that discovery, in political affairs as in other things, will not be made by rhetoric, however eloquent. The truth must be searched for, patiently and unweariedly: it must be slowly and perhaps painfully disentangled from popular superstition and interested mis-representation. When we know the actual facts underlying a problem of politics we can begin to consider its solution. Until we do know the facts any attempt at solution is the idlest and most futile of occupations.

To any observer not obsessed by tradition nor blinded by prejudice the conjunction of the disastrous course of events, social, economic, and political, since the war of 1914-18, both at home and abroad, on the one hand, and the utter inability of governments and politicians to deal with them, or even to realize their nature and significance, on the other, is terrifying. One may concede that there are few people harder worked or more burdened with responsibility than premiers, foreign secretaries, and others who have to face the day-to-day tangles of events and policy at home and abroad. There is no need to belittle their efforts or under-estimate the toil they put in; but there is every need to draw attention to their general futility.

To say this is not to suggest that the application of scientific method to political, economic, and social problems can provide a panacea for the manifold ills from which human society suffers. There is no short cut to the millennium. The social, economic, and political problems that face us are immensely complex and immensely difficult: it would be futile to suggest that they can be solved quickly, even in part, by any means whatever.

The point to be driven home is that the methods generally in use, now and in the past, show no promise of even beginning to lead to a solution: the methods of "statesmen" and politicians, in all too many cases, amount to little more than floundering about in the hope that somehow, sooner or later, we shall find a way out by chance; and, as is to be expected, their flounderings only make matters worse. True, there are in all parties, and outside party, men and women of clearer vision, who realize that research is as essential in political and social problems as in the problems of physical science and technology;* but they are as yet in a minority, and neither party leaders nor "practical" politicians nor academic political writers pay much heed to them.

To go on as we are going is next door to hopeless, and the sooner we realize it the better. Even if our methods of tackling political and social problems were reformed drastically and at once, it would take long enough in all conscience to make serious progress. With our "states-men" running round in circles and trying to "muddle through" blind-fold, we shall not even begin to straighten out the appalling mess.

---

* The names of H. G. Wells, Sidney and Beatrice Webb, Eleanor Rathbone, Harold Macmillan, and others will occur to the reader: also those of such bodies as P.E.P. and the New Fabian Research Bureau. These, however, are not the people and bodies that rule us.

It is time that we made drastic changes. It is time that we said, with the best type of enlightened modern business man, "We'll take nobody's say-so; not even that of the man who has been in the business all his life. We'll make tests and experiments, use surveys, researches and specialized counsel, and work our way toward our goal coolly and without the slightest preconceived prejudice, and cheerfully reverse our own ideas, everybody's ideas, if necessary."*

Again: "The very breath of our modern day is impregnated with the research spirit. Farmers are feeding their livestock on a measured calory basis decided by experts, not on their personal hunches, traditions, or enthusiasms. New York clothing makers are counting with hand-counting machines the number of women on Fifth Avenue, Bar Harbor, or Palm Beach who wear blue or black or what length of skirt—instead of getting up style hunches or enthusiasms of their own. There is no detail too small to be measured nowadays; instruments exist capable of measuring the heat of a match lit twelve miles away. The whole world of life is a research adventure, and the smallest task in modern business and industry is full of factors of genuine research importance."

Yet again: "We are just beginning to grasp the significance of the research idea in industry. Our own organization is learning that young men from the schools and colleges are happier and contribute more to the business when they are encouraged to work in the research spirit and are dominated by the research idea rather than by the old, routine idea which deadened initiative, ambition, and the finer capacities. An organization steeped in the research idea, its executives and workers all thinking of problems and studying carefully their solutions with something of the zest the scientist brings to his work, is something more than an organization. It is an organism with opportunities for growth stretching out both for the individual and for the company."

Contrast that attitude with the attitude of the average cabinet minister, member of parliament, or party organizer: is not the difference startling—and alarming? How long shall we remain content with the incompetent amateurishness, the out-of-date traditionalism that now rule us?

This book, then, is an attempt to apply the spirit of research, the methods of science, to one small part of our political problem: that of parliamentary representation. It *is* only a small part; but, as every scientific worker knows, research involves a great deal of labour if even a small part of any field is to be adequately explored. It is only the neophyte who attempts to reform a whole science in one epoch-making treatise: the more experienced worker is humbler, and is content if he can contribute new light on a small branch of it; or, to vary the metaphor, if he can lay truly a few small bricks in the edifice of a newer and better civilization.

It may be that some critics will assert that the whole of this is beside the point: that the matters discussed in this book are merely matters of

* *For Top Executives Only*, Business Bourse, New York, 1936.

machinery, and that, as such, they are of little or no importance. "It is not likely," says Laski, "that the difficulties of the modern State are such as to be at all seriously remediable by reforms of electoral machinery. Mainly, those difficulties are moral in character. We shall meet them rather by the elevation of the popular standard of intelligence, and the reform of the economic system. . . ."*

This attitude is difficult to understand. No one of any breadth of outlook will imagine for one moment that reforms of machinery *alone* will bring about the political enlightenment and development that he would like to see: the issues are, as Laski says, mainly moral in character, or at least largely so. But though good machinery will not of itself remedy our troubles, bad machinery may, and I believe does, seriously increase them.

Let me illustrate the point I wish to make. The swift, safe, and comfortable conveyance of the passengers in a car to their destination depends mainly on three things: the skill and care of the driver, the quality and quantity of the motor spirit available, and the make and condition of the engine and its accessories. If the engine is out of date and in bad condition, progress will be neither swift, safe, nor comfortable. No doubt, even so, it would be advantageous to have a skilful driver and plenty of high-grade motor spirit—but these could only mitigate, they could not compensate, the deficiencies of the engine. Equally, of course, the latest and best engine would be useless without both petrol and driver; but who would suggest otherwise?

Those who despise reforms of social and political machinery and put their whole trust in the petrol of "moral rearmament" (as it is now the fashion to call it) and the driving of party leadership should reconsider their position: the value of both will be depreciated, if not completely stultified, if the chassis of the political car is antiquated and rusty. Let us seek to elevate the popular standard of knowledge and judgement (if not of intelligence) by all means: such an elevation is fervently to be desired. Let us reform the economic system: heaven knows it needs reform! But why impede the attainment of these desirable aims, and diminish their value when attained, by clinging to out-of-date and inefficient political machinery?

Let us be clear about this. No one in his senses would suggest that the reform of parliamentary representation would of itself suffice to restore democracy to a state of health. The troubles that beset our political institutions are not as simple as that. This, however, is no reason at all why parliamentary representation should remain unreformed. The critic who would have us reject proposals for the solution of a specific problem on the ground that the proposals will not solve a number of other outstanding problems is both unreasonable and unhelpful. Progress towards a better state of affairs would be indefinitely postponed if we were to take up such an intransigent attitude all round; for, pushed to its logical conclusion, such an attitude implies that no

* H. J. Laski, *A Grammar of Politics* (1931), page 317.

improvement in our political and social scheme is worth while unless it may be expected to produce the millennium.

I believe that the present state of our representative institutions is thoroughly unsatisfactory: that representation is, in fact, largely a sham. I believe that it is vitally important to put those institutions into a state of vigorous health, and to make representation an effective reality. I believe that until this is done all attempts at wider and more far-reaching reforms will be hampered and impeded at every turn, and their achievement indefinitely postponed. But I do not claim that the attainment of honest, vigorous, and efficient representation will do more than clear the way for the attainment of these ideals.

When every allowance is made for the immense complexity of modern civilization and the colossal difficulty of the social and political problems it presents, is it not nevertheless worth while, most emphatically worth while, if we can clear out of our way even one of the obstacles that impede our progress to better things? We cannot hope, we should not look, to evolve any immediate Utopia. Let us rather address ourselves to the solution of problems that are at once urgent and within our grasp. Let us set aside alike the defeatism that says that the problems are too vast, that nothing can be done, and the utopianism that thinks to evolve a new heaven and a new earth within our own lifetime.

Here, in the subject of parliamentary representation, is one problem that urgently needs solution, one problem that it is within our power to tackle. Let us first get a clear view of the nature of the problem, of the facts of the present position: and then let us try to find a solution. That we shall succeed fully in either aim is improbable: but if we can make some advance the attempt will be worth while.

The plan of this work is very simple: Part I is devoted to a statistical and analytical study of parliamentary representation as it has functioned in inter-war Great Britain; Part II is an attempt to determine, in the light of the ascertained facts, what is wrong and why; while Part III suggests what can best be done to set it right.

The method followed in the preparation of Part I was as follows.* A number of quarto sheets were printed with carefully planned headings and divisions. One of these was filled up for each member who had sat in the House of Commons at any time from the general election of December 1918 to the end of 1936. When this stage of the investigation was completed there were 1,823 sheets available, each containing, systematically and uniformly arranged, the essential data relating to the age, education, occupation, etc., of one of the 1,823 members of parliament.

To obtain these data, and so far as possible to check them, use was

* I gratefully acknowledge my indebtedness in this to Sidney and Beatrice Webb, *Methods of Social Study* (1932), chapter IV, *The Art of Note-taking*. The analysis of the facts, laborious enough even with this apparatus, would have been almost impracticable without it—at least in my circumstances.

made of the works of reference to which acknowledgement is made in Appendix I. Great care was taken in the compilation of these sheets, and so far as practicable every entry on them was verified by consultation of independent sources; in some cases as many as four or five different works of reference were used in relation to a single entry.

Difficulties arose in several ways. It would appear that certain members of parliament have a great aversion from letting anyone know their age, education, occupation, or, indeed, anything about their experience or qualifications: a strange perversity in a public representative. At any rate, in these cases—fortunately comparatively rare—hardly one of the reference works in question has succeeded in getting out of these secretive people even the essential particulars. In other cases the member concerned seems to have supplied each book of reference with different information, so that he is credited with several different dates of birth, more than one educational history, and several inconsistent accounts of his occupation! These cases, again, are fortunately rare, but some of them are really amazing. In yet other cases the information supplied is so vague or so ambiguous that it is difficult to know what to make of it.

These cases caused endless trouble and delay, but in the end, by careful searching, it was possible to clear up many of the ambiguities and inconsistencies, and even to find out some facts about the people who seemed so anxious to conceal their previous history. Fortunately, too, in the great majority of cases difficulties of this kind did not arise. Hence it was possible to make the final results reasonably complete and, so far as can be judged, reasonably free from serious error. Gaps there are and, it is to be feared, errors; but I am satisfied that they are not so extensive, nor of such a character, as to impair the general accuracy of the conclusions reached or invalidate the criticisms made.

In this connexion it may be as well to point out that the different kinds of information recorded have different characteristics, and are subject to greater or less possibilities of error. For example, every member has one date of birth and one only. This date may be (a) given differently in different books of reference, (b) incorrectly given, or (c) not given at all. But whether we succeed in ascertaining it accurately or not, it is a single, definite date. Similarly, every member either is or is not a baronet: there may be a doubt as to the facts, but if they are known they are free from ambiguity. By contrast, education and occupation are often of a somewhat indeterminate character: if a member claims to be an author, not only may the facts be a little difficult to ascertain, but they are incapable of exact delimitation. At what stage between the writing of, say, a single letter to *The Times* and the making of a living, year after year, by the writing of books does a man become "an author"? Who shall say?

These are just illustrations, but they serve to indicate the basic fact that the different kinds of information are subject to different kinds and degrees of error. Interpretation comes in more in some cases than in others, both in determining the facts and in drawing conclusions from them. These provisos should be borne in mind when considering the results of this investigation.

From the data on these 1,823 sheets statistics were prepared as set out in the following chapters. For purposes of comparison with the analysis of members' ages, educations, occupations, etc., the corresponding figures for the general adult population of Great Britain were obtained, so far as was found practicable, the chief, though not the only, sources of information being the various reports of the 1921 and 1931 censuses.

It will be noticed that all the figures are confined to Great Britain. The inclusion of the Irish members (and, correspondingly, the general adult population of Ireland) would have offered many difficulties, with no corresponding advantages. During the period of 1918-1922 the majority of Irish members were Sinn Feiners and did not take their seats. Since 1922 Ireland has ceased to be represented in the House of Commons, except for the thirteen "six counties" members, whose presence is anomalous, since the "six counties" have a parliament of their own.

One more point before we pass on to the results of the investigation. Part I consists almost entirely of the ascertained *facts*, other matter being confined to the explanations necessary to make clear the course of the analysis, and to such comments as seem desirable to illuminate its significance; Part II, on the other hand, contains a more oroadly critical study of the results and of the causes which underlie them; while Part III embodies suggestions for reform. Every endeavour has been made to present the facts in Part I with scrupulous impartiality and exactness so far as the nature of the data allows. In Parts II and III, again, I have tried to make my criticisms as objective as possible, but here it is obviously harder to preserve strict impartiality.

It is my hope that even those who disagree strongly with some (or all) of my criticisms and suggestions in Parts II and III will nevertheless find in Part I much useful information and a new light on what *is*. They can rely on this: that whatever errors may have crept into the book, no pains have been spared to present the facts with scientific accuracy and freedom from bias. Disagreement with my expressed opinions will not, I hope, lead to doubt of my facts: the former are inevitably personal and coloured by my ideas of what is politically desirable; the latter are as accurate and precise as scientific care can make them.

I desire particularly to stress this point because, while I believe the views expressed in Parts II and III to be both sound and useful, I attach great importance to such a detailed and factual exposure of the present realities of a problem as I have attempted in Part I. As H. G. Wells says, "The new world as a going concern must arise out of the old as a going concern,"* and we cannot facilitate the process unless we are aware of the facts about the old world.

* H. G. Wells, *The Open Conspiracy* (1928), page 31.

THE PERSONNEL OF PARLIAMENT

CHAPTER II

THE AGES OF MEMBERS

AT what ages do most members first enter the House of Commons? What is the average age of the House at any given time? Does one party favour younger members than another? Is the average age of the House increasing or decreasing? These are some of the questions we shall be able to answer as a result of this part of the investigation. We shall also be able to see how the ages of members compare with those of the electorate, and what truth there is, so far as the House is concerned, in the saying that the government of the country is too much in the hands of old or elderly people. In short, we should be able to form a clear picture of the age-composition of the House at any given time, see how it varies from party to party and from election to election, and have some basis on which to form a judgement as to the desirability or otherwise of the present state of affairs in the matter.

It is convenient to divide this part of the investigation into two sections, the first dealing with the ages of members on their first election to the House of Commons, and the second with the ages of members, new and old, immediately after a general election. The first section will be considered in this chapter, and the second in that following.

1. AGE ON FIRST ELECTION

Table 1 gives the ages on first election to the House of Commons of all *new* members at each general election from 1918 to 1935 inclusive, with the exception of a few members whose ages it was not found possible to ascertain. For convenience the ages are taken in groups of five years each. The first age-group comprises the members who entered the House at ages ranging from 21 years 0 month to 25 years 11 months, the second those who entered at ages ranging from 26 years 0 month to 30 years 11 months, and so on.

Table 1 gives the figures: but it is not easy to grasp the significance of such an array by simple inspection. In Fig. 1, therefore, the totals from the last column of the table are displayed in the form of a diagram, which shows the state of affairs much more clearly. It is suggested that Table 1, and most of those that follow, should be used chiefly for reference, and that in general the reader should pay more attention to the text and diagrams than to the tables. It is necessary to give this tabular matter—it is the basis and proof of the contentions set forth—but most people find long arrays of figures more than a little wearisome, and the free use of diagrams makes it possible to follow the argument without close study of the tables.

TABLE 1.—AGE ON FIRST ELECTION: NEW MEMBERS AT EACH
GENERAL ELECTION

5-Year Age-Range *	Number of Members							
	1918	1922	1923	1924	1929	1931	1935	Total
21-26	1	2	5	5	3	2	4	22
26-31	10	14	12	15	12	38	8	109
31-36	18	22	18	13	15	31	13	130
36-41	31	34	19	15	19	26	11	155
41-46	33	35	36	27	26	18	11	186
46-51	52	33	30	22	19	36	12	204
51-56	45	46	22	20	20	26	4	183
56-61	28	25	8	12	14	12	7	106
61-66	22	17	5	3	6	4	4	61
66-71	9	3	—	1	1	5	—	19
71-76	1	—	—	—	1	—	—	2
Total ...	250	231	155	133	136	198	74	1,177

* Age-range 21-26 includes all ages from 21 years 0 month to 25 years
11 months, and so on.

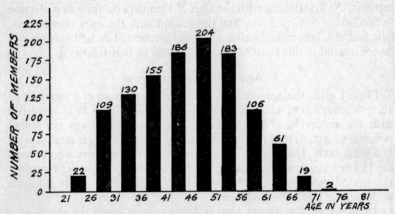

FIG. 1.—Age on first election: new members at general elections, 1918
to 1935 inclusive.

It will be seen that relatively few members entered under the age of
26 or over the age of 66, while the most popular five-year range was
that from 46 to 51 years of age. The entries increase rapidly up to that
group and then decline again, the fall after the 51-56 group being rapid.
There was, in all the seven general elections, only one entrant at the
lowest age, 21, and only one at 75, which was the highest age.

Table 1 gives the actual numbers in each age-group for each election,
and Fig. 1 displays the general effect for the seven elections considered

together; but a more generally useful quantity, and one which enables us more readily to compare one election with another, is the *average* age of entry. This is given, for each election separately and for all seven together, in Table 2. The figures in this table, by the way, have not been calculated from those in Table 1, but from more detailed tables in which each member's age is recorded to the nearest month. Fig. 2 shows graphically the results recorded in Table 2.

It will be seen that the new members elected in 1918 were much the oldest set for any of the elections, with an average age of 48 years $5\frac{1}{2}$ months, and that, after that, the average age fell fairly steadily until at the last two elections it was only 42 years $0\frac{1}{2}$ month: a drop of 6 years 5 months in the average age of entry compared with 1918.

The high age of entry in 1918 and the fall since may be taken, perhaps, as a significant indication of the tragic loss of life of the younger manhood of the nation in the last war, and its—probably regrettable—effect in throwing the control of affairs in the crucial post-war years into the hands of a House abnormally elderly in composition.

The temporary rise in 1929 is due to the fact that, as will appear later, members of the Labour party on an average enter the House 3 years 4 months later than do members of the Conservative party, and 3 years 1 month later than members of the Liberal party: 1929 was the year in which more Labour members entered than at any other of these elections. When this is taken into account it will be seen that the fall in the average age is really remarkably steady. Judging by the 1931 and 1935 figures, the drop had then more or less reached its end.

In considering this aspect, however, it should be borne in mind that Table 2 and Fig. 2 refer only to *new* members: the average age of the House as a whole at each general election will be considered later. Naturally the average age of the whole House depends not only on the ages of the new members, but also on the ages of the re-elected members. The latter will tend to be greater than the former, and a House which contains many new members will therefore tend to be younger than one which contains relatively few.

So much for the age on first election of the *new* members elected at each general election. We pass now to the age on first election of *all* members who sat in the House at any time during the period from the 1918 general election to the end of 1936, irrespective of the date at which they were first elected. Table 3 gives the figures, arranged by parties, and Fig. 3 the corresponding diagrams. For convenience of comparison each diagram is taken on the same basis of 1,000 members.

The three party diagrams present a rather curious contrast. The most popular age-group for Conservatives is evidently 46-51, while for each of the other two parties it appears to be 41-46, though for Labour the 46-51 group runs the 41-46 group very close. Yet the average age for Conservatives is lower than the average age for either of the other two parties. The explanation of this paradoxical state of affairs is to be found in the fact that, while there is a substantial inflow of Conserva-

TABLE 2.—AVERAGE AGE OF NEW MEMBERS ON FIRST ELECTION

General Election	Average Age* of New Members	
	Years	Months
1918	48	5½
1922	46	9½
1923	43	9
1924	43	10½
1929	44	8½
1931	42	0½
1935	42	0½
All seven elections	45	1

* In computing these averages each member's age has been taken to the nearest month.

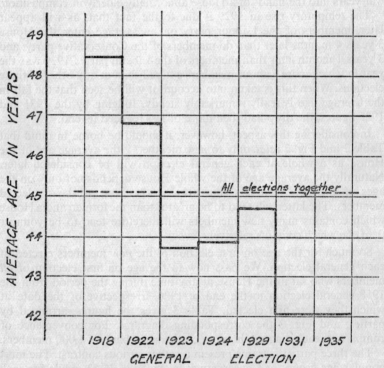

FIG. 2.—Average age of new members on first election.

tives at all ages between 26 and 46, relatively few Liberals enter before 31 and relatively few Labour members before 36.

It will be noticed, too, that whereas both the Conservative and

Labour entries fall off rapidly after the age of 51, the decline in Liberal entries is delayed until after 56. The numbers of Liberal and Labour members concerned, however, are not so great that much significance can safely be attached to these particular results.

When all parties are considered together the two age-ranges 41-46 and 46-51 show a very close similarity of numbers, and it would be unsafe to say decisively which represents the more popular. What can, however, be said with certainty is that the ten-year range 41-51 is the most popular for first entry to the House: the number of new members in this is 582, against 476 for the age-range 31-41 and 392 for the age-range 51-61. The ten-year ranges 21-31 and 61-71 are much smaller again, with only 200 and 111 entries respectively.

TABLE 3.—AGE ON FIRST ELECTION: ALL MEMBERS, 1918 TO 1936

5-Year Age-Range *	Number of Members				
	Cons.	Lib.	Lab.	Ind.	Total
21-26	32	10	2	—	44
26-31	116	29	11	—	156
31-36	130	58	26	6	220
36-41	132	57	65	2	256
41-46	134	69	83	3	289
46-51	158	54	80	1	293
51-56	118	58	64	3	243
56-61	82	25	39	3	149
61-66	44	16	24	1	85
66-71	21	1	4	—	26
71-76	—	1	1	—	2
76-81	—	1	—	—	1
Total ...	967	379	399	19	1,764

* Age-range 21-26 includes all ages from 21 years 0 month to 25 years 11 months, and so on.

A few other points to which attention may be drawn are: (a) the fact that, even proportionally to total party entrants, for every Labour member who enters the House between the ages of 21 and 31 there are, roughly, three Liberal entrants and five Conservative*; (b) the high proportion of Labour members who enter between 41 and 51 (41 per cent of the total); and (c) the comparatively small differences in party entries after the age of 51 (5 Conservative to 5 Liberal and 6 Labour entries). These facts stress the initial financial disadvantage of Labour, and to a less extent Liberal, candidates and its partial disappearance at a later age.

* The actual disproportion is, of course, much greater (the ratio is roughly 11:3:1) owing to the larger total number of Conservative members.

The distribution of first-entry ages in the three parties is shown in a somewhat different way in Fig. 4. This again shows the ages at which members enter the House of Commons, and again on the basis of 1,000 members of each party; but here we have superimposed continuous graphs, of which the points represent the numbers of members entering

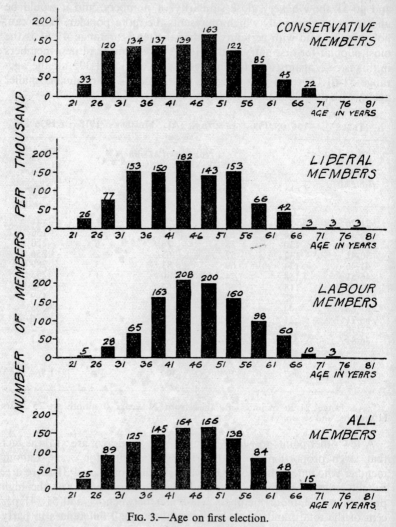

FIG. 3.—Age on first election.

at each year of age. The graphs have all been smoothed, but even so are somewhat irregular. This is only to be expected in view of the small magnitude, from a statistical point of view, of the numbers under consideration. Nevertheless, the graphs show marked differences from each other. It is interesting to observe that at most ages the Liberal curve lies between the other two curves, a phenomenon that will be observed again and again in the course of this survey.

The causes already mentioned obviously account to a very considerable extent both for the differences in form of the three graphs and for their irregularities. It would, however, be rather interesting to make further investigations with a view to accounting for them somewhat more precisely—*e.g.*, by considering the occupations of members and how the age of entry varies with these. One may speculate why the Conservative entries, after rising both steadily and steeply up to the age of 29 or 30, suddenly become very nearly constant for all ages up to 45; whether the apparent three peaks for Liberal entries—at 33-34,

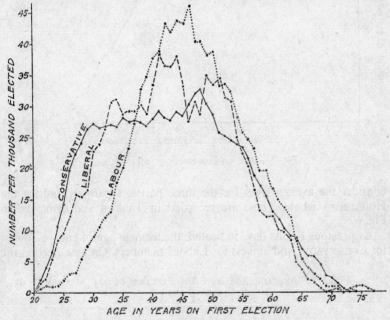

FIG. 4.—Age on first election: distribution by parties.

at 41-43, and at 49-51—are merely accidental and can be explained by the smallness of the numbers concerned, or whether they represent some real difference in the type of entrants; and so on.

Finally, in Fig. 5 a smoothed curve is given for the ages on first election of all members of parliament who sat in the House of Commons at any time from the 1918 general election to the end of 1936 (with the exception, as before, of a few whose ages it has not been possible to ascertain). The graph, like those in Fig. 4, is based on reduction to a total of 1,000 members, to facilitate comparison. It seems clear from this last graph that the years from 41 to 49 are the most popular for entry, and that within these limits there is very little difference in popularity between the various ages, though there is some reason to suppose that the peak at 44 may represent a genuine climax.

So much for the general distribution of ages of entry. We must now

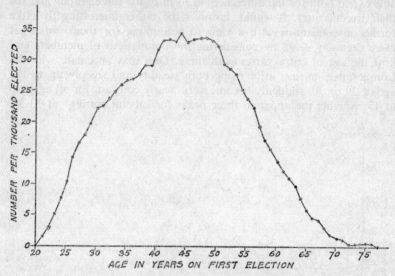

FIG. 5.—Age on first election: all members.

consider the average ages for the three parties separately and for the House as a whole. These are recorded in Table 4 and displayed in Fig. 6.

As previous results have indicated, the average age of entry is lowest for Conservative and highest for Labour members. On first election the

TABLE 4.—AVERAGE AGE ON FIRST ELECTION OF ALL MEMBERS, 1918 TO 1936

Party			Average Age *	
			Years	Months
Conservative	...	...	43	7½
Liberal	...	...	43	10½
Labour	...	...	46	11½
Independent†	...	...	44	9
All parties ...	...	...	44	5

* In computing these averages each member's age has been taken to the nearest month.

† Independent members are included for the sake of completeness, but their average age has little significance in view of their heterogeneity and the smallness of their numbers.

average Conservative is 3 months younger than the average Liberal and 3 years 4 months younger than the average Labour member: a rather striking difference. It can hardly be doubted that this is a mirror of the advantages, not only financial but also in the way of social prestige, which the Conservative party, and to a less extent the Liberal party, enjoys by comparison with the Labour party. How easy it is for the Conservative peer's son, from Eton and Oxford or Harrow and Sand-hurst, to find a seat at any age, and how difficult by comparison for the son of the shopkeeper or farm labourer, whatever his personal abilities!

It is interesting to notice that in average entrance age the Liberal

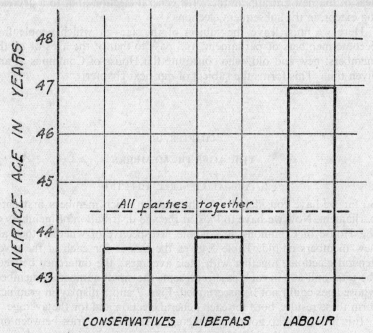

FIG. 6.—Average age of all members on first election.

party approximates more closely to the Conservative than to the Labour party. One may doubt whether this would have been so between 1906 and 1918.

Before passing on it is instructive to compare Table 2 with Table 4. Both deal with average age on first election, but Table 2 is concerned only with members who entered the House of Commons for the first time at the general elections from 1918 to 1935 inclusive, whereas Table 4 includes all members who sat in the House at any time during the period from the 1918 general election to the end of 1936, irrespective of the date of their first election, and therefore includes many whose début in parliament took place before the 1918 election.

The average age on first election for the 1,764 members in Table 4 was 44 years 5 months; the average age for the 1,177 members in Table 2 was 45 years 1 month. A simple computation shows that the average age on first election for the 587 members included in Table 4 but not in Table 2 was 43 years 0 month. In this 587 members are included some who entered the House for the first time at by-elections during the period under review, but most of them first came in before December 1918. Comparing this figure of 43 years 0 month with the averages for new members at each of the general elections given in Table 2 emphasizes the point already made about the abnormal elderliness of the new entrants in the 1918 general election and, to a decreasing extent, in the subsequent elections.

Here we must leave the subject of the ages at which people first become members of parliament, and pass to that of the ages of *all* the members, new and old, who constitute the House of Commons at any given time. This forms the subject of our next chapter.

CHAPTER III

THE AGES OF MEMBERS

2. AGE AT GENERAL ELECTION

So far we have considered only the ages at which members first enter parliament. Now we have to look at the age distribution of members of the House of Commons as a whole, irrespective of whether they are new members or old. Table 5 gives the figures for each of the seven general elections, together with their averages: the difference between the total and 602 in each case represents the small number of members whose ages could not be ascertained. Figs. 7 and 8 display in graphical form these results, both for each general election and for the average.

It is interesting to notice how the age distribution varies between one election and another. It has already been observed how relatively elderly the new entrants in the 1918 election were, and how in the subsequent elections the age of entrance fell. We now find the same tendency observable in the ages of *all* members. Take, in particular, the series of three five-year age-groups covering the ages from 21 to 36 years: in the 1918 election the number of members in these three groups together was 36; in 1922 it rose to 58, in 1923 to 61, and in 1924 to 72. In 1929 the number fell to 58; but, as indicated in the previous chapter, this was due to the influx of Labour members, who are, in general, older than the members of the other parties. In 1931 the number of "young" members (under 36) rose to 106—nearly three times the figure for 1918—and though in 1935 the number fell to 75, it was still, at that figure, higher than in any election except 1931. Moreover, two factors in 1935 tended to reduce the number of "young" members:

the return of more Labour members and the abnormally low number of new members.

Allowing for these factors, therefore, there has been a pretty steady rise in the number of "young" members from 1918 onwards, marking undoubtedly the gradual replacement of war losses. How far the abnormal elderliness of the House in the immediate post-war period affected policy it is impossible to say, but it is a question that may interest students of political history, as may the similar question whether the relative elderliness of the Labour party in the House is reflected in its policy and its vigour (or lack of vigour).

TABLE 5.—AGE AT GENERAL ELECTION: 1918 TO 1935

5-Year Age-Range *	Number of Members								
	1918	1922	1923	1924	1929	1931	1935	Total	Average
21-26	2	3	6	7	4	2	5	29	4
26-31	11	17	21	30	17	52	18	166	24
31-36	23	38	34	35	37	52	52	271	39
36-41	64	58	61	61	47	64	61	416	59
41-46	73	82	101	89	88	67	64	564	81
46-51	107	96	98	99	101	87	77	665	95
51-56	107	114	109	111	94	93	93	721	103
56-61	84	89	82	82	95	78	83	593	85
61-66	69	56	49	50	65	54	71	414	59
66-71	40	28	22	22	28	29	38	207	30
71-76	9	8	8	9	9	9	19	71	10
76-81	3	2	3	3	2	2	3	18	3
Total...	592	591	594	598	587	589	584	4,135	591

* Age-range 21-26 includes all ages from 21 years 0 month to 25 years 11 months, and so on.

The whole age-range of the membership of the House covers a period of almost exactly sixty years—21 to 81—and it is instructive to divide the members into four groups of equal age-range—viz., fifteen years. These four age-groups may for convenience, and without any intention of exact description, be termed the "young" group, comprising members between 21 and 36 years of age; the "younger middle-aged" group, comprising those between 36 and 51; the "older middle-aged" group, from 51 to 66; and the "elderly" group, from 66 to 81.

Inspection of Figs. 7 and 8 from this point of view reveals the fact that the great majority of members fall into one or other of the two "middle-aged" groups, and that those two groups are closely similar in size. The "young" and "elderly" groups are much smaller and, again, are roughly similar in size to each other; though in every election but that of 1918 the "young" group is bigger than the "elderly."

Fig. 9 displays the percentage composition of each House, and of the average House, in terms of these four age-groups. It is instructive both in respect of the general similarities that it shows and in respect of the

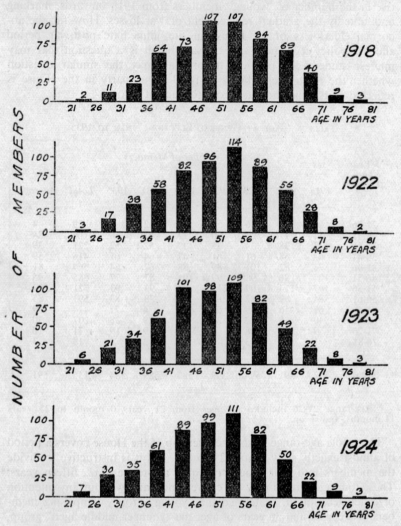

FIG. 7.—Ages of members at general elections.

differences, particularly the chronological differences in the "young" group to which attention has already been called.

A different aspect of the age distribution of members is shown in Fig. 10. Here curve (a), "Age proportions for M.P.s at general elections," has been obtained by taking the figures in the "Total" column of Table 5, reducing to a basis of 1,000 members (i.e., reducing proportionately all the figures, so that the grand total for all ages is 1,000 instead of 4,135, as in the table), and smoothing the curve so obtained. This curve, then, shows fairly accurately what may be termed the

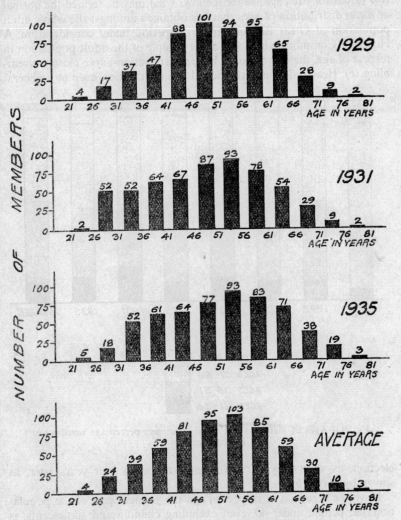

FIG. 8.—Ages of members at general elections.

normal or mean distribution of ages that has obtained amongst members at the inter-war general elections.

The dotted curve (b) has been obtained by shifting curve (a) to the right through a distance representing four years; hence it shows (neglecting the effect of by-elections, which is very small) the normal or mean distribution of ages of members four years after a general election.

Finally, curve (c) has been obtained by determining the age distribution per thousand of the whole *adult* population of the country at each of the inter-war censuses of 1921 and 1931 and taking the mean of the two values for each age; hence it shows what may be termed the normal or mean distribution of ages that has obtained amongst the whole adult population of Great Britain during the period under consideration. A House of Commons which was a fair sample of the adult population in respect of age, therefore, would have a distribution-curve closely resembling (c). How different is the actual age distribution even at a general

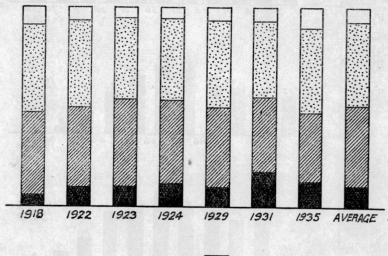

FIG. 9.—Ages of members at general elections: percentage numbers in 15-year age-groups.

election, as shown by curve (a), and still more four years later, as shown by curve (b)!

It will be seen that in respect of age the younger part of the population, the people under 40, even excluding children and adolescents, is grossly under-represented, the section of the population between approximately 45 and 65 is much over-represented, while the section aged 70 and over is more or less reasonably represented.

It is not here argued that an age distribution of members of parliament corresponding to the age distribution of the whole adult population would necessarily give a better House than the actual age distribution; attention is merely drawn to the fact that the House is not in any sense a fair sample of the general adult population in respect of age.

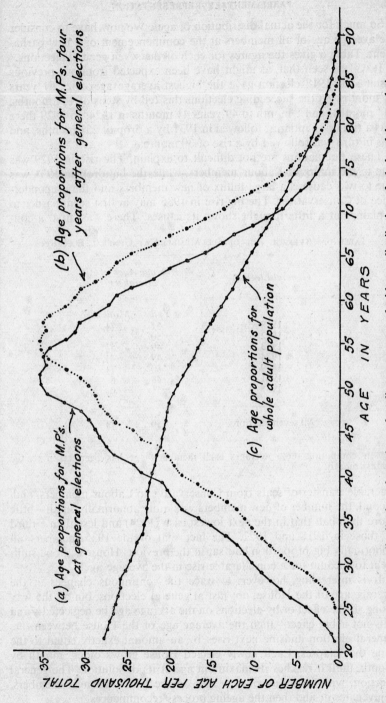

Fig. 10.—Age-distribution of members of parliament compared with age-distribution of whole adult population.

(b) Age proportions for M.P.'s four years after general elections

(a) Age proportions for M.P.'s at general elections

(c) Age proportions for whole adult population

AGE IN YEARS

NUMBER OF EACH AGE PER THOUSAND TOTAL

So much for the actual distribution of ages. We now have to consider the average age of all members at the commencement of a new parliament. Table 6 gives the figures for each of the seven general elections.

It will be seen that, as might have been expected from our previous results, the 1918 election gave the highest average age—viz., 51 years 7½ months. At the succeeding elections this fell by steps of 14½ months, 11½ months, and 1 month to 49 years 4½ months in 1924. In 1929 there was a rise of 15 months, followed in 1931 by a drop of 25½ months, and this in turn was followed by a rise of 30 months.

These fluctuations are not difficult to explain. The rise in 1929 was due to the influx of Labour members, while the big drop in 1931 was due to two causes: a large influx of new members and the preponderance of Conservatives. The big rise in 1935 may at first seem harder to explain, but a little thought shows its causes. There was, first, a con-

TABLE 6.—AVERAGE AGE OF ALL MEMBERS AT GENERAL ELECTION

General Election	Average Age* of All Members	
	Years	Months
1918	51	7½
1922	50	5
1923	49	5½
1924	49	4½
1929	50	7½
1931	48	6
1935	51	0
All seven elections	50	1½

* In computing these averages each member's age has been taken to the nearest month.

siderable transfer of seats from Conservative to Labour members, and, second, the number of new members was quite abnormally small—little more than half that in the next lowest case (1924) and less than a third of those in 1918 and 1922. The fact that of the 1935 members an abnormally big proportion had sat in the previous House is alone sufficient to account for a considerable rise in the average age.

It is interesting, however, to trace the continuous changes in the average age of the House, not just at general elections, but all the way along. If the effect of by-elections on the average age be neglected—and it is not a big effect—then the average age of the House between one general election and the next rises by an amount exactly equal to the time that elapses. Each newly elected House grows older, month by month, until it reaches its maximum age at its dissolution. The general election, with its influx of new and on the whole younger members, rejuvenates it; and then the ageing process recommences.

We find that, within the inter-war period, the House was at its oldest at the 1922 dissolution, when the average age was 55 years 6½ months, and at its youngest immediately after the 1931 election, when the average age was 48 years 6 months—a difference of 7 years and half a month. The biggest "rejuvenation" was in 1922—5 years 1½ months—and the smallest in 1924—11 months. But the House is now (December 1942) older than at any time since 1918, having reached the astonishingly high average age of 58 years 1 month.* It looks as though when the next general election does at length take place the average may well be over 60.

How does the average age of members of parliament compare with

TABLE 7.—AVERAGE AGE: HOUSE OF COMMONS COMPARED WITH
ADULT POPULATION

Date	Average Age				Difference	
	House of Commons		Adult Population			
	Yrs.	Mths.	Yrs.	Mths.	Yrs.	Mths.
1918 Election	51	7½	42	10½	8	9
Dissolution 1922 ...	55	6½	43	2½	12	4
1922 Election	50	5	43	2½	7	2½
Dissolution 1923 ...	51	6	43	3½	8	2½
1923 Election	49	5½	43	3½	6	2
Dissolution 1924 ...	50	3½	43	4½	6	11
1924 Election	49	4½	43	4½	6	0
Dissolution 1929 ...	53	11½	43	9½	10	2
1929 Election	50	7½	43	9½	6	10
Dissolution 1931 ...	53	0½	44	0	9	0½
1931 Election	48	6	44	0	4	6
Dissolution 1935 ...	52	7	44	4	8	3
1935 Election	51	0	44	4	6	8
December 1942 ...	58	1	44	11½	13	1½

the average age of the whole adult community? I calculate that the average age of all the adults in Great Britain at the time of the 1921 census was 43 years 1 month, and at the time of the 1931 census 43 years 11½ months. There being no violent fluctuations of the birth-rate to affect the average age of the *adult* population during the period under review, and no heavy war casualties, it may legitimately be assumed that the change in the average has been continuous and practically uniform.†

Making this assumption, we have an ageing of the adult population

* The new entrants at recent by-elections have mostly been unusually elderly (possibly owing, in part at least, to the "party truce"), and so have done even less than in normal times to delay the "ageing" process.

† This may not be strictly true of the last few years, but it is doubtful whether either factor mentioned has yet had much effect on the *average* age.

3

of 10½ months in 10 years, or 1·05 months a year. This gives average ages for the whole adult population at the time of each dissolution and subsequent general election (and at the present time) as shown in Table 7, where they are contrasted with the contemporary average ages

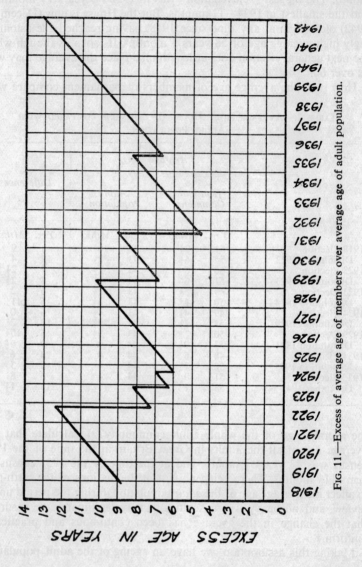

FIG. 11.—Excess of average age of members over average age of adult population.

of the House of Commons. Fig. 11 displays the differences set out in the last column of Table 7. For simplicity, dissolutions have been taken as simultaneous with the subsequent general elections.

It will be seen that the average member of parliament is considerably older than the average adult he represents, the smallest difference being 4½ years at the 1931 election. With the repeated prolongations of the life of the present parliament the difference has now (December 1942) risen to the record height of 13 years 1½ months; and it is, of course, still rising.

The mean value of the difference of average age between the House and the adult population for the whole period from December 1918 to December 1942 is about 8 years 7½ months. Hence, taking a broad view, we may say that members of parliament are on the average 8½ years older than their constituents—a remarkably high difference of age.

If we compare the average age of members with the average age of the *whole* population, the difference is, of course, much greater. The average age of the whole population of Great Britain at the 1921 census was 30 years 6 months, while at the 1931 census it was 32 years 6 months. Hence members of parliament are, on an average, roughly 20 years older than the average of the whole population.

These figures suggest that the average age of members of parliament is so high as to put the House of Commons in some danger of being out of touch with the feelings, beliefs, wishes, and needs of the people they are supposed to represent. However, here we are concerned with the facts: their discussion must come later.

CHAPTER IV

PREVIOUS SERVICE OF MEMBERS

WHEN a new House of Commons is elected, to what extent is it composed of novices? To what extent are its re-elected members experienced in the work of the House? There is, I think, a fairly general impression that the new member on entering the House finds himself exceptional in his inexperience, and is surrounded by fellow-members of whom a large proportion are old hands with many years of previous service. How far is this impression justified by the facts?

Table 8 gives the material for answering these questions. It records the amount of previous service possessed by the members of each new House, together with the average for the seven elections. The general position, however, will be more readily grasped by reference to Fig. 12, where the averages from the last column of Table 8 are displayed graphically. The black dots on this graph show the actual figures, while the chain line shows their general trend. This line, in other words, indicates the distribution of previous service in an *average* House: in any actual House the distribution would, of course, be considerably more erratic and would not give a smooth curve.

Looking at this graph, we see at once that a newly elected House contains a remarkably large proportion of members with little or no

TABLE 8.—PREVIOUS SERVICE AT GENERAL ELECTIONS

Previous Service* in Years	Number of Members							
	1918	1922	1923	1924	1929	1931	1935	Average
Nil	260	238	159	133	146	206	79	175
0-5	57	203	303	263	146	119	192	183
5-10	130	31	21	104	177	155	132	107
10-15	91	69	63	54	69	72	126	78
15-20	26	34	33	30	35	10	38	29
20-25	17	13	9	7	19	24	8	14
25-30	12	6	4	5	3	10	18	8
30-35	4	5	7	4	3	3	4	4
35-40	2	1	1	—	2	2	3	2
40-45	1	1	1	1	—	1	1	1
45-50	—	—	—	—	1	—	1	—
Total	600	601	601	601	601	602	602	601

* Group 0-5 includes all periods of service from 1 month to 5 years 0 month, group 5-10 all periods from 5 years 1 month to 10 years 0 month, and so on.

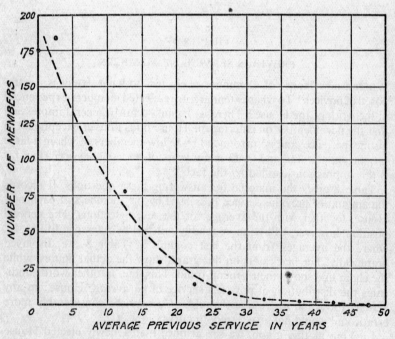

FIG. 12.—Average previous service at general elections.

previous service, and that. on the other hand, very few members have anything that could justly be described as long service. When a new House assembles after the election there are, on an average, nearly 30 per cent of novices in it: in 1918 the figure rose as high as 43 per cent—not far short of half the House. Moreover, in the average House nearly another 50 per cent have less than ten years' service, while those with twenty or more years' service number less than 5 per cent of the whole. Long experience is therefore the exception and not the rule.

Having looked at the distribution of previous service in the *average House*, we may now consider the *average length of service* of members at the commencement of each new parliament. This enables us to compare one House with another much more readily than the perhaps rather confusing figures given in Table 8. This average length of service

TABLE 9.—AVERAGE PREVIOUS SERVICE AT GENERAL ELECTIONS

General Election	Average Service* of All Members	
	Years	Months
1918	6	3½
1922	5	1
1923	4	11½
1924	4	11
1929	6	2
1931	5	11
1935	8	1
All seven elections	5	11

* In computing these averages each member's service has been taken to the nearest month.

is set out in Table 9, which also gives the average length for the seven elections taken together.

We can now see that, judging by average previous service, the least experienced House was that of 1924. The members of that House had, on election, an average previous service of only 4 years 11 months. Their average would have been just as high had none of them been elected before November 1919, providing that they had all served continuously since that date. The effect, of course, would have been different, but that way of looking at the matter serves to show how rapidly the personnel of parliament changes. Even the most experienced House, which it may surprise many people to learn was that of 1935, with an average of 8 years 1 month of previous service, was only equivalent in that respect to a House elected in October 1927 and serving continuously from that date.

Taking the seven general elections together, the average previous service of all the members on election was only 5 years 11 months. This seems surprisingly short. Indeed, the whole of these figures of previous service are such that any idea of a close continuity of one parliament with its predecessors gets rather a shock from them.

However, as time passes after its election the House steadily gains in

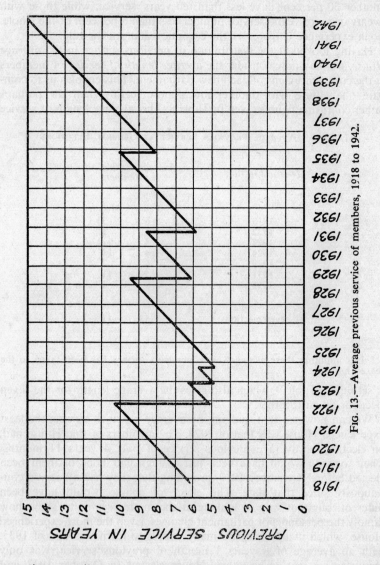

Fig. 13.—Average previous service of members, 1918 to 1942.

experience until a new general election replaces many of its older members by novices, and the maturing process recommences. This sequence of maturing and replacement is shown as a continuous diagram in Fig. 13. As in previous graphs of similar type, the effects of by-elections and of the intervals between dissolutions and the subsequent general elections have been disregarded, the errors so introduced being negligible.

The number of entirely new members returned at each general election is recorded in Table 8, and some reference has already been made to it. It may be of interest, however, to see the proportions shown graphically, and they are so displayed in Fig. 14. As already noted, the House with the largest number of novices was that of 1918, which had no fewer than 260; that with the smallest number was the 1935 House,

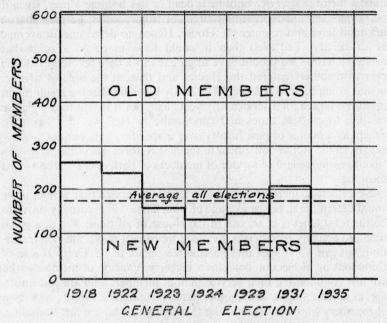

FIG. 14.—New and old members at general elections.

NOTE.—New members are those entering the House of Commons for the first time: old members those who have been members at any time before the election in question (not necessarily during the previous parliament).

which had only 79. The average number for the seven general elections was nearly 175—a little under 30 per cent of the whole membership.

At the other end of the scale we have a marked contrast: although there are generally a few members who have very long service, running to 40 or 50 years, yet the number who can claim even 20 years is small. The maximum was 40 members (1931) and the minimum 19 members (1924), with an average of 29. Out of 602 members that is not as big a proportion as one would expect. It has, however, to be remembered that, with the present method of election, very few members, however distinguished their parliamentary service may have been, can count on uninterrupted membership of the House over a long period. There is a so-called "swing of the pendulum"; a few thousand or even a few hundred votes are transferred—and out goes a member, perhaps at the zenith of his powers. Out he goes, and it may be years before he can get back; when he does his "previous service" stands where it did when he lost his seat, though a whole parliament or more may have elapsed since.

These considerations suggest another question: What is the average *total* length of service of members of parliament? This is not an easy question to answer, even approximately, since we cannot finally determine a member's service until he is dead or has become a peer. Even if he resigns and announces his retirement from politics, he may change his mind later and re-enter the House. Hence, to determine an average at all exactly—and even then it would have to be on a somewhat arbitrary basis—we should have to go back to a date before any of the present members entered the House; and that, at the time of writing, means going back to before 1890. Clearly if we did that the result might give the average total service fifty years ago, but it would have no close relation to modern times and conditions. In fact, we may say that, except as a matter of past history over a specified long term of years— say, from the Act of Settlement to the first Reform Act—the expression "average total length of service of members of parliament" *has* no exact meaning.

Nevertheless, there must be some length of service that would, if we could determine it, be the average of what Time will eventually prove to be the total lengths of service in the House of all those who at a given time are actually members. Obviously we cannot make this determination; but can we at least make a rough estimate of it? Every House of Commons at its election contains a bigger proportion of members who are just commencing their service than of members who are just finishing; at its dissolution, on the other hand, it contains a bigger proportion of members who are just finishing than of those who are just beginning. Hence it would seem that if we compute the average previous service of members halfway between election and dissolution and then double it, we shall get an approximation to the figure we are after; it will, in fact, be as close a measure of average total length of service as we can hope to get.

From Table 9 we see that the average previous service at election for all the seven general elections together is 5 years 11 months. The seventh parliament is still in being, but to date (March 1941) the average duration of the seven Houses is about 3 years 2 months. Hence the average House is halfway through its course at 1 year 7 months after election, and its average previous service at this point is 5 years 11 months plus 1 year 7 months—that is, 7 years 6 months. Doubling this, we get 15 years as the average total length of service for the inter-war period; and that is as close an estimate as we can hope to make.

CHAPTER V

THE EDUCATION OF MEMBERS

1. School Education

It may seem a simple matter to classify the education of members of parliament according to the type of school they have attended, but actually it is by no means easy to find a satisfactory method of doing so. Take the well-known term "public school", for example: setting aside any comment on the inappropriateness of the term for schools which are not, in fact, publicly owned or controlled,* it is by no means easy to define just what constitutes a public school. To most people probably a public school means Eton or Harrow, Rugby or Winchester, or one of a few other schools closely resembling them in general organization; that is, a large non-profit-making boarding-school, of traditional reputation and somewhat expensive character, which places considerable stress on classics and still more stress on games.

Actually there is no watertight definition of a "public school". Even the traditionally accepted nine "great" public schools—Eton, Harrow, Rugby, Winchester, Westminster, Charterhouse, Merchant Taylors', Shrewsbury, and St. Paul's—are by no means uniform in type. Winchester is purely a boarding-school, but Merchant Taylors' is purely a day-school; while Westminster, with roughly equal numbers of boarders and day-boys, is midway between.

Probably the most commonly accepted definition of a "public school" is "a school whose Head is a member of the Headmasters' Conference." But the schools on the Headmasters' Conference list vary greatly in type, in size, in reputation, and in importance: at one end we have huge, expensive, and world-famous boarding-schools such as Eton; at the other small day-schools with low fees and only a local reputation.† There is really no common group of characteristics which they all possess to the exclusion of other schools.‡ Moreover, there are schools not on the list that more closely resemble some of the schools on the list than the latter, as a whole, resemble each other.

The more closely the position is investigated, the more nebulous and unsatisfactory appear the boundaries between "public" schools and other types of school. It is impossible to formulate any precise definition which will include even the better-known public schools and will at the same time exclude all schools that are not accepted as entitled to that description.

* "An American wag, commenting on the name English Public Schools, said that they were called English because they taught so much Latin, Public because they were private, and Schools because two-thirds of the time they taught nothing but games" (*Comparative Education*, ed. Peter Sandiford). It is interesting to note that in Scotland a "public school" is an elementary school.

† Eton has 1,156 boys and George Watson's College has 1,422: there is a school on the list with only 50 boys, and many schools with few more than 100.

‡ For the criteria for admission to the list, see *Whitaker's Almanack*.

In these circumstances, after a prolonged attempt to find a better criterion, I have been driven to take inclusion in the Headmasters' Conference list as the standard for acceptance as a public school. It is, as we have seen, an unsatisfactory standard, since the schools included have no common body of characteristics that belong to them all and to them exclusively; its one saving grace is its definiteness.

The term "secondary school" also requires comment. The modern connotation of the term is that of a school providing definitely post-primary education—that is, education after the age of 11+. But the common usage, which still largely continues, is to contrast "secondary" with "elementary", not as a different stage, but as a different type of education; and, incidentally, to separate "public schools" from other secondary schools. This ambiguity is not an easy one to resolve fully, even at the present day; but in the case of an investigation such as this the difficulty is greatly increased by the fact that the members of parliament whose education is under consideration were at school at very different periods, ranging from the forties of last century to the twenties of this. During the greater part of this period, however, secondary and elementary education were largely alternative to each other: it is reasonable, therefore, so to take them for our purposes.

Hence in this investigation the schools attended by members have been classified as (a) public, (b) secondary, or (c) elementary. Under (a) are taken the schools now included in the Headmasters' Conference list; under (b) all other secondary schools, including boarding-schools, grammar-schools, and high-schools; and under (c) all public elementary schools, "National" schools, "British" schools, and schools that so far as can be ascertained fall into the same category.

It will be evident that the classification is by no means an exact or highly dependable one, especially in view of the widely different dates at which members received their education and the many changes that have taken place during the period, not only in the general organization of education, but also in the status and character of individual schools. Nevertheless, when all allowances are made, the classification does represent something real; it corresponds with significant categories of education. Moreover, when we come to compare the education of members with that of the general population, it provides a fairly definite standard of comparison.

Adopting, then, this method of analysis, Table 10 gives the school education of all members who sat in the House of Commons at any time from the general election of 1918 to the end of 1936, so far as it has been possible to ascertain it. As will be seen, in spite of all difficulties, it has been found possible so to classify nearly 82 per cent of the total membership.

These are the actual statistics on which much of our analysis must be based, but the position will be clearer if we restate them in two rather different ways. In doing this let us also simplify them: first, by ignoring the Independents (who are, after all, not a party, but just a few members with widely differing views); second, by assuming that *within each party* the members whose education is unknown were at the different types of school in the same proportions as those whose education is known (this may not be strictly accurate, but is most unlikely to introduce any but trifling errors); and, third, by employing percentages instead of actual numbers.

Making these simplifications, let us restate our statistics so as to see, first, how the product of each type of school is distributed between the three main parties; and, second, how the membership of each party is derived from the three types of school. It will be realized that these are separate and distinct aspects of the subject.

The first of these two ways of looking at the state of affairs is presented in Table 11 and illustrated in Fig. 15, which show the differing

TABLE 10.—SCHOOL EDUCATION: ALL MEMBERS

Party	Number of Members				
	Public School	*Secondary School*	*Elementary School*	*School Unknown*	*Total*
Conservative...	632	155	29	190	1,006
Liberal ...	109	114	35	96	354
Labour ...	40	71	285	48	444
Independent ...	3	7	1	8	19
Total ...	784	347	350	342	1,823

political tendencies of members in relation to the schools at which they were educated. Here we at once come up against some remarkable contrasts; for whereas no less than 80 per cent of the public-school members belong to the Conservative party and only $4\frac{1}{2}$ per cent to the Labour party, when we look at the elementary-school members the position is reversed, 79 per cent of these belonging to the Labour party and only 9 per cent to the Conservative party. It is noticeable that the secondary schools, which are socially intermediate between the public schools and the elementary schools, distribute their product much more evenly between the three parties.

Now let us turn to the other aspect. This is set forth in Table 12 and displayed graphically in Fig. 16, both of them showing the proportions in which each party derives its membership from the three types of school. It will be seen that out of every 40 Conservative members 31 were educated at public schools, while only 1 in 30 was educated at an elementary school; or, to put it in a slightly different way, there are over 22 public-school members in the parliamentary Conservative party for every member with an elementary-school education. In the Labour

TABLE 11.—PARTY AFFILIATION OF MEMBERS FROM EACH TYPE OF SCHOOL

Party	Type of School		
	Public	Secondary	Elementary
	%	%	%
Conservative	80	45	9
Liberal	15½	36½	12
Labour	4½	18½	79
Total	100	100	100

party in the House, on the other hand, nearly 3 out of every 4 members have only an elementary-school education, while only 1 in 10 has been at a public school, almost exactly reversing the position in the Conservative party. The Liberal party membership is more equally distributed, but secondary schools provide a bigger proportion—4 out of

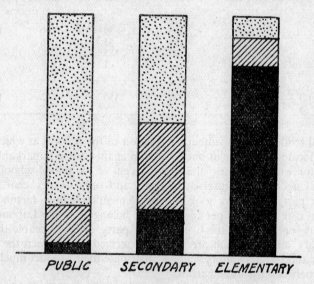

PUBLIC   SECONDARY   ELEMENTARY

CONSERVATIVES
LIBERALS
LABOUR.

FIG. 15.—Party affiliation of members from each type of school.

TABLE 12.—SCHOOL EDUCATION OF MEMBERS OF EACH PARTY

Type of School	Party		
	Conservative	Liberal	Labour
	%	%	%
Public	77½	42½	10
Secondary	19	44	18
Elementary ...	3½	13½	72
Total	100	100	100

every 9 members—than either of the other types, though public schools
are a good second. So far as public schools and elementary schools are
concerned, the party membership in both cases lies between that of the
other two parties, rather significantly.

There is another interesting and rather curious point that emerges
from the figures recorded in Table 12. Of the Conservative members, the
great majority (77½ per cent) come from the public schools, of the

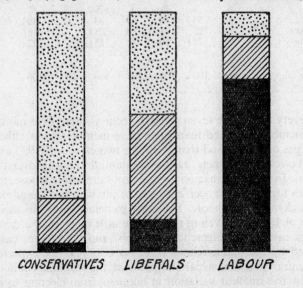

CONSERVATIVES   LIBERALS   LABOUR

PUBLIC
SECONDARY
ELEMENTARY

FIG. 16.—School education of members of each party.

Liberal members the largest number, though not actually a majority (44 per cent), come from the secondary schools, while of the Labour members the great majority (72 per cent) come from the elementary schools. To a remarkable extent, therefore, we should be justified in calling the Conservatives the public-school party, the Liberals the secondary-school party, and Labour the elementary-school party. We shall refer to this point again later.

So far we have considered all the members of parliament for the inter-war period as a whole, irrespective of the times at which they sat in the House of Commons. Let us now turn our attention to the seven general elections and see how they compare with each other so far as the school education of members is concerned. Table 13 gives the necessary data, expressed for convenience in percentages. It will be seen

TABLE 13.—SCHOOL EDUCATION OF EACH HOUSE

Type of School	General Election							Average House
	1918	1922	1923	1924	1929	1931	1935	
	%	%	%	%	%	%	%	%
Public	60	55½	48	59	43	66	59½	56
Secondary ...	23½	23	23	19	21½	22½	18½	21½
Elementary ...	16½	21½	29	22	35½	11½	22	22½
Total	100	100	100	100	100	100	100	100

that at every one of the seven general elections there were more public-school members returned than there were members from either of the other types of school, and that in all but two elections (1923 and 1929) the public-school members have a substantial majority over the other two types. In the 1931 election two-thirds of the whole House, including all parties together, had been educated at public schools, and only one-ninth at elementary schools. The most plebeian House in this respect was that of 1929, but even in that House little more than a third of the members came from elementary schools, and these were easily out-numbered by the public-school men. As is only to be expected from their "centre" position, social and political, the secondary-school members show the smallest variation in numbers from election to election, never rising above 23½ per cent and never falling below 18½ per cent of the House.

It is interesting in this connexion to trace how the numbers of members from the three types of school vary with the numbers of members of the three political parties with which, as already pointed out, they seem to have affinity. In Fig. 17 this affinity is displayed graphically. Here we have the fortunes of the public-school members compared with

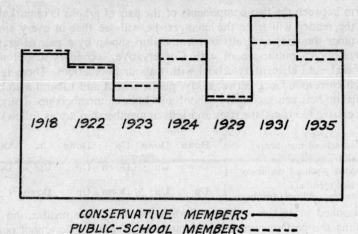

1918 1922 1923 1924 1929 1931 1935

CONSERVATIVE MEMBERS ———
PUBLIC-SCHOOL MEMBERS – – – – –

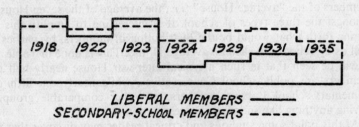

1918 1922 1923 1924 1929 1931 1935

LIBERAL MEMBERS ———
SECONDARY-SCHOOL MEMBERS – – – – –

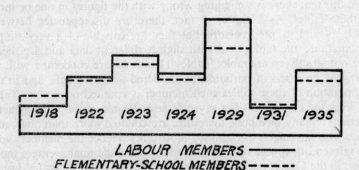

1918 1922 1923 1924 1929 1931 1935

LABOUR MEMBERS ———
FLEMENTARY-SCHOOL MEMBERS – – – – –

FIG. 17.—Comparison of numbers: parties and types of school.

the fortunes of the Conservative members, the fortunes of the secondary-school members compared with those of the Liberal members, and the fortunes of the elementary-school members with those of the Labour members. In each of the three cases, it will be seen, the resemblance in form between the two components of the pair of graphs is remarkable. If the reader will trace the changes, he will see that in every single instance the rises and falls in membership shown by a pair of graphs correspond: public-school with Conservative, secondary-school with Liberal, and elementary-school with Labour fluctuations. There is no such correspondence between, say, public-school and Liberal membership, or between secondary-school and Labour membership. Thus, in successive elections, the rises and falls in membership are as follows:

Conservative members Public-school members }	Down	Down	Up	Down	Up	Down
Liberal members Secondary-school members }	Down	Up	Down	Up	Up	Down
Labour members Elementary-school members }	Up	Up	Down	Up	Down	Up

Looked at in this way, the figures provide ample justification for calling the parliamentary Conservative party the public-school party, the Liberals the secondary-school party, and Labour the elementary-school party.

The last column of Table 13 gives the percentage distribution of the members of the "average House" (*i.e.*, the average of the seven Houses) amongst the three types of school. It is interesting to amplify this by setting forth what would be the distribution of numbers, by parties as well as by schools, in such an average House. This is done in Table 14. It will be seen that in such a typical inter-war House nearly half the members are public-school Conservatives, while nearly one-fifth are elementary-school Labour members, no other comparable grouping having anything like so large a representation.

At this point some studious and critical reader may discover that the distributions given in Table 14 are not in exact agreement with those previously given in Tables 11 and 12, and may be inclined to conclude from this that there is something wrong with the figures in one or more of these tables. As a matter of fact, there *are* discrepancies between Table 14 and its predecessors, but they are capable of a very simple explanation: the tables deal with slightly different data and are therefore not strictly comparable. Tables 11 and 12 are concerned with all inter-war members of parliament considered as individuals, and in the computation of these tables each member is counted once only. Table 14 gives the average for the seven Houses elected at the seven general elections: many members, therefore, are counted more than once, and those who sat longest are counted most times. Hence the members with the safest seats appear most often and influence the final averages most. Now, in the Conservative party the safest seats are, in general, given to the upper-class members, and *vice versa*: hence in the average House the Conservative party includes more public-school and fewer elementary-school members than the earlier tables would indicate. In the Labour party the tendency is just the reverse: here the safest seats are given, in general, to the trade-union members, so that in the average House the

Labour party includes more elementary-school and fewer public-school members than the earlier tables would indicate. These opposite tendencies throw an illuminating sidelight on the attitudes of the respective party machines.

The other discrepancies between the tables are similarly explainable by the different methods of compilation: they are not errors, but are due to the causes already set out. For example, the smaller proportion of Liberal members in the average House, by comparison with the proportion amongst all members, is largely due to the considerable number of Liberals who sat only in the brief 1923 parliament.

TABLE 14.—SCHOOL EDUCATION OF AVERAGE HOUSE

Party	Type of School			
	Public	Secondary	Elementary	Total
Conservative	277	62	9	348
Liberal	44	41	10	95
Labour	14	23	116	153
Independent ...	1	4	1	6
Total	336	130	136	602

Let us now consider how the school education of members of parliament compares with that of the population of Britain as a whole. For several reasons no exact comparison is possible, but nevertheless some interesting and significant results can be reached.

In determining the distribution of the school population between the three types of school, even at the present time, we are faced with the difficulty that results from the passage of pupils from one type of school to another. Since the elementary-school and secondary-school numbers that we require must include only those who do not subsequently pass on to the other types of school, the actual numbers of pupils in these schools at the moment do not give us just what we want. Moreover, the varying lengths of school life affect the position: what we want is not the totals, nor even the net totals, in attendance at each type of school, but the proportionate output of each.

For this the information immediately available* is neither sufficient nor suitably arranged. However, a rough estimate can be made, and it will probably be reasonably accurate if we take the present effective distribution of output to be, in round figures, as follows:

Public schools ...	...	...	...	...	3%
Secondary schools	...	...	...	...	11%
Elementary schools	...	...	...	...	86%

* *E.g.*, in the *Annual Reports* of the Board of Education.

Now, this represents the approximate distribution of *young people* from the three types of school *at the present time*; but the education of those who were *adults* at any time during the years from 1918 onwards was, like that of the inter-war members of parliament, spread over a period extending well back into the nineteenth century. Hence the scholastic distribution of the average inter-war adult population will differ considerably from the figures just given. The true distribution is necessarily indeterminate, however, and the most we can do is to hazard a guess at it. Taking into account the great development of post-primary education in recent years, especially since 1918, we shall probably be much nearer the truth if we take the mean distribution for the adult population of the whole inter-war period as being approximately as follows:

Public schools	2%
Secondary schools	5%
Elementary schools	93%

If the inter-war members of parliament had had, proportionately to their numbers, the same school education as the general population of the period, on this estimate, then their distribution would be, in round figures:

Public schools	12
Secondary schools	30
Elementary schools	560

How does this compare with their actual (average) distribution? Turning back to Table 14, we find that the figures for the latter are:

Public schools	336
Secondary schools	130
Elementary schools	136

It will be seen at once that, in relation to school education, the House is not in the least a fair sample of the general population. Elementary schools have less than a quarter of their proportionate representation, secondary schools have more than four times their proportion, while public schools have no less than twenty-eight times as many members as their strength in the population would entitle them to have.

Even allowing for a considerable margin of possible error, these disproportions are astonishingly high, and provide much food for thought. The wideness of the divergence between the two sets of figures will perhaps be made even more evident by a glance at Fig. 18, where they are displayed graphically.

Nothing in this discussion, of course, must be taken as assuming that the House of Commons would be improved if its education corresponded more nearly with that of the general population. Our object at this stage is to ascertain the facts and to point out their more immediate significance, not to draw final conclusions from them.

We now turn to another point. In investigating the school education of members of parliament one is struck not only by the big proportion of public-school men in the House of Commons, but also by the marked preponderance of Eton and, to a less extent, Harrow. It will probably astonish most people to learn that roughly one-fourth of all the Conservatives who sat in the House at any time during the whole inter-war period were old Etonians, while one-third of the whole number were from either Eton or Harrow. The proportions in the other parties were, as one would expect, much smaller; but even so we find that one in every seven of all the members of all parties together, including Labour,

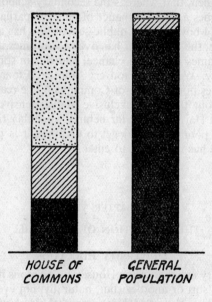

HOUSE OF COMMONS   GENERAL POPULATION

PUBLIC
SECONDARY
ELEMENTARY

Fig. 18.—School education: average House of Commons compared with general population.

was an old Etonian, and that one in five was either an old Etonian or an old Harrovian.

Eton is a big school, but even so its annual output of boys cannot be more than about 250. The corresponding output for all the schools of the country may be taken as round about 750,000. Hence it will be seen that only about 1 in 3,000 of the population of the country is educated at Eton. It follows that, if the House of Commons were a fair sample of the population in respect of education, the proportionate representation of Eton would be one-fifth of a member. The actual number of old Etonians in the House naturally varies from time to time, but the average for the period under review is about 105. Eton, therefore, has well over 500 times as many members as she should have on the basis of proportion. Harrow is a smaller school than Eton, having an annual output of roughly 120 boys. Hence, proportionately, less than one-tenth of a member of parliament should be an old Harrovian. The actual number in the House averages about 43, or nearly 450 times as many as proportion would give.

We may say, then, that whereas the secondary-school boy has *prima facie* about 18 times as good a chance of entering parliament as has the elementary-school boy, and the public-school boy has about 115 times as good a chance, the Harrovian has over 1,800 times and the Etonian well over 2,000 times as good a chance; and this in spite of the rise of the Labour party. Well may Eton cry "Floreat Etona!"—the school certainly flourishes in the House of Commons.* The reader should note that Eton is about the most exclusive and expensive school in the country, and that Harrow is not far behind it in either respect. The boy of ability from a poor home *may* get to Oxford—it is possible, though not easy—but he has no chance to enter Eton.

CHAPTER VI

THE EDUCATION OF MEMBERS

2. UNIVERSITY EDUCATION

PRACTICALLY every member of the House of Commons has had a school education of one sort or another; but, naturally, not every member has been at a university. Nevertheless, the number of university men—not necessarily graduates—in parliament is considerable, as Table 15 shows. From this we find that exactly half of the inter-war Conservative members have had a university education, about three out of seven of the Liberals, and about two out of nine of the Labour members. If we allow for cases where university education has not been recorded, the actual proportions may be just a little higher, but such cases are probably very few.

The dominant position of the two old universities will be noticed. Of the Conservatives with a university education, over 80 per cent were at Oxford or Cambridge, and of the Liberals over 57 per cent; while even in the Labour party the proportion was 42 per cent. For all parties together it was over 71 per cent. If we take all members, non-university as well as university, we find that Oxford and Cambridge claim over 40 per cent of the Conservatives, over 24 per cent of the Liberals, and about 8 per cent of the Labour members; or nearly 30 per cent of all parties together.

* In the House of Lords it is even more dominant, having a solid majority of no less than 60 per cent of the whole House!

As between Oxford and Cambridge, it will be seen that amongst the Conservatives Oxford predominates, there being four members from Oxford to three from Cambridge; amongst the Liberals there is little to choose, with 22 Oxford to 21 Cambridge; whilst amongst the Labour members the position is reversed and there are roughly five from Cambridge to four from Oxford. For all parties together the ratio is roughly five from Oxford to four from Cambridge. Of the whole number of members, non-university as well as university, Oxford claims almost exactly one in every six, while Cambridge claims rather more than one in every eight.

TABLE 15.—UNIVERSITY EDUCATION: ALL MEMBERS

Party	Number of Members					
	Oxford	Cam-bridge	London	Other British	Over-seas	Total *
Conservative ...	232	174	33	78	20	503
Liberal	44	42	15	56	9	150
Labour	15	19	18	31	5	81
Independent ...	3	2	3	2	2	9
Total	294	237	69	167	36	743

* Apparent discrepancies in these totals are due to the fact that some members have attended more than one university.

It will be seen that Oxford and Cambridge amongst universities occupy a favoured position in the House comparable with that of Eton and Harrow amongst schools. Oxford and Cambridge are much bigger institutions than Eton and Harrow—Oxford's output is perhaps four times that of Eton—so their preferential position is not as marked as that of the schools, though it is outstanding.

Even with the development of the public scholarship schemes, Oxford is still largely the university for men of wealth and social position, and Cambridge is a good second to it: at the time when the members we are studying were there the two universities were even more exclusive. It is, therefore, significant that (a) roughly one Conservative member out of every four was at Oxford and two out of every five at either Oxford or Cambridge, (b) one member out of every six of all parties together was at Oxford and two out of every seven were at either Oxford or Cambridge, and (c) all the other universities together, British and overseas, cannot nearly equal these figures.

The poor position of the University of London in parliament is remarkable. It has been established over a century and its output is considerably greater than that of Oxford and Cambridge together; yet of

TABLE 16.—PARTY AFFILIATION OF UNIVERSITY-EDUCATED MEMBERS

Party	University			
	Oxford	Cambridge	Other	All
	%	%	%	%
Conservative ...	80	74	49½	68½
Liberal	15	18	30	20½
Labour	5	8	20½	11
Total	100%	100%	100%	100%

the 1,823 members of parliament included in this survey only 69 can be traced as members of London against 530 who have been at Oxford or Cambridge. Size for size, therefore, Oxford and Cambridge together are perhaps a dozen times as well represented as London. When it is borne in mind not only that London is by far the biggest university in the country, but also that parliament itself meets in London, the position disclosed by these figures is astonishing.

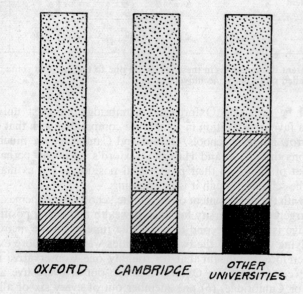

OXFORD　　CAMBRIDGE　　OTHER UNIVERSITIES

CONSERVATIVES
LIBERALS
LABOUR

FIG. 19.—Party affiliation of university-educated members.

The rest of the English universities are smaller institutions and mostly of recent growth—a considerable factor in the case—but collectively their output is greater than that of Oxford and Cambridge together. They provide 44 members against the 530 from the two old universities, and have therefore a representation that is roughly one-fourteenth as good. The long-established Scottish universities, with their 98 members, do relatively well compared with the modern English universities, though poorly by comparison with Oxford and Cambridge. Size for size they have roughly one-sixth of the latter's representation, though they are nearly three times as well represented as the former. Wales and the Irish universities are also better represented than the English, even though it is only the members for Great Britain that come within this survey.

Let us now consider how the university-educated members are distributed between the three main parties, ignoring the Independents and employing percentages for clearness instead of numbers. Table 16 presents this point of view, and the state of affairs it discloses is most interesting. Notice how 80 per cent of the Oxford men are Conservatives against 74 per cent of the Cambridge men and only 49½ per cent of the rest of the university alumni. Observe how in the other parties the position is reversed, the Liberal percentages rising instead of falling, and the Labour percentages rising more steeply than the Liberal. Notice, too, that Oxford and Cambridge are "right-wing" and the other universities "left-wing" by comparison with the average for all universities given in the last column. Whether we study the figures in this table down each column or across each line, they give food for thought. Fig. 19, which presents them graphically, may help to drive home their lessons: see how as the Conservative areas decrease the Liberal and Labour areas increase, the latter more sharply than the former. It is exactly the same type of social pattern as we found in studying school education.*

Now, instead of seeing how the university product divides itself between the parties, let us take the alternative way of looking at the subject and see in what proportions the three main parties draw their strength from Oxford, Cambridge, and the other universities respectively, again ignoring the Independents and using percentages. These proportions are set out in Table 17† and shown diagrammatically in Fig. 20.

We see again that Oxford is the university most favoured by the Conservatives, with Cambridge next, and the other universities a long way behind. The Labour party reverses the process, while the Liberals, as usual, come in between.

It is now evident that, just as school education and party are strongly

* See, for comparison, Table 11 and Fig. 15.
† The differences between the figures given in this table and those given in the text earlier in this chapter are due to the fact that some members have attended more than one university; the present table gives the *proportionate* distribution, whereas the earlier percentages, though perfectly correct, involve some overlapping.

TABLE 17.—UNIVERSITY EDUCATION OF MEMBERS OF EACH PARTY

University	Party		
	Conservative	Liberal	Labour
	%	%	%
Oxford	43	26½	17
Cambridge ...	32½	25½	21½
Other	24½	48	61½
Total	100	100	100

correlated, so are university education and party. If a member of parliament has been at Oxford, it is 4 to 1 that he is a Conservative and 19 to 1 that he is not a Labour member; just as, if he has been at Eton, it is 9 to 1 that he is a Conservative and 34 to 1 that he is not a Labour member. As we go down the scale from Oxford to Cambridge and from Cambridge to the newer universities, so does the party complexion change; just as it does when we pass from Eton to Harrow, from

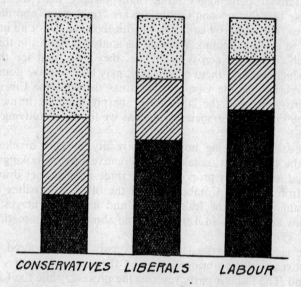

CONSERVATIVES　LIBERALS　LABOUR

OXFORD

CAMBRIDGE

OTHER UNIV.

FIG. 20.—University education of members of each party.

Harrow to the other public schools, thence to the secondary schools, and thence to the elementary schools. The older, the more expensive, and the more socially exclusive the university or the school, the more certainly will its product be found on the right wing in politics, and *vice versa*. Incidentally we note that in university education, as in age and school education, the Liberal party occupies an intermediate position between the Conservative and Labour parties.

We may conclude this chapter with a glance at the position at each of the seven general elections, as set out in Table 18. It will be seen that the number of Oxford men has varied from a minimum of 13½ per

TABLE 18.—UNIVERSITY EDUCATION OF EACH HOUSE

University	General Election							Average House
	1918	1922	1923	1924	1929	1931	1935	
	%	%	%	%	%	%	%	%
Oxford	17	16	15	17½	13½	22½	21	17½
Cambridge ...	12½	13	11	14	13	17	16	13½
Other	13½	12½	12½	13½	14½	15	12	13½
Total*	40	39	37	42	38	51	46½	42

* Apparent discrepancies in these totals are due to the fact that some members have attended more than one university.

cent of the whole House in 1929 to a maximum of 22½ per cent in 1931, with an average of 17½ per cent. When it is borne in mind that less than one in a thousand of the population of Great Britain goes to Oxford, it will be seen that the Oxford man has something like 180 times as good a chance of entering parliament as has the average member of the public. As already remarked, Oxford in this respect does not come out in such a privileged position as Eton, but she is nevertheless remarkably well placed. In the case of Cambridge the number of members has varied from a minimum of 11 per cent of the whole House in 1923 to a maximum of 17 per cent in 1931, with an average of 13½ per cent. The Cambridge man's chance of entering parliament is therefore not so good as the Oxford man's, though it is at least 140 times as good as that of the average member of the public.

CHAPTER VII

THE OCCUPATIONS OF MEMBERS*

1. General Survey

MOST people are aware that lawyers and trade-union officials are plentiful in the House of Commons, but few people know much more than that of the distribution of occupations amongst members. It is the business of this chapter to supply the facts: to give in some detail the occupations of members and, in order to bring out the significance of the figures, to compare them with the corresponding figures for the adult population as a whole.

This comparison serves two related purposes: first, it enables us to see the figures for members in reasonable perspective; and, second, it provides further evidence on which to decide whether the House is or is not a fair sample of the general population.

In order to carry out such a comparison, however,. and, indeed, in order to record the facts at all, it is necessary to decide on a basis of classification: for the complexities of our modern mechanized civilization are so great that the number of distinct occupations runs into many hundreds. Almost inevitably we turn to the Occupation volumes of the Census of Great Britain, 1921 and 1931, for the basis of classification, for, though their system is far from ideal, there appears to be no better alternative available.

The reason why we say that the census classification is far from ideal is because, though the census now claims to distinguish between *occupation* and *industry*, in actual fact it fails to do so. A man's occupation is determined by the work which he actually does, and is irrespective of the industry by which he is employed. A clerk is a clerk whether he works for a brewer or a stockbroker or a government department. A joiner is a joiner irrespective of the industry that uses his services. Unfortunately, the census is amazingly blind to this very obvious fact: its compilers cannot get *industry* out of their heads when they are supposed to be thinking of *occupation*, and the results are deplorable. On the one hand, persons whose actual work is closely similar are placed by the census in different groups; on the other hand, persons whose work is utterly different are placed in the same group. Instances of both kinds are numerous, but it will suffice to mention a few of each.

An aviator is placed in Group XXII if engaged in civilian flying, but in Group XXIV if in the R.A.F. An engine-driver is placed in Group XXII if the engine he drives is a locomotive, but in Group XXX if it is a stationary engine or a crane. An accountant is placed in Group XXIII if employed by a bank, in XXIV if employed in the civil service, in XXV if in private practice, and in XXVIII if employed as a company registrar.

In Group XXII we find such dissimilar occupations as those of rail-

* See also Chapter XXIX.

way signalman, shipowner, aviator, and postal sorter; in XXIII are brought together such diverse workers as shop assistants, bankers, and valuers; XXIV includes civil servants, admirals, and policemen; while in XXV we find a heterogeneous collection indeed—judges and metallurgists, Scripture readers and naval architects, journalists and sculptors.

Moreover, the census fails seriously in another respect: it lumps together employers and managers, a proceeding which has no justification but that of simplicity. It is true that many employers are their own managers; but the functions of an employer, *qua* employer, are not the same as, or even closely similar to, those of a manager. In essence the manager is normally either the expert administrator or technician, or the promoted foreman, whereas the employer may be a functionless or nearly functionless owner with no expert knowledge and no share in the day-to-day management. Take Group III (Mining and Quarrying): a mine manager must be a man of considerable experience and technical training, and must hold a statutory Certificate of Competency; a mineowner needs no qualifications. On what grounds can mere ownership, of a mine or of anything else, be held to constitute an occupation? The census treats landowners as "not gainfully occupied": why not mineowners also?

There are, of course, real difficulties in the way of more accurate classification: border-line cases always present a problem, and there are other snags. Nevertheless, a much better analysis could and should have been achieved. The great trouble is that the census authorities fail to concentrate on what a man *does*; they get themselves muddled up by letting their thoughts stray to the industry in which or the employer for whom he does it.

Against these defects in the census, however, must be set the great advantages it offers. It is based on the record of occupations actually followed in the country; it is in general very thorough; it is authoritative; and, finally, it gives us a means of comparing the occupations of members with those of the general population. Before we can utilize it, however, we must make some important adjustments.

In the first place, in dealing with members of parliament we are concerned to know what are or have been their occupations, but not whether they are or are not still following them. Now, the census places the retired in Group XXXII (Not Gainfully Occupied); hence for proper comparison with members of parliament these retired workers must be transferred back to the groups in which their former occupations belong. Next, the census treats students and persons employed abroad as being also not gainfully employed: for our purpose they would be more reasonably allotted to Group XXXI (Other and Undefined Workers), and they must accordingly be transferred to that group. Finally, in dealing with the occupations of the general population, we have to eliminate that portion of it which is under 21, and we have to combine the returns for Scotland with those for England and Wales, and the returns for females with those for males.

Here is another point. In allocating members of parliament to their appropriate occupational groups, difficulties are occasionally encountered, either because of the vagueness of the information available or for other reasons. For example, when a member has followed in succession a number of different occupations, or has carried on more than

TABLE 19.—OCCUPATION: ALL MEMBERS

Group	Abridged Description *	Number of Members				
		Con.	Lib.	Lab.	Ind.	Total
I ...	Fishermen	—	—	—		—
II ...	Agriculture	22	7	7	—	36
III ...	Mining ...	4	7	87	1	99
IV ...	Non-Metal Products ...	—	—	1	—	1
V ...	Brickmakers	2	—	2	—	4
VI ...	Chemical Workers ...	7	6	—	—	13
VII ...	Metal Workers	12	6	32	2	52
VIII ...	Precious Metals	—	—	—	—	—
IX ...	Electrical Workers ...	1	—	—	—	1
X ...	Watches and Clocks ...	—	1	1	—	2
XI ...	Leather Workers ...	1	1	—	—	2
XII ...	Textile Workers ...	18	12	19	1	50
XIII ...	Clothing Makers ...	5	5	5	—	15
XIV ...	Food, Drink, Tobacco ...	27	2	3	—	32
XV ...	Wood and Furniture ...	1	2	16	—	19
XVI ...	Paper Workers	3	—	2	—	5
XVII ...	Printers	15	14	5	—	34
XVIII ...	Builders	13	3	8	2	26
XIX ...	Painters	—	1	5	—	6
XX ...	Other Materials ...	—	—	—	—	—
XXI ...	Mixed Materials ...	15	2	3	—	20
XXII ...	Transport	35	13	25	—	73
XXIII ...	Commerce and Finance	132	69	21	3	225
XXIV ...	Admin. and Defence ...	181	14	10	3	208
XXV ...	Professional ...	330	160	132	13	635
XXVI ...	Entertainment ...	6	2	4	—	12
XXVII ...	Personal Services ...	4	—	2	—	6
XXVIII...	Clerks and Draughtsmen	25	3	27	—	55
XXIX ...	Warehousemen	—	—	1	—	1
XXX ...	Engine Drivers ...	—	—	2	—	2
XXXI ...	Miscellaneous	2	1	—	—	3
XXXII ...	Not Gainfully Occupied	142	23	19	2	186
——	Total	1,003	354	439	27	1,823

* For the full official description of each group see Appendix II.

one occupation at a time, it is not always easy to determine into which group he may most reasonably be placed. However, these complications arise only in a small minority of cases, and where they do great care has been taken to make the allocations as accurately as the circumstances permit. While, therefore, it is useless to expect the tables that

TABLE 20.—OCCUPATION: GENERAL ELECTIONS

Group	Abridged Description	General Election							Average
		1918	1922	1923	1924	1929	1931	1935	
I	Fishermen	11	11	9	10	16	16	13	12·3
II	Agriculture	34	52	52	46	50	25	40	42·7
III	Mining	1	1	1	1	1	1	1	1·0
IV	Non-Metal Products	—	1	1	2	2	1	1	1·1
V	Brickmakers	8	5	3	2	1	1	—	2·9
VI	Chemical Workers	19	22	23	24	23	13	18	20·3
VII	Metal Workers	—	—	—	1	1	—	—	—
VIII	Precious Metals	—	—	—	—	—	1	—	0·1
IX	Electrical Workers	1	1	1	1	1	—	1	0·9
X	Watches and Clocks	—	—	—	—	—	—	—	0·7
XI	Leather Workers	18	15	18	15	19	2	10	14·6
XII	Textile Workers	4	4	6	2	5	2	—	3·4
XIII	Clothing Makers	17	12	12	13	9	8	7	11·1
XIV	Food, Drink, Tobacco	4	6	9	7	11	5	8	7·1
XV	Wood and Furniture	—	2	—	2	2	2	2	1·7
XVI	Paper Workers	16	17	18	15	8	7	10	13·0
XVII	Printers	9	9	8	7	8	7	6	7·7
XVIII	Builders	1	1	3	1	3	1	2	1·7
XIX	Painters	—	—	—	—	—	—	—	—
XX	Other Materials	7	5	6	6	7	7	6	6·3
XXI	Mixed Materials	33	28	29	24	24	13	21	24·6
XXII	Transport	86	59	72	59	54	77	76	69·0
XXIII	Commerce and Finance	67	71	58	91	66	95	84	76·0
XXIV	Administration and Defence	190	199	201	188	206	220	196	200·0
XXV	Professional	—	3	5	5	7	4	4	4·0
XXVI	Entertainment	2	2	2	3	4	2	3	2·6
XXVII	Personal Services	10	15	17	16	27	14	30	18·4
XXVIII	Clerks and Draughtsmen	—	—	1	1	1	—	1	0·4
XXIX	Warehousemen	2	1	—	—	—	—	—	1·0
XXX	Engine Drivers	—	—	2	2	1	2	—	—
XXXI	Miscellaneous	—	—	—	—	—	—	1	1·3
XXXII	Not Gainfully Occupied	62	60	42	57	44	70	57	56·0
	Total	602	602	602	602	602	602	602	602

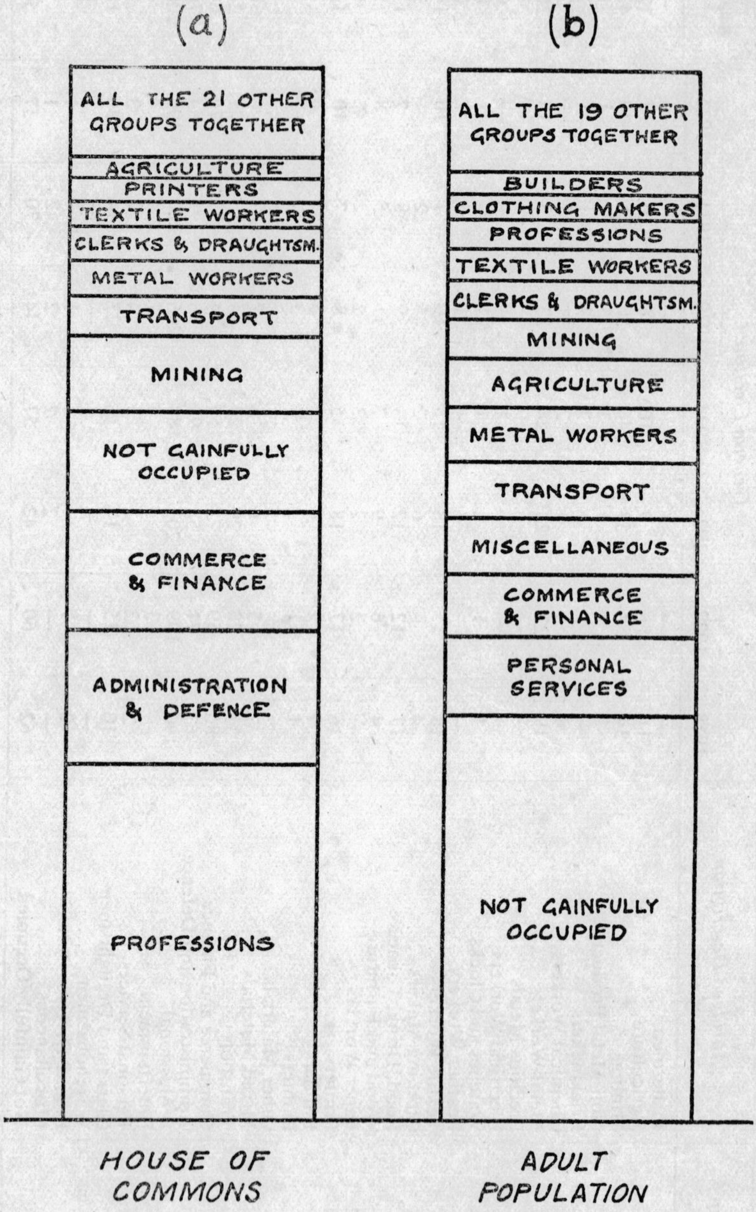

(a)

ALL THE 21 OTHER GROUPS TOGETHER

AGRICULTURE
PRINTERS

TEXTILE WORKERS

CLERKS & DRAUGHTSM.

METAL WORKERS

TRANSPORT

MINING

NOT GAINFULLY OCCUPIED

COMMERCE & FINANCE

ADMINISTRATION & DEFENCE

PROFESSIONS

HOUSE OF COMMONS

(b)

ALL THE 19 OTHER GROUPS TOGETHER

BUILDERS

CLOTHING MAKERS

PROFESSIONS

TEXTILE WORKERS

CLERKS & DRAUGHTSM.

MINING

AGRICULTURE

METAL WORKERS

TRANSPORT

MISCELLANEOUS

COMMERCE & FINANCE

PERSONAL SERVICES

NOT GAINFULLY OCCUPIED

ADULT POPULATION

FIG. 21.—Occupations of members and of adult population.

follow to give mathematically precise figures, the reader may take it that they are substantially correct.

We can now turn to our first set of data. Table 19 records the occupations of all members of parliament who sat in the House of Commons at any time during the inter-war period, arranged by parties and census groupings, subject to the modifications indicated above. It is at once apparent how unequally the various occupations are represented in parliament; comment on this will be made at a later stage. It will also be observed that certain groups are much more strongly represented by one party than by the others. It would be a mistake, however, to attach much importance to these facts as they stand. They are of interest as showing certain general tendencies, but they need amplification and closer scrutiny before they can be made to yield results of much significance.

Let us turn to the occupations of the members returned at each general election; these are recorded in Table 20, together with the averages for the seven elections. On the whole the numbers in the various groups do not fluctuate very widely, so that their averages give a fairly accurate indication of what we may term the normal occupational composition of the House. Before discussing in detail the figures in Table 20 we must complete the next stage of our investigation, the determination of the occupational distribution of the whole adult population of Great Britain, but even at this stage some interesting results emerge.

Notice the predominant position of certain groups. Observe particularly how Group XXV (Professional Occupations) provides no less than a third of the House, while the three groups XXIII (Commerce and Finance), XXIV (Public Administration and Defence), and XXXII (Not Gainfully Occupied) provide between them another third, so that two-thirds of the House consists of members having professional or semi-professional occupations or not gainfully occupied. We have the astonishing result, therefore, that Agriculture, Mining, Transport, and the whole of the manufactures of the country, including the important metal and textile industries, together with all the manual workers, all the clerks, draughtsmen, etc., all the people engaged in Personal Services, and all the people of miscellaneous occupations, are, together, represented by one-third only of the House. We shall return to this later. Meanwhile section (a) of Fig. 21 displays the occupational distribution of the House in diagram form. (The other section of the figure will be dealt with later.)

We must next determine the occupational distribution of the whole adult population of Great Britain. The census returns of 1921 and 1931 give us the means of doing this, but, as already indicated, they need considerable adjustment and rearrangement. What we require, for each occupation-group, is the number of workers comprising (a) both sexes, (b) all ages over 21, (c) the whole of Great Britain, and (d) retired as well as present workers. What the census supplies is the number of

TABLE 21.—NUMBERS OF MEMBERS IN PROPORTION TO ADULT POPULATION

Group	Abridged Description	Census, 1931			Census, 1921			Average Total
		Men	Women	Total	Men	Women	Total	
I	Fishermen	0·9	0·0	0·9	1·2	0·0	1·2	1·0
II	Agriculture	24·1	1·2	25·3	27·2	2·1	29·3	27·3
III	Mining	20·2	0·1	20·2	24·2	0·1	24·3	22·3
IV	Non-Metal Products	0·5	0·0	0·6	0·5	0·0	0·5	0·5
V	Brickmakers	1·4	0·4	1·8	1·3	0·4	1·6	1·7
VI	Chemical Workers	0·9	0·1	1·0	0·7	0·1	0·8	0·9
VII	Metal Workers	27·9	1·2	29·1	32·4	1·2	33·5	31·3
VIII	Precious Metals	0·5	0·2	0·6	0·6	0·2	0·8	0·7
IX	Electrical Workers	3·4	0·3	3·7	2·6	0·2	2·7	3·2
X	Watches and Clocks	0·4	0·0	0·6	0·6	0·0	0·6	0·6
XI	Leather Workers	1·0	0·3	1·3	1·1	0·3	1·4	1·4
XII	Textile Workers	6·3	10·6	16·8	6·8	11·3	18·0	17·4
XIII	Clothing Makers	5·6	8·3	13·9	6·2	9·2	15·4	14·7
XIV	Food, Drink, Tobacco	3·7	1·2	4·9	3·6	1·2	4·8	4·8
XV	Wood and Furniture	10·1	0·3	10·4	10·0	0·3	10·3	10·3
XVI	Paper Workers	0·8	0·9	1·7	0·7	0·8	1·5	1·6
XVII	Printers	2·9	0·5	3·4	2·7	0·5	3·2	3·3
XVIII	Builders	15·3	0·0	15·4	12·4	0·0	12·4	13·9
XIX	Painters	5·3	0·5	5·8	4·6	0·4	5·0	5·4
XX	Other Materials	0·7	0·3	1·0	0·6	0·3	1·0	1·0
XXI	Mixed Materials	1·4	0·2	1·6	1·7	0·3	2·0	1·8
XXII	Transport	31·8	1·0	32·8	31·1	1·0	32·1	32·5
XXIII	Commerce and Finance	30·0	10·2	40·2	23·6	9·5	33·0	36·6
XXIV	Administration and Defence	6·8	0·1	6·8	10·9	1·6	12·5	9·7
XXV	Professional	8·5	9·2	17·7	7·1	9·1	16·3	17·0
XXVI	Entertainment	1·9	0·4	2·3	1·4	0·4	1·8	2·1
XXVII	Personal Services	9·6	33·0	42·7	7·6	31·6	39·1	40·9
XXVIII	Clerks and Draughtsmen	15·0	9·0	23·9	12·0	7·6	19·7	21·8
XXIX	Warehousemen	4·9	1·8	6·7	4·6	1·6	6·3	6·5
XXX	Engine Drivers	3·6	0·0	3·6	4·0	0·0	4·0	3·8
XXXI	Miscellaneous	31·2	2·9	34·1	29·8	3·7	33·5	33·8
XXXII	Not Gainfully Occupied	4·3	226·9	231·3	5·6	228·1	233·7	232·5
	Total	280·9	321·1	602	279·1	322·9	602	602

workers (*a*) of each sex separately, (*b*) of all ages over 14 together, and in small age-groups such as "14 and 15", (*c*) in England and Wales and, separately, in Scotland, and (*d*) excluding retired workers, who are given separately in tables not conveniently divided in respect of age.

Hence much manipulation and recalculation are necessary to get the figures in the form we need. There is no need to specify all the steps in detail; it suffices to say that, taking first the 1931 census, we start with the figures for males given in Table 2 of the England and Wales Occupation volume, deduct the workers under 21 and add the retired workers, using Table 12 for the necessary information about the latter. This series of age-adjustments and transfers having been completed for the males of England and Wales, the same processes must be carried through for the females of England and Wales, the males of Scotland, and the females of Scotland. A series of simple additions then gives us the total numbers of adult workers in each occupation-group for the whole of Great Britain, based on the 1931 census.

The next step is to determine what would be the number of members of parliament elected from each occupation-group if the groups were represented proportionately to their strengths. A total adult population of 29,323,163 was in 1931 represented by the 602 members of parliament, so that on an average 48,710 adults were represented by each member. Hence the number of adults in each occupation-group divided by 48,710 gives the number of members of parliament to which it would be entitled on the basis of the 1931 figures. This information, for the sexes separately and together, is set out in columns 3, 4, and 5 of Table 21.

When we turn to the 1921 census we come up against a serious difficulty. The census tables for 1921 employ a different set of age-groups, and these, unlike those of 1931, give us no means of determining directly the number of adults in each occupation-group. It is true that Table 9 of the 1931 census gives, for England and Wales, a rough measure of the changes of occupation numbers that had taken place between the two censuses, but it is not a very satisfactory table for our purpose. For one thing, it not only includes adolescents, but it commences at 12 years of age in 1921 against 14 in 1931. For another, the adult population of Great Britain was not the same in 1921 as in 1931, so that the basis of one member of parliament to each 48,710 adults employed in calculating the number of members proportionate to each occupation-group in 1931 will not be correct for 1921. Finally, the sex-distribution was by no means the same in 1921 as it was in 1931, so that we cannot determine the proportionate numbers of male and female members without a further correction.

Unfortunately, the census tables do not give us the means of making any of these corrections with exactness, and it is consequently not possible to compute the numbers of members of parliament proportionate to the strength of the occupation-groups for 1921 with the same accuracy as those for 1931. However, by making various assumptions it

5

is possible to calculate figures for 1921 that are not likely to be seriously in error, and these are given in columns 6, 7, and 8 of Table 21, while the last column gives the averages of the 1931 and 1921 totals.

It is not suggested that the reader need study the figures in this table in detail; he will for the most part find it quite sufficient to use this and other tables for reference only. But if anyone scrutinizes the figures closely he may detect some small discrepancies between individual items and their totals or averages. These arise from giving the figures in the table correct to one place of decimals only, whereas all the items, with their totals and averages, are calculated separately from more exact data. Each is consequently correct to the degree of accuracy stated, even when they do not seem to agree precisely amongst themselves.

Let us look for a moment at the last column of Table 21. The figures in this column show how the House of Commons would be composed if the occupation-groups were represented in proportion to their mean inter-war strength in the general population. It should be clearly understood, however, that no expression of opinion as to the desirability of such proportionality is implied. This proportionate representation is shown graphically in section (b) of Fig. 21.

Now compare the two sections of Fig. 21. It will be seen at a glance how utterly unlike the actual distribution is to the proportionate. Compare, for example, the Professions groups in the two sections, and also the Not Gainfully Occupied groups. Notice, too, that the Public Administration and Defence group, which is the second largest in section (a), is too small to be shown separately in section (b); while the converse is the case with the Personal Services group. Clearly there is no resemblance between the two distributions; not only do the sizes of the groups vary greatly between them, but also there is no similarity in the orders of importance. These are matters that need fuller discussion; this chapter has given us the essential data, and the next will be devoted to a closer scrutiny of the facts and a consideration of their significance.

CHAPTER VIII

THE OCCUPATIONS OF MEMBERS

2. FURTHER ANALYSIS

LET us now see how the actual composition of the average House of Commons in respect of occupation compares with the composition that the House would have if each occupation were represented proportionately to the number of people engaged in it.

In the absence of any disturbing factors the ordinary laws of chance or probability would ensure a fairly close correspondence between the number of adults engaged in a particular occupation and the number of members of parliament drawn from it. It stands to reason, for example, that Group XI (Workers in Leather) with a population of some 63 thousand is likely to be represented by fewer members than Group XII (Textile Workers) with a population of some 820 thousand; and this is actually the case, the numbers of members drawn from the two groups being one and fifteen respectively.

Obviously, however, many factors, apart from pure chance, enter into the matter. It is one thing to compare workers in leather with textile workers: it is quite another to compare either of them with, say, professional workers or the big Not Gainfully Occupied group. Before discussing the causes, however, let us see what are in fact the chief

TABLE 22.—OCCUPATION: UNDER- AND OVER-REPRESENTATION OF GROUPS

Group	Abridged Description	Number of Members Proportional	Actual	Ratio of Actual to Proportional
XXXI ...	Miscellaneous	33·8	1·3	0·04
XXVII ...	Personal Services	40·9	2·6	0·06
XIII ...	Clothing Makers	14·7	3·4	0·23
XXXII ...	Not Gainfully Occupied ...	232·5	56·0	0·24
II ...	Agriculture	27·3	12·3	0·45
XVIII ...	Builders	13·9	7·7	0·55
VII ...	Metal Workers	31·3	20·3	0·65
XV ...	Wood and Furniture	10·3	7·1	0·69
XXII ...	Transport	32·5	24·6	0·76
XII ...	Textile Workers	17·4	14·6	0·84
XXVIII	Clerks and Draughtsmen ...	21·8	18·4	0·85
XXIII ...	Commerce and Finance ...	36·6	69·0	1·9
III ...	Mining and Quarrying ...	22·3	42·7	1·9
XIV ...	Food, Drink, Tobacco ...	4·9	11·1	2·3
XVII ...	Printers	3·3	13·0	3·9
XXIV ...	Administration and Defence ...	9·7	76·0	7·8
XXV ...	Professional	17·0	200·0	11·8

divergences between the actual and the proportional representation of the various groups.

We may disregard all groups in which the actual and proportional numbers are each less than ten members, since the smaller the group the greater will be the effect of pure chance on its representation, and the less the significance of any comparison. Taking the figures for the actual and proportional representation from the last columns of Tables 20 and 21 respectively, we have in Table 22 the remaining (larger) groups in order, from the most under-represented at the top to the most over-represented at the bottom.

We find that the most inadequately represented group, proportionally, is XXXI (Other and Undefined Workers). This, however, is the least determinate of the groups, and therefore the one for which the figures are most likely to be in error; the ratio is therefore unreliable.

Moreover, this group, from its miscellaneous character, least needs and is least capable of direct representation.

Next comes XXVII (Personal Services). Here the disproportion is extreme; the group has only one-sixteenth of the representation that it would have on a proportional basis. It is not surprising that there are few domestic servants, waiters, or hairdressers in parliament, but it means that, occupationally, this half-million men and million and a half women are practically unrepresented. The group's few members of parliament are untypical, being mostly hotel or restaurant keepers or beersellers.

After this comes XIII (Makers of Textile Goods and Clothing), with less than one-fourth of its proportion of members. Even this scanty representation is untypical; three-fourths of it consists of employers and managers, and the small remainder is nearly all boot and shoe workers. So the great bulk of the group's quarter-million men and half-million women are, occupationally, unrepresented.

Next we have what is easily the largest group of all—even after our transfers from it—namely, XXXII (Not Gainfully Occupied). It is unfortunate that this group is not subdivided, for it includes, apart from oddments of one sort or another, two main sections that, though lumped together by the census, are entirely dissimilar: first, the "idle rich", and, second, the women engaged in unpaid domestic work. Before we discuss their representation, however, let us consider some of the characteristics of these dissimilar sections.

Are we justified in speaking of the "idle rich"? If we intend it as a term of abuse to be applied indiscriminately to all people who are not directly earning their living, we are certainly not. Such people fall roughly into three categories: (a) those who, after earning their living in one occupation or another, have retired and are living on their pensions or savings; (b) those who, though they do not live on their earnings, nevertheless in effect earn their living—we will explain this seeming paradox in a moment; and (c) those who do not earn their living, directly or indirectly, and are not retired workers.

So far as category (a) is concerned, we have already eliminated it from Group XXXII and returned its members to the occupations in which they were formerly engaged: they are not included in the section which we have termed the "idle rich".

Category (b) is an interesting one. It consists of those people who, having "independent means"—i.e., owning property or investments on such a scale as would enable them to lead idle lives—nevertheless devote themselves seriously to useful occupations which are either unpaid or from which the proceeds form only a secondary and relatively unimportant source of income. In this category we find those landowners who, though their rent-roll would keep them in comfort, nevertheless devote their energies seriously to farming; those professional men—officers in the armed forces of the Crown, for example—who take their profession seriously, though they do not need its emoluments; and those people who, having an unearned income sufficient for their needs, devote their whole lives to unpaid public service. We are justified in saying of such people that, though they do not live on their earnings, they do, in a very real sense, earn their living. Now, most of the well-off people who fall into this category are shown by the census as "occupied"—as farmers, as officers in the navy, army, or air force, and in many another occupation—and so are excluded from our "idle rich" section. Some, of course, will have been placed by the census in Group XXXII; but against these must be set the mineowners, shipowners, etc., who are included by the census in the occupied classes, though in many cases they do little or no real work, and the men who, entering the army and other professions for social reasons, soon retire and spend most of their lives in idleness.

Clearly the dividing lines are more than a little vague in either case; but so long as we bear in mind this vagueness and do not imagine a precision that does not exist, we may safely conclude that this section of the *adjusted* Group XXXII suffers no substantial injustice when, for brevity, we term it the "idle rich". Here are the people who devote almost their whole lives to sport and the social round—race meetings, hunting, the London season, grouse-shooting, and so on. (You can—or could in peace-time—see them pictured *ad nauseam* in the art-paper weeklies.) Here also, lower down the social scale, are the idle dependants (chiefly women) of comfortably-off professional and middle-class men; the devotees of golf, bridge, and motoring, and the keepers-up-of-appearances; hardly rich, perhaps, but idle and futile and sharply to be distinguished from the "idle poor"—the unemployed.

We turn to the other big section of the adjusted Group XXXII, the women engaged in unpaid domestic work. While recognizing the possible difficulties in the way of identifying these working housewives for inclusion in Group XXVII, where they properly belong, it must be pointed out that their description as "not gainfully occupied" is doubly misleading. They are not only, in most cases, very fully *occupied*, but they are in fact *gainfully* occupied, since they work for their living and have no private means of their own. Let us take an illustration. Suppose a man employs a working housekeeper and pays her so much a week; she is then classified as a member of Group XXVII (Personal Services). Now suppose that her employer marries her, and that she continues to carry out the same household duties and to receive the same remuneration as before. She is now regarded by the census as "not gainfully occupied" and transferred to Group XXXII, though there has been no change in either her daily work or her remuneration. Clearly the transfer is unjustifiable; and equally clearly all bona-fide domestic workers belong properly to Group XXVII. Their relationship to the householder and the amount and form of their remuneration are beside the point: the essential fact is that they earn their living by "personal service".

We have, then, in our revised Group XXXII two entirely different sections: idlers on the one hand and domestic workers on the other.

Let us endeavour to estimate in what proportions these make up the group. This, of course, is only possible because of the fact that practically the whole of the unpaid domestic workers are women, so that we may safely assume that the vast majority of the men in the group—as modified by us—belong to the other section, the idlers. In 1931 these men numbered 210,242, while the women in the group numbered 11,054,333.

Now, there are more women than men in the "idle" section. This arises from the fact that amongst people of "independent means" more men enter an occupation—the army, for example—than do women, and also from the fact that many men who earn their living have idle womenfolk. It is not easy to estimate the proportions, but if we take it that for every genuinely unoccupied man there are three genuinely unoccupied women we shall probably not be very far out. On this assumption we have as idlers about 840,000 adult men and women, leaving about 10,400,000 adult women engaged in "unpaid" domestic duties. Of course, not all of the latter work equally hard: with some of them—how many it is impossible to say—housework is only a part-time job.

On the basis of 48,710 adults to one member of parliament, then, the idlers would in 1931 have been entitled to about 17 representatives (4 men and 13 women), while the unpaid domestic workers would have been entitled to about 214 (all women). Now compare this with the actual (average) representation, which is 56 members, practically all of whom are idlers and men. Clearly the disparity between the proportional and the actual representation of this group is much greater than is indicated by Table 22. The idlers have well over three times their due representation, while the domestic workers are practically unrepresented. If we now transfer these unpaid domestic workers to Group XXVII, where they properly belong, it indicates for that group a proportional representation of over 250 members against an actual representation of perhaps 4 or 5, a ratio of actual to proportional of at most 2 per cent. Hence "Personal Services" workers are easily the least adequately represented in the House of Commons.

Before leaving Group XXXII we should notice that it is far from including all rentiers and members of the propertied classes generally, since, as we have already seen, the census treats all mineowners and shipowners as occupied, whether they are or not, whilst many other people who appear as occupied are in fact only so for a few years (as in the case of many army officers) or for a mere fraction of their time. If we could pick them out these people would be more realistically placed in the idle section of Group XXXII. That section would then be seen to be very much more over-represented in parliament than even our figures show.

Reverting to Table 22, the next group is II (Agriculture). Taken as a whole this is much better represented than the preceding groups, but nearly 90 per cent of its members of parliament are farmers, land-agents, etc., and only 10 per cent labourers or farm servants. Farmers are considerably over-represented, especially as a proportion of members classified as landowners are to some extent farmers too, while ordinary farm workers are very badly represented indeed. This is typical of many other groups: employers over-represented, employees under-represented.

The next few groups do not call for much comment. In Group XVIII (Building, etc.) the employers and managers carry off 80 per cent of the representation, but in Group VII (Metal Workers) they get less than 40 per cent, while in Group XV (Wood and Furniture) the figure drops much lower still. It is interesting to speculate why, apart altogether from the total representation of a group, the internal distribution between employers and operatives varies so greatly from group to group. That there are specific reasons cannot be doubted, but they are seldom obvious.

Group XXII (Transport and Communications) comes next, with over three-quarters of its proportionate representation. As already noted, this is a highly heterogeneous group, with its agglomeration of signalmen, bus conductors, shipowners, bargemen, aviators, postal sorters, etc.: it is obviously, despite the census, an industrial and not an occupational group. About three-fifths of the members of parliament drawn from it are shipowners, employers, managers, and officials. Similarly, Group XII (Textile Workers), taken as a whole, does not fall very far short of proportionate representation, but two-thirds of the members drawn from it are employers and managers and only one-third operatives.

With Group XXVIII (Clerks and Draughtsmen) we come nearer still to proportionate representation. About 10 per cent of its members in the House are secretaries and registrars of companies, etc., whose proper place would seem to be in Group XXV, but with the other 90 per cent drawn from the general run of workers this group does approximate to proportionate occupational representation.

We now come to the over-represented groups. The first is XXIII (Commerce and Finance), with nearly twice its due share of members. This is another very heterogeneous group, including such diverse elements as merchants, shop-assistants, bankers, commercial travellers, valuers, and stockbrokers. The affinity between butchers and bankers and between stockbrokers and drapers' assistants—if any—must be industrial; it is certainly not occupational. Once again, too, the various occupations by no means have their due proportion of the group's representation. Here are just a few instances. Proprietors and managers of wholesale businesses have roughly 16 times their proportion, bankers about 18 times theirs, and stockbrokers no less than 80 times theirs! As may be imagined, other occupations in the group—shop-assistants, for example—go correspondingly short.

Next we have Group III (Mining and Quarrying). This, like the previous group, has nearly double its proportionate representation, but, unlike that group, well over 90 per cent of its members of parliament are operatives, the balance being owners, agents, and managers. It should be noticed, however, that many coalowners are in the House besides those who so describe themselves. *Owning* is not an occupation at all, and owners may be found amongst bankers or bakers, army officers or idlers. Leaving these people out of account, the miners themselves have not far short of double their ratio of members. As we have seen, it is rare for any group of operatives to have even its fair share of members; why, then, are the miners so favoured?

The explanation is simple. Mining is, by its nature, concentrated into special localities, unlike agriculture and building, for example, which are widely scattered over almost the whole country. Hence there are many constituencies in which miners dominate the elections to an extent that has no parallel in any other occupation; they can practically choose their own members of parliament, and the rest of the electorate has little voice in the matter. Contrast mining and agriculture. There were during the inter-war period approximately a million adult miners in the country; these were represented in parliament by, on a rough average, 40 of themselves, or one member to each 25,000 miners. There were during the same period nearly as many adult rank-and-file agricultural workers; these were represented by at most a member or two—say, at best, one member to some 500,000 workers. Miners, therefore, are at least 20 times as well represented in parliament as farm workers, though mining and agriculture employ closely similar numbers.

Next in Table 22 comes Group XIV (Makers of Food, Drinks, and Tobacco). This has well over twice its proportionate share of representation, but almost all its members of parliament are employers and managers. The next group, XVII (Printers and Photographers), has nearly four times its due number of members, but, again, six out of seven are employers or managers.

We come now to Group XXIV (Public Administration and Defence). As already noted, its components are not linked together by what they *do*, but by the irrelevant fact that they are employed by the state or by local authorities. What justification can there be for collecting as an *occupational* group people as diverse as admirals, policemen, and the higher civil servants? It reduces the grouping to a farce. Clearly civil and municipal officers belong to the professional group, and so do the officers of the fighting forces. If these are grouped with private soldiers and seamen, then architects should be grouped with bricklayers and engineers with mechanics.

However, taking the group as it is, we find that it has nearly eight times as many members of parliament as its strength in the adult population would give. But 80 per cent of these members are commissioned regular officers in the navy, army, and air force: these officers have about 80 times the representation in the House that their numbers would justify. Moreover, there are other members who have held regular commissions, but, having since acquired other occupations, are entered elsewhere: when these are taken into account the regular commissioned ranks of the fighting services are seen to be even more over-represented than the figures indicate. (It should be noted that temporary war-time service and service in the territorial army have *not* been counted as occupations.) Most of the remaining members of parliament in this group are drawn from the higher civil service. There are hardly any army "other ranks", and no naval ratings or aircraftmen. Thus with extreme over-representation of the commissioned ranks there is practically none of the "other ranks".

Last of all we have Group XXV (Professional Occupations). This is the most over-represented of all the groups, with 200 members of parliament in place of the 17 that proportionate representation would give it. Of this huge body of members well over half are either barristers or solicitors, with three of the former to one of the latter. It is well known that lawyers have a partiality for the House—indeed, it is notorious that ambitious barristers use it as a means of advancement in their profession—but it is doubtful if it is generally realized to what lengths this has gone. We shall discuss this more fully later.

The next strongest section in the group is that comprising authors, editors, and journalists; these are collectively about as numerous as the solicitors. Most of them are journalists rather than authors, though the absence of any specifiable qualification in either case makes this a very ill-defined section. Journalists notoriously have a penchant for parliament, and, though they are very easily beaten by the barristers in the proportion as well as the number of seats they succeed in capturing, they occupy about 62 times as many as proportion would give them.

Next come teachers, engineers, medical men, and accountants, in that order, and then a number of other professions, none of them with outstanding membership.

Here let us leave the question of group representation for the time being, and turn to another question to which, so far, only incidental reference has been made. Let us attempt to analyse the membership of the House of Commons according to the *occupational status* of the members. It is not easy to do this at all precisely, for not only is status hard to define in any completely satisfactory way, but also in the vast range of occupations there are so many that do not fall into any readily recognizable category in this respect. We might, of course, follow the census, in which the categories are: managerial, operative, workers on their own account, out of work, and retired. This, however, seems a pointless way of looking at the matter. It may be useful to know how many people are out of work or retired, but that is not a question of *status*; it is a matter of conditions at the moment. The category of "workers on their own account", again, which lumps together tinkers and barristers, jobbing gardeners and clergymen, really cannot be taken seriously. Moreover, the census takes the astounding course of placing the whole of Group XXIV (Public Administration and Defence) in the category of "operatives".* It may be amusing to see admirals, field-

* In Scotland, for some unaccountable reason, a very few (82) civil servants are classed as "managerial", but none are in England or Wales!

marshals, and permanent secretaries in the civil service grouped with miners, farm labourers, bricklayers, and so on, as "operatives": but why on earth are these people excluded from the "managerial" category? In Group XXV, again, about 75 per cent of the professional workers are treated as "operatives". This sort of thing reduces "status" to nonsense.

Let us, then, make our own analysis. Simplifying the problem as much as possible, we may specify five categories as the minimum into which occupations may be divided. First we have the people classified by the census as "employers and managers" and under similar descriptions. Obviously this includes a wide range of occupations differing considerably in detail, but it has the unifying bond that its members are the people in authority in industry. Next we have the rank-and-file workers, the labourers, craftsmen, clerks, and so on, including fore-

TABLE 23.—OCCUPATIONAL STATUS (1931)

Occupational Status	Number of Members		Ratio of Actual to Proportional
	Actual	Proportional	
Employers and Managers ...	152	27	5·6
Rank-and-file Workers	125	321	0·4
Professional Workers	272	23	12·1
Unpaid Domestic Workers ...	—	214	0·0
Unoccupied	53	17	3·1
Total	602	602	—

men, charge hands, and other petty officials: the equivalent, in short, of what the army would call "other ranks". The third category comprises the professions, together with a number of occupations—for example, those of pilot, bank manager, army officer, registrar—in which the members, though they may not be professional men in the narrower sense, yet have that expert knowledge, independence of action, and responsibility that are marks of a profession. The fourth category consists of the unpaid domestic workers, while fifth and last we have the unoccupied—the rentiers, landowners, etc., and the idle dependants of occupied people. The "out of work" and "retired", of course, must be re-classified according to their former occupations.

In transposing the census figures for status into the five categories adopted, then, we observe the following rules:

1. Exclude the adolescents.
2. Re-transfer the "out of work" and "retired".
3. In Group XXIV treat the "other ranks" of the police and defence forces as rank-and-file workers and all the other members of the group

as professional workers. Transfer the whole of Group XXV to the category of professional workers, together with a proportion (estimated) of Group XXVI.

4. Subject to the above exceptions, (a) treat "workers on own account" as rank-and-file workers, and (b) place the census "managerial" people in our employers and managers, and the census "operatives" in our rank-and-file workers.

5. Divide the balance of Group XXXII between our categories of unpaid domestic workers and unoccupied.

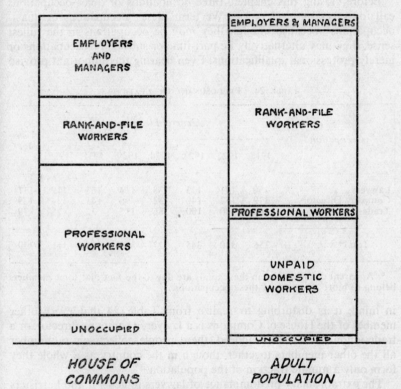

HOUSE OF COMMONS   ADULT POPULATION

FIG. 22.—Occupational status.

Table 23 gives the results of our analysis. The column headed "Actual" shows the occupational status of the average House of Commons, while that headed "Proportional" shows what the distribution would be if it followed that of the adult population (in 1931). Fig. 22 displays the two distributions graphically.

It will be seen that out of every 20 members in the average House roughly 5 belong to the category of employers and managers, 4 are rank-and-file workers, 9 are professional workers, and 2 are unoccupied. But proportionate representation would give roughly 1 employer or manager to 10 or 11 rank-and-file workers, 7 unpaid domestic workers, and 1 or 2 professional workers or unoccupied. When full allowance has been made for unavoidable errors, it is abundantly clear that, proportionately, the general body of workers, including unpaid domestic workers, is greatly under-represented in parliament, while employers, managers, professional workers, and unoccupied are much over-represented. Whether this is an evil is another matter; our object at present is to establish the facts, leaving the discussion of their good or ill effect until later.

Before closing this chapter, three occupations or quasi-occupations call for special consideration. We term these "occupations or quasi-occupations" because, though they *may* be occupations in the fullest sense, they may alternatively be part-time or subsidiary occupations or merely professional qualifications. Even bearing this important proviso

TABLE 24.—PREDOMINANT OCCUPATIONS

Occupation	General Election							Aver-age
	1918	1922	1923	1924	1929	1931	1935	
Lawyers	150	141	133	138	114	165	119	137
Company Directors ...	179	152	140	132	96	143	134	139
Trade-Union Officials	62	80	100	86	115	32	78	79
Total*	356	340	345	327	309	316	311	329

* Apparent discrepancies in these totals are due to the fact that some members belong to more than one of these occupations.

in mind, it is disturbing to realize from Table 24 that every other member of the House of Commons is a lawyer, a company director, or a trade-union official; that, indeed, these people collectively outnumber all the other members together, though in the country as a whole they form only a minute fraction of the population.

The extraordinary predominance of lawyers in general and barristers in particular in the House has already been pointed out, and, indeed, is fairly well known. But few people are aware *how* extraordinary this predominance is; pretty nearly one member in every four is a lawyer, by training if not in actual employment, and there are 200 times as many lawyers and 970 times as many barristers in the House as there are in the country, strength for strength. These figures speak for themselves.

Company directors are shown by the table as equally numerous with lawyers, but it is probable that the actual number is even higher, since so many men of the classes from which the membership of the House is chiefly drawn hold directorships in addition to their main occupations.

It is probable, too, that the figures for trade-union officials are slightly on the low side, though it is unlikely that the differences in this case would be great.

Table 25 shows another aspect of the matter: the proportion of each party in the House that falls into these categories. It will be seen that more than half of both the Conservative and the Liberal members are lawyers or company directors, while almost half of the Labour members

TABLE 25.—PREDOMINANT OCCUPATIONS IN THE AVERAGE HOUSE

Occupation	Proportion of Parliamentary Party belonging to Occupation			
	Conserv.	Liberal	Labour	All Parties
	%	%	%	%
Lawyers	26½	35½	7	23
Company Directors ...	31½	27	3	23
Trade-Union Officials ...	0	2	49½	13
Total*	52½	58	58½	54½

* Apparent discrepancies in these totals are due to the fact that some members belong to more than one of these occupations.

are past or present trade-union officials. The realization of the predominance of these three sets of people in the House of Commons gives much food for thought. Is it wise to have these few special interests so tremendously over-represented? Can a House so composed deal at all impartially with questions affecting their special interests? It is true that few men make a whole-time occupation of company directing, but none the less their position must impart a certain bias to their outlook.

One final point: lawyers, company directors, trade-union officials (and perhaps one should add journalists)—these are the "talking classes" of the country, the people who declaim and argue and make a trade of words. Are we not giving them too big a share in controlling our destinies, by comparison with the people who *do* things instead of holding forth about them?

CHAPTER IX

MEMBERS AND HEREDITARY TITLES

THERE is in this country no rigidly defined aristocracy or nobility such as existed, for example, in the old Austria. Nor is such aristocracy as we have conterminous with the families which possess hereditary titles, for on the one hand some of the most aristocratic and exclusive people are to be found in the county families without title, and on the other hereditary titles are given to uncultured people of obscure origin who have acquired great wealth and contributed handsomely to party funds or charity. Nevertheless, we are justified in considering that a certain section of the population does form an aristocracy in the generally accepted sense of the term, and that this aristocracy is roughly synonymous with the people who hold hereditary titles and their families. The untitled county families intermarry freely with the titled families. The unlettered manufacturer of soap or stout or motor-cars who makes

TABLE 26.—HEREDITARY TITLES: ALL MEMBERS

Classification	Number of Members				
	Con.	Lib.	Lab.	Ind.	Total
I. By Descent:					
Irish Peers, Baronets by Inheritance, and Heirs to Peers or Baronets	90*	13†	3	1	107
Other Descendants of Peers and Baronets	100	18	11	1	130
Total I	190	31	14	2	237
II. By Creation or Marriage:					
Created Peers or Baronets ...	114	33	3	—	150
Married to Peers, Baronets, or their Relations	57	5	1	—	63
Total II	171	38	4	—	213
Grand Total ...	361	69	18	2	450

* Includes one Hereditary Royal Standard-Bearer.
† Includes one foreign title (Baron).

a fortune and acquires a peerage sends his sons to Eton and Trinity and has his daughters presented at court. In a generation or two they are absorbed into their new *milieu* and have completely severed all connexion with their humble origins. The aristocracy of this country differs from older continental forms in that it has no rigid boundaries and in that it does not exclude outsiders: it absorbs and transmutes them. But these characteristics do not disprove its existence; they merely condition it.

It is, then, of interest to inquire how far the House of Commons is aristocratic in composition in the sense we have indicated, and it is convenient to take membership of an hereditary-titled family as an indication of aristocracy. As we have seen, this is an inexact procedure; but it is not unreasonably so, provided that we bear its limitations in mind.

Even on this understanding it is not easy to determine how far the House may be considered aristocratic, but Table 26 gives the facts so far as it has been found possible to ascertain them. The members of parliament under consideration fall into two categories: those who have *inherited* titles, or are descendants of holders of hereditary titles, on the one hand, and, on the other hand, those who have themselves been *created* peers (and so relinquished their seats in the House of Commons) or baronets, together with those who have married persons of hereditary title or relations of such persons.

Clearly only the first category fully possesses even such limited claims to aristocracy as we have set forth. But newly created peers or baronets are not all parvenus—many are sons or grandsons of peers, or belong to old families—and much the same is true of the members who have married into titled families.

In Category I it may be taken that the figures for peers, baronets, and their heirs are substantially correct, the facts in these cases being in general readily ascertainable. The figures for "Other Descendants" are less definite: they are almost certainly understatements, but they indicate the position sufficiently clearly for our purpose.

In Category II the figures are necessarily even less complete, since both new creations and marriages are constantly taking place. It may be taken as certain that the true numbers are considerably in excess of those given; but even as they stand they draw attention to the number of members of parliament, especially Conservative members, who are created peers or baronets.* But indeed the predominance of the Conservatives in all sections of Table 26 is overwhelming.

Now look at the grand totals. Incomplete though the figures are, they give us a rough measure of the extent to which the House is permeated, and perhaps dominated, by the aristocratic element. They show that, while this element forms a mere 4 per cent of the Labour membership and barely one-fifth of that of the Liberals, it forms more than one-third of the Conservative membership. For members of all parties taken together the proportion is roughly one-fourth.

These figures, however, refer to *all* members who sat in the House during the inter-war period, and, since no account is taken of length of service—an important factor—they have no close relation to its normal composition. For the latter we must look at Table 27, which gives the position at each of the seven general elections. Here it is desirable to give a word of warning. For obvious reasons the figures for successive general elections are progressively less and less complete, and therefore

* The number of new baronetcies created for Conservative members is particularly striking. It was 86 at the time the table was prepared: it must be considerably more now.

more and more of understatements. Making allowance for this progressive inadequacy of the recorded figures, we are forced to conclude that the true strength of the aristocratic element in the Commons averages something like 40 per cent of the total membership, and that, though it fluctuates with the variations in the political complexion of the House, it shows no sign of any real diminution.

Evidence to this effect is to be found by considering the numbers of members known to belong to the first category; that is, those who are descendants of holders of hereditary titles. The numbers in this category, as already noted, can be ascertained to a higher degree of accuracy than the numbers in the other category, and, moreover, they are by nature more stable than the latter. Accordingly, Table 28 gives the numbers of members of parliament known to belong to the first category who were returned at each of the seven elections. With these more limited figures

TABLE 27.—HEREDITARY TITLES (BOTH CATEGORIES TOGETHER)

Party	General Election							Average
	1918	1922	1923	1924	1929	1931	1935	
Conservative	186	152	123	168	109	142	127	144
Liberal	46	22	27	13	10	11	15	21
Labour	—	8	7	7	14	3	4	6
Independent	—	2	1	—	—	—	—	—
Total	232	184	158	188	133	156	146	171

there is no evidence of any falling-off in the proportion of members belonging to the hereditary-titled class. Fluctuations there are, but that is only to be expected in view of the changes of party strength and the much more aristocratic character of the Conservative party.

It is clear that in the average House of Commons more than two-fifths of the Conservative party, at the lowest estimate, belong to families of hereditary title, and we may hazard a guess that if the full strength of this element were known it would be found to include not less than half the party. Similarly the average strength of this element in the parliamentary Liberal party may be estimated at nearer one-fourth than one-fifth. In the case of the Labour party the percentage remains very low, as might be expected. For the average House as a whole, Table 27 shows that the titled-family element provides at least two-sevenths of the total membership; but this again is probably much below the true proportion.

If we wish to compare the aristocratic quality of one parliament with that of another, then clearly Table 28 provides a better indication than Table 27. It shows the 1931 House as the most aristocratic, with that of

1924 second and those of 1935 and 1918 not far behind, which is what we should expect from the Conservative predominance in those parliaments. Fig. 23 displays the numbers, for the House as a whole, recorded in Tables 27 and 28, and serves to illustrate the conclusions that have been reached.

Particularly interesting are the fluctuations of the titled-family element in the parliamentary Conservative party in relation to its total strength. The figures show that this element was proportionately at its strongest in the 1923 and 1929 Houses, when the party as a whole was at its weakest. This is a pretty clear indication that, in general, this element takes the safest seats for itself and leaves the more difficult contests to the less aristocratic elements. *Noblesse oblige?*

Let us now try to see how the strength of the hereditary-titled element in the Commons compares with its strength in the country as a whole.

TABLE 28.—HEREDITARY TITLES (FIRST CATEGORY ONLY)

Party	General Election							Average
	1918	1922	1923	1924	1929	1931	1935	
Conservative	71	67	65	87	65	97	80	76
Liberal	22	8	13	6	4	6	11	10
Labour	—	5	4	4	12	3	4	5
Independent	—	2	1	—	—	—	—	—
Total	93	82	83	97	81	106	95	91

The incompleteness of the data does not allow this to be done with any close accuracy, but we can, at least, gain a general idea of the position.

There are, roughly, 850 hereditary peers* at the present time and some 1,400 baronets, so that we have a total of approximately 2,250 persons holding hereditary titles: of these some 80 or so are minors. How many adult relations have they, alive? It is difficult to say; but if we allow ten for each hereditary peer or baronet we shall probably be overestimating the number, bearing in mind that quite a number are bachelors or childless, and that so many titled families are inter-related. On this assumption we have about 2,170 adult peers and baronets and about 22,500 adult relations. Hence the total adult strength of the hereditary-titled element in the country would be about 24,670. Now, as we have already seen, there were in 1931 about 48,710 adults in the general population for each member of parliament. Hence if the titled-family people were given representation in the House of Commons pro-

* The number of *peerages* is, of course, greater, owing to the number of peers who hold more than one title.

6

portionate to their strength in the country, they would be entitled to a shade over half a member.

Turning back to Table 27, we see that their *known* strength in the House has varied from 133 to 232, with an average of 171. But, as we have noted, this is almost certainly an understatement, and there is reason to suppose that the true average would be in the neighbourhood of 240. Let us, however, take a very moderate view and put the figure at somewhere about 200. Even on this cautious estimate the hereditary-titled element has 400 times its due representation.

This is, on the face of it, a rather startling figure; but the true element of surprise is not the minuteness of the numbers of the titled-family people compared with those of the general population; for, after all, in spite of their prominence in *The Times* and the illustrated weeklies,

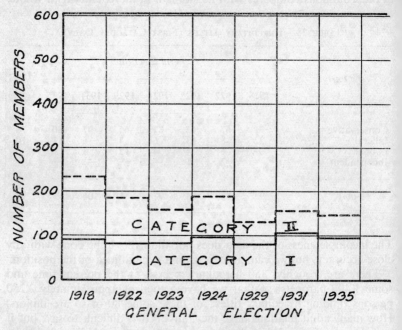

Fig. 23.—Hereditary titles (see Tables 27 and 28).

people of hereditary title are only found as a rule in a very small and exclusive section of society. Explore the general residential areas—professional class, middle class, or working class—of any town in the country (excluding certain parts of London), and it is long odds that, though you may find a knight or two living there, you will not find any person belonging to a titled family in the whole of them. Hereditary titles are not distributed evenly over the population, even to people of outstanding character, ability, experience, and achievement. They are, with rare exceptions, reserved for people of wealth, or of "good family", or of both. Unless the recipients possess these attributes, even political honours usually take the form of non-hereditary titles.

No doubt this is inherent in the nature of the case. People selected for hereditary titles are expected to have the means (and the willingness) to live up to them in conformity with accepted social standards. But that being so, the conclusion is inescapable that these people form a distinct class, an aristocracy if you like, apart from the common run of the community. Newcomers are admitted—yes, but on the understanding, or at least the strong expectation, that they will conform with the social usages of their new circle, and will sooner or later become merged in it. Even the most exclusive clubs, after all, admit new members—on conditions.

No, the truly surprising thing is not the smallness of this section of the community in comparison with the whole, but the hugeness of the share which it obtains in the membership of what is supposed to be a democratic House of Commons; and this in spite of adult suffrage and the rise of the Labour party.

We must not, of course, lose sight of the facts that the data on which our conclusions are based are far from exact, and that the conclusions themselves are correspondingly approximate. But, when the fullest allowance has been made for this, it remains indisputably true that the holders of hereditary titles, and their near relations, have representation in the House of Commons out of all proportion to their numbers in the community. The significance of this result will be all the more appreciated when it is borne in mind that the other House, the House of Lords, is composed almost entirely of holders of hereditary titles. Hence the hereditary-titled element combines undisputed control of the Upper House with immense over-representation in the Lower. Whether this is necessarily a bad thing is another matter: what we are concerned with for the moment is the establishment of the facts and some appreciation of their meaning.

CHAPTER X

MEMBERS AND PARTY

1. GENERAL SURVEY

IT is notorious that party strengths in the House of Commons do not correspond at all exactly with party strengths in the country, as disclosed by the votes of the electorate, and from time to time figures have been published to show how, in a particular election, this or that party has been under- or over-represented by its successes at the polls. For a clear understanding of the position, however, a more orderly and systematic presentation of the facts, covering the whole inter-war period, is desirable.

There are many difficulties in the way of ensuring that even such a systematic survey shall be an exact picture of the state of affairs. We need not concern ourselves with all of these, but there are two which cannot be ignored, and some attempt must be made to overcome them if a reasonably accurate understanding of the state of affairs is to be reached.

We have, first, the difficulty in certain cases of determining the proper party affiliations of members. We need, of course, only consider the Conservative, Liberal, and Labour parties. Very small but definitely separate parties, such as the Prohibitionists, Communists, and Irish Nationalists (each of which has succeeded in electing one or more members in Great Britain during the period) need give us no trouble: we group them together as Independents, and set them aside as, for our purpose, of little account. But trouble arises (a) where one of the major parties has been seriously split on questions of policy or tactics and has suffered something of a civil war between its contending factions—a state of affairs often accompanied by "pacts" between one of the factions and another party; and (b) where candidates have given themselves ambiguous descriptions.

Case (a) arose in 1918, when all three parties were divided into coalition ("coupon") and anti-coalition (or at least non-coalition) candidates. It occurred also in a very marked form in 1931, when electors were faced with three brands (at least) of Liberal candidates: "National Liberals", "Liberal Nationals", and "Independent Liberals"; and also with "Labour" and "National Labour" candidates. The rivalry and even enmity between these factions, especially in the latter case, was considerable. No doubt in this instance many people might consider that "Liberal National" and "National Labour" candidates, being hand-in-glove with the Conservatives and at daggers drawn with other members of their respective (original) parties, should be treated as Conservatives. The analogy with the "Liberal Unionists" of 1886 onwards, who in the great majority of instances never returned to the Liberal party but became completely assimilated with the Conservatives, is obvious. But "heresy-hunting" is no business of ours, and it seems better for our purpose to treat as Conservatives, Liberals, or Labour all candidates who claimed and used these descriptions, whether or no they were acceptable to the respective main party organizations. Hence "Independent Conservatives" and I.L.P. candidates are here treated as Conservative and Labour respectively, and similarly in other comparable cases. The justification for this is plain. We are concerned with the three main streams of political thought during the period—Conservative, Liberal, and Labour—and the dissensions and splits of party organizations are beside the point. What we want to ascertain is how far these main streams of political thought are represented in the House of Commons in proportion to their strength in the country.

Case (b) overlaps to some extent with case (a), as in the instance just mentioned of "Independent Conservatives". Some books of reference treat these as Independents and others as Conservatives, but our rule easily settles the point for us. Much more troublesome is the spate of freak party designations which occurred in 1918 and to a less extent in other elections. How are we to deal with the "National Democratic Party", "New Party", "National Party", and other miscellaneous and, in general, shortlived parties that are not so clearly independent as, say, the Prohibitionists? There is really no possibility of solving this problem with exactness. The easiest way would be to dub them all "Independents". But that would not only be inconvenient for our purpose; it would also disregard the realities of the situation, since many of these ephemeral parties, whatever their ostensible *raison d'être*, had in fact fairly close affinities with one or other of the three major parties. Hence, following the same principle as in the previous case, we place members of these small and transient groups in one or other of the major parties wherever circumstances indicate that as a reasonable course, and only the remainder for whom no such identification appears justifiable are labelled "Independents". The latter designation, then, signifies that those to whom it is applied supported policies hostile to or outside the range of the policies of the three major parties: not that they were rebels within the ranks of those parties.

Clearly this involves a good deal of approximation, and necessitates some amount of personal judgement. But universal agreement on such questions is hardly to be expected when even the standard books of reference disagree with each other.* It is desirable to give this explanation in order to avoid misunderstanding, but the matter is not of outstanding importance in our comparative analysis, since (i) cases of doubtful party designation, even in the most ambiguous elections, such as that of 1918, occur in regard to only a small minority of candidates; and (ii) any undesirable effects of misjudgement are minimized by the fact that voters are allocated in the same way as candidates: we are concerned not so much with how many candidates of any party were elected as with how the successes of each party were related to its voting strength.

The nature of the other major difficulty can best be made clear by a comparison between the 1929 and 1931 elections. In the former only three candidates were returned unopposed, and in the great majority of constituencies there were three-cornered contests. For the 602 seats the Conservatives put forward 578 candidates, the Liberals 507, and Labour 570, not to mention 52 Independents, so that in a large proportion of divisions electors had a choice between candidates of all three

* Here are some figures for the 1929 election. It will be seen that no two of these authorities are in exact agreement, even though this is one of the least ambiguous elections of the whole series.

	Con.	Lib.	Lab.	Ind.
Constitutional Year Book	249	59	288	6
Debrett's House of Commons	248	59	288	7
Dod's Parliamentary Companion	249	58	289	6
Whitaker's Almanack	249	59	287	7

major parties, and in most of the others they had a choice between at least two candidates. Hence the total number of votes recorded for each party gives a very fair indication of its strength in the country at that time, and a good basis for estimating to what extent the division of opinion in the House of Commons corresponded with that in the country as a whole. For this purpose the 1929 election was admirable also in the fact that each party ran its candidates with a freedom, not often found in inter-war elections, from entangling alliances with other parties on the one hand and distracting internal dissensions on the other.

Yet even in these favourable conditions the voting aggregates do not measure the political views of the country quite as closely as might appear at first sight. Apart from the fact that political opinion cannot be neatly separated out into three distinct streams, and three only, and apart also from the influence that local and personal considerations exert in most elections, there are two reasons for this. First, there is the fact that in about 95 divisions Liberal electors had no Liberal candidate for whom to vote, while Labour electors had a similar disability in about 32 divisions, and Conservative electors in about 24. Clearly to this extent the total votes polled by each party are an understatement of its strength in the country. But the constituencies in question will be those in which the parties not putting forward candidates had little or no hope of success, and could claim only a minority of supporters: hence the errors introduced into the party aggregates will be relatively small. To put the matter in another way, the Liberals contested 84 per cent of the seats, but well over 84 per cent of their supporters had the chance to vote for Liberal candidates. Let us take it, as a rough estimate, that the number was halfway between 84 per cent and 100 per cent—that is, 92 per cent. On this basis the Conservatives polled 98 per cent of their strength and Labour 97 per cent of theirs. Hence the errors due to uncontested seats, in taking the total votes as a measure of the party strengths, are not serious *in this case*.

But while some Liberal electors will simply abstain from voting if there is no Liberal candidate, others will vote on the principle of "keeping out" the candidate whose politics they most dislike. There is, therefore, not simply a loss of Liberal votes that could not be recorded; there is also an accretion of Liberal votes to Conservative and Labour candidates. The same thing will occur, *mutatis mutandis*, where there is no Conservative or Labour candidate. It is impossible to say how far this will happen, but it will certainly tend to increase unduly the total vote obtained by the parties that put forward most candidates, since they will not only secure the maximum effect for their own voting strength but will also attract voters from other parties.

Now for the other reason why the aggregate votes cast for the three parties do not measure their respective strengths as closely as might at first sight appear. Even in a three-cornered contest an elector who sees no prospect of success for his own party may decide to vote for one of the other candidates in the hope of "keeping out" the third candidate whose policy he dislikes still more. To what extent this actually happens it is, again, impossible to say, but in the country as a whole its effect will be still further to reduce the chances of the party which initially has, or is thought to have, the least prospect of success.

Generally, therefore, there is a tendency for the aggregate votes of the more successful parties to exaggerate their real strength in the country, and for the aggregate votes of the less successful parties to provide an under-statement of their real strength. This, it should be noted, has nothing to do with the number of *seats* won; it refers solely to *votes* recorded.

Let us now turn to the 1931 election. If even in the favourable circumstances of 1929 the aggregate votes cast for the three parties cannot be taken as a close measure of their real strength in the country, how much less can the aggregates in 1931, when the conditions were so adverse! The panic induced in many electors by the "crisis"—a panic wilfully fostered by certain politicians—the serious splits in the Liberal and Labour parties, and perhaps a good deal of resentment in the Conservative party over the "National" pacts, all tended to confuse the issues and to discourage straight party voting. But these matters, though important, are outside the scope of this survey, and we turn our attention to the large number of constituencies in which electors had no chance to vote for a candidate of their own party. There were 89 seats without a Labour candidate, 96 without a Conservative candidate, and no fewer than 441 without a Liberal candidate; the fact that one seat had two Conservative candidates, 18 had two Labour candidates each, and one had three Labour candidates, only made the position worse.

It may be estimated that perhaps 8 per cent of the Labour electors, a slightly higher proportion of the Conservative electors, and anything up to 40 or 50 per cent—possibly even more—of the Liberal electors were more or less disfranchised by having no chance to vote for a candidate of their own views. So far as aggregate votes go, the effects more or less cancel out as between the Conservative and Labour parties, but not as between them and the Liberal party: it would be farcical in such circumstances to regard the votes actually cast for the Liberal candidates as an adequate measure of the voting strength of the party in the country as a whole. But the shortage of Liberal candidates did not merely wipe out some millions of potential Liberal votes. It would have done this if all the Liberals affected had simply abstained from voting, but actually a good many must have voted for the Conservative candidate in order to "keep Labour out", or *vice versa*. Hence in addition to the reduction of the Liberal aggregate there were increases, of uncertain size, in the aggregates of the other parties. The same thing would, of course, occur in varying degree with the other parties, but it obviously affected them much less (in 1931) because of the much smaller number of constituencies in which they had to face a similar situation.

In such circumstances, then, we cannot even estimate what correction to apply to the respective total votes in order to obtain the true party strengths in the country. All we can safely say is that the aggregate votes actually recorded are far from being true indications, and that relatively the aggregates will give an unduly favourable assessment of the strengths of the more successful parties, and an unduly adverse assessment of those of the less successful.

Divisions in which only one candidate was nominated present a special problem. It is sometimes boldly assumed* that all the electors in such a constituency are of the same party as the "unopposed" member: this is obviously wrong. In *every* division there is at least a minority, and in many a substantial body, of opponents of the success-ful party. A more usual and more reasonable method of allowing for unopposed returns is to allot for each "unopposed" member a number of votes equal to the average poll of all the candidates of his party in contested constituencies in the same general election. This is likely to be an underestimate in most cases, since unopposed returns usually occur in divisions where the successful party is particularly strong; but as nothing at all is allowed for the opponent electors in the division it is probable that in a rough-and-ready way the final result metes out fairly even justice all round. The method has, too, the merit of simplicity. It has therefore been adopted in this investigation. No attempt has, how-ever, been made to provide any correction in contested elections: as we have seen, such a correction, though eminently desirable, is impractic-able.

Summing up, we may say that in elections such as that of 1929, where there were no serious party splits and where all three parties con-tested a high proportion of the seats, the final total party strengths in the country can be estimated pretty closely; where there were party splits on the one hand and "pacts" or "coupons" on the other, but nevertheless a fairly high proportion of three-party contests, as in 1918, the figures will still be moderately accurate, but will have less signifi-cance; where a large proportion of seats are uncontested by one of the parties, as with the Liberals in 1931 and 1935, the real strength of that party in the country will be considerably greater than the final aggregate voting figures indicate, even when corrected for unopposed returns.

It may be as well at this stage to deal with a point that may occur to some readers. Are we not, it may be asked, taking too much for granted when we assume that the vast majority of electors belong to one or other of the three great parties? Would it not be truer to say that a large proportion of them have no definite party affiliations, voting empirically at each election according to their reactions to the events and propaganda of the moment?

The answer is that we do not, in fact, assume any *fixed* party allegiance on the part of electors. When we say that the strength of such-and-such a party at a given election was so many votes, we mean

* See, for example, the *Constitutional Year Book*, 1933, pages 259 and 261 to 264.

simply that at that election that number of electors did in fact vote for candidates of that party or would have done so had they had the opportunity. The effective strength of a party consists not only of the stalwarts who always vote for it, whatever the circumstances, but also of the less constant—or more critical—electors who make up their minds and give their votes as they conceive the issues of the moment to require. If there were not this considerable "floating vote" of electors there would be little difference between the results of successive elections. But a voter who, however detached from active party life, gives his vote to party A rather than to party B or party C is for the time being a unit in the strength of party A, and must be so counted.

These discussions may seem a little lengthy, but if the statistics that follow are to be appreciated at their proper value it is important that the points made should be borne in mind.

TABLE 29.—VOTES AND MEMBERS: 1918 ELECTION

Party	Candidates	Effective Votes	Number of Members		Excess or Deficit
			Elected	"Ideal"	
Conservative ...	410	4,265,000	358	246	+ 112
Liberal	425	3,015,000	165	174	− 9
Labour	442	2,690,000	72	155	− 83
Independent ...	134	465,000	7	27	− 20
Total	1,411	10,435,000	602	602	—

Let us now turn to the figures for the seven general elections. These are set out in tables which show for each election and party the number of candidates nominated and their "effective" total poll. This "effective" total consists of the aggregate vote actually received by the party candidates in contested elections, together with an allowance for each *unopposed* candidate equal to the average received by *opposed* candidates of the same party. Next in each table we have the number of members of parliament actually elected by each party, and then the "ideal"* number obtained by dividing the total of 602 seats amongst the parties in proportion to their respective effective total votes. Finally, we have the excess or deficiency of the number of members of each party elected by comparison with the "ideal" number.

It is perhaps desirable to reiterate that the data on which these results are based are not of such a nature as to allow of mathematical precision, and it would be possible by alternative readings of the more

---

* It should be clearly understood that the term "ideal" is here used in the strictly limited sense of "proportionate to effective voting strength". No wider meaning is intended, and none should be read into it.

ambiguous data to arrive at results which differed slightly from those given. The differences would not, however, affect the general position disclosed.

These remarks are particularly appropriate with reference to Table 29, which gives the results of the 1918 election, because of the "coupon", the consequent party dissensions, and the number of ephemeral new parties. But though alternative interpretations might lead to some variation of the figures, their general effect would remain unchanged. The Conservatives succeeded in electing nearly 50 per cent more members than their voting strength deserved, while the Liberals obtained about 95 per cent of their proper representation, and the Labour party less than half of theirs. The Conservatives secured a clear majority of 114 (not counting the Ulster members) over all other parties together, whereas by rights they should have been in a minority of 110. To speak

TABLE 30.—VOTES AND MEMBERS: 1922 ELECTION

Party	Candidates	Effective Votes	Number of Members.		Excess or Deficit
			Elected	"Ideal"	
Conservative	484	5,880,000	336	244	+92
Liberal	492	4,200,000	117	175	−58
Labour	412	4,270,000	142	178	−36
Independent ...	40	125,000	7	5	+ 2
Total	1,428	14,475,000	602	602	—

of such results as expressing "the will of the people" or as giving "a mandate from the country" is clearly ludicrous.

We shall discuss these and other results more fully later, but meanwhile let us pass on to Table 30 and the 1922 election. The "coupon" stunt had become discredited, the coalition had broken up, and the party system had returned to something like normal working; but though the circumstances were very different from those of 1918, the result was similar in giving to the party securing most votes an altogether disproportionately large number of seats. The Conservatives, who, on voting strength, should have been in a minority of 114, were in a majority of 70 over all other parties together, while the Liberals only secured two-thirds of their due representation, and the Labour party, though doing better than at the previous election, had, even so, only 80 per cent of their fair share of seats. Once again "the will of the people" did *not* prevail.

That the present "system" makes a general election a huge gamble was rubbed in—to those who were capable of perceiving it—when Mr. Baldwin (as he then was) "appealed to the country" a year later. So far

as votes went, the country gave him almost exactly the same answer as
it had given to Mr. Bonar Law in 1922. Yet how different was the result
measured in seats! Consider the figures set out in Table 31 and compare them with those in Table 30. The Conservative vote diminished by
only 4 per cent, yet the number of Conservative members fell by 26 per
cent. The Liberal vote increased by less than 5 per cent, but the number
of Liberal members rose by 36 per cent. The Labour vote increased by
little more than 2 per cent, yet there were nearly 35 per cent more
Labour members elected. Moreover, the total vote was little changed,
being just over 1 per cent greater. So, with hardly any change in the
distribution of political opinion in the country, there was a drastic
change in the political complexion of the House of Commons.

Actually at the 1923 election the state of opinion in the country was
reflected much more nearly than at the 1922 election (or, indeed, any of

TABLE 31.—VOTES AND MEMBERS: 1923 ELECTION

Party	Candi-dates	Effective Votes	Number of Members		Excess or Deficit
			Elected	"Ideal"	
Conservative ...	522	5,630,000	248	231	+ 17
Liberal	454	4,400,000	159	181	− 22
Labour ...	433	4,365,000	191	180	+ 11
Independent ...	14	250,000	4	10	− 6
Total	1,423	14,645,000	602	602	—

the other inter-war elections). Even so, the Conservatives secured 17
seats too many and the Labour party 11, while the Liberals, in spite of
better luck than they had in 1922, were 22 below their proper strength.
Had seats corresponded with votes, the Liberals, instead of being the
smallest party in the House, would have had a member more than the
Labour party, and so would have had at least as good a right as the
latter to form a government when Mr. Baldwin was defeated and
resigned in January 1924.

At the next election (1924) the gamble again turned out heavily in
favour of the Conservatives. As Table 32 shows, they secured a clear
majority of 198, whereas they should have been in a minority of 46;
that is, they again had nearly 50 per cent more seats than they should.
The Labour party secured less than three-quarters of their fair share,
while the Liberals, severely hit by the vagaries, not of the electorate,
but of the electoral "system", had little more than a third of their due.
As a matter of fact, even this is an underestimate of the hardships that
befell the Liberals. The party secured its aggregate with only 339 candidates: had it been able to run another 200 or so, as the other parties

did, it would have displayed a voting strength entitling it to some 160 seats, or four times the number it actually won. The injustice of these electoral results hardly needs stressing.

Coming now to Table 33, we see that in 1929 the so-called "pendulum"—pendulums do not really behave in such an erratic manner—swung over and benefited the Labour party, though not at the cost of

TABLE 32.—VOTES AND MEMBERS: 1924 ELECTION

Party	Candi- dates	Effective Votes	Number of Members		Excess or Deficit
			Elected	"Ideal"	
Conservative ...	532	7,600,000	400	278	+122
Liberal	339	2,980,000	40	109	− 69
Labour	508	5,580,000	151	204	− 53
Independent ...	25	300,000	11	11	—
Total	1,404	16,460,000	602	602	—

the Conservatives. In this election Conservatism and Labour, with closely similar numbers of candidates, secured almost exactly equal aggregate votes, and on these should each have won 227 seats. Actually the Conservatives got 22 more than they deserved, while the Labour party were lucky enough to secure no less than 62 more. Once again the Liberals were the victims of the gamble, being deprived this time of

TABLE 33.—VOTES AND MEMBERS: 1929 ELECTION

Party	Candi- dates	Effective Votes	Number of Members		Excess or Deficit
			Elected	"Ideal"	
Conservative ...	578	8,340,000	249	227	+22
Liberal	507	5,200,000	58	141	−83
Labour	570	8,365,000	289	227	+62
Independent ...	52	260,000	6	7	− 1
Total	1,707	22,165,000	602	602	—·

nearly 60 per cent of the seats their aggregate vote should have given them. As they were without candidates in nearly 100 constituencies, that aggregate did not represent their full strength in the country, and their luck was even worse than appears at first sight.

As already pointed out, this election is particularly instructive because, with neither "pacts" nor "splits" to complicate matters, and with only three members returned unopposed, almost all electors had some choice of candidates and most had a straightforward choice between the three parties. Yet even in these favourable conditions the results, as we have seen, were anomalous and unjust.

We turn to Table 34 and the cataclysm of 1931. In this election—the

TABLE 34.—VOTES AND MEMBERS: 1931 ELECTION

Party	Candidates	Effective Votes	Number of Members		Excess or Deficit
			Elected	" Ideal."	
Conservative	507	12,730,000	460	340	+ 120
Liberal	161	2,510,000	68	67	+ 1
Labour	533	7,050,000	65	188	− 123
Independent ...	75	275,000	9	7	+ 2
Total	1,276	22,565,000	602	602	—

only one in all the seven—the Conservatives secured a clear majority of the total votes cast. If seats had gone accordingly they would have received a clear majority of 78 over all other parties in the House, but actually their majority was 318: an undeserved "bonus" of 240. The Labour party, on the other hand, which should have been in a minority of 226, was actually in a minority of 472: a "penalty" of 246 for losing

TABLE 35.—VOTES AND MEMBERS: 1935 ELECTION

Party	Candidates	Effective Votes	Number of Members		Excess or Deficit
			Elected	"Ideal"	
Conservative ...	508	10,640,000	379	288	+ 91
Liberal	205	2,340,000	54	63	− 9
Labour	589	9,000,000	166	244	− 78
Independent ...	31	255,000	3	7	− 4
Total	1,333	22,235,000	602	602	—

the gamble. As for the Liberal party, if we include the equivocal "Liberal Nationals", it secured approximately its rightful number of seats according to the votes actually given; but nearly three-fourths of the constituencies had no Liberal candidate of any kind, so that a large proportion of Liberal electors had no chance to vote for their party.

Hence the aggregate Liberal vote probably represented less than half the real strength of the party in the country. The Conservatives' real strength must therefore have been even less than indicated by their aggregate vote, and their over-representation even greater than stated. No doubt this was offset to some extent by Conservative votes given to "Liberal Nationals", but the latter were not sufficiently numerous for their effect to be great. Moreover, many Liberals preferred to vote for Labour rather than support "Liberal Nationalism". For similar reasons we may surmise that the real under-representation of Labour was less than the apparent. In any event the historian may well see in the deplorable results of this "stunt" election, with its practical annihilation of parliamentary opposition, one of the major causes of the disastrous sequence of events, particularly in foreign affairs, since 1931.

Finally we come to the 1935 election and Table 35. Here the discrepancies are not so extreme as those of 1931, but they are bad enough. The aggregate votes indicate that the Conservatives should have been in a minority of 26, whereas in fact they obtained a clear majority of 156, while the Labour party, which should have been in a minority of 114, was actually much worse off, being in a minority of 270. The Liberals again had candidates in only a few (one-third) of the constituencies, and so did not poll anything like their total strength. Even so, they should have received on the votes given 63 seats instead of the 54 that came to them. Notice that while the Conservatives had nearly *four*-thirds of the number of seats corresponding to their aggregate vote, the Labour party had little more than *two*-thirds of *their* due share.

In concluding this chapter there are two points that may be noted. The first is that the voting strength of the three parties, even as it stands, indicates that throughout the inter-war period they were much more nearly equal in the country than their numbers in the House of Commons imply; and, as we have seen, there is good evidence that if the aggregate votes could be corrected they would show these strengths as still more nearly equal.

The other point, which has not been generally recognized, is that in the latest (1935) election the Labour party secured the highest proportion of the grand total of votes that it has ever had. In 1929, which is usually regarded as its peak year, it secured nearly 38 per cent of the total, but in 1935 its share rose to over 40 per cent. It illustrates the dangerously irresponsible and unpredictable character of the electoral "system" that in 1929 the Labour party's bare 38 per cent of votes secured 48 per cent of seats and gave us a Labour government; whereas in 1935 its full 40 per cent of votes secured less than 28 per cent of seats and we were given a violently anti-Labour government. Could anything be less worthy to be termed a "system"? How, in the face of such happenings, can we take the results of a general election as expressing, even in the most general terms, "the voice of the people"?

CHAPTER XI

MEMBERS AND PARTY

2. FURTHER ANALYSIS

HAVING compared the party allegiances of members of parliament with those of the general population, as revealed by their aggregate votes election by election, we may now look a little closer at the results as a whole. We have already computed, as nearly as the data allow, what would have been the strength in the House of Commons of each of the three major parties if the wishes of the corresponding sections of the electorate had been given equal effect, size for size, and, comparing these "ideal"* strengths with the actual strengths in the House, have seen that in no single election of the series have the two tallied at all closely, while in most of the elections they have differed almost incredibly.

Table 36 brings together for each election and party these differences between the "ideal" and the "real" membership. One of the first things that strikes the observer is the fact that in every one of these seven elections, covering the whole inter-war period, the Conservative party succeeded in obtaining greater representation than it was entitled to on voting strength, and in all but the 1923 and 1929 elections very substantially greater strength. Its average excess representation appears in the table as just over 82 members: this, however, is merely the average of the figures for the seven elections. When allowance is made for the different lengths of the parliaments—a vital consideration—the true average excess representation of the Conservatives for the twenty-three years 1918 to 1941 is, in round figures, 96. That is to say, the Conservative party has had on an average nearly a hundred more members in the House of Commons during the past quarter of a century than its aggregate voting strength (including an allowance for unopposed returns) could justify.

The Liberal party, on the other hand, has been persistently under-represented. That was so even in 1931, despite the "Liberal Nationals'" dependence on Conservative votes, because in that year and again in 1935 the party, counting all its dissident sections, was able to put but few candidates in the field, so that Liberal electors in many divisions had no chance to vote for *any* brand of Liberal candidate. The average under-representation shown in Table 36 is nearly 36 members, but if we allow, as before, for the varying duration of the seven parliaments, this figure drops to about 30. The true figure, however, must be much higher.

The fortunes of the Labour party were more chequered. In 1923 and 1929 it won more seats than its aggregate vote justified; at all the other elections it won fewer, and mostly many fewer. Its true average under-

* *I.e.*, proportionate to effective voting strength.

representation, allowing for varying duration, works out at over 62, against the 43 given in the table.

Hence the average House of Commons during the twenty-three years from 1918 to 1941 has contained, in round figures, 96 more Conservatives, 30 fewer Liberals, and 62 fewer Labour members (together with 4 fewer Independents) than the respective voting strengths would justify. This is no doubt a very satisfactory state of affairs to the Conservative party organizers and leaders; but to the man or woman who believes in democratic government it is a very disturbing one. What is the root cause of this dangerous and indefensible position? Why has the luck of the gamble so persistently favoured the Conservatives, so persistently proved adverse to the Liberals (though with queer fluctuations in each case), and sometimes smiled and more often scowled upon Labour?

A certain amount of light is thrown upon the problem by plotting a

TABLE 36.—EXCESS OR DEFICIT OF PARTY SEATS

Party	General Election							Average *
	1918	1922	1923	1924	1929	1931	1935	
Conservative	+112	+92	+17	+122	+22	+120	+91	+82½
Liberal	+ 9	−58	−22	− 69	−83	+ 1	− 9	−35¼
Labour	− 83	−36	+11	− 53	+62	−123	−78	−43
Independent	− 20	+ 2	− 6	—	− 1	+ 2	− 4	− 4

* Average of figures for the seven elections: for true average for whole period see text.

curve (Fig. 24) to show the relationship between the "ideal" numbers of members for each party at each general election and the corresponding "real" numbers.* In this diagram we are not concerned with the fortunes of the parties separately, but are endeavouring to ascertain what general relationship exists between corresponding "real" and "ideal" numbers of members. The diagonal straight line shows the location that the points would have if in each case the "real" number had the same value as the "ideal". Points above this line mark cases where "real" exceeds "ideal"; points below it those where "real" falls short of "ideal".

If now we draw a line (the fine dotted line) vertically through the point A, which corresponds to 200 on both the "ideal" and "real" scales, we get the interesting result that nearly all points on the *right* of

* For the benefit of anyone who is unfamiliar with graphs of this sort it may be explained that the point marked B, for example, represents the results for the Conservative party of the 1931 election. The *horizontal* distance of the point from the origin O represents the "ideal" number of members which their aggregate voting strength would have given the Conservatives: the *vertical* distance of the point from the origin represents the "real" number of members who were elected. The point C similarly represents the Labour figures, "real" and "ideal", for the 1929 election. Cases where the figures are very small have been omitted.

this vertical line are *above* the diagonal line, while all points but one on the *left* of the vertical line are *below* the diagonal line. What does this signify? The point A corresponds pretty closely to one-third of the House (excluding Ulster, of course), and the distribution of the points shows that, with rare exceptions, a party obtaining more than one-third of the grand aggregate of votes given in a three-party general election will secure more than its due proportion of seats, while a party obtaining less than one-third of that aggregate will obtain less than its due

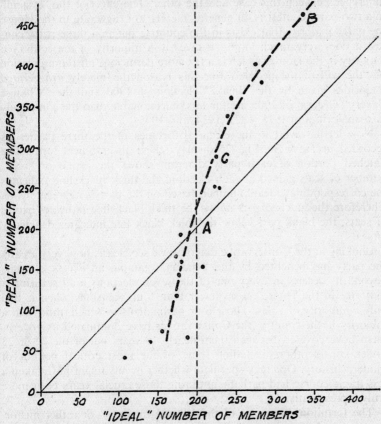

Fig. 24.—Relation between "ideal" and "real" representation.

proportion. In other words, the present system tends to give to the stronger parties more seats and to the weaker parties fewer seats than they respectively deserve. What makes the position worse is that these exaggerations of strength and weakness often run to extremes and at the same time are spasmodic and uncertain in their action. This is shown by the fact that the plotted points are too scattered for any definite curve to be drawn through them, though the chain line indicates their general trend.

Hence, in a three-party contest, any party which can secure more than one-third of the grand total of votes can be almost certain of securing a dominating position in the House of Commons and in all probability a clear majority of seats; while any party which is unlucky enough to secure less than one-third of the total votes must expect less —often much less—than its fair representation. Similarly, in a two-party contest the party that secures a bare majority of votes will almost certainly secure a substantial majority of seats: but there is one vital difference between this case and the other. The effect of the "system" in a two-party contest is, in general, merely to exaggerate in the House the party majority that exists in the country; but in a three-party contest it does very much more: it gives to a minority in the country a majority in the House, which is a far more pernicious misrepresentation of "the will of the people". For this reason the merely *exaggerated* majorities given by the "khaki" election of 1900 and the "Chinese slavery" election of 1906 are far less objectionable than the completely *false* majorities of 1918, 1922, 1924, and 1935.

Now let us revert to the electoral fortunes of the three parties as recorded in Table 36. Fig. 25 displays these in graphical form. The hatched portion of each party diagram shows the actual or "real" number of seats gained at each election; the thick black line indicates the corresponding "ideal" number, based on the party's aggregate vote. Therefore the hatched part *above* the thick black line indicates excess of seats; the blank part *below* the thick black line indicates deficiency of seats.

Looking at the Conservative diagram, we see clearly how very greatly the party has benefited by the "system", gaining an excess of seats beyond its deserts in every one of the seven elections, and securing a majority in the House on no fewer than four occasions when it had only a minority of votes. Those four parliaments in which, though in a minority in the country, the Conservatives have dominated its government have covered between them nearly 16 years out of the 22 or 23 under consideration, including some of the most critical periods of modern history. One may speculate whether events might have taken a less tragic course had parliament during those crucial years been more truly representative.

The fortuitous character of the Liberal fortunes—or rather misfortunes—stands out plainly in the diagram. Notice that in 1918 the party was already a little under-represented; yet in 1922, when its proportion of the total vote was slightly *higher*, it lost another 48 seats. The next year its voting strength rose still higher, but though it gained some seats, it failed to reach even the inadequate 1918 level of representation. In the two following elections its voting strength suffered a severe decline —in 1924 partly at least through leaving so many seats uncontested— but its strength in the House went down much faster; indeed, to a mere fraction of what it should have been. After these undeserved disasters (undeserved in the sense that they came, not from lack of aggregate

voting strength, but from the caprice of the electoral machine; we are
not here concerned with the merits or demerits of party policy) it is

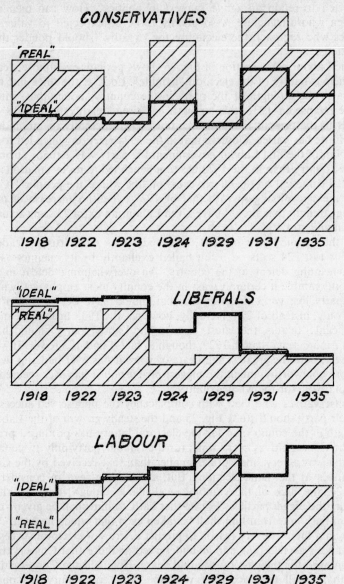

FIG. 25.—Party representation, "real" and "ideal".

hardly surprising that in the subsequent elections the party has made
but a poor showing. Consider, for example, the fact that in 1929 the
Liberals polled nearly 5¼ million votes, yet only secured seats corre-

sponding to a bare $2\frac{1}{4}$ million, so that in effect over 3 million Liberal voters were disfranchised. How can electors in such circumstances be expected to retain an active interest in politics? How can men and women whose franchise is so plainly futile be expected to value it? Critics who reproach the electorate for "apathy" should ponder these questions.

The Labour party section of Fig. 26 shows perhaps even more clearly the vicious nature of the electoral "gamble". Look at the thick line that indicates the strength of the party in the country; notice that, with a single relapse in 1931, this strength has risen steadily from 1918 onwards to the present time, and see how very differently its strength in the House has varied. Observe that in the 1924 election which led to the downfall of the first Labour government the party was actually stronger in the country than in the 1923 election which led to its installation: an ironical comment on the effectiveness of "the will of the people"! Contrast these results again with that of 1929, when an increase of total voting strength that should have given Labour an extra 23 seats actually gave it an extra 138.

In the "panic" year of 1931, betrayed by its most trusted leaders, Labour lost 224 seats—a result hailed exultantly by its enemies as an overwhelming defeat in the country. An overwhelming defeat in the electoral gamble it certainly was; in the country most emphatically not! The party lost *votes* to an extent that should have deprived it of 39 seats only, instead of 224. Actually, however, the 1935 figures are more significant: in this, the latest, election the Labour party should have had 17 more seats than in 1929, though in fact it had 123 fewer. It won, however, both the greatest aggregate of votes it has ever had and, what is more noteworthy, much the biggest *proportion* it has ever secured of the total vote for the whole country.

Conservatives who view with complacency the undeserved successes of their party should study Fig. 25 and the steady growth of the Labour strength in the country. So far the electoral lottery has produced prizes for the Conservatives every time; for the Labour party only twice (and the first was a very small prize, smaller than that received by the Conservatives at the same election). But, as we have seen in considering Fig. 24, the luck of the gamble, incalculable though it is, definitely favours the bigger parties. "For he that hath, to him shall be given: and he that hath not, from him shall be taken even that which he hath." On these data there is every reason to predict a series of electoral successes for Labour as sweeping and as undeserved as those that Conservatism has enjoyed for the past twenty-odd years. How will the Conservatives like that? Will they accept it with the same equanimity—to put it mildly—as they have shown over their own unearned victories?

It should be remembered that, in all this discussion, nothing has been said about party programmes and policies; with them we are not concerned. Our business is to show how the present electoral "system" works, to demonstrate both its injustice and its utter unreliability, and incidentally to point out that though the benefit of these eccentricities has so far (since 1918) accrued very largely to one party, there is no guarantee, and indeed no likelihood, that this will continue.

We turn now to another aspect of party representation. Among the causes of the lack of interest in politics and the apathy over elections that are so often criticized (and that are indeed regrettable) must be placed the practical monopoly of representation enjoyed in various parts of the country by one or other of the parties. It is bad enough that in certain single constituencies no one but a Conservative or a Labour candidate, as the case may be, has any chance of success; that is bound to have a deadening effect on local political activities. But when the representation of a whole group of adjacent constituencies is confined to a single party the effect is naturally worse.

Let us consider some actual instances. In selecting these, however, we

TABLE 37.—CORNWALL COUNTY ELECTIONS, 1929

Party	Votes Obtained	Seats	
		Deserved	Secured
Conservative	63.875	2	—
Liberal	70,481	2	5
Labour	30,047	1	—
Independent	1,976*	—	—

* With one candidate only.

are in a difficulty. In order that we may be able to ascertain, at least approximately, the political views of the electorate for comparison with the resulting distribution of seats, we need an area and an election in which as many as possible of the divisions were contested by all parties. But the most glaring cases of monopoly representation are just those in which contests, being almost hopeless for the minority parties, seldom occur. Our examples must therefore be in the nature of a compromise between contending requirements. Areas and elections in which each of the three major parties put forward a candidate for each seat, so that every elector had a full choice and we can consequently determine the distribution of party allegiances with some accuracy, are the most useful for comparing what is with what should be; but the very fact that so many contests have occurred there shows that these are not the worst examples of monopoly.

However, making the best of this quandary, let us consider three cases in turn, one for each party. First let us take the five county divisions of Cornwall in the 1929 election; the relevant results are summarized in Table 37. These five divisions cover an area of about 1,360 square miles in all, and had, in 1929, a population of 321,000, with an electorate of 210,000. Each party put forward a candidate for each seat, and the aggregate votes recorded show that at that election nearly 39 per cent of the voters were Conservatives, 42 per cent were Liberals, 18 per cent were supporters of the Labour party, and the small residue gave their votes to an Independent. Yet to represent the whole of this huge area and its politically diverse population only Liberals were returned. The 70,000 Liberal voters secured five members to put forward their views: the 96,000 anti-Liberal voters secured no one to represent them.

Cornwall, however, is not really "safe" for the Liberals. Although they secured all the seats in 1923 as well as in 1929, yet in between, at the 1924 election, the position was reversed, and all the seats went to the Conservatives; while at the other inter-war elections they were distributed between the two parties, Labour alone failing to secure any

TABLE 38.—WESTERN DURHAM ELECTIONS, 1935

Party	Votes Obtained	Seats	
		Deserved	Secured
Conservative	37,438*	1	—
Liberal	31,685*	1	—
Labour	99,206	3	5

* With candidates in three divisions only.

representation. As a matter of fact, there are now few, if any, seats that can be considered really "safe" for the Liberal party, though before 1918 there were many.

Let us now take an area in which the Labour party has a predominant position. Probably our contending requirements can be met as well as is possible by taking a group of five adjacent divisions in western Durham at the 1935 election. These five divisions are Barnard Castle, Bishop Auckland, Consett, Sedgefield, and Spennymoor, and the essential results are summarized in Table 38. These divisions together cover an area of about 720 square miles, and had in 1935 a population of about 347,000, with an electorate of 209,000. The votes recorded show about 22 per cent of the voters as Conservatives, 19 per cent as Liberals, and 59 per cent as Labour. Yet the whole of the seats went to Labour. The 99,000 Labour votes secured five representatives, the 69,000 anti-Labour votes none. Actually the position was worse than these figures show. In two of the divisions there were no Conservative candidates, and in two others no Liberals put up, so that Conservative and Liberal voters in these divisions respectively had no chance to record votes for candidates of their own parties.

How would the distribution of votes have gone had there been candidates of all three parties in each of the five divisions? It is impossible to say with exactness, but by making certain assumptions we can form an estimate that will probably give us a truer picture of party strengths than is given by the actual voting. Such an estimate indicates 24 per cent as Conservatives, 23 per cent as Liberals, and 53 per cent as Labour; so that though Labour won all five seats it had probably little more than half of the electorate behind it. This area is, however, not really "safe" for Labour. In 1929 and 1935 it won all the seats, and in 1922 and 1923 all but one, but in 1931 the exceptional conditions gave two seats to the Conservatives and two to the Liberals, while in 1918 and 1924 Labour secured only two and three seats respectively. There are not many *areas*, as distinct from single seats, in which Labour appears to be in an unchallengeable position.

Let us now take an area and an election in which the Conservatives

TABLE 39.—SUSSEX COUNTY ELECTIONS, 1924

Party	Votes Obtained	Seats	
		Deserved	Secured
Conservative	108,593	4	6
Liberal	29,477*	1	—
Labour	22,962†	1	—

* With candidates in four divisions only.
† With candidates in five divisions only.

had things all their own way. We select the six county divisions of Sussex, East and West, in the 1924 election, our choice, as before, being governed by the necessity of finding an area in which, while one party was outstandingly successful, the others put up enough candidates to give us a good idea of the respective party strengths. These six divisions together cover an area of about 1,440 square miles, with a population in 1924 of about 473,000 and an electorate of 236,000. The votes recorded (see Table 39) show about 67½ per cent of Conservatives, about 18½ per cent of Liberals, and about 14 per cent of Labour supporters. Two-thirds of the votes sufficed to give all six seats to the Conservatives: the other third of the votes failed to gain any representation at all.

Further, in two divisions there were no Liberal candidates and in another division no Labour candidate. If we estimate, on the same basis as before, what would have been the distribution of the aggregate vote had there been three-party contests in all six divisions, we get about 63 per cent of Conservative voters, about 24 per cent of Liberals, and about 13 per cent of Labour. Hence the 63 per cent of electors who were Conservatives had six members to represent them in parliament, while the 37 per cent of electors holding Liberal or Labour views had not a single representative.

In Sussex, moreover, unlike Cornwall and Durham, electoral history shows that the predominant party not only secured all the seats at this particular election, but has been able to maintain its favoured position throughout the inter-war period. In this period the Sussex county area has seen seven general elections and five by-elections, making forty-seven contests. Of these the Conservatives have won forty-six, the solitary exception being the winning of Chichester by the Liberals with a small majority in 1923, only to lose it again ten months later. The Conservative party, therefore, has a virtual monopoly of the parliamentary representation of Sussex; and, since even in 1924 (a year particularly favourable to that party) about 37 per cent of the electors were Liberal or Labour, we may conclude that in general some 40 per cent of the Sussex electorate are, for all practical purposes, permanently disfranchised in present conditions.

These three cases—Cornwall, Durham, and Sussex—are by no means mere abnormalities, rare eccentricities due to special circumstances. On the contrary, they are fairly typical examples of a feature of the electoral "system" that is widely prevalent, for to "safe" areas must be added many "safe" individual divisions. In all too many constituencies the electors belonging to two out of the three parties might almost as well have no votes for all the use they are. Is it any wonder if these electors regard politics as just something in the newspapers, and elections as a solemn farce?

Our investigations, then, show that not only is the party complexion of the House of Commons no true index of the views of the electors of the country as a whole, but also that there are widespread disfranchisements of large bodies of electors: for what is the use of a vote that is doomed, from the start, to complete sterility?

CHAPTER XII

REVIEW

WE have now investigated the chief characteristics of the personnel of the House of Commons that concern us, and have amassed a considerable amount of information about the ages, education, occupations, party affiliations, and other attributes of members of parliament. We have also seen how the personnel of the House compares in these respects with the general adult population by whom it is elected, and whom it is supposed to represent. Before passing on to a more general discussion of the issues involved, let us review as concisely as possible the facts we have ascertained; such a review may serve as an epitome as well as a reminder.

AGE ON FIRST ELECTION

We have studied the ages at which members first entered the House of Commons, both with respect to *new* members who first entered the House in the inter-war period, taking them election by election and as a whole, and with respect to *all* members who have sat in the House during that period, taking them party by party and as a whole. What do we learn from our statistics and graphs? Many interesting facts emerge and we cannot recapitulate them all; let us recall a few of the more significant.

Consider first the *new* members: relatively few entered the House under the age of 26 or over the age of 66, while the most popular five-year range was that from 46 to 51 years of age. The entries increase rapidly up to that group and then decline again, the fall after the 51-56 group being rapid. There was, in all the seven general elections, only one entrant at the lowest age, 21, and only one at 75, which was the highest age.

If we consider the *average age* of entry, we find that the new members elected in 1918 were much the oldest set for any of the elections, with an average of 48 years 5½ months, and that subsequently the average declined until at the last two elections it was only 42 years 0½ month, a drop of 6 years 5 months compared with 1918. The high age of first entry in 1918—obviously due to the war of 1914-18—had the deplorable effect of giving the control of affairs in the crucial post-war years into the hands of an abnormally elderly House.

When we turn to the age of first entry of *all* inter-war members, new and old, we find that the two age-ranges 41-46 and 46-51, closely similar in numbers, were the most popular. There were, again, few entrants below 26 and few over 66. (The actual lowest age was 21 years 6 months and the highest 76 years 1 month.)

Comparing the three parties, we find a rather curious contrast. The most popular age-group for Conservatives is evidently 46-51, while for each of the other two parties it appears to be 41-46, though the average age for Conservatives is lower than that for either of the others. The explanation is that, while there is a substantial inflow of Conservatives at all ages between 26 and 46, relatively few Liberals enter before 31 and relatively few Labour members before 36. We note that, even proportionately to total party entrants, for every Labour member who enters the House between the ages of 21 and 31 there are roughly three Liberal entrants and five Conservative, and we also observe the high proportion of Labour members who enter between 41 and 51. These facts stress the initial financial disadvantage of Labour, and to a less extent Liberal, candidates, and, of course, they are reflected in the *average age* of entry. This is lowest for the Conservatives (43 years 7½ months) and highest for the Labour members (46 years 11½ months), with the Liberals in between (43 years 10½ months): the over-all average for all members is 44 years 5 months. On first election the average Conservative is therefore 3 months younger than the average Liberal and 3 years 4 months younger than the average Labour member; a rather striking difference. Hence the average age of the new members entering parliament at any general election, as well as the average age of all the members elected, is affected by the party character of the results.

Finally we note that whereas the average age of entry of the inter-war new members was 45 years 1 month and the average age of the 1918 new members was 48 years $5\frac{1}{2}$ months, the average age of the members who first entered before 1918 was only 43 years 0 month.

AGE AT GENERAL ELECTION

Here we are concerned, not with the age of first entry to the House, but with the ages of *all* members, new and old, at each of the seven general elections. We observe that, as with new entrants, so with members as a whole, the 1918 House was abnormally elderly, while the later Houses were (with some variations) successively younger. The *average age* on election was highest in 1918 (51 years $7\frac{1}{2}$ months) and lowest in 1931 (48 years 6 months). As the influence of the last war has receded into the past, the average age on election has gradually fallen, except when it was raised temporarily in 1929 by the influx of elderly Labour members and in 1935 by the abnormally small number of new members.

The *lowest age* of any member at a general election was 21 years 6 months; the *highest* was 80 years 7 months. These limits give a *range* of very nearly 60 years, and enable us to divide members into four age-groups of equal range: 21 to 36, or "young"; 36 to 51, or "younger middle-aged"; 51 to 66, or "older middle-aged"; and 66 to 81, or "elderly". At each of the seven elections the "middle-aged" greatly preponderate, with a total strength varying from 85 per cent of the House in 1918 to 75 per cent in 1931, and averaging 81 per cent. The two "middle-aged" groups are closely similar in size, as are the much smaller "young" and "elderly" groups.

We are not concerned, however, only with the figures for members of parliament. We have to see how these compare with the corresponding figures for the *adult population*. We find that the average member of parliament is very considerably older than the average adult member of the public. The difference fluctuates, but over the whole period to date (December 1942) its mean value is about 8 years $7\frac{1}{2}$ months, the average member of parliament being approximately 52 years $6\frac{1}{2}$ months of age, while the average adult is only 43 years 11 months old. This is a big difference, though not nearly so big as that between the mean age of the average member of parliament and the mean age of the average member of the *whole* population; the latter is approximately 32 years $5\frac{1}{2}$ months. Hence the average member of parliament is a good twenty years older than the average member of the whole population—not far short of a generation difference!

But averages, useful though they are, give only limited information, so we compare the *age-distribution* of members of parliament with that of the adult population in detail by means of a graph (Fig. 10) which is particularly interesting. Such a comparison does not lend itself to summarization, but, as we have seen, the general effect is to show that the adult population under 40 years of age is severely under-represented, the population between, say, 45 and 65 is much over-represented, while the population of 70 years of age and over is more or less reasonably represented.

Previous Service

The outstanding result of our investigations into the previous service of members was the discovery that the personnel of the House of Commons changes much faster than might have been thought; that members in general have, in fact, only a comparatively short record of previous experience. The long service of a few outstanding members is apt to give an impression of continuity in the composition of the House that the facts do not warrant.

The *distribution* of previous service amongst members at each general election has been given in some detail, together with the average distribution for the seven parliaments. We find that in the average newly elected House 175 members are complete novices, and another 183 have not more than five years' experience; while only 136 have more than 10 years, and only 29 more than 20 years of previous service. The new House is much "greener" than one might expect!

Judged by *average* previous service, the least experienced House was that of 1924, which had on election an average previous service of only 4 years 11 months. The most experienced, by the same standard, was that of 1935, with 8 years 1 month of average previous service. For all the elections together the average was only 5 years 11 months.

The House of Commons with the largest influx of *new members* was that of 1918, which had 260, or 43 per cent of the total membership. The 1935 House, with 79 new members, or 13 per cent of the total, had the smallest influx. The average for the seven elections was 175, or 29 per cent.

As for *long service*, though a few members retain seats in parliament for as long as 40 or 50 years, yet few reach even a total of 20. The maximum number with 20 years' previous service at a general election was 40 (in 1931), the minimum was 19 (in 1924), and the average was 29; these out of a total of 602 members. Broken service (absence from one or more intervening parliaments) probably accounts to a considerable extent for the lowness of these figures.

The average *total length of service* of members cannot be computed directly or exactly. An indirect and approximate calculation suggests that it is in the neighbourhood of 15 years.

School Education

In dealing with the school education of members, we drew attention to the difficulty of classifying schools and defining the various categories: the discussion of this difficulty should be borne in mind. The classification finally adopted was threefold: public schools, secondary schools, and elementary schools.

We first considered the school education of *all* members who sat in the House of Commons during the period under investigation, irrespective of the date of election. Let us recall some of the more significant results.

In the first case we found that of the members who were known to have had a public-school education 80 per cent were Conservatives, 15½ per cent were Liberals, and only 4½ per cent were Labour members. Of those who had had a secondary (other than public-school) education, 45 per cent were Conservatives, 36½ per cent were Liberals, and 18½ per cent were Labour. Of those with only an elementary education 9 per cent were Conservatives, 12 per cent were Liberals, and no less than 79 per cent were Labour.

Next, looking at the matter the other way round, we found that of the Conservative members 77½ per cent had had a public-school education, 19 per cent a secondary education, and only 3½ per cent an elementary education. Of the Liberal members, 42½ per cent came from public schools, 44 per cent from secondary schools, and 13½ per cent from elementary schools. The Labour members' education is just the reverse of that of the Conservative members, for they derive 10 per cent from the public schools, 18 per cent from secondary schools, and no less than 72 per cent from elementary schools.

It will be seen that of the Conservative members the great majority come from the public schools, of the Liberal members the largest number, though not actually a majority, come from the secondary schools, and of the Labour members the great majority come from the elementary schools. To a remarkable extent, therefore, we should be justified in calling the Conservatives the public-school party, the Liberals the secondary-school party, and Labour the elementary-school party.

Looking next at the results of the seven general elections separately, we find that at every one of them there were more public-school members returned than there were members from either of the other types of school, and that in all but two elections the public-school members had a substantial majority over the other two types. In 1931 no less than two-thirds of the whole House had been educated at public schools, and only one-ninth at elementary schools. The most plebeian House in this respect was that of 1929, but even in that House little more than a third of the members came from elementary schools, and these were easily outnumbered by the public-school men. As might be expected from their "centre" position, social and political, the secondary-school members show the smallest variation in numbers from election to election.

Tracing how the numbers of members from the three types of school vary with the numbers of members of the three political parties with which, as already noted, they seem to have affinity, we find a remarkably close correspondence: public-school with Conservative, secondary-school with Liberal, and elementary-school with Labour. There is no such correspondence between, say, public-school and Liberal membership, or between secondary-school and Labour membership. We note, too, that in the average inter-war House nearly half the members are public-school Conservatives, while nearly one-fifth are elementary-school Labour members. Another interesting point is that in the Conservative party the safest seats are, in general, given to the upper-class members, while in the Labour party the tendency is just the reverse: here the safest seats are given, in general, to the trade-union members. These opposite tendencies throw an illuminating light on the attitude of the respective party machines.

Comparing the school education of members of parliament with that of the adult population as a whole, we find an astonishing contrast; in this, as in so many other respects, the House is not in the least a fair sample of the general population. Elementary schools have less than a quarter of their proportionate representation, secondary schools have more than 4 times their proportion, while public schools have no less than 28 times as many members as their strength in the population would entitle them to have. When the social and financial exclusiveness of the public schools is borne in mind, this is a very significant result.

Still more astonishing and significant is the very marked preponderance of Eton, and to a less extent Harrow, in the House of Commons. Roughly one-fourth of all the Conservatives who sat in the House at any time during the whole inter-war period were old Etonians, while one-third were from either Eton or Harrow. One in every seven of all the members of all parties together, including Labour, was an old Etonian, and one in five was either an old Etonian or an old Harrovian. Eton, about the most exclusive and expensive school in the country, averages well over 500 times as many members as she should have on the basis of proportion, while Harrow, not far behind, has nearly 450 times her due representation. The Harrovian has over 1,800 times and the Etonian well over 2,000 times as good a chance of entering parliament as has the elementary-school boy—in spite of the rise of the Labour party!

UNIVERSITY EDUCATION

The number of university men—not necessarily graduates—in parliament is considerable. Half the Conservative members, three-sevenths of the Liberal members, and two-ninths of the Labour members have had a university education.

The dominant position of the two old universities is noticeable. Four-fifths of the university-educated Conservatives were at Oxford or Cambridge, as were four-sevenths of the Liberal and three-sevenths of the Labour members so educated: for all parties together the proportion is five-sevenths. If we take *all* members, non-university as well as university, we find that Oxford and Cambridge claim nearly 30 per cent of the grand total. As between the two, amongst the Conservatives Oxford predominates, amongst the Liberals there is little to choose, while amongst the Labour members Cambridge is the more favoured. We find that Oxford and Cambridge amongst universities occupy a preferential position comparable with that of Eton and Harrow amongst schools.

We note the astonishingly poor position of the University of London in parliament—and parliament, be it remembered, meets in London. Size for size, Oxford and Cambridge are perhaps a dozen times as well represented as London; indeed, they are far and away better represented than any of the other universities.

Some interesting facts come to light when we consider party in relation to university education. Four-fifths of the Oxford men are Conservatives, against three-fourths of the Cambridge men and only half of the rest of the university alumni. In the other parties the position is reversed, the Liberal proportions rising instead of falling, and the Labour proportions rising more steeply than the Liberal. These facts disclose the same type of social pattern as we found in studying school education: just as school education and party are strongly correlated, so are university education and party. If a member of parliament has been at Oxford it is 4 to 1 that he is a Conservative and 19 to 1 that he is not a Labour member; just as, if he has been at Eton, it is 9 to 1 that he is a Conservative and 34 to 1 that he is not a Labour member. The older, the more expensive, and the more socially exclusive the university or the school, the more certainly will its product be found on the right wing in politics, and *vice versa*. Moreover, the Oxford man has something like 180 times, and the Cambridge man something like 140 times, as good a chance of entering parliament as has the average member of the general public.

OCCUPATION

In considering the occupations of members, we drew attention to the complexity of the subject and the difficulties in the way of a satisfactory classification: that discussion should be borne in mind. We adopted, with some modifications, the Census grouping of occupations, and recorded the number of members of each party belonging to each group. We note at once the markedly unequal representation in parliament of the various groups, and the predominance of Conservatives in some groups and of Labour members in others.

Turning to the occupations of members elected at each general election, we find that the numbers in the various occupation-groups do not fluctuate very widely, so that their averages give a fairly accurate indication of what we may term the normal occupational composition of the House. The outstanding fact at this stage of the investigation is the predominant position of the Public Administration and Defence, Commerce and Finance, Not Gainfully Occupied, and Professional Occupations groups. These four groups together fill two-thirds of the House: an astonishing result when it is remembered that Agriculture, Mining, Transport, all the manufactures of the country, and other large and important groups, have to squeeze into the remaining one-third.

Next we compare members' occupations with those of the adult population of the country. The Census returns provide the distribution figures for the latter, but need considerable manipulation for our purpose: in particular, we are concerned only with adults, and we do not want retired workers separated from those still occupied. Having made the necessary adjustments, and taken into account the Censuses of both 1921 and 1931, we compute the composition of an imaginary House of Commons in which each group of occupations is represented proportionately to its strength in the country. Comparing this with the average actual House of Commons, we find extraordinary differences in composition. In the latter most groups are, by comparison, either over- or under-represented; and the variations are in some cases extreme.

Neglecting small groups and passing over Other and Undefined Workers, we find that the worst-represented groups are those of Personal Services, Makers of Textile Goods and Clothing, Not Gainfully Occupied (more of this anon), and Agricultural Occupations, all of which have less than half of their proportionate representation: the best represented are those of Makers of Food and Drinks, Printers and Photographers, Public Administration and Defence, and Professional Occupations, all of which have more than twice their proportionate representation. The Personal Services group has only one-sixteenth of its proportionate strength: at the other end of the scale Professional Occupations have nearly twelve times their due. Moreover, in many cases the actual representatives are far from typical of the group as a whole. For instance, in many groups representation is almost monopolized by "employers and managers" to the exclusion of the far more numerous operative workers.

An important point about the Not Gainfully Occupied group is that, even after we have simplified it by the removal of the retired and other incongruous elements, it still contains two entirely dissimilar and ill-assorted sections. On the one hand we have the "idle rich"—the unoccupied people of "independent means" and the idle dependants of occupied people—and on the other the vast army of unpaid domestic workers, who should really be classified as engaged in Personal Services. We cannot separate out these two classes accurately, but we estimate that there are about five-sixths of a million adult "idlers" to $10\frac{1}{2}$ million adult unpaid domestic workers. On this basis the "idlers" have about three times their proper representation, while the domestic workers, paid and unpaid, are practically unrepresented.

The occupation-groups of the Census are largely arbitrary, artificial, and based on industry rather than occupation: hence the under- or over-representation of a group as a whole does not completely expose the position. We have noted the incongruous elements in the Not Gainfully Occupied and the preponderance of "employers and managers" in many groups, but there are many other cases in which it is necessary to look at individual occupations rather than groups. No summary can deal adequately with what is so much a matter of detail, but a few instances may be recalled.

Proprietors and managers of wholesale businesses have roughly 16 times as many members of parliament as proportion would give them, bankers have 18 times, and stockbrokers no less than 80 times as many. Commissioned officers in the fighting forces also have about 80 times their due share of members: "other ranks" are almost unrepresented. Miners are at least 20 times as well represented as are agricultural workers.

More than one-sixth of the entire (average) House of Commons consists of practising lawyers; while lawyers, practising and non-practising, constitute nearly one-fourth of the total membership. There are nearly a thousand times as many barristers in the House as their numbers in the country warrant. Solicitors, with only 55 times their due number, are more modest. Taking both branches together, there are 200 times as many lawyers in parliament as there are in the general population, strength for strength. Journalists have 60 times and teachers 6 or 7 times their proportionate representation; but in view of the indeterminate boundaries of these occupations these figures must not be taken as exact.

When we consider *occupational status* we find that the Census categories are arbitrary in conception, imperfect in application, and useless for our purpose. By redistribution, however, into the categories of (a) employers and managers, (b) rank-and-file workers, (c) professional workers, (d) unpaid domestic workers, and (e) unoccupied, we obtain a classification that, though admittedly imperfect, has real significance. Comparing the average House of Commons with the general population, we find that the "unpaid domestic workers" are practically unrepresented and the "rank-and-file workers" have little more than one-third of their proportionate share of the membership, while the "unoccupied" have three times, the "employers and managers" five or six times, and the "professional workers" more than twelve times as many members as their respective numbers in the community would justify. Clearly the general body of workers, paid and unpaid, is much underrepresented, while employers, managers, and professional workers are greatly over-represented.

Three occupations, or quasi-occupations, collectively provide more than half the membership of the House of Commons; for every other member is a lawyer, a company director, or a trade-union official. More than half of the parliamentary Conservative party and more than half of the parliamentary Liberal party are composed of lawyers and company directors, while almost half of the parliamentary Labour party consists of trade-union officials. Pretty constantly one member of the House in every five is a barrister and one in every four is a lawyer of some kind.

HEREDITARY TITLES

Holders of hereditary titles and the near relations of such holders have representation in the House of Commons far and away greater than their numbers would entitle them to receive. This element forms in the average House from two-fifths to one-half of the Conservative party and just half that proportion of the Liberals. By contrast, it contributes only about one in 25 to the Labour party membership of the House. For all parties together the titled-family element provides at least two-sevenths of the average House.

The 1931 House was the most "aristocratic" in this sense, and the 1929 House the least so. The parliamentary Conservative party is most "aristocratic" when it is numerically at its weakest: a clear indication that, in general, the hereditary-titled element takes the safest seats for itself and leaves the more difficult contests to the less "aristocratic" elements.

It is difficult to estimate with any high degree of accuracy the strength of the hereditary-titled element in either the House of Commons or the country as a whole, but a cautious estimate indicates that this element has at least 400 times the representation that it would have on a proportional basis.

PARTY

Many factors need to be taken into account in considering the relationship between party strengths in the House of Commons and party strengths amongst the electorate. We are concerned only with the three major streams of political thought, Conservative, Liberal, and Labour, but even so difficulties arise. The proper party affiliations of members are not always easily determined, especially in cases where there are "splits" or "pacts" or where ephemeral "parties" have made a fairly wide but transient appeal to the electorate. Again, where all three parties contest a seat it is possible to ascertain with some degree of accuracy their relative strengths amongst the voters; but when there are only two candidates this is not so easy. Not only have voters of the third party no means of indicating their allegiance, but, since some of them will perforce vote for the other parties, the strengths of the latter will be inflated by votes that they only receive *faute de mieux*. In the case of uncontested elections the position is even less clear. We find that, for these and other reasons, there is a general tendency for the aggregate votes to exaggerate the strength of the more successful parties and to underrate that of the less successful. This, be it noted, refers purely to *votes* and has nothing to do with the number of *seats* gained.

In analysing the votes cast we made allowance for uncontested elections, but decided that further adjustments were impracticable. The "effective" votes recorded are therefore simply the actual aggregates plus an allowance for unopposed returns.

Turning to the successive elections, we find that there is little correspondence between votes cast and seats won: in none of the elections do they tally at all closely, and in most they are seriously divergent. The facts amply justify the description "a gamble" often applied to general elections: they demonstrate the absurdity of speaking of the results as expressing "the will of the people" or as giving " a mandate from the country".

8

In 1918—the "coupon" election—the Conservatives gained nearly 50 per cent *more* seats than their voting strength entitled them to; the Labour party gained over 50 per cent *less* than their proper representation. In 1922 the Conservatives were again unduly successful, gaining nearly 40 per cent more seats than their aggregate vote merited. The Liberals won only two-thirds and Labour only four-fifths of their due share.

In 1923 the state of opinion in the country was more nearly reflected in parliament than at any other inter-war election. Even so, the Conservatives had 17 and Labour 11 more seats than their due, while the Liberals had 22 fewer. Compared with 1922, the Conservative vote only fell 4 per cent, yet their representation dropped 26 per cent; the Liberals gained less than 5 per cent in votes, but won 36 per cent more seats; the Labour vote rose little more than 2 per cent, but gained nearly 35 per cent more seats. With hardly any change of political opinion in the country there was a drastic change in the political complexion of the House.

In 1924 luck reverted to the Conservatives: they won 44 per cent more seats than their voting strength merited. The Liberals correspondingly had 64 per cent less seats than their due, and Labour 26 per cent less. In 1929 the Conservatives obtained a mere 10 per cent of undeserved seats, whereas the Labour party secured 27 per cent, though the aggregate votes of the two parties were practically equal. These undue successes deprived the Liberals of nearly 60 per cent of the seats they should have had.

In 1931 the Conservatives, profiting yet again by the "gamble", secured over 35 per cent more seats than their votes justified. Labour's strength, traduced by the results, gave it 65 per cent less seats than it deserved. The Liberals secured seats roughly corresponding to their votes; but they contested so few divisions that millions of Liberal votes must have gone unrecorded. In 1935 the Conservatives, lucky yet again, secured 32 per cent too many seats, while Labour was mulcted of a like percentage. The Liberals were about 14 per cent down, but as they again put up very few candidates their true under-representation must have been much greater.

The erratic nature of the present "system" is strikingly demonstrated by the fact that, whereas in 1929 an aggregate Labour vote of 38 per cent of the grand total gave us a Labour government, in 1935 an aggregate Labour vote of 40 per cent of the grand total gave us a strongly anti-Labour government. The Conservative party has, since the last war, profited extremely by the electoral gamble, but there is no guarantee that this will continue: there are signs that before long it may be the turn of the Labour party to have a similar, and equally undeserved, run of luck. Its voting strength steadily increases, and in 1935 it secured the highest percentage of the total vote it has yet had. Soon our capricious "system" may give it an overwhelming majority in the House while it is still only a minority in the country.

This is no fanciful picture; for four times since the last war the Conservatives have secured a substantial majority of seats in the Commons when they had only a minority of votes in the country. For 17 years out of 24 the Conservatives have dominated the government while markedly in a minority in the country. The sweeping changes in the party complexion of parliament at such elections as that of 1931 do not represent any corresponding change of view on the part of the electorate. Labour lost 224 seats at that election; its loss of voting strength only corresponded to a loss of 39 seats.

We observe another defect of the present system of election in the virtual disfranchisement of electors belonging to minority parties in many constituencies and in quite a number of extensive areas. For example, in the inter-war period the County of Sussex, with a population of nearly half a million, has had forty-seven electoral returns, and the Conservatives have secured the seat in forty-six of these. The 40 per cent of Sussex electors who belong to the Liberal and Labour parties are completely unrepresented and likely to remain so; nor is this area unique.

Looking back over our investigations as a whole, what are the outstanding results? I think we may note the following matters as having special significance.

The first point is the *elderliness* of the House of Commons. The average member does not even commence his parliamentary service until nearly a quarter of a century after becoming an adult, while the mean age of members is $8\frac{1}{2}$ years higher than that of the electorate and 20 years higher than that of the whole population.

The next point is the dominating position of *public-school* men in the House, and particularly the amazingly high proportion of members educated at Eton and (to a less extent) Harrow. These two schools have a share of the membership about 500 times as big as their share of the electorate.

Next we note that occupationally the House is in no sense a microcosm of the community: the distribution of occupations is utterly dissimilar. Moreover, a huge proportion of members belong to the *talking classes*, and in particular to the legal profession.

Another point is the big proportion of members who hold, or are related to the holders of, hereditary titles. This *aristocratic* element, which forms only a tiny fraction of the community, secures a share in the membership of the House 400 times as great.

A final point is the conspicuous failure of the House as a representation of the political opinion of the country, even as recorded in votes. The common description of a general election as a *gamble* is seen to be founded on fact: for its results are not merely an exaggeration of prevalent public opinion—they are a capricious and unpredictable distortion of it.

These are the salient characteristics of the House in respect of certain important matters considered separately. But there are some more general qualities to be detected when we survey the field as a whole.

First we note that the House is not in any sense what Professor Laski calls "an average sample of ordinary men". In no single respect—age, education, occupation, sex, social standing, party—does the composition of the House of Commons reflect that of the community. The differences, moreover, are not the minor deviations inseparable from any system of representation: they are radical divergences.

Studying these divergences, we are driven to the conclusion that parliament is recruited to a very marked extent from what are, in one way or another, privileged classes. In the Labour party the dominant position of the trade unions gives to the officials of those unions the status of a privileged class: they secure their huge share of the party's parliamentary seats, not on general political grounds, but because of their services, past, present, and future, to the interests of the unions.

Outside the Labour party it is social position, as measured by the factors of birth, education, and financial means, that determines the privileged class. Here we find ourselves forced to join issue with those who assert that "the belief in the existence of social classes . . . is the result of studying social theory of doubtful value and of neglecting social facts."* This assertion has already been answered,† and we need spend no time on any general refutation of it. But if we face honestly the "social facts" with which this book is concerned we are compelled to recognize the existence of social classes, irrespective of "social theory" (whether "of doubtful value" or otherwise), and it may be as well to make this point clear.

If there were no social classes we should find little or no correlation between the political views and the social attributes of members of parliament. If there were no social classes we should be unable to predict from a member's education or occupation what his political views would be. If there were no social classes we should expect to find old Etonians and old Oxonians equally at home in any of the political parties: we should not be able to say, as we can now, that if a member is an army officer, a stockbroker, or the heir to a peerage, it is next door to certain that he is a Conservative, whereas if he is a miner or a joiner it is a pretty safe bet that he is a Labour member. We need not multiply examples: throughout this investigation the accumulating facts drive home the point. Politics are strongly correlated with education, with occupation, with parentage, with financial means, and the rest of it: and these are correlated with each other.

If there were no social classes, why should this be so? In a classless society a man's political views would be the reflection of his individual personality, the outcome of his individual experience as a human being. But, indeed, the existence of social classes is obvious if one will but

---

* A. M. Carr-Saunders and D. Caradog Jones, *A Survey of the Social Structure of England and Wales* (1927), chapter VI.
† *E.g.*, by R. H. Tawney, *Equality* (1931), chapter III.

look at the facts that stare one in the face. Are there no class distinctions between, shall we say, the officers' mess and that of the sergeants? —or between the grand stand at Ascot and the stablemen's quarters?— or between the débutantes at a Court and the flower-girls in the street outside?

The facts that social classes are not *discontinuous*,* but shade off gradually into one another, and that they are not entirely *rigid*, but allow a certain amount of passage to and fro in individual cases from one class to another: these facts are not a denial of the existence of class—they are merely an indication of the conditions in which it functions.

We conclude, then, that outside the Labour party (and even to some extent within it) parliament is very largely recruited from certain favoured sections of the community. Whether we label these sections "the upper classes", or "the wealthier classes", or, as some prefer, "the political classes", the essential fact remains that they form what we may safely term a privileged class. Their attributes of birth, education, and means give them many advantages in life generally; and the abnormal share of the membership of the House of Commons which they secure reflects these advantages and enables them to dominate the political life of the community. †

Here we can leave our study of the personnel of the House of Commons as it now is: we have the basic facts and can pass on to study the causes underlying the present state of affairs, to discuss what changes may be desirable, and to consider how such changes could be brought about.

* It appears that Professor Carr-Saunders and Mr. Jones fall into the error of assuming that there can be no classification without sharp dividing lines, for they say: "But since incomes and holdings of property are continuously graded, it is clear that amount of income and holding of property cannot of themselves form the basis of classification into anything of the nature of discontinuous social classes." And again: ". . . there is seldom or never to be found a sharp dividing line between wage-earners and the rest." But discontinuity and sharp dividing lines are by no means essential to classification: ask the biologists, the physicists, scientists generally. There is no discontinuity between day and night, and no "sharp dividing line" between the animal and vegetable kingdoms; yet the distinction in each case is clear enough and important enough for all practical purposes. It simply will not do to require "sharp dividing lines" and "discontinuity" as a prerequisite of all classification.

† For a remarkably able and penetrating study of this aspect of British public life by an observer who stands outside it, reference may be made to *King, Lords, and Gentlemen*, by Karl Heinz Abshagen (1939).

PART II

CAUSE AND EFFECT

CHAPTER XIII

THE HISTORICAL BACKGROUND

WE now know what sorts of people represent us in parliament. We have ascertained their characteristics and peculiarities in age, education, occupation, party, and other matters. We have compared them in these respects with the general adult population, and have discovered that there are marked differences between the composition of the House of Commons and that of the electorate: the House is not a reproduction of the nation in miniature, but something quite different.

Certain kinds of people preponderate in the House of Commons, with no corresponding preponderance in the community at large. Why are we represented by these kinds of people and not by other kinds? What considerations govern the choice of the personnel of parliament? Do the divergences between the qualities of this personnel and the qualities of the community arise from the operation of any principle, or are they the fortuitous outcome of parliamentary evolution, the accidental product of social conditions and historical events?

These are the questions that we have next to consider. To answer them we have first to analyse the conditions that govern the selection of candidates for parliament, and the choice between those candidates; and then to study the relation between those conditions and the resulting composition of the House of Commons.

Now, it is no part of the scheme of this book to present a history of parliamentary institutions in this country, or even to record the origins of the House of Commons and the story of its development into its present form. But, in order that the matters to be discussed in the succeeding chapters may be seen in proper perspective, it is desirable that we should at least notice briefly the salient characteristics of that history, and should pay some attention to the phases of it that are most closely related to our subject.

Amongst these historical characteristics we may observe first the doctrine, or if you prefer it the way of thinking, that the government of this country is not to be regarded as a despotism, that its rulers have no totalitarian rights over the community. It may well be that this doctrine was not consciously present in the minds of those who in the remote past first helped to establish it. It is probable that it long remained implicit in actions rather than expressed in words. It is certain that, even when it came to be expressed, its scope was limited, its outlines nebulous, and its implications not fully grasped. It is indisputable, also, that kings and priests and landholders were constantly striving, and often with considerable success for the time being, to overthrow or ignore it. But, when all is said and done, it seems clear that the principle has been there, however latent or ill defined, and that it has exercised a powerful, if intermittent, influence on the growth of our political institutions. It is deeply rooted in our traditions and has become almost instinctive in our race, though, like most instincts, it is largely taken for granted.

Next among these characteristics we may note that the growth of the House of Commons from its remote origins in Saxon times to its present forms and powers has been a slow and lengthy process. It was never deliberately planned as the House of Representatives was planned in the United States of America and as most other modern legislative bodies were planned. By comparison it is an organism, evolved by the interaction of many factors during many centuries, where they are consciously-designed machines; and, as with other organisms, it retains vestigial traces of ancestral forms. Lacking perhaps the neatness of the modern artificial product, it possesses instead an almost biological capacity for growth and adaptation. Superficially its history may seem spasmodic and even discontinuous, with many fluctuations and regressions; but taking a longer view there is a continuity about it that is not only remarkable, but has been, in all probability, of extreme value in maintaining the vitality and durability of our political activities and consciousness.

If slow growth and continuity may be taken as the second salient characteristic of the development of the House of Commons, we may regard as the third the adaptability to changing circumstances that goes with them. The history of the House is a long record of changes in composition, in function, and in procedure, brought about by changing conditions and unfolding ideas. As the social and industrial life of the country has expanded and as its civilization has developed in complexity and amenity far beyond the rude simplicity of Saxon times, so have the bases of its parliamentary organization and the range of its parliamentary activities broadened out far beyond those of the witenagemot.

Concurrent with these changes, and perhaps hardly separable from them, there has been the long struggle between the few who have acquired and would retain for themselves a privileged position in the government of the country and the increasing number who have sought the right to participate in the determination of their political destinies. The struggle takes many forms down the centuries: now as a contest between a feudal king and his turbulent barons, now as a quarrel between a monarch seeking to establish the doctrine of divine right and his refractory parliament, now as the opposition of the great landowners to the sharing of power with the new industrial magnates, now as the effort of the common man to demand a place in the political scheme of things: but through it all we can see, as the combatants can rarely have seen, the gradual development of something that approximates more and more nearly to a democratic way of government. As Pollard*

* A. F. Pollard, *The Evolution of Parliament* (1920), page 15.

observes: "The state has gone on from strength to strength because its parliamentary organization provided for an ever-widening national representation, and government became increasingly the affair of the English people." Here is no completed tale, however; the struggle still goes on, and the end is not yet in sight.

These essential characteristics of the growth of the House of Commons to its present powers and status suggest certain lines of thought in connexion with any scheme for the improvement or further development of the House, including the solution of the problems of personnel which it is the purpose of this book to discuss. We have not yet reached the stage in our investigations at which concrete proposals for reform can be considered—there are still many matters to be taken into account before we can do that—but if our reading of the trend of parliamentary history is substantially correct it seems to indicate the general attitude of mind which should inform our approach to the question of reform.

One general consideration that suggests itself is that in a country with so lengthy and, on a long view, so consistent a record of political development we should be guided as much by tradition as by pure logic in any proposals we may put forward. Stating the matter in another way, we may postulate as a fundamental principle that schemes for reform should grow out of the history of the institutions to be reformed, in so far as that is possible or practicable. To say that is not to suggest that no violent departure from tradition can ever be justifiable or successful. There may be conditions that render such a departure almost inevitable; the bold course may succeed in spite of its risks and of the turmoil which it almost inevitably causes. We have such an instance in the establishment of the new régime in Russia. But a course which may be justified in the case of a country in desperate straits is not therefore to be recommended for a country with a settled way of life and a proved capacity for constitutional evolution. It is almost certainly the failure to observe this principle that has been one of the greatest, though not the only, cause of the breakdown, partial or complete, of parliamentary institutions in countries where they have been imposed in spite of the lack of any previous traditions or experience of a comparable kind.

If we accept this view, then we must conclude that the best line of advance is to start from things as they are and find ways of improving the House as we know it and as it has evolved through the centuries, rather than to take a clean sheet of paper and attempt to start all over again from abstract considerations of logic and efficiency. This is no plea for "gradualism" as a basic political philosophy, nor is it in any way an advocacy of timidity in facing our problems: it may be that drastic remedies are required to meet the needs of the case. What we are asserting is that proposals for reform, whether drastic or otherwise, should take account of our deeply rooted ways of living and thinking, should build on what is best in our long national experience and tradition, rather than attempt to begin afresh from some different and non-historical basis. It seems to me that the really serious criticism of such a proposal as that of the Webbs for a Political Parliament and a Social Parliament side by side* is not so much to be found in considerations of either political theory or practical mechanical efficiency as in the fact that the scheme involves an abrupt break with tradition and a fresh start on a totally new basis.†

Of course, if an institution or a tradition has outlived its usefulness and is moribund, then the only thing to do is to scrap it completely, start afresh, and substitute something that we hope will prove not only new but better. But in spite of all its defects—and they are many—I can see no ground for deciding that the House of Commons has reached such a state. Even the present war, with all its upheavals and stresses, has not demonstrated any such failure of the House as would warrant us in consigning it to the scrap-heap or even in remaking it on a completely new basis.

A further consideration suggested by the characteristics of its history is that any alteration in the constitution or in the personnel of the House should be in the direction of making it more and not less democratic. Not so long ago there were people in this country who quite seriously contended that the need was for a more authoritarian form of government. The present war has largely silenced if not converted them, since it has engaged us in a life-and-death struggle with the three great authoritarian states, Germany, Italy, and Japan, and since the evils of dictatorship and despotism have been demonstrated anew in the actions of those states. But, quite apart from the war and the lurid light it has thrown on such forms of government, I suggest that our own history is sufficient to indicate beyond a doubt that for us at least the true line of development is to be found in seeking to widen the distribution of effective political power, to utilize more and more fully the political capacities of our people in whatever walk of life they are to be found. For us there seems no natural tendency towards totalitarianism on the one hand or the dictatorship of the proletariat on the other. We are in the happy position of having found a broad way of advance which, in spite of its manifest imperfections and its tendency to resemble Chesterton's "Rolling English Road", suits us and has given us an almost unexampled political stability: let us continue to pursue it, though now, it is to be hoped, with a clearer vision of our aims, a bolder effort to achieve them, and a better sense of direction.

It would be interesting to pass from these general considerations and trace in detail the steps in the evolution of the House of Commons as a separate chamber, its gradual change of function, and its development

---

* Sidney and Beatrice Webb, *A Constitution for the Socialist Commonwealth of Great Britain* (1920).

† I am aware that this might be disputed by the authors of the scheme, who say: "Each society can only reconstruct itself on the lines of its own past development, and out of the social materials that are, for the time being, available." It does not seem to me, however, that the scheme complies with this requirement: it involves a fundamental departure from our accustomed ways of development.

into its present form. Leaving that to the constitutional historians,* however, we may just note one or two points of special interest. It was in 1254 that the "knights of the shires", the forerunners of our present county members, were first summoned to parliament, and only eleven years later that representatives of cities and boroughs were included; whilst in 1295 or a few years later, and more by chance than of set purpose, parliament first met as two houses, the prelates sitting with the greater feudal lords, and the knights of the shires with the citizens and burgesses. So, within the short space of a generation or two, the great council of the realm changed from a feudal assembly to a parliament of two houses, lords and commons: the essential germ of parliament as we know it to-day.

We must, however, avoid the mistake of reading into these happenings an immediate significance that they did not possess. It is doubtful whether a contemporary observer would have seen in them anything more than adjustments made to meet current needs: their significance to us arises from the fact that they were the first steps taken on a path which has led to enormously important results, and that had those steps been taken—as they so easily might have been taken—in some other direction, the political development of the country would in all probability have followed a wholly different course. It must be borne in mind, moreover, that the functions of the "model parliament" of 1295 differed greatly from the functions of its modern descendant. It was the germ from which the latter sprang; but it was not a modern parliament in mediaeval dress.

Now, although any comprehensive study of the history of parliament would be out of place here, it is pertinent to our inquiries to survey in outline the stages by which the personnel of the House of Commons and its method of election have varied and developed from 1254 to the present time: seven hundred years of growth and experiment and adjustment.

Initially the "knights of the shires" were of the same feudal class as the barons: they were, indeed, the lesser "barons" in the original sense of the term, the difference being simply that, whereas the greater barons were summoned to parliament by individual writs addressed to them personally, the knights were summoned by writs addressed to the sheriff, and each county had to elect two *representatives* to attend parliament: the rudimentary beginnings of representative government. There were at first thirty-seven counties so represented, Wales and the counties palatine being excluded, and the county representation of England remained remarkably constant right up to the Reform Act of 1832. The Welsh counties were brought in by Henry VIII and, of course, the Scottish and Irish counties on the union of their parliaments with those of England and Great Britain respectively.

The election of the knights for service in parliament was made by the

* There is an admirable summary of this evolution in Sir Courtenay Ilbert's *Parliament* (ed. 1929), chapter I.

county courts from amongst their own members. These county courts were, of course, very different bodies from the county courts of the present day: they had administrative and fiscal functions to perform as well as judicial. At first there was no machinery of election specified. The sheriff was in charge of the proceedings, but otherwise the method of choosing representatives appears to have been left to each county to determine for itself. In 1430, however, an act of Henry VI laid it down that the electors (and therefore the representatives) must be resident in the county and must hold land—freehold or tenement, not leasehold or copyhold—of the net annual value of at least forty shillings. This act remained in force for a remarkably long time. For four centuries its provisions endured untouched, and even the Reform Act of 1832, though it enfranchised certain copyholders, leaseholders, and occupiers, left the forty-shilling freeholders practically undisturbed.

It may be noted that as early as 1294 freeholders with land of a net annual value of less than forty shillings were *excused* from attendance at county courts and therefore from service in parliament, though it was not until 1430 that they were *excluded*. But in those early days such duties were regarded as onerous and unwelcome: to be excused was a boon and not a deprivation. The change made in 1430 is probably symptomatic of a changing attitude to parliamentary service, the dawning consciousness that such service might have its advantages as well as its disadvantages.

The history of city and borough representation is much more complex and tangled than that of the county. The first writs merely instructed the sheriff to secure the return of two members for each city and borough in the county, no towns being mentioned by name. As with the counties, electors and elected belonged to the same category in each case: the citizens of each city and the burgesses of each borough chose, or had chosen, from amongst their own numbers the two representatives who were to serve for them in parliament. As with the counties, too, service in parliament was not originally a privilege, but an unpleasant duty, to be shirked whenever possible: moreover, apart from individual reluctance to undertake this service, towns were often anxious to be excused, since they had to pay wages to their representatives and were taxed at a higher rate than counties. In this connexion it must be borne in mind that the early parliaments were, on the one hand, judicial bodies and, on the other, a means of securing the taxes that the king needed. It was only in the course of centuries that they became to any appreciable extent bodies for the enacting of legislation and the discussion of policy. The reluctance of knights, citizens, and burgesses alike to undertake the dangers and discomforts of the journey to Westminster, and to assume the responsibilities involved, is therefore easily understandable.

The number of boroughs returning members varied greatly from time to time, and the qualifications for participating in elections varied amazingly from place to place: the borough franchise never had the uniformity imposed on that of the county by the act of 1430. It is remarkable that there should have been such differences between counties and boroughs, both in regard to the number of constituencies and in regard to the qualifications of electors; but so it was, and not until the Reform Act of 1832 were borough representation and franchise put on to anything like a sound and uniform basis.

At first the selection of towns to be represented seems to have been left to the sheriff, though no doubt in the course of time custom tended to fix the choice. As, however, the functions of parliament developed and membership gradually changed in aspect from a disagreeable duty to a valuable privilege, the right to representation became something to be sought instead of shirked, and the number of boroughs represented in parliament rose considerably. New boroughs were created by royal charter, particularly by the Tudors, and borough representation was correspondingly increased. There seems some doubt how far this expansion was due to the desire of monarchs—Elizabeth, for example—to create "pocket boroughs" as a means of controlling the House of Commons, and how far it was due to the increasing desire of citizens and burgesses to have a voice in affairs of state: probably both influences were at work at different times and places.

Certain it is that the early and widespread reluctance to serve that caused two Oxfordshire knights to flee the country on their election to parliament, and Torrington to obtain a charter giving it perpetual exemption from representation,* underwent a change in the course of time. About the middle of the fifteenth century the number of boroughs returning members to the House of Commons began to increase again after having fallen from the 166 of early days to the 99 of 1445; and by the sixteenth century the former position was reversed, membership of the House was eagerly sought, and seats were even bought and sold. As Pollard says: "The burden of representation had become a privilege, because people had grasped the fact that through it they could impose their will on the crown, instead of the crown through it imposing its will upon them. The forms of the partnership remained, but the predominance was changing hands."†

The age of the Tudors, indeed, marks the transformation of parliament from an assembly of mediaeval organization and functions to something recognizably similar in general effect to the modern institution. From that period until 1832, though there were innumerable changes in forms and procedure and outlook, yet in essentials the House of Commons remained much the same, and its constituencies and franchises underwent no substantial reorganization or modification.

From that point of view the Reform Act of 1832 is of much greater significance than its immediate results betoken. It fell far short of fulfilling the hopes that had been placed upon it by ardent reformers of the time; it gave power rather to commercial and industrial magnates than to the people generally. But it marked the transition from an out-

* Pollard, *op. cit.*, page 154. † *Op. cit.*, page 159.

worn post-mediaeval franchise and distribution of seats to something that is definitely modern, and it paved the way for the Representation of the People Acts (the very title of which is significant) of 1867, 1884, 1918, and 1928, together with the Ballot Act of 1872 and the Redistribution of Seats Act of 1885. By these acts the franchise and the distribution of seats, which had not varied greatly in essentials from 1254 to 1832, were completely transformed. The franchise especially was expanded out of all knowledge, so that in less than a century we pass from the era of rotten boroughs with a mere handful of male electors to an age in which adult suffrage for both sexes is the rule and seats are distributed with at least some regard to population. One needs to sit back and take a bird's-eye view of the changes as a whole to realize how sweeping they have been and how great is their significance in the democratization of politics.

There would be little point in attempting to survey in detail the changes in the franchise in the intervening period between 1832 and 1928: particulars of them are readily accessible elsewhere, and they have little direct bearing on the issues with which we are concerned in this investigation. We pass over them, therefore, and conclude this chapter with a brief statement of the present position, which, it will be seen, is a great deal simpler and more straightforward than was the case at any previous time.

To be eligible to be placed on the register of electors, and hence to be eligible to vote in a parliamentary election, a person must be a British subject, must be twenty-one years of age, and must (a) have resided in the same constituency or a contiguous constituency for the previous three months, or (b) have been in occupation for the previous three months of business premises of a yearly value of ten pounds or more in a constituency other than that in which he or she resides (or be the wife or husband of a person in such occupation), or (c) hold a degree of a British university. Inmates of prisons, lunatic asylums, workhouses, and similar institutions are not entitled to the franchise.

At a general election a person may vote *once* on account of a residence qualification, and also *once* on account of *either* a business-premises qualification *or* a university qualification. No one may vote more than twice, however many qualifications he or she may possess. At a by-election, however, anyone on the register of electors for the division may vote. There are special provisions for absent voters, including those in the fighting services, and there are a number of rules dealing with exceptional cases. These, however, are not material to our discussion and need not be given here.*

It will be seen that practically every adult British subject of either sex who is resident in this country is entitled to a vote, and the number of electors on the register—over 31 millions (excluding Northern Ireland)—bears this out, even when allowance is made for "plural voters".

* For fuller particulars see the *Constitutional Year Book* and other works of reference.

Even so recently as 1885 the number of electors was under 5 millions, while in 1832, even after the Reform Act, there were only about 1 million. These figures speak for themselves.

When we turn from the qualifications necessary in order to become an *elector* to the qualifications necessary in order to become a *candidate*, we find a corresponding simplicity and straightforwardness. Legally the restrictions on candidature for membership of the House of Commons are few in number and not very onerous. On the positive side, a candidate must be a British subject, must be twenty-one years of age, must be nominated in writing by ten electors of the constituency he seeks to represent, and must deposit the sum of one hundred and fifty pounds in cash or notes with the Returning Officer. If the candidate succeeds in obtaining not less than one-eighth of the total number of valid votes recorded, his deposit is refunded to him after the election; otherwise it is forfeited.

On the negative side, the following classes of persons are debarred from membership of the House: peers of England, Scotland, and the United Kingdom; Irish representative peers; judges of the High Court; members of the permanent Civil Service; clergymen of the Established Church; priests of the Roman Catholic Church; bankrupts; lunatics; and persons convicted of treason, felony, and certain electoral offences.

It is typical of the anomalies still remaining in the constitution that though Irish peers who have no seats in the House of Lords may enter the House of Commons, Scottish peers may not; and that though members of the permanent civil service are excluded from parliament, ambassadors and members of the navy, army, and air force are under no such ban. Furthermore, a candidate need not reside in the constituency he seeks to represent, nor need he even be an elector in that or any other constituency. He may have spent his whole life abroad, in the dominions or elsewhere, and have neither knowledge of conditions in this country nor place of residence in it; so long as he is a British subject he is eligible for election.

Apart from the comparatively small number of persons disqualified as set out above, then, any British subject of full age who can secure ten electors' signatures and find a hundred and fifty pounds to deposit can become a candidate. The finding of the deposit may in some cases be a hardship, but otherwise the conditions could hardly be easier.

Freedom from legal restrictions, however, is not the only governing consideration, and we pass in the succeeding chapters to the discussion of other matters which have a powerful effect in determining the character of our representation in parliament.

CHAPTER XIV

THE COST OF ELECTIONS

As we have seen in the last chapter, seven centuries of parliamentary evolution have brought us to the stage of universal adult suffrage and almost negligible restrictions on election to the House of Commons. Legally the position could hardly be simpler, for almost every adult British subject is entitled to a vote and eligible to become a candidate. But removal of legal barriers, though of the first importance, is not the whole story: it is one thing not to be prohibited from a given course of action, and quite another to be able to follow that course. As Tawney remarks, the law "is even generous, for it offers opportunities both to those whom the social system permits to seize them and to those whom it does not."* So, in this case as in many others, the value of legal opportunity is largely nullified by the stringencies of finance: it is an expensive business to contest an election, and a more expensive one to sit in the House of Commons.

Take first the question of the cost of contesting an election. The amount of money that may be expended by or on behalf of a candidate is limited by Act of Parliament, but is nevertheless considerable. The maximum permissible expenditure consists of an allowance based on the number of electors on the register of the division at the time of the election, together with certain other allowances. The limit per elector is 6d. in a county division, 5d. in a single-member borough division, and 3¾d. in a double-member borough division. Let us see what this allowance amounts to in practice.

The smallest number of electors in a county division at the last general election (1935) was 27,309, at Barnard Castle, Durham, and the largest was 167,939, at Romford, Essex. Hence the *per elector* part of the permissible expenses for each candidate ranged from £683 to £4,198 in county divisions, with an average of about £1,230. An additional sum of not more than £75 may be paid in remuneration to the election agent. To these sums must be added the personal expenses of the candidate himself: these are not limited to any precise amount, though they must, of course, be *bona fide*. The maximum permissible expenditure per candidate for all purposes, therefore, ranges in county divisions from about £900 to about £4,400, with an average of about £1,500.

In the single-member borough divisions the smallest number of electors was 27,484, at South-West Bethnal Green, and the largest was 106,936, at Ilford. Hence the *per elector* part of the permissible expenses for each candidate ranged from £573 to £2,228 in such divisions, with an average of about £1,000. Adding the £50 allowed as remuneration to the election agent in a borough division, and also the personal expenses of the candidate himself, it may be taken that the maximum permissible

* R. H. Tawney, *Equality* (1931), page 139.

expenditure per candidate for all purposes in single-member borough divisions ranges from about £750 to about £2,400, with an average of about £1,200.

It should be observed that there are rules governing the exact purposes for which expenses may be incurred and the manner in which they must be paid, but these rules do not concern us here. It will be realized, also, that the figures given are in all cases maxima, and that no candidate is under any obligation to spend sums of this size on his election expenses; but clearly if he curtails his expenditure unduly a candidate is likely to reduce the effectiveness of his electoral campaign and correspondingly to damage his prospects of success.

It is of interest, therefore, to inquire what amounts are actually spent by candidates. Every candidate has to declare to the returning officer, after the election, the amount and details of his election expenses; and the whole of the returns so made after a general election are printed by order of the House of Commons and published as a blue-book. Let us glance at the returns for the general election of 1935.*

The first thing we notice is that, in general, the actual expenditure of candidates falls considerably short of the legal maximum. As we have seen, the average *permissible* expenditure for candidates in county divisions is about £1,500: against this the average *actual* expenditure in 1935 was £576. The average in contested divisions is, however, rather higher, as the lower average costs when there is no contest tend to bring down the general average a little. Assume it as £600 in round figures for contested seats; then we see that the actual expenditure was only 40 per cent of the permissible, taking the averages for the whole of the county divisions.

In borough divisions the actual average for the whole country was £515: say £520 in contested elections only. The permissible amount averaged about £1,200, as we have seen. Hence, for the borough seats, the actual expenditure was only about 43 per cent of the permissible, on the average.

An interesting and significant fact disclosed by the official "Return" is that in almost every constituency the Conservative candidate's election expenses are much higher than those of his Liberal or Labour opponent. It is rarely, indeed, that the Conservative expenditure is equalled by that of any opponent: a clear indication of the greater wealth of the Conservative party. In the 1935 election the average amounts of election expenses for contested elections were, in round figures, as follows:

Conservative candidates	...	...	...	£780
Liberal candidates	...	...	...	£520
Labour candidates	...	...	...	£360

so that the average Conservative candidate spent half as much again as the average Liberal candidate, and more than twice as much as the

* *Return of the Expenses of Each Candidate at the General Election of November 1935* (H.C. 150, 1936).

average Labour candidate. It should be added that these figures do not include "Liberal National" and "National Labour" candidates. The expenses of these were on the high side, equalling or even exceeding those of their Conservative allies: an interesting sidelight on these products of "National" government.

The same financial position is seen from a slightly different aspect if we consider the cases where a candidate's election expenses exceeded £1,000. There were 95 such candidates in the 1935 election, and 83 of them were Conservatives or their allies,* while only 7 were Liberals and 4 Labour, the remaining 1 being an Independent. No less than 30 per cent of the National Labour candidates spent over £1,000 each on their election expenses, and so did over 18 per cent of the Liberal Nationals and nearly 14 per cent of the Conservatives. But only a little over 4 per cent of the Labour candidates exceeded £1,000. The contrast speaks for itself.

The total bill for election expenses for the whole country was no less than £722,093, very nearly three-quarters of a million pounds. Who pays this bill? The practice varies considerably, both as between one party and another and as between one constituency and another. It is not easy to ascertain the facts very closely, and, indeed, it is only in the Labour party that there is any definite scheme for dealing with expenses. We can, however, discern the broad trend of each party's practice.

In the Conservative party the official view is that the financial and other arrangements in connexion with a candidature, including the question of who is to pay the election expenses, are matters to be settled between the candidate and his constituency party association. The Central Office of the party, however, I am told, uses its influence, whenever possible, to ensure that no local association limits its freedom of choice by making too heavy financial demands upon any prospective candidate. What in this context are to be considered as excessive demands, how much freedom of choice is considered necessary, and how far the influence of the Central Office is actually exerted or successful, I have not been able to discover.

According, however, to one Conservative candidate, Mr. Ian Harvey, ‡ a prospective Conservative candidate must be willing to pay "at least half" of the election expenses out of his own pocket to have even "a reasonable chance" of being adopted, while his prospect of adoption will be "excellent" if he is willing to pay the whole of the expenses. § Any part of the expenses not paid by the candidate himself is presum-

---

* 69 Conservatives, 8 Liberal Nationals, and 6 National Labour.
† The candidature is, nevertheless, subject to the approval of party headquarters.
‡ Ian Harvey, *A Plutocratic System*. This memorandum was issued to the press in January 1939: the essential passages are reproduced, by permission, in Appendix III.
§ He must also, according to Mr. Harvey, be willing to pay a substantial annual subscription to the local Conservative association; see Chapter XV.

9

ably found by the local association. Mr. Harvey estimates the actual amount of the election expenses as "anything between £400 and £1,200": * hence, if he is correct, no one can expect to be adopted as a Conservative candidate, in any but exceptional constituencies, unless he is prepared to contribute towards his election expenses at least £200, and possibly as much as £2,000.

At first sight there may seem to be some inconsistency between Mr. Harvey's statements and the official view of the party; but that inconsistency, I suggest, may be only superficial. So long as there are would-be Conservative candidates available who are willing to meet the financial demands indicated by Mr. Harvey, the Central Office may perhaps consider that the local associations are not limiting their freedom of choice by making too heavy financial demands upon prospective candidates: it is a matter of interpretation. In any event there can be little doubt that what has been termed by leading Conservatives the "selling of seats" does take place; and as this is not just a matter of domestic interest for the Conservative party, but one which has an important bearing on the whole question of parliamentary representation, I propose to give a brief account of some evidence in support of Mr. Harvey's general accusations.

The Scarborough conference of the Conservative party in October 1937 passed a resolution which led to the setting up of a committee under the chairmanship of the late Earl of Crawford to consider the problem "as a matter of supreme importance". It has been stated that the committee reported to the then party leader, Mr. Neville Chamberlain, but the nature of the report is unknown, and it does not appear to have led to any action.† The London conference of the Federation of University Conservative Associations on 5th January 1939 unanimously adopted a resolution, submitted by Mr. Hugh Fraser, deploring that "considerations of personal fortune rather than of natural talent" influence local associations in their choice of parliamentary candidates.‡ The annual meeting of the University of London Conservative Association on 22nd February 1939 passed a resolution "viewing with concern and alarm the present practice in many strongly held constituencies of selecting candidates with less regard for their fitness and ability to play their part in public life than for their willingness to defray the whole costs of their election and to make substantial contributions to the funds of the local Conservative association".§

Individual Conservative members of parliament have also given evidence in the same direction. Sir Reginald Blaker, M.P. for Spelthorne, Middlesex, is reported to have said of the "selling of seats" accusation:

* Actually the range is even greater, varying from £325 (in a Scottish division) to £2,334 in 1935. In no fewer than 29 cases Mr. Harvey's maximum of £1,200 was exceeded by Conservative candidates, though very few fell below £400. As we have seen, however, the average is, in round figures, £780.

† *Evening Standard*, 4th January 1939; *Yorkshire Post*, 5th January 1939; *Daily Telegraph*, 5th January 1939.

‡ *Manchester Guardian*, 6th January 1939.

§ *Manchester Guardian*, 23rd February 1939.

'I think it is perfectly true. I think such methods do more harm to our party than any other thing."* Mrs. Mavis Tate, M.P. for Frome, Somerset, is stated to have decided in April 1939 not to stand again because she could not afford to keep up the payment of heavy election expenses and subsidies to the local Conservative association. At the 1935 election Mrs. Tate's election expenses amounted to £1,153† and were, apparently, all paid by herself. In addition she agreed to hand over the whole of her salary as a member of parliament (at that time £400 per annum) to the local Conservative association. On top of this, Mrs. Tate added, "I keep a house in the district, which, with donations to charity and other expenses, costs another £500 a year."‡

The case of the Hendon division of Middlesex is also instructive. From the correspondence published in the *Daily Telegraph*§ it appears that "the next candidate will have to find £1,000 a year and his election expenses",‖ and that "a candidate absolutely unknown to the constituency—an entire stranger" and, moreover, "one whose chief recommendation (beyond the possession of 'ample means') seems to be that recently he lost a seat to the Socialist Opposition", is to be adopted by the divisional association as Conservative candidate.

If any further evidence were necessary it could be found in a leading article in the Conservative *Yorkshire Post*,¶ and in correspondence and notes in that paper, the *Daily Telegraph*, and the *Evening Standard*, following the issue of Mr. Harvey's memorandum.

I have been at some pains to stress this practice in the Conservative party because of its obvious bearing on the subject of this investigation. Men and women of means inevitably enjoy considerable advantages in many ways over their poorer fellows, and a practice that greatly augments those advantages in relation to the political life of the country is inconsistent with democratic government. It gives to the wealthy a dominating position in the parliamentary Conservative party, and an unduly strong, often a dominating, position in the House as a whole. As the other House is also in the main composed of wealthy men, this means that parliament as a whole is ruled by the wealthier classes to an extent that must colour its outlook and influence its decisions in a very undesirable way. Writers as diverse as John Stuart Mill** and H. J. Laski†† have pointed out that one class cannot adequately represent another; and a parliament of rich men cannot adequately represent a community that is in the main composed of poor men.

Let us turn to the Liberal party. I am informed on good authority that, while there may be cases in the party comparable with those dis-

---

* *Evening Standard*, 6th January 1939.
† *Return of Election Expenses, 1935*, page 57.
‡ *Daily Express*, 18th April 1939.
§ *Daily Telegraph*, 5th, 13th, and 16th January 1939.
‖ At the last election these expenses amounted to £1,145 for the Conservative candidate (*Return of Election Expenses, 1935*, page 54).
¶ *Yorkshire Post*, 5th January 1939.
** J. S. Mill, *Representative Government*, chapter III.
†† H. J. Laski, *An Introduction to Politics*, chapter I, section II.

cussed above, they are far rarer than in the Conservative party. The view is taken that, while it is naturally an advantage to a candidate if he possesses private means, it is by no means a *sine qua non*. I have not come across any evidence of the "selling of seats" to Liberal candidates, and it would seem that if anything of the sort goes on it must be on a smaller scale altogether than in the Conservative party. It is noticeable that the whole organization of the Liberal party is more flexible than that of the other two major parties, and that correspondingly the local associations have more freedom, and probably more self-reliance. It may be judged that, in general, they are more self-supporting and more ready to provide their own financial backing.

In the Labour party the financing of elections is governed by regulations adopted by the party conference of 1933.* Under these regulations the constituency party must undertake to pay not less than 20 per cent of the election expenses, while any affiliated organization (*e.g.*, a trade union) promoting the candidature must not undertake to contribute more than 80 per cent of the expenses, with a further limitation that its contribution shall not exceed 80 per cent of 60 per cent of that part of the legal maximum that is based on the number of electors in the constituency. The effect of this is that the contribution from the trade union or other affiliated body is limited to a maximum of 48 per cent of 6d. per elector in county divisions and of 5d. per elector in borough divisions. The constituency Labour party must provide the remainder of the expenses.

Though not explicitly stated in the regulations, it is apparent, from the published form of financial agreement that has to be signed in respect of every candidature, that a candidate not put forward by an affiliated body is under the same limitation to 48 per cent of the legal *per elector* maximum in respect of any contribution that he may personally make towards the election expenses as would apply to the contribution of any such affiliated body, and I am informed that this is, in fact, the case.

It is also not explicitly stated in the regulations whether the *total* election expenditure is to be limited to 60 per cent of the legal *per elector* maximum, though that appears to be implied. I am informed, however, that it is recognized that in certain contests a larger expenditure than 60 per cent of the legal maximum may be required, and that that is the reason why the 60 per cent line has not been made an absolute limit. Where a constituency Labour party spends on a parliamentary election a larger sum than 60 per cent of the legal maximum, the whole of the expenditure above that line must, of course, be met by the constituency party itself.

This 60 per cent proportion of the legal *per elector* maximum gives an allowance ranging, at the 1935 election, from £410 to £2,520 in county divisions and from £345 to £1,340 in single-member borough

* *Report of the Thirty-Third Annual Conference of the Labour Party, Hastings, 1933.*

divisions. These are not so far away from the amounts mentioned by Mr. Harvey as the actual costs for Conservative candidates. As we have seen, however, the average amount of the actual expenses of Labour candidates in contested elections in 1935 was only about £360. It is evident, therefore, that even the 60 per cent line is not nearly reached by Labour candidates in most cases, since the latter would give an average of about £670.

It is clear that in general the legal maximum is well above the amounts actually expended even by Conservative candidates. Even so, the bill for election expenses is not one to be faced with equanimity by a candidate of moderate means. It is only a wealthy man who can plank down "anything from £400 to £1,200" to pay the expenses of a single election, with the prospect, too, of having to repeat the expenditure within, at most, something less than five years. Yet the candidate who cannot produce such a sum, or at least a substantial part of it, has only very restricted opportunities of adoption, let alone election. As we have seen, his chance in the Conservative party is but slender. In the Liberal party it is probably better, but he will have to be an attractive candidate in personality and reputation to overcome the handicap of lack of means. In the Labour party his chance is better still; but unless he has the backing of a trade union—which means, in most cases, unless he is a successful trade-union official—he may have great difficulty in finding a constituency ready to adopt him.

For the great majority of people of any party, then, no matter what their ability and keenness, the expense of contesting an election rules out any chance they might otherwise have of entering parliament. For the man or woman of independent views the position is even more definitely hopeless; only in quite exceptional circumstances can a non-party candidate hope to succeed unless he combines the possession of private means with established reputation and some degree of popularity. This, of course, is partly due to other circumstances, which we shall discuss later; but the one we are now considering is usually a more than sufficient deterrent in itself. Hence in many ways the cost of elections is a big factor in determining the character and quality of the personnel of the House of Commons.

CHAPTER XV

OTHER FINANCIAL MATTERS

WE have seen how important a part is played by election expenses in connexion with membership of the House of Commons. They are, however, not the only financial burden that may, and all too frequently does, fall on the member of parliament, and in particular on the Conservative member. We must now turn our attention to the other expenses that he must expect to have to meet. These include contributions to local party funds, contributions to charities, etc., and increased costs of living. Let us take first the question of contributions to local party funds; this is a question of great importance to Conservative candidates, of less importance to Liberal candidates, and in most cases of little or no importance to Labour candidates.

According to Mr. Harvey,* to have "an excellent chance of being adopted" as a Conservative candidate a man or woman must not only be willing to pay the whole of his election expenses, but must also be willing "to subscribe between £500 and £1,000 a year to the local association". Now, the average interval between general elections in the inter-war period was about three years, so that election expenses may be expected to average anything from, say, £140 to £400 a year. Hence this type of Conservative candidate will have to pay over, for the combined purposes of election expenses and support of the local association, an annual sum ranging from £640 to £1,400 a year. Allowing for income tax at pre-war standard rate, this means that a part of his gross income amounting to from £900 to £2,000 a year, approximately, must be set aside for these purposes. The man who can afford to do this is well off indeed.

Let us look at this a little more closely. A candidate who is willing to pay over even £900 a year in this direct expenditure on his candidature will necessarily be in receipt of an income considerably in excess of this sum. Let us assume that his income is £3,000 a year or over: the number of people in this country receiving such an income may be roughly estimated as 60,000.† The adult population of the country is, in round figures, 30 millions: hence only one adult person in 500 has an income sufficient to allow of his allotting £900 a year to cover election expenses and party subscription. But £900 a year is the figure for the cheapest constituency: let us see how things work out in the dearest, where at least £2,000 a year is required for these purposes. To be able to spare this £2,000 a year a candidate may be assumed to possess an income of, say, not less than £5,000 a year. The number of persons with an income of £5,000 a year or over is roughly 26,000. Only one adult person in 1,150 has such an income. Hence we are justified in saying that only a minute fraction of the population is wealthy enough to have —if Mr. Harvey is correct—"an excellent chance of being adopted" as a Conservative candidate.

For Mr. Harvey's second class—those who have "a reasonable chance" of being adopted—the corresponding figures are as follows. Half their election expenses amounts to a sum of from £200 to £600; say, in round figures, £70 to £200 a year. The expected subscription to the local association is from £250 to £400 a year. The total contribution by the candidate is therefore from £320 to £600 a year, or, allowing for income tax at pre-war standard rate, a share of his gross income

---

* Ian Harvey, *op. cit.* (See Appendix III.)

† This estimate and those following are based on the figures given by Carr-Saunders and Jones, *The Social Structure of England and Wales* (1927), page 102.

amounting to roughly £450 to £850 a year. To set aside the *minimum* sum of £450 a year for these purposes a candidate may be presumed to possess a gross income of not less than £2,000. There are round about 90,000 people in the country with such an income, or 3 in every thousand of the adult population.

Hence we may say that—again, if Mr. Harvey is correct—997 adults out of every thousand are excluded, *by the demands of the local associations alone*, from having even "a reasonable chance" of being adopted as a Conservative candidate for parliament, while to have "an excellent chance" one must belong to the wealthiest one-five-hundredth, or even the wealthiest one-thousandth, part of the population. These figures are necessarily very rough, and allowance must be made for the possibility, or even probability, that Mr. Harvey has taken an unduly pessimistic view of constituency financial demands: it is almost certain that a healthier state of affairs exists in some constituencies. Nevertheless, when all allowances are made, it is evident that the possession of a substantial income is a *sine qua non* for Conservative candidates and members in many divisions, and a great asset in most of the others. The man who cannot provide party funds on such a scale may not be as completely excluded as Mr. Harvey contends, but he is evidently very severely handicapped.

So much for election expenses and regular contributions to party funds: but even these do not exhaust the financial demands on a candidate, and still less those on a member. It would be interesting to know how many requests a member, or prospective member, receives inviting him to become a president, vice-president, or patron of cricket clubs, football clubs, horticultural societies, charities of all kinds, and what not; with, of course, the expectation that he will subscribe to the funds of the soliciting body; and also what average expense this form of mild blackmail inflicts on members. The amount no doubt varies greatly from constituency to constituency, from party to party, and from individual to individual; but it may be surmised that the sum is sufficient in many cases to add appreciably to the cost of being a member.

Finally, apart from election expenses, party contributions, and subscriptions to clubs, societies, charities, bazaars, and the like, the current personal expenses of living will usually be considerably increased by becoming a member of parliament or even a candidate. A member must visit his constituency with reasonable frequency, and he must attend innumerable public functions, there and elsewhere. If his home is at a distance from his constituency, and both are at a distance from London, he may have to have, in effect, three separate places of residence: one in or near London for use when parliament is sitting, one in or near his constituency, and, of course, his permanent home. Moreover, a member must deal with a considerable, or even at times a huge, correspondence. This will entail an appreciable bill for postage, and may in some cases necessitate the special engagement of a private secretary or personal assistant of some kind. In a hundred ways, small in themselves, perhaps, but cumulatively considerable, he is likely to find his expenses, direct and indirect, rising beyond their former level, however careful he may be.

As we have seen, Mrs. Tate has stated that, in her case, these extra expenses, apart altogether from the cost of her election and of her contributions to the local association, amount to £500 a year. In this matter there will obviously be much variation between one member and another, depending on occupation, interests, tastes, personal ideas as to what is necessary, and, of course, the location of constituency and home. No doubt many members contrive to spend much less than £500 a year on these extras, but even so, to a member of moderate means, the additional cost may be an appreciable burden.

It may be judged, then, that *ceteris paribus* life as a member of parliament is likely to be a good deal more expensive than life as a non-member. It should be realized, moreover, that this additional cost of living is likely to press much more heavily on the man of moderate means than on the man of wealth; not merely because his margin of available income is less, but also because the changes in his mode of living brought about by his election will be more marked, and correspondingly his increase of expenditure may be actually and not merely relatively greater.

What sort of an income, then, is necessary to a member of parliament in order that he may live and carry out his duties with reasonable comfort and convenience? Naturally a working-class member, used to making ends meet on a few pounds a week, and living in a small house in a small way, may, if he is wise enough not to change his style of living more than is absolutely unavoidable, manage on a considerably smaller income than a professional or business man used to some degree of comfort and obliged to maintain a fairly high standard of appearances. But, if report is correct, even the Labour party, in which appearances are not regarded as of the first importance, does not find that its members can pay their way on a total income of much under £1,000 a year, though I understand that in actual practice many of them have to manage as best they can on considerably less. What will be necessary to members of other occupations, other traditions, and other ways of living will vary greatly; but it may be hazarded as a rough estimate that no ordinary middle-class or professional man can adequately fulfil his functions as a member of parliament, and maintain his family in their customary style of living, on a total income of less than £1,500 or £2,000 a year.

As is well known, a member of parliament now receives from the state, while he is actually in the House of Commons, a salary and certain allowances. How far do these payments go towards meeting his necessary outlay on the maintenance of himself and his family and on the expenses which, as we have seen, are incurred as a result of his membership? Let us see what he receives, and compare it with the various rates of income that our investigations have led us to believe are required, according to his party and social status, if he is to be reasonably free from financial cares.

First and foremost he receives an annual payment of £600,* of which £500 is treated as salary and is therefore subject to income tax, while £100 is treated as expenses and is therefore free from tax. He is also entitled to free first-class railway travel between London and his constituency. Beyond this the only assistance he receives is the right to free use of House of Commons stationery. There have been one or two attempts to secure free postage for members of parliament, but these have not been successful. Taken as a whole, the average value of these emoluments in terms of ordinary income cannot be put at a higher figure than, say, £650 a year.

Such a sum forms a substantial grant-in-aid, but it is pretty clear that it is insufficient, in normal circumstances, to enable even a working-class member to live in reasonable comfort, support his family, and meet the innumerable expenses of membership. Hence, quite apart from any contribution that he may be called upon to make towards his election expenses or to the funds of his local party association, it is hardly possible for a member of parliament to live on his official salary and expenses allowance, even supplemented by railway travel vouchers and official stationery. The working-class member will need another £350 or so a year, while the middle-class or professional-class member will need anything up to another £1,000 or more, if he is not to be continually harassed by a struggle to make ends meet.

In the Labour party this difficulty is, no doubt, met to a certain extent by the selection of candidates who are trade-union officials and receive salaries or allowances of some sort in that capacity (together with, in some cases, a promise of re-employment if they should lose their seats). This may obviate, more or less, the need of a private income, but it means that the members concerned are tied hand and foot, not only to the policy of the Labour party, but also to the interests and prejudices of their respective trade unions. Those who pay the piper will expect to call the tune. One need not take a cynical view of trade unions and trade-union policy to see how undesirable this is. As Laski says: † "A member is not the servant of a party in the majority in his constituency. He is elected to do the best he can in the light of his intelligence and his conscience. Were he merely a delegate, instructed by a local caucus, he would cease to have either morals or personality. . . . Burke's classical explanation ‡ of the relationship is as true to-day as when it was first spoken." When a member depends not only for his election expenses, but even for his living, on a party and, even more narrowly, on a particular section of that party, how can he avoid being to a great extent the servant of that party and that section, rather than of the community?

* Since 1936: previously the amount was only £400.
† H. J. Laski, *A Grammar of Politics* (ed. 1931), page 319.
‡ For Burke's famous address to the electors of Bristol in 1774 reference may be made to Sir Courtenay Ilbert, *Parliament* (ed. 1929), page 157.

It may be of interest at this point to inquire how far the Labour party in parliament is in fact composed of members who are backed by trade unions and comparable bodies. Taking the party's official list of Labour members in the House of Commons in October 1937,* we find that exactly half—80 out of 160—were backed by specified trade unions, while 9 were backed by the co-operative societies. A majority—roughly four out of every seven—of Labour members, therefore, are financially and in other ways dependent to a greater or lesser extent on bodies that are only *sections* of the Labour party, and these members are correspondingly under some sort of obligation to represent sectional interests. Even the 69 candidates who are backed by divisional Labour parties might conceivably be regarded as liable to be unduly influenced by their financial dependence, more or less, on the local party funds; but it is the dependence of the others, the majority, on specific sectional bodies within the party that is the really objectionable thing.

To say this is not to blame the trade unions and other bodies concerned so much as to draw attention to the general position that makes this about the only way in which the Labour party can secure a reasonable share in parliamentary representation. There is, of course, no necessary opposition between trade-union interests and the general welfare of the community; but the fact remains that if such a clash should occur, the member will almost certainly put his trade-union interests first, and in any case, apart from a clash, he will have a strong inducement to concentrate his energies on a particular set of political issues—wages, working conditions, and allied questions—instead of distributing them fairly over the whole political field. Parliament is concerned with many issues that do not directly affect trade unions as such, and the member should not be under the temptation to treat those wider issues as secondary.

Only two of the 160 Labour members on the list are backed neither by trade unions and co-operative societies on the one hand nor by divisional Labour parties on the other. These two may be presumed to be largely financing their own candidatures, but evidently there is little or no "selling of seats" to rich men in the Labour party.

In the Conservative party, however, as we have seen, a member must not only be self-supporting, but must also in many cases, probably the majority, contribute substantially to the payment of election expenses and to the maintenance of the constituency party organization. It must never be forgotten that conditions vary greatly from constituency to constituency, but it is probably a fair statement of the general position to say that a man cannot normally be a Conservative member of parliament unless he possesses a private income of from £1,500 to £5,000 a year, according to the division for which he sits and his own social status. The analysis of the education, occupation, etc., of Conservative members given in Part I of this book tends to confirm this view of the

* *Report of the Thirty-Seventh Annual Conference of the Labour Party. Bournemouth, 1937,* Appendix II.

state of affairs. The typical Conservative member is clearly a man of means: the "working-class Conservative" candidate, about whom so much was heard a few years ago, is a rarity indeed, while the number of Conservative members who belong to the general run of ordinary middle-class people—excluding the wealthy manufacturer or stock-broker—is an inconspicuous minority of the party. It is evident that if it were possible to analyse the incomes of members of parliament on the lines on which we have analysed their ages, educations, occupations, etc., it would be found that Conservative members, at least, are no more "an average sample of the general population" in respect of means than they are in any other respect; that is, they are not an average sample at all.

In the Liberal party conditions are less clearly defined than in either of the other parties. The Liberal member cannot normally expect the financial backing of any trade union or comparable body, but on the other hand he is not so likely to be the victim of excessive demands from his constituency party as is the Conservative member. It may therefore be estimated that, in normal circumstances, a man needs a private income of from, say, £800 to £2,000 a year to be a Liberal member of parliament. This is borne out by the results of the investigations recorded in Part I: the Liberal parliamentary party by no means consists of poor men, but it is not nearly so conspicuously a party of wealthy men as is the Conservative party in the House.

The Independent member, who must pay the whole of his election expenses and, having no party organization behind him, must meet additional secretarial and organizing expenses, can hardly hope to pay his way without a private income of at least £1,200 a year.

We may sum up, then, by saying that the state emoluments of a member of parliament are insufficient to meet his normal living and other expenses. How much he needs, in practice, to supplement those emoluments depends on his social class, his personal habits and circumstances, and his party. A working-class member may need, roughly, another £350. In the Labour party he probably gets something towards this from his trade union or similar body, though it may not be really sufficient: in the other parties he is practically non-existent. A Liberal member will usually need from, say, £800 upwards; an Independent member (having to pay his own election expenses, etc.) will need from, say, £1,200 upwards; and a Conservative member (having to contribute substantially to his local association, as well as to his election expenses) will need from, say, £1,500 upwards.

All these estimates take into account the state allowance of salary and expenses that the member receives. They also assume that he is a married man with the usual family responsibilities: if he is a bachelor there will naturally be some corresponding reduction in the supplementary income needed. It cannot be too strongly emphasized, in any case, that these are broad general trends, to which there are many exceptions: all we can do is to deal with the normal, typical cases.

Since the official emoluments are inadequate for the proper maintenance of a member of parliament, we must next inquire how far it is
possible for him, setting aside subsidies and private means, to earn a
living while actually serving in the House of Commons. It is difficult to
give any precise answer to this question, and, in any case, before
attempting an answer, we must define what we mean by "earn". Apart
from purely unearned incomes, derived from investments, parental
allowances, and so on, many men of means derive their income, or a
considerable part of it, from a business or businesses in which they
combine ownership or partnership with some share of the management.
This share of the management, or its equivalent the directorship of a
company, may involve duties, but not necessarily absorb anything like
their whole time. An income of this kind is clearly intermediate in
character between earned and unearned, and the duties in connexion
with it may well be compatible with membership of the House.

Turning to purely earned incomes, what is the position? What opportunity has a member to earn a living? What amount of time has he free
for this purpose?

The House of Commons normally sits for about forty hours a week
when in session, its meetings occupying every afternoon and evening
from 2.45 to 11.0 or 11.30 on Mondays, Tuesdays, Wednesdays, and
Thursdays, and from 11 a.m. to 4 p.m. on Fridays. In addition the
member may serve on Standing or Select Committees, and these, though
they *may* meet simultaneously with the House, are not limited to the
same hours. Moreover, party meetings, meetings with constituents,
correspondence arising from membership, social functions of an official
or party character, and many other matters, will make claims upon his
time, and these claims cannot all be discharged while the House is
sitting. It is evident that for the member who takes his duties seriously
they constitute pretty well a whole-time job. It is true that the House
does not sit right through the whole year, but the length of the sessions
is considerable, and even when the House is not sitting the member has
many duties to fulfil in his constituency, at party conferences, and
elsewhere.

Clearly no full-time occupation in the ordinary sense, requiring
regular hours of work five or six days a week throughout the year (apart
from short holiday breaks), can be followed by a member concurrently
with proper attention to his parliamentary duties. But how about occupations which do not necessarily require such regular hours: the law,
for example?

Many—it may be suggested far too many—practising barristers are
members of parliament and contrive somehow or other to combine the
two occupations. It is to be feared that all too frequently they are in the
House more to serve their professional ambitions than from any great
regard for the interests of their country. Let us, however, take the more
charitable view and assume that cause and effect are the other way
about, that they have adopted this profession in order to obtain the

income necessary to follow a political career: this is almost certainly so in many instances. In any event, whatever their motives, they have an arduous time, practising in chambers and in the courts by day and attending the House by night. They must of necessity work exceedingly hard, and it is almost inevitable that their value and efficiency as members of parliament must suffer, both because their practice will interfere with the regularity of their parliamentary attendance and because they will come to their political duties with jaded faculties and with thoughts elsewhere. So, though an active career as a barrister in full practice is by no means impossible for a member of parliament, it cannot be considered as desirable. However conscientious such a member may be, the heavy calls on his time and energy made by the law must inevitably detract from his freshness and efficiency as a member.

Many other members combine journalism with their parliamentary duties in a somewhat similar way, and, if they depend for a living on it, the effects on their health and on their efficiency as parliamentarians are likely to be detrimentally affected to a corresponding extent. Part-time journalism—the writing of occasional articles or the contribution of political notes to a review, for example—is another matter.

It is not impossible for men of certain other professions—consulting physicians, surgeons, or engineers, for example—to combine remunerative occupation with parliamentary membership; but unless the remuneration arises really from investment or goodwill (in a partnership, for instance)—that is, if it is really earned by the member's *work* and not by his reputation—he can as a rule only follow it by toiling excessively long hours, and with adverse effects on his health and political efficiency. Here again, of course, if his professional work is merely part-time and secondary, no such trouble may arise, but that is quite a different matter.

The vast majority of employments, however, are totally incompatible with membership of the House of Commons. Men and women who are wage-earners or salaried workers (other than trade-union officials) are in most cases completely shut out; and it must be remembered that an overwhelmingly big proportion of the gainfully employed population comes under this heading. Working housewives, shopkeepers, and small employers generally, who actively direct and work in their own establishments, are similarly barred. Moreover, even consulting professional men cannot seriously combine earning an income with membership unless their practice is in or near London.

Hence it is safe to say that for the general run of men and women membership of the House of Commons is impossible, because, apart from all other reasons, they would have to give up their employment on entering the House and would have nothing but their official salary and expenses allowance on which to live; and these, as we have seen, are not adequate for the purpose. The prospect, too, of losing their seats at perhaps the next election and finding themselves suddenly penniless and unemployed would be a further deterrent if any were needed.

To all intents and purposes, then, the possession of private means is a *sine qua non* to the would-be member, unless he is a trade-union official standing for the Labour party, or is a member of one or other of a very few professional or semi-professional occupations; and in these cases he will be unusually fortunate if neither his health nor his efficiency suffers from his attempt to do two jobs concurrently.

To sum up: membership of the House of Commons, if taken seriously, is a full-time job and, in the public interest, the member ought for the time being to devote all, or practically all, of his working energies to it. He ought not to have to earn his living in any outside occupation; for if he has to do that he cannot devote adequate attention to his parliamentary duties inside and outside the House, and if he is forced to make the attempt one or other, if not both, sets of interests will suffer, to say nothing of his own health. To assert this is not to advocate a class of permanent professional politicians: it is simply to point out that the pressure of public duty on a member of parliament is so heavy that he cannot adequately discharge it if he has simultaneously to earn his living.

Moreover, under the present system the great majority of people are shut out altogether from any real, as distinct from purely legal, eligibility to enter parliament, not primarily by lack of ability, but simply because they lack financial resources. X, who is unsuitable but wealthy, can buy a seat: Y and Z, who are infinitely better fitted for the job, are permanently excluded, because election would deprive them of their present income and subsequent loss of their seats would leave them penniless and unemployed.

The abolition of "rotten boroughs" in 1832 marked a great step forward; but while finance continues to play so great a part in determining the sort of member of parliament we get we are still a long way from a democratic system of representation.

CHAPTER XVI

ELECTORAL METHODS AND PARTY

HAVING seen how big a part finance plays in the choice of candidates for parliament, we have now to examine another important aspect of our subject and see how the present electoral methods affect both the choice of candidates and their chances of success at the polls.

Since 1884* the standard method of election to the House of Com-

* "The system of 'single-member' constituencies and (approximately) equal electoral districts is a very modern innovation, dating only from 1884. Until that date, with only slight modifications, members were always elected for counties and boroughs as a whole—that is, for organised communities with a character and tradition of their own." (Ramsay Muir, *How Britain is Governed* (ed. 1933), page 157.) See also the *Report of the Royal Commission on Electoral Systems* (1908), pages 1-3.

mons has been by what is termed the single-member majority system. Under this system, with certain exceptions which we shall consider later, the whole country, borough and county alike, is divided into constituencies that are intended to have approximately equal numbers of electors. In practice the size of constituencies, as measured by their numbers of electors, varies considerably even immediately after a redistribution-of-seats act, and subsequently the growth or decline of the local populations tends to make them still more unequal. Nevertheless, the general principle holds, and we need not here concern ourselves with the discrepancies, regrettable though they are. In each single-member constituency, then, each elector has one vote, and one vote only, which he gives to the candidate of his choice by putting a cross (×) against that candidate's name on the voting-paper. When the poll is over the votes are counted and the candidate who has received most is declared to be elected as member for the division.

The effects of this method of voting need to be considered from two aspects: first, as they affect the representation of the division itself; and, second, as they affect the representation of the country as a whole. Let us take them in that order.

In the old two-party days, given a "straight fight" between a Conservative and a Liberal, the result of an election, though it left the minority—often nearly as numerous as the majority—unrepresented, nevertheless had a substantial measure of justice in it, so far as that division was concerned, since it gave the seat to a candidate who had received an actual majority of the votes given. Even so, the results were by no means entirely satisfactory. For one thing, the ordinary elector, having had no voice in the selection of candidates, had a correspondingly limited choice in voting for a member. He had to make that choice either on party lines or on the personality of the candidates: he could not do both. At one of the earliest elections in which I had a vote the candidate put forward to represent the party with whose views I was nearest in accord was a man of mediocre ability, dubious record, and doubtful integrity. His opponent, though inexperienced, gave evidence of better ability and greater integrity. I happen to know that I was not the only voter who was much exercised at having to make such a choice, but I think that in the end we mostly voted, though with considerable qualms, on party lines.

The voter's dilemma was not always as definite as that, of course, but it was often of that type, and it frequently happened that neither candidate was of a calibre to command respect. The parties put up their respective nominees, and the electors had no means of indicating their disapprobation of a candidate except by voting for his opponent—and, as already indicated, party considerations usually ruled that out—or by the very ineffective way of not voting at all. Let us, however, defer further discussion of this point until a little later.

With the rise of the Labour party as an independent force the single-member majority method of voting, never very satisfactory, became highly unsatisfactory. What was merely inefficient under a two-party system became positively dangerous with three parties in the field. In a large proportion of cases the successful candidate no longer had a majority of the votes cast, even by the narrowest of margins; he was the representative of a minority, having more votes cast against him than for him. All that could be said was that he had more votes than either of his opponents *singly*; and all experience—not only in parliamentary elections, but elsewhere—indicates that with more than two candidates in the field the one who scores highest on a first vote is not necessarily the one whom the majority of voters would choose if they had any effective way of making known their wishes. The present crude method of voting, superficially satisfactory with only two candidates in the field, is totally unfitted for enabling a genuine choice to be made between a larger number.

Needless to say, this particular defect, brought into prominence by the incursion of a third party into politics, was almost equally obnoxious and equally resented whenever, as not infrequently happened, there were more than two candidates in an election in the old two-party days: the advent of the third party merely stressed the defect and made its results more widespread and so more serious.

It is not surprising, then, that since the Labour party first became an effective force in parliamentary elections early in the century the failure of the electoral system in this respect has caused endless heartburning and much recrimination. Various remedies have been proposed, the second ballot, the alternative vote, and the single transferable vote (proportional representation) being those most advocated. There is no need at this stage to discuss their respective merits and demerits: their significance for us at the moment lies in the evidence they provide of the intense dissatisfaction the present system causes, the widespread conviction that it is erratic and untrustworthy, that it all too often gives a result that does not adequately represent the wishes of the electorate.

We must now go back again for a few moments to the question of the calibre of the candidates put forward at an election by the respective parties. Let us take a glance at the process of selection. The man in the street has very little idea how the candidates put before him are chosen. So far as he is concerned he is faced at the election with two, three, or more candidates from whom he must choose; but how these people have become the recognized party candidates he does not know, and, as we have already noted, he sometimes finds them not much to his liking.

Now, when we speak of "the candidates put forward by the respective parties" what exactly do we mean? Such-and-such a "party" in this connexion certainly does not signify that party as a whole, even within the division, for the many thousands of electors of like views on whose votes the candidate depends are not in any way consulted when he is selected as their champion: they have no voice in the matter at all. Nor does it even mean the local party association as a whole: for whatever may be the theory of the matter and its superficial appearance, the essential reality is that the candidate is chosen by a very few people, the party caucus, or even an inner ring within the caucus. There is, of course, no strict uniformity in the process of selection: it varies between one party and another, between one constituency and another, and from one time to another. In general, however, those who have the really effective say as to who shall be the party candidate are few in number. Even when the prospective candidate is submitted to a larger body for approval—yes, and even when more than one prospective candidate is so submitted—the really effective choice has usually been made behind the scenes already.

There is little doubt also that in particular cases specific groups or even individuals exercise a determining voice in the selection of candidates. In some rural areas, for example, a Conservative candidate must be acceptable to the local territorial magnate: if the magnate does not choose the candidate himself, he has *sub rosa* a powerful voice in the matter and a pretty effective veto on candidates who are not agreeable to him. On the other hand, in mining districts as a rule only a man who is or has been a working miner stands much chance of selection as Labour candidate; and though more than one candidate may appear for consideration at the final stage, the nominee of the inner ring of the Miners' Federation is pretty certain to be adopted against all comers. Apart from these special cases, however, the main point stands: the *effective* choice is made by some small inner circle of the party. From our point of view the exact constitution of this inner circle is immaterial: the vital fact is that the local party as a whole has no real voice in the matter.

On what lines does this inner circle make its choice? Clearly a matter conducted so confidentially cannot be analysed in any detail, nor in any case will there be any general uniformity. The most we can do is to draw attention to factors that pretty obviously influence the decisions of the selectors.

In the first case there is the financial issue: somebody or other has to shoulder the costs of the election. Since, however, we have discussed this problem in Chapter XIV, all we need do here is to point out the important part it is bound to play when candidates are being chosen.

Next there may be the question of services rendered to the local association and party: here both seniority and popularity may come into the picture. Closely related to this is the question of "pull": the would-be candidate who has a considerable personal following, or who is the protégé of an influential group or trade union or even individual within the party, starts with a great advantage.

Of great importance, too, is the question of "soundness". Is the aspirant for adoption a good party man, one who can be relied upon to support his leaders if elected? Here, of course, the right of veto exercised by the central organizations of both the Conservative and Labour parties comes into play. In either of these parties a candidate must promise complete and absolute party obedience, and must be definitely

10

and formally approved by party headquarters before he can be adopted or recognized as the party candidate. In the Liberal party, on the other hand, selection by the local organization constitutes the person selected the official Liberal candidate, and no such rigid vows of party loyalty are exacted.

Other factors that may be taken into account are the would-be candidate's popularity in the district, actual or potential, his capacity for public speaking, his qualities as a "good mixer", and even his personal appearance. It may be surmised that these personal factors are a relatively minor consideration in choosing a candidate for a "safe seat" but will carry more weight in the case of a doubtful or hostile division.

Other things being equal, a local candidate is, of course, likely to be preferred to one from outside the district. There may, however, be no local man or woman who is both willing to stand and acceptable to the party organizers, or there may be a doubt about the matter. In that case the local committee will probably apply to party headquarters for assistance. Party headquarters will then send down a list of prospective candidates who are available from outside the constituency. The local committee, or its inner circle, will choose from this list one or more people for interview, and perhaps for comparison with any local alternatives, before making their final choice. It may be assumed in this connexion that any list from party headquarters is likely to be composed chiefly, if not entirely, of people who are thoroughly "sound" from the party point of view: in other words, largely of "yes-men".

Amongst these various factors that we have been considering—finance, services to the party, "pull", "soundness", and so on—some will have more weight in one division and others in another: it depends on the party, the locality, and the circumstances of the occasion. It may be observed that amongst them we have not included, in any specific way, the question of the innate ability of the candidate, his fitness to fulfil the manifold and exacting duties of a member of parliament, his qualifications to serve the community as well as the party. It is to be feared that such matters come in only for secondary and incidental consideration in the great majority of cases.

To say this is not to suggest that unsuitable or inferior candidates are habitually or deliberately chosen, though, as many members of parliament will be the first to agree, the general level of the membership of the House in respect of intellectual capacity, breadth of experience, and integrity of spirit falls a long way below that which we should desire to see and have a right to expect in so important and powerful a body. Nor is it to imply that those in whose hands rests the selection of candidates act irresponsibly or from unworthy motives. I have no doubt that in the great majority of cases they honestly try to pick the best candidate they can. But they are themselves not always well equipped for their exacting and delicate task, and in any case they have to make their decisions in circumstances that narrowly limit the range of their choice. Financial difficulties must be met somehow, while services to the party, seniority, and "pull" are not lightly to be set aside—or so it must no doubt seem to the selectors.

We need not, then, attribute any ill motives to those responsible for the selection, even when the chosen candidate is quite unworthy of a place in parliament and ill fitted to discharge its obligations. We must look rather to the interaction of prevailing conditions, the circumscription of choice by the burden of expense, and the secondary and unperceived effects of the method of election, if we are to explain the low calibre of the average candidate or to seek a remedy for this unsatisfactory state of affairs.

So far as finance is concerned, little more need be said at this stage. We have shown how tiny a fraction of the population can afford the cost of standing for parliament or meet the expense of life as a member, and we note accordingly how restricted is the field from which candidates can be drawn. Probably 99 per cent of the men and women of the country are excluded from consideration by this factor alone.

Let us pass on to consider how the present method of election plays a part in determining the calibre of candidates. By long-standing tradition elections in this country are conducted on party lines, and the majority of electors have correspondingly a deeply rooted attachment to one or other of the three major parties. Consequently, in anything like normal circumstances, the votes a candidate receives are determined to a very great, if not overwhelming, extent by the party label he bears. There is no need here to argue whether this attachment to party is in itself a good or bad thing: for our present purpose it is sufficient to note the fact, and to observe how it carries with it as a corollary a marked tendency to disregard the personal qualities of the candidates when it comes to the actual giving of votes. The elector may grumble at his party's choice of a candidate, but as a rule he will vote for him just the same.

Smith, standing in the Conservative interest, may be a man of little or no useful experience and with more money than brains, but he will get the Conservative vote every time in preference to Brown, his Labour opponent, who has a keen intellect and an ardent interest in all branches of politics; while in another division Jones, worthy but ignorant and uninspired, will carry off the Labour vote in its entirety, though Robinson, who stands for the Conservatives, is a man of genuine culture, widely travelled, well read, and high-minded. Once again, I am not here criticizing this loyalty to party: I am merely pointing out its inevitable effect under the present single-member majority system: it depreciates the influence of the intrinsic personal qualities of candidates on the voting at elections, and in consequence encourages party organizers to ignore those qualities in selecting their candidates.

If the Conservative elector were choosing between Smith and Robinson, or the Labour elector between Brown and Jones, so that the intelligence and integrity of the candidates were weighed up by the electors untrammelled by party bias, the better man would usually win hands down. But it is just that sort of choice that the present system never gives, or gives only accidentally and uncertainly on the rare occasion of a serious and irreconcilable party split.

Moreover, it is not merely that in every constituency there is a "hard core" of party adherents who will vote Conservative, Liberal, or Labour as the case may be, irrespective of the issues of the moment or the personal merits or demerits of the candidates. Apart altogether from the party stalwarts, the ordinary voter who for one reason or another—ignorance, indifference, or genuine independence of mind—is unattached to any party in the ordinary way will nevertheless vote as a rule on party lines. This "floating vote" may be given differently at different elections, but there seems little doubt that in the main it is given to the party candidate rather than to the man himself. Here and there local and personal considerations will have a marked effect on the voting, but the general rule stands: under the present system it is party that decides the result in all but a few marginal cases, and the general level of character and ability in the House of Commons is detrimentally affected in consequence.

To sum up, then: the two really fundamental and serious defects of the present method of electing members of parliament as it works *within a single constituency* are (a) that it all too often results in the election of a minority candidate* whose views are unacceptable to the majority even of the electors actually voting, and (b) that it gives the elector no choice between candidates of his own party and therefore no effective means by which he may endorse a wise choice of candidate or register his disapprobation of an unsuitable one, so that in consequence there is not the incentive that there should be for the selectors to seek really able men.

So much for the effects within a single division: they are serious in themselves, since their result is that in many a case the member of parliament is the spokesman of a minority only, or is a man of poor calibre, or even suffers from both defects. But when we turn from the division considered by itself to the country as a whole the position is even more serious, for the repetition on a large scale of these failings produces magnified results injurious to the prestige of the House of Commons and inimical to the good government of the country.

As we have seen in Part I, the system of election often leads in actual fact to a party that is well in the minority in the country gaining a substantial majority of seats in the House. This results not only from the repetition in division after division of the success of a minority, but also from the fact that, apart from such cases, the present system, even when it gives the seat to a majority candidate, usually leaves a very substantial minority unrepresented, and these cases do not necessarily nor usually cancel out amongst themselves. The complete lack of represen-

---

* There were no fewer than 315 minority members returned at the 1929 general election—*i.e.*, well over half of the members of the House of Commons represented only a minority of their constituents.

tation for the Liberal and Labour voters of Sussex, for example, is not automatically balanced by an equal and opposite lack of Conservative representation elsewhere. *Some* amount of such compensation there certainly is from time to time, but it is spasmodic and uncertain in action and hardly ever results in a reasonable total representation, quite apart from the local injustices involved.

This vice of irresponsibility, this lack of any rational relation between votes given and seats won, is inherent in the system. Take a single example. In the Penryn and Falmouth division in 1935 the Conservative candidate was elected, though he received less than 40 per cent of the votes cast and more than 60 per cent were given against him: such a result repeated throughout the country would have given an entirely Conservative House of Commons with a country that was more than 60 per cent opposed to Conservatism. That extreme result is unlikely to happen, but there is nothing whatever in the system to prevent it, and in actual fact we go dangerously far in that direction at some elections. In that same general election of 1935, for instance, less than 48 per cent of the votes given secured to the Conservative party 63 per cent of the seats in the House of Commons.

Hence we get the situation, both farcical and tragic, that a general election is a gamble of which not even the most experienced politician can predict the result. He may be aware of a turn in the tide of public opinion, but how much effect it will have, measured in seats won or lost, is beyond human ability to foretell, since it is in fact largely a matter of pure, incalculable chance.

Of the other aspect little more need be said at the moment. It is clear that a system that encourages the putting forward of mediocre candidates in the constituencies must result in a House of Commons in which the level of intellect, experience, and integrity is much below that which we have a right to expect. The House contains many worthy, sincere, and able men now; but how much higher a general standard we could and should set for people burdened with such arduous tasks and entrusted with such tremendous powers!

In the succeeding chapters we trace a little more closely the relation between the causes we have just been studying and the effects they produce as shown by the actual characteristics of the personnel of the House of Commons disclosed in Part I. But before we end this chapter we must glance for a moment at those seats which involve a departure from the single-member majority system. These fall into two categories: boroughs with two members elected within a single constituency, and university seats.

The twelve borough two-member divisions are a curious and anachronistic survival from an earlier age, vestiges of the long period in which borough and county alike were represented by two members each, irrespective of the sizes of their electoral rolls. Their continuance in an age in which (nominally) equal electoral areas are the rule is one of those illogicalities that our race seems to love. There appears to be no sound reason why, when other two-member boroughs are divided into two single-member divisions, these few should be left undivided.

In these divisions each elector has two votes, which he gives by putting a cross against the names of the two candidates he favours. He is not allowed to "plump"—that is, to give both his votes to one candidate—but he is free to give one vote only if he so chooses. As a rule the contending parties put up two candidates each, and the voting appears to be pretty strictly on party lines, since both seats usually go to the same party (or to two parties working together as allies and putting up only one candidate each), and there is little difference between the number of votes recorded for one candidate of a pair and that recorded for the other. It is rare for one each of two opposing pairs of candidates to be elected, and when it does happen so it is usually because the party voting strengths are nearly equal, so that a slight difference in the popularity of a pair of candidates may lead one to success and the other to defeat.

In 1935 six of these twelve divisions returned two Conservatives each, four returned one Conservative and one "Liberal National" running in double harness, and one returned one Conservative and one "National Labour" fighting as allies. In the remaining seat one Conservative and one Liberal were returned, but the two parties, though not allies, put up only one candidate each. There was not a single case of one of a pair of candidates being successful and the other unsuccessful.

It seems clear that the two-member divisions are normally just as unkind to substantial minorities in a "straight fight" as are the standard single-member divisions. In Blackburn, for instance, both seats went to the Conservatives in 1935, though 48 per cent of the votes were given to the Labour candidates. This is a clear case, on common-sense grounds, for each party to have one member; but the system does not work out like that, except accidentally in rare marginal cases. Similarly, where there is a three-party contest in a two-member division the same evils of minority representation and majority non-representation are liable to occur as in the single-member constituencies.

Hence we may say that in general the two-member divisions do nothing to secure a more equitable distribution of seats between the parties: in fact, as in the instance of Blackburn just quoted, the results often serve to emphasize the illogicality and injustice of the system by giving both seats to one party when the most elementary common sense and fairness would allocate one to each.

The eleven university seats involve another curious and illogical departure from the single-member majority system, and they also are, though in a different sense, something of an historical vestige. The Speaker's Conference on Electoral Reform appointed in 1916 recommended the adoption of both the single transferable vote and the alternative vote, and both were included in the bill that followed. The House of Commons, however, rejected the one and the House of Lords the other, and in the end a rather fantastic compromise was inserted in the act of 1918. The single transferable vote was applied to university constituencies returning more than one member, and *could* also be applied to a further hundred seats if a scheme to be prepared by commissioners were approved by both Houses. The scheme was prepared, but was rejected by the House of Commons.

Consequently the university seats are the only ones to which the single transferable vote actually applies. Moreover, whether through failure to understand the principles of that system or from a malicious desire to sabotage it I am unable to say, it was so applied to those seats that it could not possibly work properly. In order that it may achieve its aims the system needs that each constituency shall include *at least* three seats: the act applies it to one three-member and three two-member constituencies. Hence there is only one division (the Scottish universities) in which the necessary conditions for success obtain.

For these reasons, while the introduction of the single transferable vote into British parliamentary elections by the 1918 act is something of a landmark, the operation of the system on this limited scale and in this mutilated form does not and cannot provide a reliable test of the merits of the system. For such evidence we must look elsewhere. We shall return to this question later, however.

We conclude, then, that the special methods of voting in the two-member borough divisions and in the university two- and three-member divisions, though presenting points of interest, are of little effect on the working of the electoral system as a whole and do practically nothing towards securing juster representation.

CHAPTER XVII

CAUSE AND EFFECT

1. AGE AND EDUCATION

THE detailed analysis of the composition of the House of Commons given in Part I showed that in age, in education, in occupation, in party, and in other respects, the House is not in any sense a fair sample of the community it is elected to represent; that certain kinds of people who form only a tiny minority in the general population secure for themselves a large proportion of the seats in the House; and that the results of a general election do not at all accurately mirror the state of political opinion obtaining in the country at the time. In Chapters XIII to XVI we have studied the circumstances in which the personnel of parliament is chosen, and have discussed influences that must largely determine the character of that personnel. We have seen how the selection of candidates is conditioned, have considered the factors that influence the elector in giving his vote, and have observed the causes that shape the results of the voting.

We have now to relate, in rather more detail, the forces at work, as displayed in Chapters XIII to XVI, with the actual state of affairs disclosed in the preceding chapters. We have to see how the peculiar characteristics of the membership of the House of Commons are brought about by the conditions that govern the selection of candidates and the election of members, and to a less extent by other subsidiary factors. Until we have done this we shall not have rounded off our study of things as they are, nor be in a satisfactory position to commence the quest for ways of bringing about a more satisfactory state of affairs.

In this chapter and the next, then, we shall consider in the light of Chapters XIII to XVI the chief attributes of members of parliament that we had under discussion in Part I, and shall attempt to relate them to their causes.

The first of these attributes is *age*. The outstanding differences between the membership of the House of Commons and the adult community as a whole in this respect are, first, that the average age of the former is a great deal higher than the average age of the latter, and, second, that the age-distributions in the two cases are altogether unlike.

As might be expected, the *difference of average ages* varies rather widely from one time to another, being in general highest at a dissolution and lowest immediately after a general election. It depends also on the party complexion of the House, the average age of Conservative members being lower than that of Liberal members, which in turn is lower than that of Labour members. It was further influenced in the earlier part of the inter-war period by the effects of the war of 1914-18. A sufficient indication of the general position is, however, afforded by the mean difference of the averages over the whole period. This mean difference, as we have seen, was 8 years 7½ months, the mean average age of members of parliament over the period being 52 years 6½ months, while the mean average age of the adult population was 43 years 11 months.

This is a big difference, especially as the lower average is that of the *adult* population only.* How are we to account for it? I suggest that the chief cause is to be found in the expensiveness of serving in parliament or even becoming a candidate for it. This view is supported by the fact that the average age of *first entry* to the House is 44 years 5 months—*i.e.*, nearly a quarter of a century after the reaching of adult age. Many young men are keenly interested in politics and would very much like to enter parliament: it is therefore hardly conceivable that the average age of first entry would be so high if there were not serious obstacles in the way of their doing so. Obviously expense is not the only factor involved: one would, for example, expect a young man to have to prove his worth before he was adopted as a candidate. But it

* The difference between the average age of members of parliament and the average age of the *whole* population is, as already noted, over twenty years.

does not take a really capable man more than twenty years to do that, and I suggest that lack of financial means is much the greatest impediment in his path.

A man on the threshold of his career will not usually have means of his own apart from whatever income he may be able to earn by his own exertions; and the latter, as we have seen, he must normally relinquish if he enters parliament. He may, of course, have inherited wealth,* but inheritance in most cases takes place in middle life rather than in youth. Short of that he can usually find the requisite means only if his father is both able and willing to make him a fairly substantial allowance. This is borne out by the fact that youthful members of parliament are as a rule the sons of peers or of men of wealth and family; no doubt their social status as well as their money helps to get them elected.

Those who have no parental income on which to draw must usually defer their political début until they have made their financial position secure—and it is only exceptionally that that can be done before middle life is reached. For very many people it cannot be done until they reach the normal age of retirement in the fifties or sixties, while for countless thousands it cannot be done at all. It is not only that in many cases election expenses, in whole or part, have to be met out of members' pockets; it is not only that a member must have some income with which to supplement his official salary. The fact has also to be faced that, apart from a comparatively small number of really "safe" seats— mainly held by the wealthier Conservatives—there is no security of tenure. A general election may come at almost any time at very short notice: in 1935, for example, the Prime Minister gave the first definite news of his intention to ask for a dissolution in a speech to his constituents on the 19th October; four days later he told the House of Commons that he had asked for a dissolution, and only two days after that the House was actually dissolved.† When the House is dissolved parliamentary salaries automatically cease, so that a member must be prepared to lose his official income at a few days' notice. If he is re-elected, well and good: otherwise he is thrown suddenly and completely on his own resources. Hence a member must not only have the means to supplement his official salary while in the House: he must also have an income immediately available if he loses his seat.‡

The difference of average age between the three parties gives further support to these contentions. It is indisputable that the Conservative parliamentary party contains a far higher proportion of people of "independent means" than either of the other parties. It is equally indisputable that the Labour party contains far more poor men than either of the other parties. The average age at which Conservatives enter parliament is, as we have seen elsewhere, 3 years 4 months less than the correspond-

---

* Such terms as "wealth" in this and subsequent passages are to be understood in a comparative sense and not as implying great riches.

† *The Times House of Commons, 1935*, page 18.

‡ I am informed that cases have occurred of members being reduced to "the dole" by losing their seats.

ing age for Labour members. It is a fairly common thing for Conservatives to enter the House young, before they have any appreciable means of their own, earned or unearned. It is quite exceptional for that to happen in the Labour party. The typical Labour member is or has been a trade-union official: 43 per cent of the parliamentary party membership is known to come within this description, and it is probable that the true percentage is even higher. These people and others of similar type will naturally enter parliament at a comparatively late age, for whatever their political ambitions they are in a position to achieve them only when they can get the financial and general backing of a trade union or similar body, and they will not ordinarily get this until they are veterans in the movement.

The question of expense, however, affects all parties to a greater or lesser extent, and has a general tendency to raise the age of entrance and the average age of members. Even in the Conservative party the rich men who "buy" seats will more often than not have reached middle age before they have amassed or inherited their wealth. Moreover, the great majority of people in the party are far from wealthy, and these people, if they are not excluded altogether by lack of means, will be just as much delayed by that lack as are similar people in other parties. There can be little doubt, then, that the financial difficulty is the most potent cause of the high average age of members of the House of Commons.* It is not, however, the only cause, and two others must be noted.

First, there is the fact that an appreciable number of men, after following a career in some other field, reach the age of retirement or become bored with their occupation and turn to parliament to find an outlet for their energies or a vent for the opinions they have acquired elsewhere. Most conspicuous in this category are army and navy officers and colonial civil servants. The influx of retired colonels and generals, commanders and admirals, colonial judges and administrators, is sufficient to raise the average age appreciably, particularly in the Conservative party, to which most of them belong. But for this factor the differences between the average age of the Conservative members and those of the Liberal and Labour members would be even higher.

It may be argued that the average age of the Labour party in the House is raised in a similar way by the influx of retired trade-union officials. No doubt there is some truth in this, but the cases do not seem quite parallel. The army officer turns to politics when the army no longer requires him or has ceased to interest him: his military career was an end in itself, not a means to an end. The trade-union official, on the other hand, follows an occupation that is itself semi-political in

---

* It is true that the average age of members of the House of Lords is even higher, being about 58 years 8 months, though the members of that House are seldom poor men. But in the great majority of cases men neither inherit peerages nor are created peers until well on in life. The causes of the high average age in that House are therefore quite different from those producing a high average age in the lower House.

character, and not infrequently does so with the deliberate intention of using it as a means towards a political career. He would stand for parliament earlier if he had the necessary financial resources, and in becoming a member he does not so much change from one career to another as reach the culmination of the career he has already followed.

The remaining noteworthy cause of late entry into parliament acts in a rather different way. It is to be found in the fact that men who have achieved distinction or at least proved their ability in other occupations have a natural advantage *ceteris paribus* over untried youth, both when competing for adoption as candidates and when standing for election. No doubt there is some overlapping between this cause and the previous one: they act together in many cases, serving as complements to each other, but they are nevertheless distinct in essence. It is to be observed also that whereas the first two causes are in a sense artificial, involving as they do external obstructions to early entry, this third cause is relatively internal and natural.

Turning to the question of age-*distribution*, we observe that there is almost of necessity a considerable difference between the age-distribution of members of the House of Commons and that of the adult population as a whole.* In the latter case the curve is naturally a falling one: that is, in the absence of abnormal circumstances such as an altogether exceptional number of births in a particular year, or of deaths, emigrations, or immigrations at a particular age, the number of people of any given age will be less than that of any lower age and greater than that of any higher age. This is the obvious result of normal mortality: the number of people who were born in any given year and are still surviving will as year follows year steadily diminish.

In the case of the House of Commons no such obvious natural law obtains (except, perhaps, at the higher ages and there only to a limited extent). It could not be expected that under any conceivable system of election the commonest age amongst members would be twenty-one, and that for each succeeding age the numbers would be less. Whatever changes in electoral law and political conditions might be brought about, we should expect that beginning at the minimum age there would be a rise in the number of members for each succeeding year of age, up to a certain point, before any decline in numbers began; that is, the *modal*† age in any circumstances is to be looked for at some point appreciably above the minimum. The causes of the actual age-distribution are to be found in the same set of conditions as we have seen affecting the average age, and it is therefore unnecessary to discuss the matter further at this stage.

The outstanding result of our inquiries about *previous service* was the discovery that this is in general considerably less than might have been expected. It was suggested that this shortness was due chiefly to the insecurity of tenure and consequent broken service experienced by

---

* It may be useful at this point to refer back to Fig. 10, page 31.
† *I.e.*, the age most frequently occurring.

many members of the House of Commons, including members of, outstanding ability and reputation. The cause of this insecurity is clearly to be found in the single-member majority system of voting. Under this system members who represent constituencies in which the rival parties are more or less equally balanced have no certainty or even probability of re-election, however distinguished their personal records. On the other hand, men or women who have the luck to sit for constituencies in which their party greatly outnumbers its opponents—the notorious "safe seats"—are so securely planted that however poor their personal quality they are practically members for life, subject only to retaining the good-will of their party caucuses. This result of the present method of voting deserves careful note; for it means that, as things are, security of tenure depends hardly at all upon a member's ability, honesty, and devotion to duty, but almost entirely upon the strength of his party in the division. A member of exceptional ability and integrity may lose his seat simply because the parties in his division are nearly equal in strength: another member of inferior ability and far less public spirit may retain his seat year after year and election after election, without even a contest, because of his party's local predominance.

Here it may be worth noticing that the so-called "fickle" constituencies are in reality no more fickle than the safe seats. Where the parties are more or less equal in strength a small turnover of votes will suffice to hand over the representation of a division from one party to another: where one party is much stronger than its opponents a turnover of the same or greater magnitude may leave the sitting member a comfortable majority. The former division is dubbed "fickle", the latter termed "staunch": both epithets are as a rule quite undeserved.

The next characteristic of the membership of the House of Commons that we have to consider is *school education*. One of the outstanding results of the investigation was, we saw, the discovery of the rather curious fact that the distribution of the different types of school education amongst members provides considerable justification for calling the Conservatives the public-school party, the Liberals the secondary-school party, and Labour the elementary-school party. Nearly four-fifths of the Conservative members have a public-school education; nearly half the Liberals have a secondary-school education; nearly three-quarters of the Labour party have an elementary-school education. We noted, too, that public-school men are proportionately eighteen times as numerous in the House of Commons as they are in the general population, secondary-school men are more than twice as plentiful in the House as in the population, and elementary-school men little more than one-fourth as plentiful.

Finally we recorded the astonishing preponderance in the House of Commons of old Etonians and, to a less extent, of old Harrovians. One-fourth of all Conservative members and one-seventh of *all* members in the inter-war period were educated at Eton, while one-third of the Conservatives and one-fifth of all members were educated at either

Eton or Harrow. Proportionately there were roughly 440 times as many old Etonians and 360 times as many old Harrovians in the list of members as in the community at large. Moreover, owing to the bigger number of "safe" seats held by Conservatives and the holding of these seats in the main by the more aristocratic elements of the party, together with the generally lower age of entry of Conservative members, there is a longer average tenure of their seats by Conservatives than by Liberal or Labour members. Hence the actual proportion of old Etonians and old Harrovians in the average House is even higher: one-sixth of the average membership of the whole House is supplied by Eton and nearly one-fourth by Eton and Harrow together.

What are the causes of the immense disparity between the education of members of parliament and the education of the general population? One obvious explanation is that, on the whole, the more capable children secure the better education, and that people who are both more capable and better educated rise—and deserve to rise—into positions of prominence and leadership, including membership of the House of Commons. There is a good deal of truth in this, and it undoubtedly goes a long way towards explaining the bigger share of membership secured by men and women who have had a secondary education of one sort or another in comparison with those who have had only an elementary education. There is every reason, both in theory and practice, why members should generally be drawn from the better-educated elements of the community.

So far so good: few people will quarrel with the simple proposition that we need capable and well-educated members of parliament, though it should be borne in mind that even now many a child who merits a secondary education is shut out from it, while at the time when our present and recently past members were children the position was distinctly worse. This was and is due not only to the inadequate number of secondary-school places available, but also to the fact that many parents cannot afford, or do not feel that they can afford, or are even plainly unwilling, to keep their children at school for the extra couple of years involved. That, however, is the fault of the social system rather than of the parliamentary system, so here we can only note it and pass on.

If, then, we consider that there are good reasons why men and women of secondary education (using that term in its widest sense) should occupy a bigger proportion of seats in the House than those without such an education, what are we to say of the position of the public-school members? Do not the same arguments apply? Is not their predominant position due to their superior education and ability?

It is often claimed that the public schools, and particularly Eton and Harrow, offer a training that is specially adapted to fit their alumni for parliament and the public service generally, and that many boys are sent there with the express intention of equipping them for a parliamentary career. It is unnecessary to dispute this intention or to enter into a discussion of the suitability of the training for this object. Without either accepting or rejecting the claims, let us assume for the moment that they are well founded. What other considerations must be taken into account?

As we have seen, the term "public school" is ill defined, and a number of the less well known day-schools claiming the title differ little in essentials from county and municipal secondary schools. The typical public school, however, is a relatively expensive institution to attend, and it usually has a considerable proportion of places reserved for boarders. At Eton, Marlborough, Winchester, and many others of the most famous schools the whole (or very nearly the whole) of the places are filled by boarders, at correspondingly high fees.* Moreover, owing to the nature of the curriculum and the methods of admission, only boys who have attended a preparatory school from an early age and come from homes of some social standing can usually secure admission.

Essentially, therefore, the public schools are schools for the well-off, and in some cases, including Eton, schools for the wealthy. There are exceptions, let us agree, but that is the general position. It is natural, then, that a parliamentary system that largely restricts the opportunity of entering the House of Commons to people of considerable means should favour the product of these schools.

That, however, is not the whole story. We have noted the claim made for the public schools, and particularly for Eton and Harrow, that in many cases parents send their sons there with the deliberate aim and expectation that they will enter parliament. If these schools were open on equal terms to all comers of the requisite character and ability, and if it were possible at the early age at which boys' names are put down for future admission to a public school—in some cases at or even before birth—to predict the possession of special political ability, there might be something in this claim to justify the achieved results. But in actual fact these schools are open only to the sons of a very small section of the community, and it is not possible to predict so early that a boy possesses exceptional capacity for a political career.

The truth is that in certain classes of society it is taken for granted that it is the inherited right of their members to exercise a dominating influence in public affairs, including amongst many other fields that of politics. Actual ability, the possession of exceptional powers of mind and character, are treated as of secondary importance. Far more essential is it that a man should belong to "the right people", that he should be "one of us", "a pukka sahib". So, in the control of the Conservative party organization and in the selection of Conservative candidates— and perhaps, to a much smaller extent, in the Liberal party similarly— the possession of the right school tie is an asset none the less valuable because its privileges are seldom openly asserted. As an acute foreign observer has remarked: "The old boys of about a dozen, indeed of

---

* The annual fees at Eton are £245, at Harrow £250, at Winchester £210, at Rugby £201, at Marlborough £135 to £185, to mention only a few of the best-known schools. These figures are taken from *Whitaker's Almanack*.

only six or seven, schools govern England and the British Empire. Anyone who is not of their number must have altogether exceptional ability if he is to come really to the very front. Even then he is not readily accepted into the inner circle of the rulers. This is not due to any conscious exclusiveness. The strength of this dominance in every sphere of public life depends precisely on its unconscious exercise, on its being taken as a matter of course."*

Nevertheless, while it is true that much of the strength of this dominance lies in its unconscious exercise, in the way it is taken for granted by those who exert it, it is not by any means always unconscious. Perhaps one might say that it is the underlying assumptions that are unconscious, rather than the exercise itself. "The predominance of Eton men among Conservative Ministers is remarkable, and it is amusing to note that a Conservative Prime Minister educated at Eton, Lord Balfour, had colleagues almost half of whom were Eton men, while the Cabinet of a Harrow Prime Minister, Mr. Baldwin, had in it the largest number of Harrow men ever collected in a single Cabinet;"† and it is said that Mr. Baldwin (as he then was) boasted of his intention to put into office as many Harrow men as he could. Be that as it may, there is no doubt that there is a freemasonry amongst men educated at the leading public schools that makes them, whether consciously or unconsciously, give a marked preference to men similarly educated. This attitude is a powerful reinforcement to the financial factor in securing the amazingly high proportion of public-school men, and particularly of old Etonians and old Harrovians, in the House of Commons.

When we turn to the question of *university education* we find a closely comparable state of affairs and one that can be traced to similar causes. Oxford and Cambridge occupy a dominant position in parliament similar to that occupied by Eton and Harrow and with similar party affiliations. As we have seen, if a member of parliament has been at Oxford it is four to one that he is a Conservative and nineteen to one that he is not a Labour member, just as if he has been at Eton it is nine to one that he is a Conservative and thirty-four to one that he is not a Labour member. The older, the more expensive, and the more socially exclusive the school or university, the more surely will its product be found on the right wing in politics.

Though there are now very much better chances than formerly for the boy or girl of exceptional ability to go up to Oxford or Cambridge, even if his or her parents are poor, thanks to the expansion of the system of state, municipal, and other scholarships, yet it still remains true that the older universities are, on the whole, places for rich men's sons and daughters. Only a minute proportion of the children who are clever but poor have any chance of getting to them, and only a small fraction of the undergraduates there come from really hard-up families. We may instance again in this connexion the fact that though the Uni-

---

* Karl Heinz Abshagen, *King, Lords, and Gentlemen* (1939), page 174.
† Harold J. Laski, *Studies in Law and Politics* (1932), page 192.

versity of London turns out far more graduates than Oxford and Cambridge together, yet London men in parliament are outnumbered by Oxford and Cambridge men by perhaps seven or eight to one.

It has been suggested that the predominance of Oxford and Cambridge in parliament is largely due to two facts: that their curricula are especially adapted to the needs of men who desire to follow a political career, and that accordingly many men go up to those universities with that end in view. There is, I suggest, some confusion of thought here. It is probably true that many men go up to Oxford and Cambridge as a preparation for a political career, but it does not follow that they do so because of any particular appropriateness of the studies they will pursue there. The honour schools at Oxford and the tripos examinations at Cambridge cover a very wide field of knowledge, but there is little in that field that is not covered also in the faculties of London and other universities. Even if we turn to more specialized studies, London has its School of Economics and Political Science, Liverpool has its School of Social Science, and so on. We must look elsewhere than at curricula to find the key to the favoured position of the older universities.

London is relatively a poor man's university, and its graduates lack the social status conferred by an Oxford or Cambridge degree; and the same thing is true, perhaps even more markedly, in the case of the provincial universities. I suggest, therefore, that when a man goes up to Oxford or Cambridge as a step towards a seat in parliament, and perhaps in the Cabinet, he does so far more because of the value of the hall-mark he thereby obtains than because of any special suitability in the course of study on which he embarks. To say this, of course, is not in any way to belittle the educational value of that course: it is merely to point out that the really effective motive for taking it is to be found in other considerations.

So we are driven to the conclusion that the predominance in parliament of Eton, Harrow, and the public schools generally on the one hand, and of Oxford and Cambridge on the other, is due in the first place to the financial conditions that make the possession of private means almost essential to a political career, and in the second place to the "open sesame" that the right school and the right university place at the disposal of their alumni. Finally it may be remarked that it is more important to have been at the right school than to have been at the right university: the boy who goes up to Oxford from a provincial grammar school does not achieve the privileged position of the old Etonian, even though the latter may have no university education at all.

CHAPTER XVIII

CAUSE AND EFFECT

2. OCCUPATION, HEREDITARY TITLES, AND PARTY

THE next characteristic that we have to consider is that of the occupations of members. Using the occupation schedule of the census as the
best available basis of classification, we found that the various *occupation-groups* have very unequal representation in the House of Commons,
both absolutely and by comparison with the size of the groups in the
general population. On making this latter comparison, we found that
there is marked over-representation* of the groups denominated as
Professional Occupations, Public Administration and Defence, Mining
and Quarrying, Commerce and Finance, and of several others. Correspondingly there is marked under-representation of the groups denominated Personal Services, Makers of Textiles, Not Gainfully Occupied,
Agriculture, and a number of others.

But, as we have seen, these groups are very unsatisfactorily constituted, being planned on an industrial rather than an occupational basis.
Looking at individual *occupations*, therefore, instead of at occupation-
groups, we discovered some astonishing facts; for example, that
bankers have 18 times, solicitors 55 times, journalists 62 times, officers
in the fighting services and stockbrokers 80 times, and barristers no less
than 970 times the number of seats they would be entitled to if representation in the House of Commons were on the basis of occupational
numbers in the general population. On the same footing many occupations are very greatly under-represented in the House: for example,
domestic servants, housewives, farm labourers, and workers in the
building and clothing trades.

Again, when we looked at the question of *occupational status* we
found that, proportionately, employers and managers are nearly six
times as numerous in the House as they are in the country, while professional workers are more than twelve times as numerous. On the
other hand, the general run of rank-and-file workers have less than
two-fifths of their proportionate representation, while the unpaid
domestic workers, though they form a very large section of the community, are practically unrepresented.

Finally, because of their peculiar position—in some cases as full-
time occupations, in others as part-time occupations, and in yet others
as mere qualifications—we paid special attention to the occupations or
quasi-occupations of barrister, solicitor, company director, and trade-
union official. We found that more than half of the Conservative members and also more than half of the Liberal members of parliament
are either lawyers or company directors or a combination of the two,

* It should perhaps be stressed that this is not a final judgement on the rightness or wrongness of the position: it is a *comparison*, made as a useful basis for
further discussion.

while almost half of the Labour members are drawn from the ranks of trade-union officials. More than half of the House of Commons is composed of lawyers, company directors, and trade-union officials.

Whatever way we look at it, the distribution of occupations in the House is extraordinarily different from that in the country: there is no resemblance between the two. Moreover, it is quite clear that this is not in the main a matter of chance, for there is comparatively little variation between one general election and another in this respect, and what there is can largely be accounted for by the fluctuations in party strengths. If the occupational distribution in the House *were* a matter of chance we might quite possibly be content to leave it at that, since in this country we have never accepted any scheme, fascist or otherwise, for the direct representation of occupations in parliament (excepting that of the bishops in the House of Lords). But in fact certain particular occupations do secure enormous representation, election after election, while others as regularly secure little or none, and this may well cause misgiving. It is desirable, then, to trace the reasons for these marked peculiarities; for when we are clear about the causes at work we shall be better placed for deciding whether such eccentricities of representation can be tolerated, and, if not, what is the best way of bringing about a more satisfactory state of affairs.

It needs little argument at this stage to make it clear that one of the major factors in the case is the opportunity which certain occupations offer for earning a living while actually serving as a member of parliament, and the complete lack of such opportunity exhibited by many other occupations. Among the favoured occupations the law notoriously comes first, and particularly the bar. There is little doubt that to the careerest who has the requisite qualities of mind and body, and particularly the ability to work hard for long hours year after year, the combination of law and politics offers many glittering prizes. For our purpose it is unnecessary to determine which of the two holds out the greater incentives, or to attempt to decide whether as a rule it is the barrister who enters parliament to further his legal career or the politician who takes to the law in order to finance his parliamentary ambitions. Doubtless both motives play their part in varying degree, and in any case it is the result rather than the motive that chiefly concerns us; that is, we are more interested to observe how this possibility of a dual career regularly floods parliament with lawyers than we are to decide exactly why the individual embarks on it.

It may be suggested, of course, that a third reason for the predominance of lawyers in parliament is to be found in a certain natural affinity between law and politics. Is it not appropriate, we may be asked, that the lawyer should have a big share in the making of laws?

Superficially the idea may seem reasonable, but reflection suggests that it has little to commend it. In the first place, the House of Commons is not solely, perhaps not even chiefly, a legislative body.* In the

* See, for example, Harold J. Laski, *Democracy in Crisis* (1933), pages 80-82.

second place, even in the process of legislation, *content* is at least as important as *form*; and it is only in connexion with the latter that the lawyer as a lawyer can be supposed to have any exceptional contribution to make. But the question of form in legislation—the preparation of bills, the embodiment of ideas in statutory language—is the province of the specialist parliamentary draftsman rather than of the barrister or solicitor in general practice. Hence we conclude that the House has no need on professional grounds to welcome the glut of lawyers that every election brings it. In any case, moreover, it would seem doubtful whether we could find in the supposed affinity of lawyers with legislation the *cause* of the presence in parliament of so many barristers and, to a less extent, solicitors. For that cause is indisputably to be found in financial conditions: first, because the doors of parliament are practically closed to men and women without a private income; and, second, because the law is one of the very few occupations that can provide such an income without simultaneously and automatically rendering membership impossible in other ways.

Much the same sort of comment applies to the familiar and traditional association between journalism and politics. While there are obvious points of contact and common interest between the two, it is unlikely that these are sufficient to account to any great extent for the large numbers of journalists who enter the House of Commons. It is much more likely that, as with the law, it is the possibility of combining money-making with politics that is the fundamental reason. The fact that stockbrokers also secure an abnormally large representation in parliament seems to bear out these contentions, for it can hardly be suggested seriously that there is any affinity between stockbroking and statesmanship, or that the selling of stocks and shares provides any special qualification for a seat in the House. Plainly it is the facility for obtaining income concurrently with membership that is the decisive factor here; and there is little doubt that in general it is the decisive factor with lawyers and journalists also.

When we turn from lawyers and journalists to company directors we have to recognize that we are dealing with an occupation or quasi-occupation that is even more ill-defined and nebulous, so that no simple statement will cover all the cases involved. At one end of the scale we have the man who is a company director by accident as it were, the man who is primarily a cotton manufacturer or a brewer, an engineer or a publisher, and is a director merely because the firm with which he is concerned has been registered as a limited liability company. At the other end of the scale is the man who makes a substantial income by acting as a company director, who is on the board of half a score or more of undertakings of whose technology and management he knows little and cares less. It is a debatable point, perhaps, whether his directorships get him his seat in parliament or whether it is not rather the magic letters "M.P." after his name that secure him his lucrative inflow of director's fees. Either way it is once again financial considerations that are chiefly accountable for his prominence in the House, though other matters—social standing, for example—may play their part too. In between, of course, come many grades and varieties of company director, and there is no need to attempt the impossible task of classifying them. From our point of view it is their massed effect, the very big if not excessive part they play as an ingredient in the make-up of the personnel of parliament, that is the interesting thing.

To much the same causes in general we can trace the high proportion of employers of all kinds and of owners—mineowners, shipowners, landowners—who secure seats in the House. Here, as elsewhere, all sorts of considerations play their part, but it is to financial considerations first, and to social influences next, that we must look for the reasons why so much representation is concentrated into so small a range of occupations and semi-occupations.

As we have already seen, it is also to financial conditions in the main that the House owes the presence of so many trade-union officials. The inability of the ordinary individual to meet election expenses on the one hand or to live on his official pay as a member of parliament on the other compels the Labour party to seek its candidates largely from those who have the financial backing of a trade union or comparable body, and such bodies will naturally give preference to their tried and trusted officials, even though the qualities needed in a trade-union secretary or a miners' agent are not necessarily those most valuable in parliament—except, of course, in matters directly concerning trade-union affairs. As, however, we have already touched on these matters we need here only stress again the importance of the financial factor: it has a profound influence on the composition of the parliamentary Labour party, as it has, with very different results, on the composition of the other parliamentary parties, and in all parties this influence is reflected in the predominance of certain favoured occupations. To stress this, however, is not to suggest that it is the only influence at work in connexion with occupational distribution, nor that it always acts in the direct ways that we have just discussed.

Let us consider one example of its direct influence before we pass on to quite different factors. In certain occupations men have the opportunity, and sometimes the obligation, to retire on pension at an early age while they are still in the prime of life. In this category come officers in the fighting services and members of the colonial civil services. This early pension provides the financial means for a political career: the cessation, while still in full vigour, of employment elsewhere in a position of responsibility and authority, and the habit of ruling engendered by that employment, provide the incentive. Probably, too, there is in many cases a desire to ventilate in parliament the strong views acquired in the course of that employment, and perhaps to embody them in legislation.

An example of an entirely different factor in the case is to be found in the geographical distribution of occupations. The difference between the representation of mining and that of agriculture illustrates this. As we have seen, the million adult miners are represented in parliament on an average by roughly forty of their own number, or one member of parliament to every 25,000 miners—about twice the proportionate number of members that their voting strength should give. The nearly a million adult agricultural workers, on the other hand, secure a member or two at most: say one member of parliament to every 500,000 workers. The miners of the country are therefore at least twenty times as well represented in parliament as are the agricultural workers.

The cause, or at least the chief cause, of this is to be found in the different geographical distributions of the two industries, in conjunction with the single-member majority system of voting. Mining is concentrated in certain limited areas: agriculture is distributed over almost the whole country. In quite a number of constituencies the miners dominate the local Labour party, and Labour can claim a majority of the electors' votes; so that, in practice, the miners, though themselves a minority of the electorate, have these seats at their disposal. Agriculture, on the other hand, is scattered: though a good many constituencies are referred to in the press and elsewhere as "agricultural", few of them in these days are without a considerable urban population, and in few, if any, is the agricultural labourer in a position to dominate the elections. No doubt the miners are better organized than the farm workers, but that in itself is partly due to this same factor of geographical distribution. No doubt, too, the political attitude of the farm worker is considerably different from that of the miner; but here again the geographical factor comes in.

This question of concentration in the one case and dispersion in the other would have comparatively little effect but for the single-member majority system of voting. With a less arbitrary system the miner, though securing proper representation, would be unable to dominate whole constituencies and whole groups of constituencies as he can at present; while the agricultural worker would be able equally to secure his fair share of representation, without depriving the other elements in an area of their shares.

Now let us glance for a moment at the other side of the picture. If lawyers, journalists, stockbrokers, and others have exceptional opportunities for serving in parliament, there is a very wide range of occupations which are altogether incompatible with a concurrent parliamentary career. Note the word "concurrent": for in that lies the crux of the matter. The barrister can enter the House of Commons and continue his legal practice (indeed, it may well become more lucrative as a result): the general run of people lose their jobs and their incomes if they do so. It is true that trade-union or similar backing may more or less overcome this difficulty in a limited number of cases; but in these cases the occupation of the member is as a rule really that of a trade-union official, and in any case it is only a tiny minority of the population that has the slightest chance of securing such backing. For the vast majority of people—accountants, engineers, chemists, teachers, doctors, no less than joiners, miners, farm workers, sailors, soldiers, clerks. shopkeepers—in short, for the ordinary run of men and women, quite apart from any question of ability or inclination, there is not the slightest chance of entering parliament at any time in their whole lives. This is because doing so would involve relinquishing their occupations; and from such a step they are completely barred by the absence of any alternative source of income.

Probably few people who have "private means" of one sort or another —whether they are also occupied in a business or profession or not— realize that the vast majority of people, including those engaged in commercial and professional work as well as wage-earners, are wholly dependent on their own earnings: to relinquish their jobs is not merely to diminish their incomes, it is to forfeit them altogether, it is to court financial disaster complete and absolute. The man who has behind him the reserve strength of income flowing in from landed property or investments has no conception of the slavery in which "earning a living" involves most of his fellow-citizens: a slavery that effectively shuts them out from, amongst other things, any chance of a career in parliament.

The fact that amongst the many persons wholly dependent on their own earnings for a living (and especially amongst the less skilled workers) the inclination that would seek and the qualities of mind and character that would merit a political career are likely to be exceptional does nothing to justify this state of affairs. The financial barriers do not merely exclude the unsuitable majority: they shut out just as inexorably the suitable minority. Meanwhile the wealthy nonentity can and does "buy" a seat.

There is thus no escaping the conclusion that the distribution of occupations in the House of Commons is primarily a result of financial conditions. Entrance to the House is effectively open only to people who have an income from some source other than their official salaries as members; and, for most people, to enter parliament is to forfeit whatever income they have.

We turn now to the consideration of *hereditary titles* in relation to the membership of the House. As we have seen, holders of hereditary titles and heirs to and relations of holders of such titles have about 350 to 400 times the representation that they would have on a proportional basis. This element forms in the average House 40 to 50 per cent of the Conservative party and 20 to 25 per cent of the Liberal party. Even of the Labour party it forms about 4 per cent, though in the general population it is less than one-tenth of 1 per cent. How shall we account for this extensive aristocratic permeation of the democratic House? Investigation shows that, as with other characteristics we have discussed, it is due to a complex of factors. Let us glance at some of them.

It is notorious that the British public "loves a lord", and it extends this love in varying degree to the wives, sons, daughters, and other relations of lords. It gives, indeed, an instinctive respect and deference

:o anyone with a title, so that a baronet or even a knight can command
an attention, and sometimes secure a vote, that would not be given to a
plain "mister". The so-called "red agitator" may inveigh as fiercely as
he pleases against the titled classes: the crowds will still turn out and
cheer when royalty drives through the streets, a duke presides over a
meeting, or a countess opens a bazaar—and this largely irrespective of
the personal merits of the aristocrat in question: it is the title that casts
the spell. Here, then, is one factor in the case.

Again, there can be little doubt that the polish and *savoir faire* of the
aristocrat have their effect on voters who hear him speak at a meeting
or make personal contact with him. Few people are entirely insensitive
to good manners and distinction of bearing; and though these are
neither confined to one class nor universal in that class, yet they will be
found on balance more frequently and more effectively displayed in
men and women bred up to regard them as normal and essential parts
of their equipment for life than in those who have had small chance to
acquire them, or have passed their lives in surroundings where such
accomplishments are of little or no account. The worker, moreover,
who might despise or resent elegance of speech or manner in his own
family or amongst his own friends will be impressed by it in people of
a different class. There is still truth in Bagehot's comment of more than
seventy years ago: "Manners and bearing have an influence on the
poor; the nameless charm of refinement tells; personal confidence is
almost everywhere more easily accorded to one of the higher classes
than to one of the lower classes: from this circumstance, there is an
inherent tendency in any electoral system which does not vulgarize the
government to protect the rich and to represent the rich."*

Rank and breeding, then, enable the peeress, the heir to a peerage,
and their like, to enter upon a parliamentary candidature with initial
advantages. What these advantages are worth in votes is impossible to
determine, but they are certainly of considerable value: in some constituencies, and especially with women voters, they are probably very
useful assets indeed. Moreover, long before the polling day is reached
these initial advantages will in many cases have played their part in
securing a favourable decision from the selection committee of the
local party association, just as later they will play their part in gaining
the member promotion to office. As a recent writer comments: "There
is simply no denying that aristocratic birth or connexions are extraordinarily useful for a political career in England, and that, even in the
age of democracy, the man of good family is preferred in many cases—
indeed, in most—to those who have come to greatness out of more
modest circumstances."†

Even so, it may be judged that the most powerful factor in securing
for people of titled family so many seats in the House of Commons is

* Walter Bagehot, *The English Constitution*, quoted by Ernest Rhys in *The
Growth of Political Liberty* (1921).
† Karl Heinz Abshagen, *King, Lords, and Gentlemen* (1939), page 106.

neither title *per se*, nor polished manners, nor family influence, but wealth. Hereditary titles are not commonly given to or found amongst the poorer classes of the community. No doubt many a titled family considers itself, and perhaps by its own standards *is*, "hard-up", but poverty of that kind is only relative. For a man whose upbringing, tastes, and family traditions prescribe a way of living commensurate with an income of ten thousand a year to have only five thousand is poverty. It is, however, not the sort of poverty that precludes a parliamentary career: it may, in his own estimation, cramp his style, but it does not shut him out as does the poverty of the working man, the shopkeeper, or the smaller professional man. Moreover, the scion of a noble house commonly has the leisure of the rentier or the landowner: however inadequate to his desires he may find his income, the acquisition of it does not as a rule absorb his time and energy or interfere with his political ambitions as does the earning of a living by those whose income is derived, not from inherited property, but from their own toil.

There is, however, another factor of which we must not lose sight in discussing the prominent position of the titled (and kindred) classes in the House of Commons, and that is the tradition of public service that is almost inborn in those classes. As Abshagen puts it: "Another factor that contributes to the strong representation of members of the aristocracy in political life is the centuries-old tradition in these circles that participation in political leadership of the state is their proper occupation."* This tradition leads its inheritors to assume, as something too self-evident to need argument or even statement, that it is both their duty and their right to take a leading part in public affairs. It is reported that when Cliveden was the property of the first Duke of Westminster he was so fully occupied as to be seldom able to visit it, and on one occasion when asked to take the chair at a public meeting consulted his engagement diary and found that the day in question was the one he had allotted for his first visit there that season. Nevertheless, he took the chair—and at the request of a political opponent.† That little incident illustrates the self-sacrificing devotion to public duty that the tradition inspires. In its other aspect the tradition is perhaps less admirable and certainly far removed from democratic in its assumption of a kind of "divine right" to rule. "Our higher classes still desire to rule the nation," as Bagehot noted.‡ At its best the tradition has given us outstanding examples of disinterested service to the community: at its worst it has been the bulwark of class privilege. Good or bad, however, it is a factor that must not be left out of account.

Yet finally, when due weight has been given to all these considerations, we are left with the conviction that the fundamental reason for the high proportion of people of the titled and allied classes that is always present in the House of Commons is to be found in the possession by these people of relatively ample means in conjunction with leisure. This is so not merely because of the direct advantages and

---

* *Loc. cit.*   † *Manchester Guardian,* 11th December, 1942.   ‡ *Loc. cit.*

opportunities that money and freedom give them, but also because the culture, style, manners, and traditions on which their influence so largely depends have been built up on, and are continually sustained by, the same resources of time and money.

Next and last of the questions that we have to consider in studying cause and effect is that of the distribution of seats in the House of Commons according to *party*. This question is on a different footing from those of age, education, occupation, and other characteristics with which we have been concerned: the latter have a personal quality, are bound up with the individuality of members, in a way that party is not. It is, however, one of the most important aspects of our subject, and it is desirable to be clear about the relation between cause and effect in this connexion.

Here the outstanding fact is undoubtedly the lack of correspondence between the party complexion of the House of Commons and the state of party feeling in the electorate. As we have seen, even the aggregate vote collected by a party in a general election cannot be relied upon as a correct indication of its true voting strength: it tends to exaggerate the strength of the stronger parties and to underestimate the strength of the weaker parties. But if the aggregate votes are subject to this defect, they are at least a rough guide to party strengths: the number of seats gained by a party is seldom even that. It is not merely that the final result of a general election does not give an exact mathematical indication of party strengths: that would not worry any reasonable person, if the broad general effect were a tolerably accurate reflection of the state of public opinion. The trouble is that the system fails all too often to give even that: a general election is a gamble of which no one can predict the result with any certainty, and that result seldom accords with the wishes of the electorate as expressed by their votes. It is not mere exaggeration of which we have to complain: it is gross irresponsibility.

The major cause of this state of affairs is, as we have seen, the single-member majority system of voting. It should be clear from Chapter XVI how cause and effect are related in this matter, and it is unnecessary to repeat the explanations there set forth. We may, however, take just one illustration to drive home the point. In the county of Cornwall in 1923 all five seats were won by the Liberals; in 1924 all five went over to the Conservatives; in 1929 all five reverted to the Liberals. Analysis of the voting shows that the Conservatives should have had two members for the county as a whole—and no more—at each of these three elections; the Liberals should have had three members in 1923 and two at each of the other two elections; while the remaining member for the county in 1924 and 1929 should have represented Labour. The actual results are therefore in each case a fantastic misrepresentation of the actual party strengths. But that is how the single-member majority system works: and violent fluctuations of this sort are not confined to relatively small areas like this—they affect in varying degree the results for the country as a whole.

It should be clear that, as we have already noted, these somersaults are not due to "fickleness" on the part of the constituencies concerned : they are natural and inevitable results of the present method of voting in divisions where the parties are more or less equally balanced in strength. On the other hand, in divisions where one party is much stronger than the others we get the "safe seat", where the stronger party has to all intents and purposes a permanent monopoly of representation, with all its attendant evils. The system therefore works badly in both conditions. Where the parties are nearly equal in strength the best of members may lose his seat through a very small turnover of votes : where one party is much the stronger a "dud" member may retain his seat indefinitely. This dilemmatic evil, it should be noticed, is separate from and additional to the misrepresentation of opinion for which the system is responsible.

Another aspect of the "safe seat" outcome of present methods of election is seen in the undesirable tendency of the latter to encourage unopposed returns to parliament. In 1918 there were no fewer than eighty seats in Great Britain for which no contest took place. Exceptionally in 1929 the number dropped to three, but in no other general election has it fallen below twenty-nine, while the average number of unopposed returns for the seven inter-war general elections is just under forty-two. Yet there is not a single constituency in the country where all the voters belong to one party. Lack of a contest, in general, simply indicates that in that constituency the present system gives no chance of representation to any party but one.

In addition to the direct injustice of this virtual disfranchisement of minorities, moreover, there is an ill effect on the political outlook of the electors (of all parties) concerned; for where the result of an election is a foregone conclusion electoral apathy is an inevitable outcome. How can people be expected to take an interest in politics when their representation in parliament is, for all practical purposes, in the gift of a small inner clique of one party, against the decisions of which they have no effective remedy? The single-member majority system is, of course, the chief factor in the causation of uncontested elections, but it is not the only one. It is reinforced by the heavy cost of contesting an election; but for this, even with the present method of voting, far fewer seats would go uncontested, and the elector might get some small satisfaction from recording his ineffective vote.

We see, then, that the inherent nature of the present system is such that it is incapable of giving satisfactory results. It leads to minority representation in division after division, it distorts the aggregate party votes in the country as a whole, and it does not allot seats even roughly according to those aggregate votes. Not even broadly does it reflect the true state of political feeling in the country. Further, it encourages the return of mediocre candidates, effectively disfranchises many areas, and promotes electoral apathy.

PART III
A SCHEME OF REFORM

CHAPTER XIX

THE AIMS OF REFORM

HAVING in Part I analysed the composition and characteristics of the personnel of the House of Commons as it actually exists in modern times, and having in Part II studied the causes underlying these results and discussed the way in which they act, we have now in Part III to turn from the present to the future and endeavour to make constructive suggestions for bringing about a more satisfactory state of affairs.

In the course of our analysis we have observed certain marked defects in the present machinery of representation, and any proposals for change that we put forward must aim at remedying those defects. A scheme of reform, however, that was directed solely to the removal of obvious faults would be merely negative in character and unlikely to produce satisfying results. To look only at present failings would be to see our problem myopically, and to set about reform on such a basis would be to limit undesirably its prospect of success.

We must endeavour at the outset, then, to form a clear conception of the sort of parliamentary representation that we desire to see in being. We must add to a realization of what is now wrong a vision of the positive ends to which our efforts should be directed. Only if we have grasped clearly what it is we wish to achieve and why we wish to achieve it are we likely to formulate a scheme of reform that will do more than patch up a faulty system. It is arguable that all too many projects for the reform of this or that—including acts of parliament— have been greatly reduced in effectiveness, if not completely stultified, by too much concentration on immediate wrongs and too little of the inspiration that comes from seeing a problem whole and getting a clear vision of the possibilities latent in its solution.

To what extent we shall succeed in putting this principle in practice remains to be seen; but however far short of it we fall, it is at least likely that we shall achieve something by making the attempt. If it is not, in this case, "better to travel hopefully than to arrive", it is certainly better to travel hopefully with our eyes on the hills than to loiter about with our eyes on the ground.

We have, therefore, to ask ourselves in the most general terms what we want from parliamentary representation. We must look, not merely at the thing itself, but at the ideas and ideals in which it is or should be rooted. We must examine its component parts and its workings in the light of those ideas and ideals. We must try to stand a little outside our preconceptions and habits of thought, try to forget for a little while our accepted notions of political expediency, try to concentrate first on fundamentals. I am not in this suggesting any mood of exalted mysticism, but only that we should cast aside for the time being our bonds of custom and routine, and that we should try to get a strategical rather than just a tactical view of our problem. If we can manage to do that even to a limited extent, we shall be all the better placed for getting down in due course to brass tacks. It would be folly to suppose that we can equip ourselves with godlike wisdom and judgement; but let us at least make as brave an attempt as we can at clear-sightedness, let us try to see something of the wood in spite of the trees.

We need attempt here no logically precise or philosophically profound exposition of political theory—there are plenty of learned treatises in that field for those who desire them—but it will help us in tackling our strictly limited problem if we can restate, informally and unacademically, what we believe to be the essentials of a democratic way of government in our own times. There are any number of ways in which this might be done, and we need not seek finality of expression so much as a clear understanding of our basic ideals and the broad lines on which we conceive they should be interpreted here and now.

"Government of the people, by the people, for the people." However open to criticism Abraham Lincoln's brave dictum at Gettysburg may be if considered as a precise statement of political philosophy, it does at least enshrine in a memorable and inspiring form a noble ideal of the basis of democracy.* Is it possible, however, for that ideal to be embodied in the political institutions of the real world as it exists in our modern mechanized age? Is it not, rather, just a rhetorical flourish that will not bear scrutiny?

The trouble lies, of course, in the words "*by* the people". Our modern civilization, with its astonishing scientific developments, is one of immense and bewildering complexity. It bristles with intricate and refractory problems that have so far baffled the wisest and most far-seeing. "The people" in the mass are unthinking and ignorant and warped to trivial ends. Is it possible, then, from men and women tangled in such a welter of sordid toil, futile pleasure, and neglected intellect, to embody anything worth calling "government by the people", consistently with the direction of the state to noble ends? Have they, the people—not some idealized personification, but the real everyday commonplace man and woman—anything of value to contribute to the processes of government?

In attempting to answer these questions we must recognize right away that the ordinary citizen is, in the great majority of cases, totally incapable of any satisfactory *direct* participation in the actual work of government. Whatever he may become in some remote utopian future, here and now he is equipped neither with the knowledge, the skill, nor

---

* Lincoln's famous Gettysburg address is well worth re-reading. It will be found in John G. Nicolay's *Short Life of Abraham Lincoln* (1906), page 376; in Frederic L. Paxson's *The American Civil War* (1911), page 183; and elsewhere.

the insight necessary for such participation. Moreover, we are not dealing with a small city-state, but with a highly populous country, and mere numbers would make it impossible for all our citizens, however capable, to take a direct part in its government.

Here, then, are drastic limitations on "government by the people": is there anything left? Can the common man, ruled out from any direct share in government, usefully take any part in it at all? Must he not be treated politically—and therefore socially and economically—as a serf, a soulless unit in the vast machine of the state, to be directed and controlled and ordered about by a dictator or a small and self-appointed ruling class? That is the fascist view, the nazi view, the age-old view of tyrants and oligarchies the world over. It is, moreover, still largely the view of the privileged classes in all countries, even though they do not shout it from the house-tops. Not everyone in a democratic country is a democrat at heart.

Here and in America and elsewhere, however, we are at least nominally democratic: what do we do about this problem? In theory, by the adoption of adult suffrage, we have given almost unlimited political power to the masses, but in practice the exercise of that power is so conditioned as to make it nearly inoperative. This arises in two ways: first, because the development of our political institutions has always been very much a matter of improvisation to meet immediate needs rather than of planned and orderly advance; and, second, because of the strong resistance put up by vested interests against the effective use by the people of the powers conferred upon them.

It is a mistake of the first order to attribute all the troubles, material and spiritual, that harass our civilization to the wicked machinations of this or that group or class or party. To a very great extent they arise from the imperfections of human nature, from the intellectual laziness and lack of vision that to a greater or lesser extent afflict us all, and from the immense difficulty of foreseeing and meeting the needs of a civilization that expands and changes with, historically, almost alarming speed. We can unhesitatingly, therefore, attribute the ineffectiveness of our democratic institutions more to chance and circumstance than to deliberate intent.

Nevertheless, there can be no doubt that these influences are reinforced by the efforts, conscious or unconscious, of those who hold the strings of power to retain them as far as possible in their own hands. That again is human nature and need occasion neither surprise nor violent indignation. What we have to do is to recognize the fact and to seek means of counteracting its ill effects.

What does all this amount to in terms of actual political practice? This, I suggest: that though every adult in this country now has a vote, the organization of our representative institutions—including both the selection of candidates and the election of members—is on such lines that the elector is precluded from using his vote in a way that is consistent with his natural dignity as a thinking human being or consonant with his rights as a citizen. This is an injustice to the individual man and woman, but it also results in our failing to extract from the electors anything like their maximum potential contribution to the good government of the country.

If we are honest we must recognize the political limitations of the great majority of ordinary men and women; but if we really believe in democratic government we ought to see that they are given every opportunity and encouragement to take that share in it of which they *are* capable. This is not merely a question of individual rights, it is a matter of political wisdom. Having chosen the democratic way of life, it is ordinary common sense for us to see that it is made to work efficiently : otherwise it would be better abandoned and something else put in its place. We ought to do all we can both to develop an alert, interested, and competent electorate, and to utilize to the full its valuable qualities. How are we to set about this considerable task?

The average elector needs education, he needs all the education he can get—and at present a great deal more than he can get—if he is to make his optimum contribution to the government of the country. Without in any way decrying the advances that have been made in popular education—they are far greater and better than many critics realize—ordinary people still need more and better school education, more and better post-school education, more and better adult education, especially in what may be broadly termed the social studies. They need to be trained to think more clearly, to write and speak and express themselves generally in a more accurate and illuminating way. They need a better idea of the broad trend of history, of the basic facts of geography and biology and economics. They need to have their interest aroused in the ways and traditions and ideas of the peoples of other countries. They need all this and more—and they need to have it presented to them in such a form that they can absorb and relish it, not choked with academic detail nor rendered sterile by abstruse theories. How this is to be achieved in general we must leave to the educationists : it will tax all their skill and wisdom and zeal.

But there is one aspect of the education of the citizen that falls strictly within the sphere of our discussion. I suggest that our political institutions, and particularly our methods of parliamentary representation, would, if placed on a sound footing, be in and of themselves a means of educating the ordinary man and woman, of awakening and developing in the general run of voters an interest in and an understanding of public affairs and political problems. In the science of mechanics we know that "action and reaction are equal and opposite",* and in the science of human relations something of the same sort obtains. In particular, we ought to realize that not merely does the elector act on the electoral system by his vote, but the system reacts on him in the process. If the system is a stupid one, giving the elector no real voice—or even no voice at all—in the choice of his representatives, it will teach him

* Newton's Third Law of Motion.

nothing, it will deaden his interest in public affairs and render him apathetic to political issues. If, on the other hand, it gives him the opportunity to use his wits, to exercise his judgement, and to feel that he counts for something in the scheme of things, he will thereby be influenced to develop his powers, to use his vote wisely, and to understand the significance of the issues he is helping to decide. There is no getting away from it: the two parts of the system act and react on each other in a continuous cycle of mutual influence. An electoral method that nullifies the value of a vote makes for apathy and ignorance in the electorate: apathy and ignorance in the electorate lead to the stultification of election results. Moreover, an incompetent and frustrated electorate encourages the return of incompetent and cynical members. If we wish to get from adult suffrage all it is capable of giving us, we must treat the voters *as* adults and not as ciphers.

Judged by these standards the present system fails lamentably. It offers little incentive to the elector to interest himself in either political problems generally or in the personnel of parliament. In the "safe seats" when there are unopposed returns he has no chance to record a vote at all (in 1918 there were no fewer than eighty such returns in Great Britain), and even when there is a contest he has merely the empty satisfaction of going to the polling station and putting his × on a bit of paper, knowing that his vote is practically futile, that the result of the election is a foregone conclusion. Beyond this, however, even in the case of a contest between parties that are more or less evenly matched, there is little to make the ordinary voter feel that he is really participating in the choice of a *member*, someone to represent *him*. All he is allowed to do, in effect, is to say which of the two or three parties concerned shall have the seat. It may be right that an election shall be primarily a test of public opinion on party issues: it is not right that it shall be solely such a test. Yet that is all it normally is at present. Elections *as a whole* must turn largely on the bigger political issues of the moment; that is right and proper. But the elector should have some voice in the choice of personnel as well as party. Given that he must be content with a member whose views are only broadly those that he himself holds, that in voting he must associate himself with one or other of the major parties, he should yet have some small share in securing the best man to represent that party. The present system denies him any such share, it reduces him from a thinking human being to a mere party unit; and in so doing it deprives the community of a valuable contribution that it might receive towards good government.

This is a point to which little attention has been paid, but I believe it to be one of prime importance. It is, I think, widely agreed, even amongst members of parliament themselves, that though there are in the House of Commons men and women of first-class calibre admirably fitted to serve there, yet the *average* level of integrity and ability in the House is a long way below what it should be. If this view is correct, then it is of the utmost importance to take every possible step to improve the position; and one such step, it seems to me, is to make better use of the qualities of the ordinary voter. Let us examine this point a little closer.

I suggest that in favourable circumstances the electors can and will choose their members wisely: but the circumstances must be, in the sense I have in mind, favourable. If the only choice left to them is between single nominees of two or three sharply differing parties, each assured of its own exclusive rightness and equipped with appropriate battle-cries, then the result will be determined, not by any judgement of fitness, but by the violence of the prejudices aroused and the strength of the party traditions invoked. With present electoral methods, moreover, the political issues of the day are seldom presented fairly to the electors or judged by them with calmness and care. There is too much inflaming of party passions, too much deliberate playing on the hopes and fears of the electorate. We are so accustomed to this sort of thing that we take it as right and inevitable, but I suggest that it is neither. We have to aim at transforming the party dog-fight into something more worthy of a great nation settling its destinies. We must so order things as to make our appeal to the best that is in our people instead of the worst.

At present, then, the ordinary elector has little or no scope for the exercise of his faculties of judgement and idealism in relation either to political issues in any true sense or to the personality of the candidates put before him. He must in effect vote on mechanical party lines or not at all. But give him a choice between two or more candidates—whether official nominees of his party or not—whose views and proposals do not constitute an outrage on all he has been brought up to believe in, give him a choice of candidates where party prejudice is at a discount, and I believe that on the whole he will choose well. He will choose well because, ignorant though he is in so many directions, he has, when it comes to weighing up one man against another, a native shrewdness, an insight, that is worth much. Hence where there is a real choice before the electorate integrity and ability have a good chance of coming into their own. The worthless candidate who romps home easily now would in such circumstances be seen through and rejected, and the party organizations would have to bestir themselves to find better candidates than they commonly do now. There would no longer be the opportunity to "sell" seats that there is at present, and the second-rate man who now gets in on the strength of his party docility or seniority or influence would be likely to prove a bad bargain for the party that put him forward. It would be all to the good that the real choice of members of parliament should be transferred from the party caucuses, where it now is, to the electors themselves, where it properly belongs.

Moreover, in circumstances which discounted excessive reliance on party slogans, policy would come in for closer scrutiny and elections be decided more on the real issues of the day and less by the wilful stirring up of fears and hopes and prejudices. A much truer estimate of the real state of public opinion would be possible, and that opinion itself, being better informed and more dispassionate, would have greater influence in the state.

We put, then, as the first aim to be kept in view in any programme of reform, such changes as will enable us to draw from the common people, the ordinary voters, all that they have to give towards good government, and will at the same time react on them in such a way as to develop their political powers, widen their outlook, and deepen their insight on public questions. It is perhaps advisable to add that the full achievement of these ends must be considered as a matter of long-term policy: improved conditions such as we seek could not be expected to produce their full effect immediately they were put into operation.

So far as the electorate is concerned, there is one other major aim to be kept in view, and that is that the electoral system should be so organized that the results of a general election give a reasonably accurate reflection of the state of public opinion on the issues before the country. What we have to seek here is not the mathematically precise representation of every shade of opinion in exact proportion to the number of electors holding it, but a broad correspondence between the political views of the community at large and the political complexion of the House of Commons. This seems so elementary a requisite for anything worth calling a democracy that it should hardly be necessary to assert it. But, as the facts and figures given in Part I prove, we are very far from such a correspondence under our present system, and, strange as it may seem, there are many nominally democratic politicians and political theorists who do not even consider it desirable. That parliament—or at the very least the House of Commons—should be so constituted that it reflects with tolerable correctness the views of the country seems of the very essence of representative government. Those who disagree, whether in the supposed interest of "strong government" or for any other reason, are either guilty of muddled thinking or, what is perhaps more likely, are not really believers in democratic institutions. It is perfectly legitimate to argue that a dictatorship or an oligarchy or a system of aristocratic rule or what not is preferable to democracy: it is not legitimate to profess a belief in democratic rule and then to defend a state of affairs that makes it a mockery. The failure of our electoral system to give us even the broadest correspondence between the views of the elected and those of the electors is not a minor matter: it undermines the very foundations of good government.

Our second aim, then, in any scheme of reform that we put forward must be to secure that what our system gives us *is* representation and not misrepresentation, that things are so ordered that the state of opinion in the House of Commons shall correspond reasonably well with the state of opinion in the country, instead of distorting or contradicting it.

We turn now from the electorate to the elected. If it is important to secure that the voters shall make their maximum contribution to the

12

political well-being of the state and that their collective decisions on policy shall not be negatived by irresponsible electoral machinery, it is no less important to ensure that the personnel of parliament shall be adequate to its tasks, that it shall, indeed, be the best that is obtainable. So far so good: few are likely to quarrel with a proposition couched in such general terms. But if we begin to consider what in this connexion we mean by "best" we shall not find it easy to give a satisfactory answer offhand, and it is probable that even after discussion agreement may be difficult to reach. It is all the more necessary to go into the matter carefully and to make a special effort to think clearly and avoid hasty generalizations.

Let us begin by surveying the field in the broadest possible way; let us determine in the most comprehensive manner we can the type of membership we should desire to see established in the House of Commons. When we have settled on some sort of general principle we can go on, if it should prove desirable, to consider in more detail the qualities to be sought in prospective members.

If, then, we ask ourselves in the most open-minded way possible what sort of representatives the community should desire to have in parliament, we shall find that all the answers that can be given may be summed up in the form of three alternatives.

Firstly, we may conclude that the men and women who are to represent us ought to have some sort of special fitness for the job, that they should possess some qualities of mind or spirit, some particular aptitudes or attainments, or some appropriate types of experience that would enable them to do their jobs as members more adequately, more efficiently, than they otherwise could.

Secondly, we may hold with Professor Laski that all that is necessary or desirable is that our representatives shall be "an average sample of ordinary men".*

Thirdly, we can decide that it just doesn't matter, that so long as members of parliament are of the right party (and, of course, not too obviously mentally or morally deficient) the rest can be left to chance and there is no need to worry.

These three alternatives between them cover all the possibilities, and we have to ask ourselves which of them we must select as our guiding principle. On our choice depends the answer to the question whether any reforms are necessary in connexion with the personnel of parliament. Clearly, if we decide on the third alternative no reform is necessary, while if we consider the first or second to embody the right view we may have to suggest reforms: the nature of these, however, would depend on which of the two we judge to be the correct criterion. Let us examine them, therefore, and see if we can determine something of the significance that attaches to each.

Taking them in the reverse order, the third alternative has only to be

* Harold J. Laski, *Democracy in Crisis* (1933), page 80.

considered seriously for it to be condemned: that is, if we really desire an efficient and democratic House of Commons. By a *reductio ad absurdum* we see that it would allow of a House that consisted of the most freakish assortment of people: one, for example, where every member was in the twenties, or for that matter in the eighties. It would allow of a House that contained nobody but lawyers or, on the other hand, contained no lawyers at all. It might result in a collection of members like a coroner's jury in the old days, made up to strength by bringing in loafers from the street. Such an assembly would be quite unfitted for debate, and when it came to a division its members could merely act as recorders of party votes, people whose age, education, occupation, etc., were of no importance because such considerations were irrelevant to the one job of voting as the party whips directed. No doubt there is a strong flavour of this in the House at present, for there seems to be an implied assumption that it does not much matter whom we have as members so long as they are of the right party and vote as the whips tell them.

This casualness, however, is modified in practice because, as we have seen, existing conditions are such that extensive classes of people—in fact, the great majority of the population—are automatically excluded from any real chance of entering the House, while other sections are as automatically favoured. Moreover, there is no doubt that with all this we mix some tincture of the first alternative, that we have a feeling, rather vague and ill defined, that some people are better suited than others for membership of the House.

Rejecting, then, the third alternative, with its implications that ignorance, inexperience, and stupidity should be no bar to membership, we turn to the second. According to the passage in Laski's writings from which we have just quoted, "A legislative assembly is neither a collection of specialists nor a body of statesmen. It is an average sample of ordinary men, deflected now this way, now that, by the drift of public opinion, and organized by its leaders to accept a policy which those leaders regard as desirable". It is, on the face of it, an unattractive picture, strongly suggestive of the life of a flock of sheep, with the party leader as shepherd and the party whip as sheep-dog. Let us, however, consider it more closely. The words may be considered as a statement of fact, as an expression of an ideal, or as both combined. It would seem probable that the last is what is intended: that the pronouncement is regarded by its author as representing both what is and what should be. How far is either view justified?

Is the actual House of Commons in any sense "an average sample of ordinary men"? The whole of the results of this investigation show that it is not, that such a description would be a flat contradiction of the known facts. The House is not an average sample in respect of age, of sex, of education, of occupation, of social standing, of financial position, or even of party. Nor is the deviation from average a mere matter of excusable approximation: it is far too marked to be passed off in that way. By no exercise of ingenuity can we justify calling the House of Commons as it is "an average sample of ordinary men".

Perhaps, however, the statement is to be taken as an expression of an ideal rather than as a description of the real. Let us consider, then, what the House would be like if it were really "an average sample of ordinary men", and see whether a House so constituted supplies the ideal at which we should aim.

Such a House would contain more women than men (unless, indeed, we are to suppose the clock put back and women excluded altogether). There would be more youngsters of twenty-one than people of any other age. Gone would be the present-day hordes of barristers, solicitors, journalists, stockbrokers, army and navy officers, company directors, and trade-union officials. In their place we should find crowds of domestic servants, working housewives, clerks, labourers, factory hands, and shop assistants. There would be fewer miners and more farm workers. The old Etonians and old Harrovians would disappear, together with the Oxford and Cambridge men. In their place would be men and women who had left school—elementary—at fourteen or even earlier and had had little or no subsequent education. The landowner, the rentier, the young sprig of nobility, the peeress, the wealthy manufacturer: these would be rare indeed. It would be an immense change from all that we have known in parliament, this "average sample of ordinary men". It would be much younger than our present House of Commons, it would be more than half feminine, it would be predominantly hard up and inexperienced and ill educated. Some of the changes would be all to the good, but taken as a whole does it offer a desirable prospect, is it an ideal to be sought, does it hold out the promise of high efficiency and wisdom?

If we are honest, if we have any sense of reality, we must return an emphatic "No!" to all these questions. One need not be a believer in the "Religion of Inequality"* to be unable to contemplate with desire, or even with equanimity, the prospect of a House of Commons consisting largely of youthful ignoramuses and with men in the minority. One has only to imagine such a House at work, to think of it facing its multifarious and intricate problems, and one realizes at once the absurdity of looking to "an average sample of ordinary men" for the fulfilment of the arduous tasks of parliament.

We are forced, then, to accept the first alternative, to conclude that some people—as yet undefined—are better fitted than others for membership of the House of Commons. Let us be clear that this decision does not in any way prejudge the question as to *what* kinds of people can best represent us in parliament. All we have so far decided is, on the one hand, that the matter cannot be left to chance and, on the other, that the "average sample" theory is untenable. In particular, we have not in any way committed ourselves to the idea that the House should be either "a collection of specialists" or "a body of statesmen". So far

---

* Matthew Arnold, *Mixed Essays* (1879), Lecture on "Equality".

as we are concerned the field is perfectly open: we have merely reached the conclusion, in the most general terms, that some kinds of people could do the job better than others. The problems involved in determining what qualifications or characteristics are desirable in members of parliament have still to be discussed, and they are so important and so complex that we shall have to devote a special chapter to them. Our aim, however, is clearly established: to bring about such changes as will facilitate and encourage, and as far as practicable ensure, the election to the House of Commons of men and women who are specially suited to the tasks they will there have to face.

We have now established three guiding principles to be kept in view in formulating proposals for reform. Let us briefly recapitulate them. They are:

1. That our system of parliamentary representation shall be so organized that it will enable us to draw from the electors as a whole their maximum contribution towards the good government of the country, and that it will in the process react on them in such a way as to develop and expand their political competence.

2. That the system shall secure that the political complexion of the House of Commons corresponds with all reasonable closeness with the state of public opinion.

3. That our representatives in the House shall be people specially suited to fulfil their functions there.

To these major aims we may add one subsidiary aim that needs little argument:

4. That the system shall be freed from anomalies and minor defects that have survived from earlier times or crept in unobserved.

These aims as a whole are based on the belief that we have in our historic parliamentary institutions and in our citizens as a whole latent possibilities of political development far beyond anything we have yet utilized or even fully recognized, and that we can, if we will, secure within the framework of those institutions a standard of democratic government immensely superior to that which we now have.

CHAPTER XX

THE IDEAL MEMBER OF PARLIAMENT

Is there such a thing, even in the abstract, as an ideal member of parliament? If by the term we are to understand a single narrowly uniform type of member, then the answer must certainly be no. But we have decided that we need as members people who have some sort of special fitness for the job, and in endeavouring to determine what constitutes that special fitness we are in a broad sense seeking the ideal member.

We can at the outset reject any idea of drawing up a "standard specification" for members. We should not desire, even if it were possible, to have all members conforming to a single pattern, however good that pattern might be. What has to be sought is that the House of Commons as a whole shall be composed in such a way that its members collectively possess the attributes that will enable it to fulfil its varied functions with maximum ease and efficiency. In order that we may be in a position to pursue that search effectively, it is clearly necessary that we should bear in mind what those functions are, and should have some conception of the demands that their fulfilment makes on the personality of members.

Let us start, then, by considering the functions of the House. For our purpose, here as elsewhere, we need not so much an academic discussion of the political philosophy of parliamentary institutions as a realization of what the House actually does and has to do as it affects the members composing it. It is unnecessary, therefore, to trouble overmuch about theories of legislation, redress of grievances, separation of powers, and so on. Important though such matters are in their proper place, they do not directly affect our problem, and in what follows we shall aim at a clear understanding of practical issues rather than a logical presentation of principles. Many questions, moreover, that would require ventilation in any general discussion of parliamentary reform can be ignored for our more limited purpose.

One of the chief functions of parliament is to provide a forum for the authoritative discussion of all questions of public policy. Discussions of this sort may arise in a variety of ways—on specific proposals for legislation, on the Address to the Crown following the King's Speech at the beginning and end of each parliamentary session, on votes of censure, on motions for the adjournment of the House, and so on. Let us for the moment ignore these various occasions and look a little at some of the general questions involved in debates on policy. The first thing that strikes us is their wide range. Here are a dozen or so topics taken almost at random from the very long list of matters discussed in recent years (excluding questions arising from and about the present war): agriculture; disarmament; education; the Indian constitution; industrial insurance; Italy and Abyssinia; juvenile delinquency; local government areas; maternal mortality; protective tariffs; relations between the dominions and the empire; rent restriction; town planning; unemployment; workmen's compensation.

This is in no sense an exhaustive list: yet what a limitless vista of problems it serves to suggest! Read the list slowly and carefully and think of the ramifications and complications involved in any single item. Bear in mind, too, that these are not debating society discussions: they are discussions by the oldest, and probably the most powerful, representative parliamentary body in the world, with traditions going right back into the roots of our national life; they are discussions which help to develop and crystallize the views of those who have the responsibility for legislation and administration at the heart of the British commonwealth of nations: discussions, moreover, which directly and indirectly exert their influence on public opinion at home and abroad.

Clearly such discussions ought to be conducted with high seriousness and a keen sense of responsibility. It would be rash to say that they are always so conducted: but at least the House of Commons provides a very critical audience that does not readily listen to ill-informed and superficial speeches, or pay much attention to members who obviously do not understand the significance of the topics they are debating. Moreover, if the subject under discussion is of any general importance it is likely that hasty and ill-considered remarks will be pretty severely handled by subsequent speakers. This is so even now, in spite of the imperfections in the composition of the House that have been surveyed in earlier chapters and the widely admitted disparity between the average quality of members and the quality that should be the rule: in a House with a higher general standard of intellect and integrity the conditions of debate would, of course, be even more exacting.

Hence a member wishing to take part in a discussion in the House of Commons must bring to it a considerable store of knowledge and understanding if he is to make his contribution effective. Moreover, even the member who does not actively participate in the debate, but merely listens to the speeches and votes in the division, cannot pull his weight unless he has some knowledge of the subject, can seize the allusions, understand the references, and follow the arguments. Without an informed and alert mind and a clear perception of the wider issues involved he cannot form a judgement of any value on the propositions placed before him or estimate the soundness of the reasoning by which they are supported. To play his part worthily, even as a silent member, he must have a considerable and orderly background of information of many kinds, a critical habit of thought, and a well-balanced sense of values.

Take, for example, such a question as that of the raising of the school-leaving age. This is merely one out of very many current questions in the single field of education: yet to participate with real effectiveness in its discussion, or to give a considered vote on any issue in connexion with it, a member needs to know something of the history of the legislation concerning compulsory education from 1870 onwards, he needs to understand the educational grounds on which the demand for a higher leaving age is based, to take into account the impact of any change in that age on industries which employ much juvenile labour, and to grasp the economic effects on the parents of the children concerned, the reactions of those parents, and the consequent problem of maintenance allowances. He must bear in mind the difficulties of accommodation arising from the retention in the schools of many thousands of children for an additional year or years, the necessity for more apparatus and equipment and more teachers that will result, and the consequent need for more training-college places. He must perceive something of the financial effects of all these matters on both rates and taxes. He must have such a sense of practical psychology and of the way things actually work out in practice as will enable him to anticipate the real effect of allowing any exemptions from the extension of school life. He must, moreover, be able to take, finally, a broad view of the subject as a whole; he must not lose sight of the wood in looking at the trees, must have the ability to weigh long-term advantages against short-term disadvantages. No doubt we could go on adding to the list; but as it stands it serves to indicate the complexities and far-reaching effects of a single issue that might at first sight seem simple. It would be much the same if we took any other issue in any other field of public affairs: analysis would reveal it as much more complex and interrelated with other matters than it might seem on the surface to be.

To say this is not to suggest that the member must be an expert on all or even on any of the questions debated. If he adds to the necessary general qualities of mind and temper a specialist knowledge of a particular subject, he can make all the more valuable a contribution to debate when the occasion arises. But, quite apart from any question of expert qualifications, a member cannot justify his place in the House unless he votes not only honestly but also intelligently, and he cannot vote intelligently if he is at sea in the discussion, misses the point of the arguments, and fails to grasp the significance of the decisions he has to make. Still less, of course, can he do so if he absents himself from the debate and merely hurries in for the division. There is, unfortunately, much to deplore in the current practice of the House in this respect: many discussions of importance are left to the comparatively small number of members who have a special interest in the questions at issue, and when the division bells ring all too many members troop from the smoke-room or elsewhere into the lobbies with the ayes or the noes, shepherded by the party whips and without any comprehension— sometimes, indeed, without any knowledge—of the questions their votes are deciding.

It does not seem to be generally recognized how essentially dishonest this last practice is, how it vitiates discussion and strikes at the roots of parliamentary responsibility. Some members talk too much and too often, while others seldom even attempt to catch the Speaker's eye and are content to go on session after session without contributing a single speech. There is no virtue in speaking unless one has something of value to say, and a member who sits silent may be far from useless: he may be learning much that he will later pass on for the benefit of his constituents or employ usefully in other ways, and in the process he may be improving his own equipment as a member. Further, if he uses his ears and his judgement alertly and votes in the divisions in accordance with his conscience, after hearing both sides of the question, he is in that degree justifying his membership. It may indicate a lack of anything positive or constructive in his make-up if he never finds occasion to speak; but he is at least taking some worth-while share in the functions of the House in so far as his vote, given on the merits of the case, is helping to shape policy. But the member who, unable to contribute anything of value to a discussion, will not even learn something from it, and then, after absenting himself from the chamber and hearing no word of the debate, hastens to ingratiate himself with the whips by voting assiduously on purely party lines, knowing nothing and caring less what the divisions are about, plays into the hands of self-willed ministers and party caucuses, weakens democracy, and brings parliament into disrepute.

So long as we encourage the election of members who come forward out of vanity or to grind their own axes, so long as we allow some people to buy their seats and others to obtain theirs by influence, so long as we accept as normal the careerist lawyer who lets his briefs and his fees take the first call on his time and energy and the House only what is left, so long must we expect this kind of thing. It is so usual that few see anything to cavil at in it. It may occasionally lead to amusement when such a member in his last-minute rush gets into the wrong lobby, but it seldom receives the contempt it deserves.

We may, however, be accused of setting impossible standards and asking more of members than is reasonable. Let it be admitted that no member alive—except perhaps Mr. Speaker—can be expected to sit through all the interminable discussions on this and that, day in, day out. Let us recognize that a member as a member has other jobs to do in addition to attending debates. Let us accept it that there are subjects of which he cannot be expected to know anything and points which it would be unreasonable to expect him to decide for himself, that he must often accept the advice of his leaders in the use of his vote. All this is very true: but it does not invalidate our argument.

The House of Commons, in this aspect, is on the one hand the means by which public opinion, gathered from the constituencies and through the various organizations—social and professional as well as political—that serve to express it, may be brought to a focus and employed to influence the course of public policy and to keep the government informed of the state of feeling in the country. On the other hand it is the vehicle by which ministers may expound the views that their position in close touch with sources of information not available to the general public leads them to take, and by which they in turn, through the ordinary members of the House as well as through the press, may reach the electorate and influence the development of public opinion. The value of the House, moreover, lies not merely in providing these opportunities for the ventilation of opinion, both popular and authoritative, but in the fact that these opinions are there brought to a head, concentrated in a single unity of time and place, and allowed their full interplay, so that in the clash of views and the setting of one argument against another the questions at issue may be seen in their full significance and the decisions that emerge may be the best available, the final resultant of all the forces that make up our democracy.

Hence the member who contributes nothing of value to the debate, spends little time or care in listening to others, and in the divisions allows himself to become a pawn in the hands of the whips, is impairing the efficiency of the House and undermining the foundations of democratic government. It stands out beyond dispute that we need in our members not only the high standard of knowledge and ability that will enable them to play their proper part in the formulation and expression of policy, but also the integrity that will ensure that they do in fact play that part. We have to seek in this, not just the negative integrity of freedom from corruption, but the positive integrity that impels to an active realization of and obedience to the call of public duty.

We turn now from the functions of the House of Commons as the sounding-board of public opinion and the anvil of public policy to its functions as a legislative body. When opinion has been collected and integrated into policy, means must be found for giving effect to it, and the chief, though certainly not the only, means is by way of legislation. There is no need here to discuss the place of private members' bills in the programme of legislation: such a discussion would turn rather on questions of procedure than on questions of personnel, and, in any case, extraordinarily valuable and successful though private members' bills have occasionally been, they must be regarded in general as no more than a useful accessory: the great bulk of legislation must almost of necessity in modern conditions emerge from the bills put forward by the government. In any case we are more concerned to study the functions of the members of the House in relation to the legislative projects put before them than to consider the origin and genesis of those projects.

So far as second-reading debates are concerned there is little to be said, since they are essentially discussions of policy, and as such are, broadly speaking, subject to the same comments as any other policy discussions. It is in the committee stage chiefly that further considerations have to be taken into account. In what way does this stage make demands on the abilities and the activities of ordinary members of parliament beyond the giving of their votes, aye or no, as each division is called? There is, of course, a series of decisions to be reached on the various proposals in the bill, each of which proposals needs to be argued and supported or opposed on grounds of general policy. But beyond this, apart from the broad issues of policy involved, there is great need for the close and watchful scrutiny both of the bill itself and of the amendments to it that are put forward, clause by clause and almost line by line. The language of the parliamentary statute is highly specialized and sometimes almost unintelligible to ordinary people. It requires all the more to be examined with the greatest care to ensure that its real effect is what it purports to be, that nothing creeps into the act that the House did not intend to be there. Further, the bill requires watching to see that all the necessary "ifs" and "buts" have been included, and it needs scrutiny to make sure that when it becomes an act of parliament it will not have consequences that were not intended and are not desirable, perhaps in fields outside its own.

Parliamentary draftsmen are highly skilled in putting legislative proposals into statutory language, but the social and political consequences of those proposals are not their province, and they cannot be held responsible for them. That responsibility rests in the first case on the government that initiates the legislation, but it is a primary duty of the House of Commons to subject all bills brought before it to a vigilant, informed, and fearless criticism, and if need be to insist on amendment in the interests of the country. It is here that the critical faculties of ordinary members and their quick-wittedness, energy, persistence, and integrity can be of great service to the nation. Incidentally it is likely that, if they are people of wide practical knowledge, experience, and sympathy, they will from time to time be able to adduce pertinent facts or bring forward important considerations that might otherwise be overlooked. The ministers who decide the general lines of a bill, the civil servants who plan its provisions, and the draftsmen who put them into statutory shape, may all do their jobs honestly and efficiently; but they are at the centre of things and are not so cognizant of the needs and reactions of people at the circumference as are the private members, who know—or should know—the lives and thoughts and feelings of their constituents all over the country.

Nothing in these observations should be taken as advocating an increase in irresponsible or factitious criticism: on the contrary, it is suggested that a more serious and alert attitude on the part of members generally, and a higher average of intelligence and integrity in the House as a whole, would tend to decrease mere party "sniping" and obstructiveness—as it should also discourage the long, windy, repetitive speeches that are all too common now. Nevertheless, it is possible that if all members of parliament were as active, as competent, and as keen as we are suggesting they should be (and as, of course, some of them are now), it might lead to further congestion of business. The inept and perfunctory member who takes no real share in the proceedings of the House, beyond voting as he is told, is no doubt useful to the party leaders, particularly on the government side, just because his docility and inanity facilitate quick decisions of the sort they desire. One can understand the point of view of the whips on such matters: but the House of Commons does not exist to serve the convenience of either party leaders or whips. It is there as the central institution for securing the good government of the country on democratic lines, and that is infinitely more important than party advantage or ministerial convenience.

I suggest, then, that if increased keenness, greater competence, and a deeper sense of personal responsibility on the part of members in general should lead to any further congestion of business—which seems unlikely—the proper remedy is not the discouragement of those good qualities, but the drastic overhauling of the procedure of the House. In particular it seems probable that sooner or later the anachronistic and inconvenient "committee of the whole House" will have to give way to a much greater use of much smaller committees. Everyone with much experience knows that, broadly speaking, the efficiency of a committee is in inverse relation to its size: and parliamentary committees are no exception to this rule. The House itself is the proper place for the discussion of policy and for the taking of major decisions: for the discussion of details the proper place is a very much smaller committee. We cannot here enter into all the considerations involved in this suggested development—there is a considerable literature about it elsewhere*— but it is pertinent to our subject to suggest that improvements in the personnel of the House will demand as a corollary improved opportunities for making use of that personnel: and, notwithstanding the opposition there is to it at present, the abolition of committees of the whole House seems an almost essential step towards that end.

Another major function of the House of Commons is to exercise control over finance and administration. The rules governing the rights and responsibilities of the House in these important matters are based on long-standing tradition and practice and are decidedly complex. They need not be expounded here, however, since they can readily be ascertained from other sources,† and we are only interested for the time being in our special aspect of the matter.

It is chiefly by means of its examination of the estimates in Committee of Supply and of taxation in Committee of Ways and Means that the House exercises control over the actions of the executive government and the departments in the extremely important (and in practice almost inseparable) spheres of administration and finance. It is generally admitted that the powers of the House in these matters are not as effective as they should be, and that the machinery of control is in some respects at least ill adapted to its purpose. This is one of the many sections of the procedure of the House in which far-reaching reform is overdue. Meanwhile what part can the private member play in securing good administration? Is it not much the same part as has been suggested for him in relation to the committee stage of legislation: the part of an alert, informed, and watchful critic, the trusted and trustworthy spokesman of the ordinary men and women of the country he is there to represent? If he is to play this part adequately he must have an extensive fund of general knowledge, common sense, and shrewdness; he must have plenty of energy and endurance; and, above all, he must feel and respond to the trust reposed in him by his constituents: he must take his duties seriously and fulfil them scrupulously.

In all this he must, of course, have regard to the principles and policy

---

* See, for example, Ramsay Muir, *How Britain is Governed* (1933), chapter VI, section II; and W. Ivor Jennings, *Parliamentary Reform* (1934), chapter IV, section (e).

† Reference might be made, for example, to Sir Courtenay Ilbert, *Parliament* (1929), chapter IV, or to books of reference such as *Dod's Parliamentary Companion*.

of the party to which he belongs; but I suggest that the inevitable concomitant of a more serious and responsible attitude on the part of members generally is a diminished regard for mere party advantage, a lessened desire to score points over the other side for the sake of scoring them. It is time that the rather childish habit of treating politics as a game in which the chief object is to diddle your opponents were dropped altogether, and a more sober and adult outlook substituted. In saying this I am not suggesting that members in general are frivolous in their attitude: there is deep sincerity and devotion to principle to be found in all parties: but I do urge that the state of affairs in this respect still leaves much to be desired. It seems to me that good government in the future must depend increasingly on the recognition of the value of co-operation, even between people who differ widely in their political views. A ding-dong battle between the "ins" and the "outs" may be amusing, but it belongs to an earlier and cruder stage of civilization and it is time it gave way altogether to a higher view of statecraft. We may note in this connexion Sir Arnold Wilson's words: "Twenty years spent in the harness of official duty abroad, and half as many in commercial occupations, have convinced me that the intrusion of considerations of party upon national problems has usually been injurious."*

Apart from its more or less effective control of administration by means of its discussions of the estimates placed before it, the House of Commons exercises a salutary check on the day-to-day doings of ministers and of the services and departments by means of its interrogatory powers at question-time. This is an extraordinarily valuable part of parliamentary procedure, and serves not only for the supervision of administration in general, but also for the protection of the rights of the individual and the redress of grievances: a function of the House dating back to very ancient times and one that it fulfils with, on the whole, outstanding success. In this connexion the member will be the better able to fulfil his duties the more intimately acquainted he is with his constituency and his constituents, and the wider his human sympathies. He should understand something of the peculiar characteristics and needs of the chief industries and occupations followed in his division, should make himself familiar with local history and traditions and ways of thought, and keep in touch with its institutions and its people, not only in politics of all shades of opinion but in other spheres also. Only so can he be their representative in any full and satisfying way and, when occasion arises, their spokesman and champion. It would be a very fine thing if more members, of all parties, were to follow the admirable example of Sir Arnold Wilson in getting about on foot amongst the ordinary folk of his constituency, talking to them and listening to them, getting to know at first hand what the people of England were really saying and thinking amongst themselves.† To

* Sir Arnold Wilson, *Walks and Talks* (1934\, page 237.
† See his book *Walks and Talks* above mentioned. It is, on top of its other merits, absorbingly interesting.

address public meetings, open bazaars, and take part in party functions is not the same thing—it is very far from being the same thing. Informal personal talks, on the level, with individual men and women of varying creed and party and class are far more revealing than public gatherings, and far more valuable to the man or woman who has undertaken the arduous and responsible task of speaking and thinking and voting in parliament on behalf of so many thousands of his fellow-citizens. "If there were more Wilsons, men with a creed, taking their politics as a vocation and a great human charge, there wouldn't be any more meetings at the Albert Hall. . . ."*

One other function of the House of Commons remains to be mentioned, and that is the provision of a large proportion of the members of the government. Not every member of the House can become, or is fitted to become, or would even desire to become, a minister of the Crown: but clearly the better the quality of the membership of the House as a whole, the wider is the field from which ministers can be chosen and the higher the standard that can be set for office. Without any desire to be uncharitable, one cannot say that the general run of ministers and ex-ministers of any party offers many impressive examples of outstanding ability and character. Even some of the men who have been spoken of as potential prime ministers are of such a calibre as to suggest that, if they are the best we can find, the field of choice must be extraordinarily limited.

The high court of parliament should attract to its membership the very flower of the country's men and women, the people of exceptional qualities of mind and spirit, and the holding of office should be the privilege of the best amongst *them*. Of how many ministers and ex-ministers, if we are honest, can we say that they conform to that high standard? Not a big proportion, I fear. To be a good speaker, to have served the party loyally and long, to come of good family, to have attended a famous school, and so on—these are not in themselves fit criteria for the holding of office and the control of the destinies of the nation and maybe even of the world.

So, on this account as on the others we have considered, we are driven to accept the urgent necessity of a much higher standard for membership of the House. Even if we take a charitable and optimistic view of present standards, even if we think that members now are on the whole pretty good, we must, if we face the issues squarely, recognize that they collectively are not good enough. Only the best will serve our pressing need—and we are not in any substantial measure securing that best.

Let us now attempt to sum up the conclusions to which these various considerations tend. Let us survey briefly the characteristics that appear to be called for in the ideal member of parliament; and in so doing let us bear in mind all the time that we do not desire to specify a single narrow type, but merely to indicate something of the fundamental

* The *Morning Post*, in a review of *Walks and Talks*.

qualities that we should seek in those who are to voice our needs and aspirations, to guide our political progress, and to shape our social and economic destiny in so many ways. In attempting this summary it may be as well to pay attention not only to the more strictly personal qualities of mind and temperament and character, but also to such matters as age and occupation.

(i) INTEGRITY.—The position of a member of parliament is eminently one of trust and responsibility. It is a debased view that regards an election as merely a choice between contending factions as to which shall form a government and rule the country, and the candidates as no more than pawns in that contest. The major decisions of the country on policy and on choice of government should emerge naturally from the decisions in each constituency, and these local decisions should turn on the sober conclusions of an electorate that takes its duties seriously and weighs carefully the merits of the policies placed before it by informed, sincere, and capable candidates. That the verdict of the nation at the polls should be a verdict on policy is right and proper, but too often now it is a verdict based rather on personalities and party cries. If policy in any true sense is to be the issue, it must be expounded honestly by men and women who both understand and believe what they are saying. The candidate must fearlessly and with scrupulous fairness place his firmly held articles of faith before the electors, and not dish out to them, with his tongue in his cheek, whatever platitudes and promises party headquarters chooses to send down to him.

The candidate, then, must be honest enough and courageous enough to put the issues as he sees them and to resist pressure, whether from his own party organizers or from outside interests, to advocate courses of action in which he does not believe, or to promise results that he knows cannot be achieved. If he is elected the demands on his integrity will be correspondingly increased. As a member of parliament he must not merely avoid the obviously corrupt, the use of his voice and vote in the House to serve selfish ends, the seeking of personal advantage and reward, indulgence in nepotism, and so on. He must have virtue in its old and true sense: not a mere abstention from evil, but a positive, active, and effective will to good. He must speak and vote as his conscience dictates: he must give full attention and attach full weight to the views and advice of his leaders, but not be overruled by them: he must resist pressure from whatever quarter to misuse his position and powers.

He must, moreover, fulfil his manifold duties conscientiously and with untiring energy. He must keep himself worthy of the trust reposed in him and avoid slackness and carelessness. He must take his full share in the work of the House and not sacrifice the interests of his constituents and country to selfish ease or indolence. He must not hide neglect of real duty by pointing to the large number of divisions in which he has, without regard to their significance, participated, nor seek to gloss absenteeism by an occasional futile speech or the asking of frivolous questions.

Here is a call for a very high standard of probity and courage and zeal, and it may be that we shall be accused of highfalutin utopianism in putting it forward. But one of the major curses of political life and one of the things that bring politics into disrepute is the view that expediency is more important than principle and appearances of more value than integrity. Only when a higher standard of personal devotion and honesty is insisted upon shall we rid politics of the reproach of being "a dirty game".

(ii) INTELLIGENCE.—The daily life of the ordinary citizen is affected in a thousand ways by the decisions of parliament on policy, by its legislation, by its attitude to finance and administration, by the acts of the executive government at home and abroad, and by the multifarious activities of the services and departments. The work of government, in a broad sense, is of extraordinarily wide range and complexity in modern conditions, covering an infinity of matters, not only political and financial, but also social, economic, and even technological. Bills and acts of parliament, estimates and accounts, orders in council, statutory rules and orders, and departmental regulations, memoranda, and reports are in general highly complicated, embody a vast amount of technical detail, and are expressed in language not remarkable for its simplicity or straightforwardness. Hence, in spite of its continual impact on his work and play, on his living conditions, health, security, safety, and recreation, the ordinary citizen would be entirely at sea in the detailed business of parliament: he would not be able to grasp its significance, unravel its complications, or even understand its language.

It follows that the member of parliament, if he is to be master of his job and not just a party hack, must have intelligence and general mental qualities far above the average. He and his colleagues form the connecting medium between the political, legal, financial, and technical experts who carry on the day-to-day business of government and administration and the millions of ordinary men, women, and children for whose benefit or at whose expense all these activities are pursued. He needs to be ever on the alert, to be quick-witted and shrewd, able to grapple with multitudinous detail on the one hand and to take a broad view on the other. He must have a keenly critical mind, able to separate the essential from the inessential, to balance one consideration against another, and to exercise foresight and independence of judgement. It is not the abstract intellectual skill of the philosopher, the mathematician, or the chess-player, however, that is wanted, so much as the possession in a superlative degree of common sense, ready perceptions, and clear-headedness.

(iii) TEMPERAMENT.—Closely related to the question of intelligence is that of temperament. A man may have intelligence of a high order and yet not be fitted for the life of a member of parliament. To be a distinguished historian, a brilliant King's Counsel, a notable naval strategist, or a Fellow of the Royal Society implies the possession of exceptional intellectual gifts, but it does not guarantee suitability for or success in the House of Commons. To be fitted temperamentally for a parliamentary career a man or woman needs first and foremost a real interest in and taste for politics and public affairs. Without this his attention is likely to flag, and he will almost certainly find much of the work inexpressibly tedious and burdensome. He must have a good store of energy and driving force, yet be able to exercise patience. He should be fired with idealism and enthusiasm, yet be able to temper both with practicality. He needs a sense of humour and wide sympathies. He must be tolerant and able to see the other man's point of view without losing grip of his own aims. He should be something of a practical psychologist, and be interested in men and women of all classes as human beings and for their own sakes. He should be able to "talk with crowds and keep his virtue, or walk with Kings—nor lose the common touch".

(iv) EDUCATION. — Neither academic achievement nor profound erudition is any guarantee of fitness to participate in the affairs of parliament: yet it is evident that ignorance of history, of geography, of commerce, of the rudiments of economics and political and physical science, and of the broad framework of legislative and constitutional practice that forms the background of our social and political life, must severely handicap any member in the service of his constituents and his country. How can anyone, for instance, take part in or even follow a discussion on agricultural reform who is totally ignorant of the history and complex organization of our farming system and has no idea of the traditions and conditions in and by which it has evolved? How can he lend a hand with the intricate problems of unemployment, of social insurance, of foreign trade, of taxation, if he knows nothing of the fundamental concepts of economics, is unaware of the elementary facts of social and industrial history? How can he comprehend, let alone contribute to, a debate on colonial or international affairs if he is unread in modern history, has no clear notion of geography, is unacquainted with the traditions and outlook of other countries?

Parliamentary debates, whether on legislative proposals, on financial matters, or on broader issues, are unintelligible without the necessary background of knowledge, and the uninformed cannot safely even vote in the divisions—except as the docile vassals of the whips. Nor can members without a considerable equipment of knowledge and understanding exercise their functions as watchers over administration on behalf of the community. The ignorant member is not merely futile: he is a public danger.

Hence we must seek as our representatives enlightened men and women who, whether or no they are in the formal sense well educated, have read and thought widely, have a good knowledge of affairs, and possess an understanding of fundamental facts and principles. Naturally these requirements are most likely to be met by people who have had the advantages of secondary and university education; but we must not assume, on the one hand, that those who have missed such a training are necessarily unsuitable, nor, on the other, that the right to wear a famous old school tie is any guarantee of competence. It is the well-stored, active mind we seek, whatever may have been its process of development.

(v) AGE.—We have to consider the question of the optimum age (or rather age-range) for members from two points of view: first, in relation to the ages of the electors they represent; and, second, in relation to the duties they have to perform.

It is clearly desirable that the present state of affairs, in which the average age of members is much higher than the average age of the electors, should be changed. While no good purpose would be served by trying to secure a close correspondence between the two figures—and still less by trying to secure a close similarity of age-*distribution* in the two cases—it is yet eminently desirable that the House should not be so elderly as to be out of harmony with the thoughts and feelings and outlook of the community it represents. At present there is considerable ground for thinking that it is so: the disparity is far too great to be dismissed as unimportant. A House that over the whole inter-war period has averaged eight and a half years older than the electorate (and is now well over thirteen years older than it) is too much rooted in the past, too likely to bring to the problems of to-day the outlook of the day before yesterday.

Looking at the question from the other point of view, we have to ask ourselves whether we can expect from such a collection of old and elderly people as we now see included in the House the vigour of mind and body necessary to carry out the exacting tasks that membership, rightly understood, imposes on them. I remember, years ago, standing in one of the lobbies talking to a member and getting something of a shock when a number of other members came streaming past. Streaming?—it was a case of tottering with not a few. I was astounded at the number who seemed more or less decrepit: and that was a long time ago, when the average age of the House was a good deal less than it is now. A man's vigour of mind and body is not to be measured solely by the date of his birth—one man will be more fully alive and active at seventy than another is at fifty—but the House is no place for the senile. We need people as members who are mentally and spiritually in the prime of life, and physically at least reasonably fit, if we are to be worthily represented.

So, from either point of view, we see the need for a marked rejuvenation of the House. I hesitate to suggest an upper age-limit: though most public servants (except judges) must retire, however fit they are, at sixty-five or sixty or even younger. But at least it should be an understood thing that it isn't done for members to cling to their seats when they are no longer able to carry out their duties properly. However great their past services, they should realize, and if necessary be told bluntly, that it is time in the public interest that they made way for fitter people.

But if the old and too elderly should drop out, we do not want them replaced by the juvenile. At twenty-one a youth is too immature, too inexperienced, to make a really competent member of parliament, and even in the middle twenties that is still usually the case. It is true that Pitt entered the House at twenty-two and Gladstone at twenty-three, but that proves little. Men of exceptional genius are always a law unto themselves, and, moreover, there is no reason to suppose that had those great men deferred their entry for a few years, meanwhile obtaining useful experience in other walks of life, the country would have been the loser. We have in any case to plan for the more ordinary men and women who must always supply the great majority of members.

The nearest approach we have to the "professional politician", in the sense of the man who is a politician and nothing more, is to be found in the youngster who enters parliament in his early twenties; and I suggest that we do not want professional politicians in that sense. (Of course, the fact that members are paid for their services makes them in the sense in which the term is used in the field of sport "professional", but that criterion is of no significance for our purpose.) We do not want dilettante members—we have too many now. We want earnest and devoted men and women who for the time being will give themselves heart and soul to their parliamentary duties, but if we wish to avoid the narrow "professional politician" it is all the more important to discourage unduly early entry. I suggest that every member of the House of Commons ought to have acquired real experience of life, outside politics, before he enters the House. This point will be developed more fully in connexion with the question of occupation, but meanwhile it indicates that there should be a lower limit of entry of, say, thirty years of age, with an optimum age of entry of, say, thirty to forty.

In his early thirties a man has ten years or so of adult life behind him, and if he has used the time well he will not only have acquired an experience of men and affairs that will be invaluable to him in the House, but will also have developed those qualities of mind and temperament and personality that he needs for his political duties. He will still be a young man, full of vigour and energy, with twenty or thirty or more years before him in which to serve the country. He will, indeed, still be some dozen years younger than the average new member is at present: a remarkable and significant fact.

It may possibly be suggested that, since so few members now enter under thirty, there is no need formally to exclude younger men. But under improved conditions, such as we shall presently suggest, there might well be an influx of very young people unless some such restriction were imposed; and in any case it would be all to the good to take a step which would serve to raise the status of membership, to indicate that it is a serious obligation calling for matured gifts and not a job that any callow youth can be allowed to undertake.

To sum up, then, we envisage a state of affairs in which the normal age of entry to the House of Commons will be in the thirties (though without excluding older entrants), and in which membership will cease as soon as a member is past giving fully efficient service. We should then have a House filled with men and women in the prime of life, experienced but vigorous and active, and with an average age not differing greatly from the average age of the adult population as a whole.

(vi) OCCUPATION.—Most thinking people in this country will agree that the basis of representation in the House of Commons should continue to be territorial rather than occupational: we do not want to change over to the Italian "corporative" system or anything like it. Most will agree, also, that we do not want a system in which members of parliament are all or mostly "professional politicians", people who are politicians and nothing else. These postulates require that members, while elected to represent places rather than professions or trades, shall nevertheless in the main be people who follow or have followed some occupation other than politics.

This, of course, is broadly the system we have at present.* But in existing conditions it leads, as we have already seen, to an unsatisfactory state of affairs on this question of occupation. Certain occupations have an enormous number of representatives in the House, while others are hardly represented at all. A man's occupation is one of the major interests of his life, and it greatly influences his outlook on all sorts of matters. It is clearly undesirable, therefore, that the distribution of occupations in the House shall be so lopsided that certain points of view are over-stressed, while others are ignored. We have accordingly to try to secure a better balance of occupational experience amongst members. This is a very different thing, and directed to very different ends, from any attempt to secure a strictly proportional representation of all occupations. We do not and cannot wish to see the House filled with labourers, factory hands, clerks, shop assistants, and domestic servants merely because those occupations are followed by large numbers of people. While they should in no sense be debarred from its membership, it is highly improbable that they could normally supply more than a very few candidates capable of fulfilling all the exacting conditions we have already seen to be desirable. All we seek in this respect is that the House should draw its members from as wide a range of occupations as is consistent with other requirements, and that the distribution of members over those occupations should be such as to avoid giving excessive emphasis to particular types of opinion.

There is, however, another aspect of the matter that deserves consideration. Laski, in declaiming against the idea of parliament as "a collection of distinguished experts", has pointed out that eminence in business, or engineering, or economics, or medicine, is no proof of

---

* It may be noted that, all the same, we now have in effect a certain number of "professional politicians" in the persons of the peers' sons and the like who enter the House straight from Oxford or Cambridge, and some amount of occupational representation in the areas where only a miner has any real chance of election.

talent for the art of statesmanship.* That is very true: but it is not the whole truth, even in this context. Parliament has to deal not merely with big political issues in such fields as foreign affairs, war and peace, and taxation. It has also increasingly to concern itself with social, economic, and technical problems, and these often involve issues that cannot be adequately solved without expert guidance and expert criticism. It is true, of course, that the government of the day has at its disposal in the services and departments an array of experts: but they are generally committed to a particular point of view—in many cases what we might term the Whitehall point of view. Moreover, they take no direct part in the discussions in the House, nor could they in any case be expected to criticize the reports or proposals they have themselves prepared, or even to see all the facets of a subject on which there may be differences of opinion even amongst those qualified to judge.

In these circumstances it is often of very great advantage to the House of Commons and the country if the House has in its ranks medical men who can speak with expert knowledge on questions of public health, agriculturists who know the problems of farming from the inside, engineers who can criticize with authority big power schemes, and so on. Hence, while it would be foolish to put people into parliament merely or chiefly because of their distinction in other fields (though cases of that sort are not unknown now), when men or women who have entered the House because of their interest in and capacity for political life can bring to the work upon occasion special gifts of knowledge or experience we should be thankful for the advantage we derive from their talents. The trouble at present is that while the House of Commons is full of specialists—legal, naval, commercial, mining, and so forth—there are far too many of some kinds and not enough of others. So for this reason also it is desirable to get a wider distribution of occupations in the House.

One more point: all the considerations we have discussed indicate the importance of having as members of parliament people who can give their whole time and energy to its duties and enter the House at a fairly early age. If changes in these directions lead to the replacement of retired generals and admirals, crusted bankers and business men, and superannuated trade-union officials by younger men and women, not too deeply enmeshed in their trades and professions yet well in touch with their current needs and outlook, it will be all to the good. Times change: and people whose thoughts and feelings and experiences are too deeply rooted in the past are not those who can best serve us in dealing with the problems of the present and future.

* H. J. Laski, *Democracy in Crisis* (1933), page 79.

CHAPTER XXI

THE FIELD OF REFORM

WE have now discussed and defined the aims to which it is suggested any scheme of reform of parliamentary representation should be directed. Before passing to the consideration of definite proposals for specific reforms, let us try to bring our various lines of thought together into a synthesis that will serve as a connecting link between those abstract aims on the one hand and concrete plans for their realization on the other. We have to determine more precisely the directions in which reforms are necessary and the field that they should cover.

We desire, in the first place, to make the electoral franchise both *real* and *effective*. It should be *real* in the sense that the elector should have the opportunity to exercise his vote at every election, and that at each election he should have a sufficient choice of candidates to enable him to use that vote with a considerable amount of discrimination. It should be *effective* in the sense that, within the limits of what is practicable, every vote should have the effect that the voter desires it to have, and every vote throughout the country should have the same weight.

The present system fails to satisfy either criterion. Under it the franchise is not *real* because (*a*) when, as frequently happens, there is no contest the elector cannot vote at all; (*b*) when there is a contest there may be no candidate who holds, even in the broadest sense, the political views of the elector; and (*c*) even if there is a candidate of the elector's own party, the elector has normally no means of expressing his opinion of that candidate's personal fitness for election. It is not *effective* because (*a*) within the constituency the elector's vote does not necessarily or even usually produce the effect he desires it to produce—often, indeed, it produces no effect at all; and (*b*) votes given by different electors do not have, even approximately, the same weight in contributing to the final result of the elections as a whole.

Let us pause here to remark, once for all, that nothing in these comments or in what follows is to be taken as suggesting that every elector can or should expect to have as his representative in parliament a member who exactly shares his own views or has precisely the personal qualities he would desire him to have. We suggest nothing beyond what can be shown to be feasible, and nothing should be read into our arguments in any other sense.

Without a franchise that is both real and effective in the sense we have specified, the elector cannot make that full contribution to good government that we have taken as one of our fundamental aims; and within the framework of the present electoral system the franchise cannot be made real and effective. The single-member majority system is intrinsically unsound for the following reasons: (*a*) Where one party is much in the majority there is a direct encouragement to unopposed returns, and even if the seat is contested the election is a farce, since the result is a foregone conclusion. (*b*) Where parties are more evenly balanced we have either a two-party contest, in which case the electors of the third party are left out in the cold, or else we have a three-party contest with the strong probability that the seat will go to a minority candidate. So whether there are candidates of one or two or three parties contesting the seat the position is, in different ways, almost equally unsatisfactory. (*c*) In any event the elector has no say in the matter of the personal fitness of the candidates, since normally there will be no more than one candidate, if that, whose views are at all acceptable to him. These are grave defects; and it should be stressed that they are not accidental, local, or occasional flaws: they are defects that are inherent in the system.

The retention of the present system of voting is therefore fundamentally inconsistent with the achievement of the aims that we have set before us, and it must give way to a totally different system if the franchise is to be made a real instrument of democratic government. What we have to seek is not merely a palliative for the grosser and more obvious defects of the present method: we need constructive reforms that will put parliamentary elections on an altogether wider, sounder, and more positively representative basis. It is not a case for tinkering: it is a case for crying, "O, reform it altogether!"

In the second place, we desire to encourage, and as far as possible ensure, the election to parliament of the men and women best fitted to carry out its varied tasks. We want to see the House of Commons composed of people who have the right kind of personality and experience and have them in the highest possible degree, and we want them to give their full attention and energies to their parliamentary duties. Let us recognize that the House already attracts to the service of the country many men and women of fine quality, well equipped for their duties and carrying them out with zeal and distinction: but do not let that blind us to the facts that there are other members poorly qualified and lacking in the right spirit, that many members give little more than their spare time to their duties, and that the general level of ability and character is not nearly as high as it could and should be. The second-rate and third-rate are not good enough: we want first-rate members and we want their full service.

We have to bear in mind also that the present composition of the House is in many respects extraordinarily lopsided: that certain elements, certain interests, certain types of personality and experience, are altogether too predominant. We cannot afford to continue a state of affairs in which relatively small and specialized sections of the community have overwhelming representation, while other and larger sections are shut out completely. We want a better-balanced House, one more truly representative of the community it exists to serve.

All these considerations point to the necessity for drawing our members from a much wider field than we do at present. The number of people in any walk of life who fulfil our exacting requirements is not likely to be great, and if we are to secure the best of them we cannot afford to neglect any potential source of supply. The wider our net is cast, the better is our chance of securing that best and at the same time of getting a more truly representative House. Moreover, although the interests of the country come first and are the main argument for this widening of the sources of supply, we should not lose sight of another aspect of the matter. The phrase "equality of opportunity" has lately become something of a catchword and, like all catchwords, has tended in the process to become discredited. Nevertheless it stands for something that should be a very real feature of democratic institutions: the right of the individual to a fair chance of using his abilities to their best advantage, irrespective of the accidents of birth and wealth and the privileges that go with them, and in this context it provides a further reason for drawing our members of parliament from all classes of the community equally instead of in the main from a few privileged sections as we do at present.

To say this is not to assert that all men are equal and equally fitted for service in parliament: it is merely to insist that we should seek the best, wherever it is to be found, without fear or favour. We have no right to behave as though because X is the son of a peer and was educated at Eton and Balliol he has a prescriptive right to a seat in the House and to preferential treatment in the choice for ministerial office, while Y, because he is the son of a mechanic and left a grammar school at sixteen, must be excluded from even the chance of standing for parliament: yet that is much the sort of way in which our present system works. If X is the better man and can give the better service, as may well be the case, let him be chosen: but let the choice be made on merit and not on the colour of his tie, the length of his purse, or the rank of his father. In any event people who are what is called "well born" will always and unavoidably have great advantages: let us not allow the dice to be further loaded in their favour by prejudice or nepotism or by so fixing the conditions of election to and service in the House that men and women of first-rate quality are excluded, while people who are intrinsically inferior, though more fortunately placed financially and socially, easily secure seats.

It is, of course, perfectly legitimate to argue that aristocratic government of one sort or another is preferable to democratic government. But if we accept democracy as the basis of our institutions the conclusions we have drawn seem irrefutable. Democracy does not require that we shall invert the pyramid and let the ignorant and incompetent rule, but it does require that people who are eminently suitable shall not be excluded from a share in government merely because they lack wealth or are of humble origin. It follows that the present arrangements are inconsistent with a truly democratic way of life, for they impose financial and other barriers that have no justification of necessity or wisdom. The fact that a limited number of people of small means secure election by reason of trade-union backing does not invalidate this contention: it merely indicates that certain people of a particular class and belonging to a particular party have found a means, more or less satisfactory, of getting round those barriers, whereas we are pleading that the barriers should not be there.

It follows that we must find means by which the cost of contesting an election shall not impose anything like so heavy a burden on candidates as it does now, so that suitable people of moderate means—ordinary professional and middle-class men and women, for example—shall not be excluded from standing for parliament merely because they cannot face the expense of the election, and so that unsuitable people of wealth shall be deprived of one of the means they are now able to employ for purchasing a seat. If it be argued against this that it would open the gates so wide that every constituency would be flooded with candidates, the answer is clear. Should it be found necessary to apply special measures in order to keep down the number of candidates to a reasonable level, then let it be done without infringing the principles of democracy: financial barriers are not a legitimate way of doing it, for wealth is not in itself any criterion of fitness for parliamentary service.

The cost of elections is, however, not the only financial obstacle that stands in the way of our getting the wide choice of potential candidates that we desire. A member of parliament must live, and the official allowance of salary and expenses is, as we have seen, insufficient for his needs. Consequently these allowances must be made more adequate. The principle of payment of members having been conceded years ago, it is illogical as well as unjust to keep the rates as low as they are at present: they should be brought up to such a standard that any member who is reasonably economical can live on them without privation and without having to supplement them by private means, by trade-union or other subsidy, or by following an occupation that interferes with his parliamentary activities or detracts from his efficiency as a member. This could easily be done without making a political career so lucrative that it would attract people whose main object in life is financial gain. The monetary rewards of success at the bar, on the stock exchange, or in commerce, industry, or banking would still be far and away greater than those of a member of parliament. Moreover, under the complete scheme of reorganization that we envisage, including fundamental changes in the methods of election, the mere careerist would not find it easy to get himself elected.

With improved remuneration for members of parliament we should not only widen the field from which we could draw members, with all the direct advantages that that would give, but should also aim a further blow at the selling of seats and do away with any excuse for members giving to some other full-time or near-full-time occupation the time and energy that they ought to devote to their political duties. Yet another beneficial result would be that, by opening the doors of parliament to people of occupations that are now almost completely excluded and placing people of many different professions and occupations more nearly on a level in this respect, we should do something to remedy the present serious lopsidedness of the House of Commons and reduce the excessive number of lawyers, company directors, trade-union officials, and certain other types that it now contains. A whole series of distinct though interrelated advantages would therefore accrue.

These financial changes, by which the burden of election costs would be lightened and the member of parliament ensured a reasonably sufficient livelihood, would, however, fail in considerable measure to secure the results at which we are aiming if we did not take account of another difficulty that the would-be member of limited means has to face. As we have seen, dissolutions of parliament take place at very short notice—in 1935 it was only six days from the first intimation that a dissolution was impending to its actual happening—and in consequence members who have no private financial resources on which to fall back are faced with the prospect of losing their seats and their remuneration as members at very short notice and so being suddenly left unoccupied and penniless. To be consistent, therefore, and to make the reforms we are envisaging a reality, we must seek to make some provision for the needs of such members in this respect also. How this should be done we shall have to discuss later, but we must put it on the map now as one small part of the field of reform.

All these financial reforms together would not in themselves, however, suffice to ensure fully the improvement in the personnel of the House of Commons that we have set out to achieve. Though they are essential to that end, they are to a certain extent negative in character in that they remove obstacles in the way of getting a better and more representative House, rather than provide incentives for the better selection of candidates in the first instance and the more discriminating choice amongst those candidates subsequently. Moreover, they remove only one set of obstacles, and other formidable ones remain in the nature of our present system of voting. Under that system we cannot expect to get the best possible members, since, in Lord Hugh Cecil's words, "The people have, in practice, only an opportunity of choosing between the party candidates submitted to their choice;"* and since, as he points out, "It is the ardent partisans . . . who choose the candidates." So long as this is the case, so long will the choice of candidates be made chiefly to serve party ends rather than the interests of the country and of good government, and so long will the electors be forced to accept second-rate and third-rate members. Party leaders, party caucuses, and party organizers have a natural preference for the "sound party man", the man who will always vote as they want him to vote and will give no trouble by thinking for himself and putting principle before expediency—in short, for the "yes-man"—and so long as the electors are compelled to vote on purely party lines, so long will candidates be selected for party reasons, with little regard for personal fitness.

* Lord Hugh Cecil, *Conservatism* (1912), page 237.

This state of affairs, moreover, encourages the exercise of undue influence in the choice of candidates, whether by local magnates or sectional bodies or by outside interests, industrial, commercial, financial, or what not. This is particularly the case with the "safe seats", where the party caucus can put in a fool, or a slacker, or even a knave, without much fear of losing the seat. Security of tenure should depend on a member's personal fitness and distinction and not on the accidents of geography. At present the dud member who has got himself a safe seat by influence or purchase can stick there pretty well for life, while the ablest and most distinguished of members, if he happens to sit for a so-called "fickle" division, may lose his seat at any time.

Further, we need to make better provision for highly qualified men and women who are genuinely independent in their political outlook and can find no proper place in any of the three major parties. Such people are never likely to be numerous, but they have a valuable part to play and should not be excluded from parliament by the pressure of the party machines operating through the electoral system. The chief justification for the university seats under the present system is that they have occasionally enabled us to gain the services of outstanding men and women—for example, Eleanor Rathbone and A. P. Herbert—who, because of their independence, might have found it difficult, if not impossible, to secure election in an ordinary single-member constituency dominated by the party struggle. But there are objections to the plural voting involved in the university franchise, and in any case it should be possible for people of distinguished mind and character to stand successfully as independent candidates in any constituency in the country.

Even within the major parties, moreover, there are from time to time people who are driven by the strength of their convictions to dissent altogether from some course of action or piece of policy adopted by the party to which they belong, and who in consequence are turned out of their seats or at the least placed in an extremely difficult position. We may instance the Unionist free-trade members in the early part of the century and the Duchess of Atholl and Sir Stafford Cripps more recently. While one can understand the party point of view in such cases, it is not right that people who add to notable gifts of mind and conscience the high quality of courage should thereby be excluded from the House: we cannot afford to lose them, whether or no we agree with their politics. Yet the present electoral system tends inexorably to squeeze them out of their seats.

So for all these reasons we see that the retention of the single-member majority system is inconsistent with the aims we have set before us of securing the very best personnel we can to represent us in the House of Commons. These arguments, based on the influence of the system on the choice of candidates and the quality of members, reinforce those that we discovered in connexion with the voters' side of the electoral question. Hence from both points of view the present system stands condemned, and we are driven to seek its replacement by a new and altogether better system.

We have now got the field of reform mapped out and are in a position to translate the general aims formulated and discussed in Chapter XIX and elaborated in certain respects in Chapter XX into specific proposals for reform in various directions. Let us see what we have decided is necessary to be done: the main headings are as follows:

1. The lightening of the burden of election expenses that at present falls on candidates.

2. The improvement of the remuneration of members.

3. The making of some provision to meet the financial difficulties of members who lose their seats.

4. The abolition of the single-member majority system of election and its replacement by a better system.

To these we may add one more heading:

5. The making of such subsidiary changes as are necessary or desirable to supplement the main reforms and to rid the system of parliamentary representation of anomalies and minor defects.

In the remaining chapters, then, we shall put forward and discuss definite and detailed suggestions for the carrying out of these reforms. It may perhaps be as well to remark here that though we have considered and must consider these matters more or less piecemeal, they should nevertheless be regarded as integral parts of a considered whole, and it should be realized that their full effect can be obtained only in combination with each other.

CHAPTER XXII

FINANCIAL REFORM

HAVING now discussed both the aims of reform and the directions which reform should take, it remains only to suggest practical ways of giving effect to our conclusions. The reader is asked to bear in mind in all that follows that we are aiming not merely to remedy this or that defect but to place the whole system of parliamentary representation on a very much sounder footing. Each individual proposal must accordingly be considered as part of a comprehensive scheme and judged in that light, for each of them can achieve its full effect only in conjunction with the rest. We will devote this chapter to the financial problems that have to be solved and then pass on to the complementary questions.

We have first to seek means of lightening the burden of election expenses that falls on candidates. It seems clear that the only way of doing this in harmony with the spirit of our aims as a whole is by the transference of some part of the burden to the state. Possibly at first sight this suggestion may arouse doubts on grounds of general principle, but a little consideration will show that there is no need for hesitation on that score. Quite apart from any question of "equality of opportunity" and of individual rights, it is in the public interest that we should secure the best possible members and therefore that candidates otherwise eminently suitable should not be shut out by reason of their inability to face the expense of an election. Expenditure necessary to secure this result is therefore a legitimate charge on public funds. It may be noted, too, that the principle has already been conceded, since free postage is at present provided for candidates' election addresses. If it is right for the state to meet this expense, it cannot be wrong for it to meet others. The proposed development therefore involves no departure from established principle, and the extent to which it should be made is simply a question of expediency.

Nevertheless it is desirable from every point of view that any assistance granted should be given in such a way as to offer the least possible encouragement to frivolous or factional candidates, and I accordingly suggest that the state should pay towards each candidate's election expenses a sum calculated on the basis of the number of valid votes recorded *for that candidate*. On this footing the amount of help a candidate received would depend on the extent to which his candidature was endorsed by the votes of the electors. Sectional and "freak" candidates would get correspondingly little aid.

At what rate should this grant be made? The answer to this question must depend to some extent on whether or no the present methods of election are assumed to be still in force. Later on we shall propose the replacement of the present system by a better one, but it will avoid complications if at this stage we assume current methods to be still in force: any modifications of detail necessitated by a different way of voting could easily be made when the time arrived. Even so, it is necessary to consider certain general aspects of election expenses before we formulate a definite answer to the question.

The present legal maximum expenditure per elector on the register is 6d. in a county division and 5d. in a borough division, but these legal maxima are seldom reached or even nearly reached in practice. Taking averages over the country as a whole, Labour candidates spend only about one-third of the permissible sum, Liberal candidates only about one-half, and even Conservative candidates only about seven-tenths. For all parties together in contested elections the average expenditure is only about one-half of the legal maximum. It seems clear, therefore, that the legal maxima have been fixed at quite unnecessarily high figures.

Now, the object of the proposed grant in aid of election expenses is not to increase the amounts spent but to decrease the strain on the resources of candidates and so to widen the field from which the latter may be drawn. Hence it is desirable that the legal maxima should be reduced to figures more in accordance with what actual experience has shown to be necessary: otherwise the effect of any grant made might be to increase outlay all round, while still leaving the poorer candidates and parties at an unfair disadvantage. Making allowance for the fact that some constituencies are necessarily more expensive to work than others, I suggest that the maximum expenditure per elector be reduced from 6d. to 5d. in county divisions and from 5d. to 4d. in borough divisions. This would still leave the maxima well above the current average expenditure of Conservative candidates and a long way above that of Liberal and Labour candidates. The amount of the grant might then be fixed at double the legal maximum; that is, at 10d. in county divisions and 8d. in boroughs. In considering this suggestion it is important to bear in mind that, whereas the legal maximum is per elector on the register, the grant would be per valid vote recorded for the candidate in question. Needless to say, the present limitations and safeguards should continue to apply: the grant would be in aid of permissible expenditure and would give no licence to go outside the existing regulations.

Let us see what this means in practice by taking an example of an actual election result. In the 1935 election for Central Portsmouth the pertinent figures were as follows:

Electors on roll	50,558
Votes given to Conservative candidate ...	21,578
Votes given to Labour candidate	10,733
Votes given to Liberal candidate	3,612

The corresponding expenditures, permissible and actual, and the grants that would have been payable on the proposed basis are therefore as follows:

	Present Legal Maximum* £	Actual Expenses Incurred*† £	Proposed Legal Maximum* £	Proposed Grant Payable £
Conservative	1,053	702	843	719
Labour	1,053	195	843	358
Liberal	1,053	566	843	120
Total	£3,160	£1,463	£2,528	£1,197

It will be observed that in the cases of the Conservative and Labour candidates the grants that would be payable under the proposed regulations are in excess of the actual expenses incurred. But three observations must be made on that point: first, that the figures given for actual expenditure do not include the agents' fees or the personal expenses of the candidates (these amounted to £115 for the Conservative, £32 for the Labour, and £81 for the Liberal candidate); second, that had the grant been payable the Labour candidate at least would no doubt have spent a more adequate amount on his campaign; and, third, that in any event grant would not be payable beyond the actual expenditure.

* Excluding in each case the agent's fee and the personal expenses of the candidate. Figures are taken to the nearest pound.
† *Return of Election Expenses, 1935* (H.C. 150, 1936).

In this particular instance two of the candidates did very badly, the Liberal indeed forfeiting his deposit, and the total poll was poor. In other divisions with a higher poll the allowances payable would have been correspondingly higher. It is one of the merits of the proposal that it would give most assistance to the candidates who proved to be most acceptable to the electorate: indeed, the electors themselves would decide by their votes the amounts of grant payable. Of course, if there were no contest no allowances would be payable; so that the scheme would tend to discourage unopposed returns. But as we should hope to abolish these in any case by changes in the method of election, there is no need to dwell on that point.

It will be seen that the proposal gives little encouragement to frivolous or "freak" candidatures: the less support a candidate gets from the voters, the less grant he receives. A candidate who polled only 451 votes, as one candidate did in 1935,* would get only just over £15 as his grant. It would, of course, be possible to insert a lower limit (for instance, the familiar one-eighth of the total votes recorded, or one-tenth of those votes) below which no candidate would receive any grant; but this would seem rather a petty rule and might do more harm than good. I would, indeed, abolish the present requirement of a deposit of £150 by each candidate, and the accompanying rule as to forfeiture. This would save much time and trouble to all parties and would be unlikely to cause any countervailing difficulty. The deposit does not now prevent an occasional "freak" candidate from standing, and on the other hand it bears hardly on many candidates who by no stretch of the imagination could be regarded as "freaks". In the 1935 election no fewer than eighty-one candidates forfeited their deposits, and of these the great majority were put forward by organized parties. †

The adoption of this proposed reform should do much to improve the conditions affecting the choice of candidates, placing the whole business on a healthier and more equitable basis. It would decrease the opportunities for the "selling of seats", and lower one of the barriers that at present keep many suitable people from coming forward as candidates. But to lower one barrier is not sufficient in itself, and unless we deal with the others also this particular reform will lose much of its good effect.

We accordingly turn to the vital question of the livelihood of members of parliament. As we have seen, the present arrangements are such that on this score alone membership of the House of Commons is, in practice, limited almost entirely to people belonging to one or other of four rather exceptional groups: (i) persons of fairly substantial private means; (ii) persons following a few particular occupations that can be fitted in, more or less satisfactorily, with membership; (iii) persons subsidized by a trade union or other body; and (iv) persons who, relatively

---

* The Independent candidate at North Camberwell.
† *The Times House of Commons, 1935*, page 168.

late in life, have retired on pension or on their savings. There are reasons why none of these categories can be regarded as particularly suitable,* and in any case we want to widen the field and be able to draw our members from the ranks of *all* suitable people, wherever they may be found and whatever their occupation—and while they are still in the prime of life.

The first and most obvious change that is needed is an increase in the salary and expenses allowance paid to a member of parliament. The present figure of £600 per annum (£500 as salary and £100 as expenses) should be increased to, say, £1,000 per annum (£800 as salary and £200 as expenses), as that seems to provide about the minimum income on which a member can maintain his position. It is essential, if the aims we have in view are to be attained, that the amount shall be fixed high enough to obviate any necessity for the member to supplement his income by following another occupation concurrently, or by accepting a subsidy from a trade union or similar body, though we do not want to see it fixed so high that the financial rewards would in themselves become a main inducement to stand for parliament. Those whose chief object in life is to make money, however, would find prizes far more glittering awaiting them in commerce and banking, stockbroking and the bar, and would see little to stir their ambitions in a mere £1,000 a year. It may be noted in passing that the corresponding figure in the United States of America is £2,000 a year.†

It is suggested that the full amount of salary and expenses should be paid to all members, irrespective of their income from other sources. That seems desirable, in the first place, in order to make it clear that members, rich and poor alike, are paid for their services and are correspondingly expected to take their duties seriously. There should be no opportunity for a member to argue that as he was unpaid he was therefore entitled to take things easily. In the second place, it is desirable in order to prevent any chance that rich would-be candidates might put forward, and local caucuses accept, the proposition that by selecting *them* economies in public expenditure would be effected. That would be against the whole spirit of the proposals we are considering.

The payment of the grant towards election expenses would make those expenses no longer a serious obstacle to the candidature of persons of limited means who were otherwise acceptable, and the payment of the increased salary and expenses allowance would make it possible for such persons, if elected, to follow a parliamentary career without being reduced to penury or forced to supplement their income in other ways. But these people would still have to face the ever-present possibility of a general election in which they might lose their seats, and consequently their livelihood, at a few days' notice. This is a risk that,

---

* To put it very briefly, the first may give us "professional politicians" without useful experience, the second are likely to treat membership as merely a spare-time extra, the third may be unduly subservient to the subsidizing body, and the fourth may be too elderly and lack vitality.

† *Whitaker's Almanack, 1943*, page 595.

if not obviated, would in many cases be sufficiently formidable to nullify the good effects that might otherwise be expected from the two reforms already suggested. It is essential, therefore, to make provision against it.

Accordingly I propose that every member of parliament should have the right, on ceasing to be a member, to continue to receive for a limited time that part of his remuneration that ranks as *salary*—that is, £800 per annum—subject to the following restrictions:

(*a*) If he has any other source of income the payment of this "continued salary" should be at such a rate that his total income will not exceed, say, £1,000 per annum. For example, with a private income of £300 per annum he would receive £700 per annum as continued salary. The objections that apply in the case of members to taking income from other sources into account do not apply in the case of ex-members.

(*b*) The length of time during which this "continued salary" should be paid should not exceed the length of the member's immediately previous service in the House. For instance, a member who lost his seat after eighteen months of service would only be entitled to "continued salary" for a further eighteen months. This proviso is desirable in order to avoid excessive payments in cases such as those of members who gain their seats at by-elections and lose them a few weeks later at general elections.

(*c*) The maximum length of time for which "continued salary" should be paid to an ex-member should be fixed at, say, three years from the date at which he ceases to be a member. This limitation is a natural and reasonable one, since the object of paying "continued salary" is not to provide the ex-member with a pension, but to give him, on the one hand, the means of bridging a short gap in his parliamentary service, and, on the other hand, if he has relinquished his means of earning a living in order to enter parliament, to give him the opportunity of re-establishing himself in ordinary life.

(*d*) Members voluntarily resigning their seats should be ineligible for "continued salary" unless their resignations were due to ill-health or some similar good reason beyond their control. Probably, however, a decision not to seek renomination at a general election should not be regarded as constituting resignation for this purpose.

With these safeguards there should be little fear of any abuse of this provision, which, on the other hand, should save members and their families from excessive anxiety about the future, and correspondingly increase their efficiency.

These three reforms, taken together as interdependent parts of a considered whole, would do much to widen the field of choice of parliamentary candidates. They would provide something like a reasonable embodiment of "equality of opportunity" and would remove the reproach attaching to the present system that it excludes from the House of Commons on purely financial grounds many men and women who are otherwise excellently qualified for membership. In remedying this

14

injustice to the individual the reforms would simultaneously give us a more representative House, with a more varied background of experience and occupation. Certain interests and professions that now get an altogether excessive share of the membership would have to be content with a more modest share, while other interests and professions that are now more or less left out in the cold would secure a reasonable chance of representation. It would be a better-balanced House in many ways, and on the whole probably a more serious and more hard-working House.

It is perhaps desirable to make it clear that it is not intended that members should be formally precluded from following some other occupation concurrently with membership. The question how far such a practice should be allowed might, I suggest, be left to the good taste and sense of responsibility of members on the one hand, and to the judgement of the electors and party organizers on the other. What we are aiming at in these proposals is not an inquisitorial control of members' private lives, but a removal of the necessity for them to follow another more or less full-time occupation while in the House. It would take time for these reforms, even when put into force, to attain their full effect, but I think that gradually it would come to be accepted that it was not "playing the game" for members to allow outside occupations to absorb any substantial share of the time and energy that they could and should devote to their parliamentary duties. Far better than any system of prohibitions would be the natural growth of a higher conception of a member's responsibility to his constituents and his country : and the suggested reforms should provide the first steps towards encouraging that growth.

Another question altogether that may be thought to demand some consideration is that of the monetary cost of putting these proposals into force. It is clearly not possible to give any close estimate of this cost, since so much would depend on the frequency with which elections occurred. Taking the average over a term of years, however, I estimate that the total cost for all three financial reforms together would not exceed about £500,000 a year and might be substantially less. At first sight that may seem a fairly large sum, but in relation to the national income it is a small one. It is probably seen in better proportion when we notice that it works out at barely 4d. per elector per annum. Fourpence per elector per annum!—not a large amount to pay for measures of reform of far-reaching value to our system of government. I suggest that the achievement of the results at which we are aiming would be well worth the outlay if the monetary cost were very much greater.

It should be borne in mind, too, that the money spent on grants towards election costs, which account for roughly half the total, would not be added expenditure : it would in the main be simply a transfer of expenditure. Instead of the costs in question falling on individual candidates, party subscribers, and trade unions, it would fall on the electors as a whole—and that is surely to the good. Why should not the community pay for the services it receives, instead of allowing the burden to fall mainly on those who already, by their zeal and enthusiasm and hard work, contribute so much to the political needs of the country? Whichever way we look at it there seems no occasion for concern at the financial cost of bringing these reforms into force.

A further financial reform of a different character that seems urgently required is an extension of the Corrupt and Illegal Practices Act so as to prohibit the payment of large sums of money by a candidate or prospective candidate to the local party organization. At the present time "It is bribery to give, lend, or promise money or money's worth in order to induce an elector to vote or abstain from voting for a particular candidate. The consequences are the same whether the payment is made directly or indirectly, and whether before, during, or after an election".* Contributions to party funds made as an inducement to secure the adoption of the contributor as candidate, though presumably not a contravention of the letter of the law, are clearly contrary to its spirit and should be treated accordingly. I suggest that contributions by candidates or members to party funds should be limited by law to a maximum of, say, £10 a year, and that any payment in excess of this should be a corrupt practice and punishable accordingly. Moreover, any such excess payment within the previous five years should render the payer ineligible to stand for election. The present practice of paying or promising large sums of money in order to secure adoption is in essence the wholesale purchase of votes: and wholesale bribery, even though indirect, is at least as objectionable as bribery of individuals.

CHAPTER XXIII

ELECTORAL REFORM

OUR investigations and discussions have shown plainly that the present method of electing members of parliament is thoroughly unsatisfactory, and we have in consequence noted down as an essential element in any scheme of reform the abolition of the single-member majority system of voting and its replacement by a better system. We have now to seek that better system.

How are we to set about this search? We might, of course, get together all the information we could about the various voting methods that have been proposed from time to time—limited vote, cumulative vote, alternative vote, second ballot, *scrutin de liste*, and so on—study them, and pick the one that seemed most attractive. But this would be both laborious and futile: laborious because of the huge number of voting methods and variants of those methods that have been put

* *Constitutional Year Book, 1933*, page 299.

forward,* and futile because those methods are by no means all directed
to the same ends or based on the same conception of what is desirable.

A much sounder and more economical line of approach suggests
itself when we look at the matter in the spirit indicated in the opening
paragraphs of Chapter XIX. We want to get at the problem initially
not as a question of this or that method, nor as a question of remedying this or that abuse, but as a question of fulfilling our fundamental
aims. Only in so far as we are quite clear what those aims are, why we
want to achieve them, and as to the implications that they involve, shall
we be in a position to choose the best practical method for carrying
them out. We have, of course, already set down certain specific aims in
this connexion, but for our present purpose it will be useful to restate
those aims in a rather different way and to get down rather more closely
to bedrock in doing so. Let us for a start be clear what assumptions we
are making.

In the first place, the whole of this book is based on the assumption
that democratic ways of government are preferable to undemocratic
ways. That assumption, of course, would be disputed by many people,
but we need not argue about it, since it *is* explicitly assumed.

In the second place, we assume, as pointed out in Chapter XIII, that
reform should not involve gratuitous departure from traditional principles and practices: that is to say, while we should not allow our
schemes to be frustrated or prejudiced by the dead hand of outworn
custom, we should not go out of our way to use a new principle or
practice where an old one would serve equally well. In the present context we proceed from this assumption to two secondary assumptions:
first, we accept the view that the primary object of parliamentary representation is to give expression to the political opinions of the electorate;
and, second, we see no reason to substitute for constituencies organized
on a geographical basis constituencies organized on some other basis.

Let us be clear that these *are* assumptions. The principles involved
are not laws of nature, and other people might prefer to make other
assumptions. The political—which in this context effectively means
party—basis of representation is comparatively modern. It is not nearly
as old as the House of Commons and is not essential to representative
government. Constituencies, again, need not be geographical. They
might be occupational, as in the so-called "corporative state" of the
fascists, or they might be organized on the basis of age and sex, or in
other ways. †

Here, however, we accept these secondary assumptions as following
naturally from our two basic assumptions, and because we see no reason
to do otherwise. Geographical constituencies and representation on a

---

* According to the *Report of the Royal Commission on Systems of Election*
(1910), over three hundred methods of proportional representation *alone* were
said to be known then, a third of a century ago.

† The present university constituencies are not in any true sense geographical;
for the electors are widely scattered over the country, need no residential qualification, and are allowed to vote by post.

political (party) basis are closely interwoven with our ways of thinking and feeling, and I suggest that we can—and therefore should—achieve our aims without abandoning either. This, however, does not mean that our representatives must necessarily be chosen *solely* on party-political grounds, nor does it mean that constituencies must necessarily be organized on the *present* geographical basis. We have already argued at length that personal fitness for his duties is essential in every member of parliament, and there is no need to repeat that discussion. It is important, however, to realize that there is no inconsistency between this contention and the assumption that the choice of members is to be made primarily on the basis of party-political opinion. In a really well-organized political world every candidate for parliament would possess in a high degree the qualities necessary in a member, and the choice between candidates could then well be made chiefly—though still not entirely—on the broad political policies they put forward.

Having thus cleared the ground and got together our materials, we are in a position to commence building up towards the electoral method necessary for the carrying out of our aims. We see that this method, while encouraging the election of personally suitable men and women, should provide the electors with the means of giving effective expression to their political views, and should do this by means of constituencies organized on a geographical basis. We have now to work out the practical implications of all this in terms of votes and seats, and, since we are concerned primarily with Great Britain, let us take the dimensions of the problem there.

We have in this country approximately thirty million electors, and these electors have by some means or other to choose approximately six hundred members of parliament to represent them. Hence, by whatever method the elections are conducted, the average number of electors to each member of parliament is in round figures fifty thousand. It is useful to keep this bit of simple arithmetic clearly in mind—fifty thousand electors, more or less, connected by some, as yet unspecified, method with each member of parliament.

Now, if we had only the geographical requirement to meet we should naturally divide the country into single-member areas, much as at present. Each area would contain roughly fifty thousand electors, and all would be well. But we have already declared that in our view the primary object of parliamentary representation is to give expression to the political opinions of the electorate : the geographical constituencies are our chosen means to this end; they are not the end itself. Hence before we settle our electoral areas we must have regard to the distribution of the political opinion that our members have to represent. Now, it is of the essence of our political system that the major parties differ substantially, and in some respects fundamentally, in their views. Unless, therefore, we take an entirely cynical view of the whole realm of politics, we must agree that no member can sincerely hold and advocate the full policy of more than one party simultaneously. The socialist cannot represent those who are opposed to socialism; the protectionist cannot speak for the free-trader; the imperialist cannot put the case for internationalism. Hence in his principal task of representing the political opinions of his constituents the Conservative member of parliament cannot speak for either Liberal or Labour electors, the Liberal cannot speak for either Conservative or Labour electors, and the Labour member cannot represent either Conservatives or Liberals.

There would be little need to draw attention to this if all the Conservatives lived in one part of the country, all the Liberals in another part, and all the Labourites somewhere else. Geography and politics would then fit in nicely together, and the electoral problem would be simple: though other problems would be acute. But the real world is—fortunately!—not made like that, and we find no part of the country that is wholly one-party in politics. The distribution of political opinion varies considerably from place to place, but in every area of any size electors of all three parties are to be found. There are many thousands of Conservative voters in the mining areas, and many thousands of Liberal and Labour voters in the "home counties". Nowhere is there political homogeneity.

Hence no one member of parliament can represent even in the broadest sense the political opinion of the electors of any area of the country, for the simple reason that even on the most clear-cut and important issues those electors are divided amongst themselves. It follows that single-member constituencies are fundamentally inconsistent with the proper representation of political opinion. The case against them does not rest on the failure of small eccentric minorities to secure members, nor does it rest on the crudities of approximation that are inevitable in the actual working of any method. Given the party system, the single-member constituency is as completely wrong in theory as it is disastrous in practice. Disregarding minor parties altogether, nothing less than a three-member constituency can give even the possibility of the electors of a locality securing representation in accordance with their political views. It does not, of course, follow that even in a three-member constituency each party would in fact secure one seat. Whether it did or not would depend on its local strength or weakness; but with *fewer* than three seats in the constituency the three parties *cannot* all secure representation, even if they are exactly equal in voting strength.

Clearly devices such as the second ballot or the alternative vote cannot cure this fatal defect, for it is inherent in *any* single-member-constituency system. They could at most only alleviate its worst symptoms.

How, then, it may be asked, does the present single-member majority system work at all? It is rather instructive to study the answer to this question, not from the point of view of the system's practical results—we have already shown in detail how unjust they are—but from the standpoint of fundamental principle. Let us try to analyse the actual working of the system, strip it of the glosses it has acquired through long-standing habit and tradition, and see it for what it really is. In doing this we need pay no attention to its history, for our present purpose is to understand the significance of the actual current process.

Under the present system, then, the ratio of fifty thousand electors to one member of parliament is recognized, as a matter of geography, by dividing the country into areas that each contain, on an average, about that number of electors and allotting one member to each. (Of course, in practice sentimental considerations, movements of population, and other factors cause substantial variations from this average figure, but these variations can be ignored for our present purpose.)

So far so good: if there were no party system, and if the representation of political opinion were of no great importance, this division into single-member constituencies might be reasonable enough. But as a device for political representation it is, as we have seen, as wrong in theory as it is in practice, for it assumes that all the fifty thousand electors in a division hold, as near as matters, the same political faith; and this, as we have seen, is never the case. Let us, however, see what actually happens.

Since the fifty thousand electors owe allegiance to (at least) three quite separate and distinct parties, there is not and cannot be any real agreement amongst them as to who is to represent them in parliament. Normally, therefore, a contest takes place, and this, of course, is quite right and proper and natural. But whereas in an efficient system the contest would determine in what proportions the respective parties should *share* the representation of the constituency, in the present system the contest determines which of the parties shall have the *whole* of the representation. Naturally in such circumstances an election is something of a gamble, for in each constituency a party must gain all or nothing. This may add to the excitement and give the contest a "sporting" atmosphere, but it is not serious politics and is not worthy of a modern civilized community.

But let us scrutinize the contest a little more closely and see just how this system gets out of the difficulty created by having only one seat to allocate between three parties. To make the method clear we will first take an extreme but by no means impossible case, and assume that in a certain division just before the poll closes on election day each of the three parties has secured, say, 12,000 votes: it is anybody's election so far. Then just at the last moment a final voter arrives—and his solitary vote decides which party shall have the seat, for that party will have polled 12,001 votes to the other two parties' 12,000 each. This is admittedly an extreme case, but it illustrates how the dilemma is solved: it is not the great bulk of the votes that decide the election, for they merely cancel each other out. It is the *surplus* votes that settle the matter; and if those surplus votes run to a dozen, or a hundred, or a thousand or more, instead of one, that only makes the system less obviously absurd. It does not make it sensible or just.

The essence of the present method, therefore, is to set off the voters against each other, three by three or two by two, according to the number of candidates, until most of the voters have neutralized each other's votes, and then allow the final surplus voters, however few in number they may be, to claim the seat for the party to which they belong, even if that party has received only a minority of the votes cast. In the general election of 1929 there were, as already mentioned, no fewer than 315 such minority successes; that is, well over half of the members of the House of Commons represented only a minority of their constituents.

Any system of single-member constituencies is therefore fundamentally incompatible with the equitable representation of political opinion, and is incapable of determining the "will of the people" on even the broadest and simplest of issues. We can now, therefore, add one more definite condition to be fulfilled by the electoral system that we seek: it must have constituencies returning at least three members each. Even this, however, is not a sufficient guarantee of better results: for a constituency returning three or more members might be, like the present two-member divisions, little more than a multiplication of one single-member division, simply repeating the latter's failings on a larger scale.

What condition, then, is still missing? To answer this question we may remind ourselves that, though we have accepted the principle of constituencies organized on a geographical basis, we have also accepted the view that the primary object of parliamentary representation is to give expression to the political opinions of the electorate. It is the people who are to be represented and not the place. The present system says, in effect, that any *place* having fifty thousand electors can have a member to represent it, thereby stressing the geographical factor and ignoring the political. We say, on the other hand, that, within the limits of what is practicable, any like-minded *group of electors* approaching fifty thousand in number in an electoral area is entitled to have a member to represent it. So the missing condition is easily seen to be that the method of voting must be such that within each constituency the seats are allocated with due regard to the voting strength of the parties in that constituency.

We have now laid down the essential practical conditions for the new electoral system that we desire. But in studying these practical conditions we must not lose sight of the aims that we have in view: let us briefly recapitulate them.

We seek to replace the present single-member majority system of election by some other system that will be less clumsy and less capricious in its action, will give more scope to and make better use of the native shrewdness and good sense of the electorate, will reflect more accurately the state of political feeling in the country, give a better-balanced House of Commons, and promote a higher general standard of integrity, ability, and zeal amongst candidates and members.

Our practical conditions are fulfilled in the method of the single transferable vote, and I suggest that this method, in conjunction with the financial reforms proposed in the previous chapter, will go a very long way towards enabling us to achieve the aims we have just restated. I suggest, moreover, that there is no other known method of election for which such claims can be made and substantiated.

Unlike the second ballot and the alternative vote, the single transferable vote is not a device to bolster up the old outworn method of election: it is a replacement of it by a new method, essentially modern in its strength and flexibility and smoothness of working. Based on proposals originally put forward by Thomas Hare in 1859 and advocated powerfully but unsuccessfully by John Stuart Mill, it has been developed and improved out of all knowledge since those early days. In its modern form it has been applied in actual practice in various countries and for various purposes; and it has stood that crucial test with marked success.

Thanks largely to the patient and persistent missionary work of the Proportional Representation Society, the general principles and methods of the single transferable vote are now known to many people. Nevertheless, as a matter of convenience and for the sake of those who may be unfamiliar with the system or may have forgotten just how it works, it will be as well to give a brief description and explanation of it.

To get the best results from the system the constituencies should be of such a size that they return from three to seven members each, with five as the optimum number. For reasons of both sentiment and convenience the boundaries of each constituency should normally be fixed so as to coincide as nearly as possible with a natural unit of population, such as a city or a county, the number of members allotted to it being, of course, dependent on the number of its electors. If we assume the system applied to this country with the total number of members of the House of Commons as at present, more or less, then cities and towns such as Bradford, Bristol, Hull, Leeds, Leicester, Newcastle-upon-Tyne, Nottingham, Portsmouth, Sheffield, Stoke-on-Trent, West Ham, Cardiff, and Edinburgh would form natural constituencies by the mere abolition of their present internal divisions. On this basis Sheffield would return seven members, Leeds six, Bristol and Edinburgh five each, and the others three or four as at present, though naturally changes of population since the last redistribution of seats, and the adjustments of external boundaries that inevitably take place from time to time, might lead to some modifications. Larger cities, such as Birmingham, Liverpool, Manchester, and Glasgow, would need to be divided according to their size into two or three constituencies, following as far as possible natural internal boundaries. London would have to be divided into perhaps ten or twelve constituencies. Towns too small to justify the minimum number of three members would have to be combined to give constituencies of the necessary size. This could often be done without much difficulty. Birkenhead and Wallasey, for example, are contiguous and would form a natural unit of the requisite population. In the industrial areas of the North and Midlands many of the present county constituencies are almost wholly urban and might well unite with adjoining boroughs to give reasonably homogeneous constituencies of the required size.

In the counties, similarly, there would be many natural units readily formed by the mere removal of internal divisions. Cornwall, Cumberland, Hertfordshire, Norfolk, Shropshire, Sussex, Glamorgan, and Lanarkshire are examples of the counties that would form ready-made natural constituencies. The more populous counties, like Yorkshire, Lancashire, and Middlesex, would, of course, have to be divided into two or more constituencies, while the less populous would form units with neighbouring counties; for example, Huntingdonshire with Cambridgeshire. Special arrangements might be necessary in such exceptionally sparsely populated areas as the Highlands of Scotland, but in general the formation of the new constituencies would present no problems that could not readily be solved with the aid of intelligence, goodwill, and a little patience.

It will be seen that in general the new constituencies would have a unity, a significance, that does not attach to the present single-member divisions. Bradford, Portsmouth, Norfolk, Edinburgh—these have a corporate existence, a tradition, an individuality that does not belong to North Bradford, Central Portsmouth, South-West Norfolk, or East Edinburgh. The new system would bring about the restoration, in an improved form, of an old unity that was only destroyed by the deliberate introduction of the present single-member system as recently as 1884.*

We turn now from the new constituencies to the method of voting. The elector would receive his ballot paper at the polling station much as he does now, but instead of finding on it two, three, or four names, as he commonly does at present, would see on it anything from, say, five to twelve or more names. How many candidates there would be would depend in part, of course, on the size of the constituency, but it would also be affected by other considerations to which we shall refer a little later.

Taking his paper to the polling booth, the elector votes by simply placing a figure 1 against the name of the candidate whom he would most like to see successful, a figure 2 against his next choice, a figure 3 against his third choice, and so on. He can go on in this way until he has indicated his order of preference for all the candidates—or he can stop short at any point he chooses. He is quite free to please himself how many or how few preferences he will indicate. When he has carried out this very simple task the voter's job is done. He places his paper in the ballot box and walks out of the polling station. The whole process takes hardly any longer than that at present in use: it could scarcely be easier or more straightforward.

The counting of the votes is a more complicated business, but it is

* See footnote on page 142.

governed throughout by exact rules and is quite free from ambiguity or uncertainty. The first step is to sort all the voting papers according to the *first preferences* marked on them. Next each candidate's first-preference votes are counted, and the sum of these gives the grand total of valid votes recorded. The *quota* has next to be determined: this is done by dividing the grand total of votes by a number which is one more than the number of members to be elected. The quota is the whole number next above the result of this division. Suppose, for example, that the total number of valid votes recorded is 184,562 in a constituency returning five members. The total vote divided by 6 gives 30,760·3, and the quota is therefore 30,761.

Now, any candidate whose total number of first-preference votes is equal to, or exceeds, the quota is immediately declared elected. Not more than five candidates (in a five-member constituency) could possibly be elected in this way: for, deducting their five quotas from the grand total, there is less than a quota left for all the rest of the candidates together. In the numerical example given, five times 30,761 amounts to 153,805, and consequently there could not be more than 30,757 first-preference votes left over for any remaining candidate or candidates, and that is less than a quota.

In practice votes are not as evenly distributed as this, and it is unlikely that more than two or three of the candidates will be elected on this first count. Those who are so elected will be likely to have received first preferences amounting to considerably more than the necessary quota: that is, they will have received considerably more votes than they need for their success. Their surplus votes are accordingly transferred to the candidates who have not yet secured election. Moreover—and this is important—each successful candidate's surplus votes are transferred proportionately to the *second* preferences shown on the *whole* of his papers (except that the second preferences shown for any other candidate already elected are ignored and the third preferences on those papers taken instead).

In the numerical example given, let us suppose that the candidate who leads the poll on the first count has 42,186 first-preference votes— that is, 11,425 more than the quota which he needs to secure election. Now suppose that on his 42,186 voting papers there are 9,284 second preferences for a particular not-yet-elected candidate. Then this latter candidate receives, as an addition to his first-preference poll, a number of votes amounting to $\frac{9,284}{42,186}$ of the surplus 11,425 not required by the top candidate: that is, he receives an addition of 2,514 votes. The other not-yet-elected candidates similarly receive their respective proportions of the top candidate's surplus. In the same way the surplus votes of each other elected candidate are distributed to the not-yet-elected candidates. When all the surplus votes of all the candidates elected on the first count have been so distributed, it will probably be found that these additional votes have sufficed to bring one or more of the remaining candidates up to the quota. Any such candidate is now declared elected.

If all the seats are filled on this second count, that completes the election. It will probably be found, however, that there are still one or more places to be filled. In that event the next step is to eliminate the candidate who is now at the bottom of the poll: the whole of his votes are transferred to the other not-yet-elected candidates in accordance with the next available preferences shown on his papers. ("Next available" means "next excluding candidates already elected.") If this does not suffice to fill the remaining seat or seats, the process is repeated by the exclusion of the candidate *now* at the bottom of the poll, and the transfer of *his* votes as a whole in accordance with the next available preferences shown on his papers. Eventually in this way all the seats are filled.

To the reader who meets it for the first time this vote-counting process may seem cumbersome and confusing. He can be reassured: every step is taken strictly in accordance with predetermined regulations, and the whole business, although lengthier than the count for a simple majority, is not really cumbersome at all.*

CHAPTER XXIV

ELECTORAL REFORM: FURTHER DISCUSSION

IN the preceding chapter we have surveyed the practical conditions that should be fulfilled by the new electoral method that we seek as a substitute for the present single-member majority system, and have reached the conclusion that the only known method that complies with these conditions and does not depart unnecessarily from traditional ways is that of the single transferable vote. We have seen how this method operates, including both the process of voting and the process of counting the votes. We have now to consider rather more definitely how far the single transferable vote system does really fulfil our requirements as a whole, and then to notice and answer some of the more usual objections that are raised against the system by hostile critics. Let us accordingly first see how far the new system meets our requirements, direct and indirect.

So far as the practical conditions that we laid down early in the preceding chapter are concerned it certainly does so. In the first place, the organization of the constituencies is indisputably on a geographical basis. In the second place, the system is adapted, as the present system is not, to the representation of the electors on the basis of their political opinions: for the minimum of three seats to a constituency allows each

---

* Readers who desire a more detailed explanation of the system, or who would like information on a number of points not dealt with in this brief account, may be referred to *The Case for Electoral Reform*, by S. R. Daniels (1938), in which they will find a particularly lucid and interesting account of it. Much information is also to be found in the reports and pamphlets published from time to time by the Proportional Representation Society.

party the *opportunity* of representation, and the provisions for the transfer of surplus votes ensure that this opportunity shall be *genuine*. Both systems have the geographical basis: but the present system, by reason of its structure, is inherently unsuitable for the representation of opinion.

If we turn from these practical conditions to the aims that underlie them, we still find in the single transferable vote system the fulfilment of our requirements. Let us briefly review the aims we have set before us and see how the old and new systems compare with respect to them.

Our first aim was to find a system less clumsy and capricious than the one we now have. At present if one party in a division is appreciably stronger than the others that party gets a monopoly of representation and the others are virtually disfranchised: if, on the other hand, the parties are nearly equal in strength the result of an election is determined by what is little more than a gamble, for the seat goes to the party that can rake up even a solitary vote more than either of the others separately, and it does not matter if the successful party is much in a minority of the total votes cast.

With the single transferable vote, however, both the clumsiness and the caprice are swept away. It is no longer possible for a minority to defeat a majority, nor for one party to monopolize representation. Every candidate must secure a quota of votes for success, but if he gets that quota he is sure of a seat. Every party that has any substantial following in a constituency is bound to obtain some representation. The fantastic results in the county of Cornwall, where in 1923 all five seats went to the Liberals, in 1924 all five went to the Conservatives, and in 1929 all five reverted to the Liberals, are typical of the present erratic system. They would be impossible with the single transferable vote, which would almost certainly have given two seats each to the Conservative and Liberal parties throughout, the fifth seat going probably to the Liberals in 1923, to the Conservatives or to Labour in 1924, and to Labour in 1929. The political views of the electors of the county as a whole changed only slightly: the violent changes in representation were due to the clumsy irresponsibility of the voting system.

Our next aim was to give more scope to and make better use of the native shrewdness and good sense of the electorate. As we have already seen, the present system makes no use whatever of the elector in its numerous uncontested elections, frequently offers him no candidate of his own party in contested elections, gives him no choice on personal grounds within his own party, and generally makes him feel that his vote is completely futile in nine cases out of ten. In such conditions there is little encouragement to the elector to take an intelligent interest in the use of his vote, or in politics generally. With the single transferable vote, however, he could always go to the poll, since there would be no uncontested elections. He would practically always find a candidate of his own party to vote for, and as a general rule would find more than one—perhaps sometimes as many as half a dozen—such candidates to choose between on their personal merits and demerits. Moreover, he knows that his vote is worth something: it may not do all he would like, but it cannot be completely futile as it so often is now. Even if he should belong to some minority party too tiny to hope for a seat itself, he can still use his vote intelligently to help the return of the candidates least objectionable to him politically and most desirable on grounds of integrity and ability. He has in every case a list of candidates to study and discuss and compare, a variety of personnel and party to choose between, that adds zest to the whole business and encourages interest in political affairs in general.

How many candidates' names would the elector be likely to find on his ballot paper? That would vary considerably according to the size of the constituency and the views taken by the various parties of their chances of success. It is unlikely that the lists would be inordinately lengthy, for, the gambling element being almost entirely eliminated, no party could hope to sweep the board in a sensational coup, and there would be no point in putting up more candidates than had any chance of success. On the other hand, since the vote is transferable, there would be no need to hesitate about putting up a sufficient number of candidates to secure the most seats possible. Roughly it means that each party may be expected to put forward enough candidates to take as many seats as an optimistic estimate would give it and no more. As an example, in Edinburgh under the new system one might expect to find three or four Conservative candidates standing, two or three Labour, a Liberal, and perhaps an Independent. That would make round about eight candidates in all for the five seats, against the thirteen candidates who stood under the present system in 1935. Each voter would have a much wider choice than before—say eight candidates to choose from instead of two or three—yet there would be fewer wasted candidatures, since only about three candidates would be unsuccessful against eight in 1935.

The third aim on our list was to secure a system that would reflect more accurately the state of political feeling in the country. The present system by its very nature is unable to reflect accurately the state of political opinion in even a single constituency; for it has only one seat to offer to an electorate that comprises three or more parties. Each result is therefore necessarily a distortion of the facts—in the case of the minority successes a gross distortion—and the sum of a series of distortions is not necessarily or even probably the truth. How far it is from the truth in actual practice we have already shown. With the single transferable vote, however, the multi-member constituencies allow of a much closer approximation to the facts in each locality, and the sum of all the results—though not mathematically precise—gives a very much truer picture of the state of political feeling in the country as a whole. There would not be, nor should we expect, exact proportionality of representation, but the final result of a general election could no longer completely falsify the wishes of the electorate as it sometimes does now, and is liable to do at any time under the present system.

The fourth and last aim on our list was to secure a better balanced House of Commons and promote a higher general standard of integrity, ability, and zeal amongst candidates and members. The fulfilment of this aim depends very largely on the financial reforms discussed in the previous chapter, but adoption of the single transferable vote would greatly help. It would abolish the party "pocket boroughs", the safe seats into which at present the respective parties can put practically anyone they choose, and it would expose all candidates to the salutary experience of a contest at every election. Hence party machines would have to pay more attention to merit and less to wealth and influence in choosing their candidates—or run the risk of alienating both their own more critical members and the discriminating non-party voters.

Further, the removal of artificial financial and other restrictions on candidature for and membership of the House of Commons will greatly increase the number of potential candidates available both locally and nationally. But the total number of candidates actually put forward by a leading party will be less than under the present system, since, though it will be likely to contest every *constituency*, it will be useless, and indeed unwise, to contest every *seat*. Consequently, with more potential candidates available and fewer actual candidates required, the process of adopting candidates will be much more selective than it is at present, and so in yet another way the standard of personal fitness required will be raised.

We may claim, then, that the single transferable vote fulfils all the requirements that we, starting from fundamental considerations, laid down as necessary in any new electoral system. We can make this claim with all the more assurance since the method has been tested pretty thoroughly in practice by now and has stood up to that test most successfully.

Objections have, of course, been raised against the single transferable vote. A full discussion of these would take too long and be out of place here, but it may be useful to mention some of the more usual and to indicate briefly the answers to them.

1. *That the system is artificial.* If by this is meant that it is not a law of nature, the answer is that in that sense the whole of civilization is artificial. If it is meant that the system involves a departure from present practice, the answer is that so does any reform. But intrinsically the present system, notwithstanding its superficial simplicity, is far more artificial as a means of determining the political opinion of the country than is the single transferable vote.

2. *That the system is complicated and could not be understood by the elector.* This objection displays a singular contempt for the intelligence of the electorate, and a generation that tackles successfully the intricacies of cross-word puzzles and football pool coupons may well smile at it. Voters so mentally deficient as to be unable to vote for

perhaps eight or a dozen candidates in the order of their preference are not fit to vote at all. As a matter of fact, experience shows that electors do not find the anticipated difficulties. In the Irish Free State general election of 1933, conducted on the single transferable vote system, the percentage of papers rendered invalid from all causes was only just over 1 per cent for the whole country, though there was a heavy poll.* The *counting* of the votes is, of course, more complex than under the present system, but it presents no difficulty whatever to a competent staff and is completely free from uncertainty or ambiguity.

3. *That the change-over from the present system would cause confusion.* This has been seriously put forward; otherwise it would seem too childish to need an answer. Naturally any change-over from one system to another, in any sphere, causes a certain amount of inconvenience for the moment, and may possibly involve an occasional mistake or misunderstanding. But there is no reason to think that this would be serious: much bigger changes in the organization of our communal life have been carried through quite easily and with little confusion.

4. *That elections would be much more expensive to candidates.* There might be something in this, though it is doubtful whether the effect would be as serious as objectors claim: but in any case the objection would lose its force if the financial reforms already suggested were put into action.

5. *That candidates would lose personal touch with the electors.* This argument is out of date. Such personal touch with electors as there was, say, before 1918 disappeared to a great extent with the repeated extensions of the suffrage, and with the final adoption of adult suffrage there is next to nothing left of it. With electorates ranging from a minimum of over 27,000 voters (Barnard Castle) up to nearly 170,000 voters (Romford) in a single division, how can any candidate, even now, make personal contact with more than a very small fraction of them?

6. *That a multiplicity of small parties would result.* This appears to be a mere assertion unsupported by any valid evidence or sound argument. True, the state of parties in France and elsewhere on the Continent (before 1939) is sometimes adduced as evidence: unfortunately for those who put it forward, these countries do not use and never have used the single transferable vote. The various "list" systems of election employed in some of them are utterly different from the single transferable vote. The fact that the general term "proportional representation" has been applied to both does not excuse the essential dishonesty of attacking one system for the alleged failings of totally different systems. Moreover, the complex of parties and groups abroad originated chiefly in religious, racial, and other causes that have nothing to do with voting systems. In many cases the small parties there have (or had) a history that antedates their present (or recent) electoral arrangements. It must not be forgotten, either, that we in this country are never free for long

* S. R. Daniels, *op. cit.*, page 55.

from small parties. At the present time the following, at least, are represented in the House of Commons in addition to the main Conservative, Liberal, and Labour parties: Liberal National, National Labour, Independent Labour, Communist, and Co-operative. Each of these has its own separate party organization.

7. *That the House of Commons would be inundated with cranks and faddists.* The objectors who put this forward must have a poor opinion of their fellow-electors. It is, again, mere assertion unsupported by any trustworthy evidence. Even under the present system an occasional member who might be dubbed a crank gets elected—a prohibitionist, for example—not to mention various independents who display eccentricities that set them apart from their fellow-independents. This would, no doubt, still happen occasionally, but there is no reason to suppose that it would be widespread. As Daniels has pointed out,* it takes considerably more votes to elect a member under the single transferable vote system than it does under the present system; where, then, would the crank find his chance?

8. *That it would increase the power of the party machines.* This objection is frankly ludicrous: the very reverse is likely to be the case, as will be gathered from our preceding discussions. If it would in fact "increase the power of the professional organizer in politics", as Laski asserts,† then we may ask why the organizations of the two biggest parties in this country are opposed to it? As a matter of fact, Laski's assertion is probably based, whether correctly or no, on the continental "list" systems, but as he applies it to proportional representation in general he must be answered on that basis. Moreover, as Laski himself points out, legislatures even under the present systems "are so driven by the pressure of party control that the private member has, for the most part, been reduced to the status of a voting machine".‡

9. *That by-elections could not be held.* Undoubtedly the present method of holding by-elections would not be available. There are, however, a number of methods by which the difficulty could be overcome. Moreover, the present supposed importance of by-elections as a kind of "political barometer" would be considerably decreased under a system not subject to the violent and irresponsible fluctuations that are inherent in the present electoral system.

10. *That it would lead to weak government and, in particular, to minority or coalition government.* Of all the arguments put forward against proportional representation as a general principle, and therefore against the single transferable vote, probably the one most deserving of serious consideration is that of the difficulty of obtaining a clear party majority and consequently—in the opinion of the critics—a strong government. Let us therefore examine it carefully.

The argument implies, perhaps, rather more than its propounders

* S. R. Daniels, *op. cit.*, page 63.
† H. J. Laski, *A Grammar of Politics* (1931), page 815.
‡ H. J. Laski, *Democracy in Crisis* (1933), page 77.

15

realize. It may be analysed into components as follows: (a) It is seldom that any party has a clear majority of votes in the country. (b) Therefore any system of proportional representation—*i.e.*, any system that allocates seats in accordance with votes—will normally not give any party a clear majority of seats in the House of Commons. (c) The present system generally gives a clear majority of seats to some one party, even if that party has only a minority of votes in the country. (d) The present system therefore avoids minority and coalition governments. (e) It is essential, or at least extremely desirable, that government should be by a clear party majority in the House of Commons and not by a minority in that House nor by a coalition of parties. (f) Therefore the present system is preferable to any system of proportional representation.

We can accept (a), for, as we have shown in Chapter X, in only one of the seven inter-war general elections (1931) did any party secure a majority of votes in the country. The acceptance of (b) follows logically on that of (a). We can also accept (c) as fairly correct, for the present voting system gave a clear majority of seats in the House to the Conservative party in every inter-war election except those of 1923 and 1929. So far, then, we have found nothing to dispute in the argument. From this point onwards, however, we are unable to accept it as either logical or in accordance with the facts. The next component (d) is a *non sequitur*, and it is in fact contradicted by experience. Under the present single-member majority system we have had, in the twenty-four years from December 1918 to December 1942, the different types of government as follows:

	Years	Months
Coalition government	15	2
Minority government	3	0
Straight majority party government	5	10
Total	24	0

We have had, therefore, less than six years of straight majority party government, and over eighteen years of what the critics call "weak" government—that is, minority and coalition government—in the last twenty-four years; and that is under the present system of voting. Whatever the evils of minority and coalition government may be, it simply will not do to use them as an argument against changing over to the single transferable vote, for the present method of voting is clearly no barrier at all against those forms of government. Consequently, component (d) above being proved untrue, component (f) falls to the ground and the whole argument collapses.

To say this is not to assert that minority and coalition governments have proved themselves "strong" or even satisfactory in the very long innings they have had in recent times. (It is nearly fourteen years since the last straight majority party government went out of office.) What is clear is that if minority and coalition governments are caused by the nature of the voting system, then it is the *present* system that is the villain of the piece, and not the single transferable vote.

Moreover, there seems good reason to believe that many of the drawbacks and vices of coalition and minority governments as we have experienced them in the last twenty-four years are due to the conditions set up by the present voting system. Under the much healthier conditions that would prevail with the single transferable vote it is probable that these drawbacks and vices would largely disappear. This has been well pointed out by Ramsay Muir,* and his words on the subject are worth studying. The new system would bring about many changes, including a different and almost certainly more civilized outlook on many questions, and there is no reason to suppose that the evils inherent in the present system would survive the extinction of that system.

It may be noted, by the way, that in the fifteen years and more of coalition government that we have had since 1918 the coalitions have in each case been formed from *all* the major parties (though not always supported by the whole of each party). Consequently they gave us the serious disadvantages that arise when the opposition is weak and lacking in cohesion. If under a reformed electoral system coalitions were to continue, it seems probable that they would normally be two-party coalitions only, with the third party unitedly in opposition: a much healthier state of affairs.

There is, moreover, another very serious drawback to the present system that detracts from its value in producing "strong" government. Indisputably the system tends not merely to misrepresent or exaggerate the views of the electors, but also to give majorities in the House of Commons—whether for a single party, as in 1906, or for a coalition, as in 1918 and 1931—that are disastrously large. The really strong government is not the one with an immense numerical superiority over a tiny and enfeebled opposition: that stands out pretty clearly as one of the lessons of political history. Such an electoral "landslide" may cause jubilation in the general run of members of the successful party or parties at the time, but the more statesmanlike leaders of that party or parties will regret and deplore it. They know that it is not in the interests of good government, and in the long run probably not even in the party interests. Bonar Law's son writes of his father: "I can recall the dismay with which he greeted the election returns of 1918 and the disasters which he foresaw piling up in the wake of that swollen majority".† Yet bloated majorities of this kind are typical of the present system, and it was only thirteen years later that the even more disastrous "landslide" of 1931 took place. This aspect of the single-member majority system is one that its supporters would do well to ponder.

I think, then, that a study of the way the present system actually works in practice, as distinct from theory, should convince any impartial person that it is not in fact a system that can be recommended or

* Ramsay Muir, *How Britain is Governed* (1933), chapter V, section VI.
† Richard K. Law, M.P., in the *Manchester Guardian*, 14th November 1942.

defended on the ground that it produces "strong government". To mis-quote a well-known saying: "The way to get cured of an excessive ad-miration for the single-member majority system is to go and look at it."

If, in spite of all these arguments, there is still a hankering after single-party majority government—which, be it noted, we have not had in operation for the last dozen years—I suggest that it could be more reliably and more honestly obtained by adopting the single transferable vote in place of the present erratic and capricious system, and then giving the Prime Minister of a minority government the right to co-opt as members of parliament a limited number—say not more than fifty—of the unsuccessful candidates at the previous general election. Since his party would normally be the strongest party in the House, this addition would usually give him a small actual majority, and in any case would appreciably strengthen the forces at his command.

I do not recommend this expedient: it is a departure from the prin-ciple of election and is open to many objections. But I maintain that if we *must* procure support for the government, beyond what it is entitled to by its real strength in the country, then this would be a saner and infinitely more honest way of doing it than by the continuance of the present vicious system.

Some of the opposition to a change is undoubtedly due to a love of the two-party system as a theory of government. The devotees of that system, however, ignore two important facts: (a) that the actual history of the supposed two-party system does not show it in nearly as favour-able a light as does the theory; and (b) that whatever the merits of a two-party system, they are beside the point if in fact we have more than two parties.

As to (a): we have not had a two-party system in real force for very many years. The Irish Nationalist party had a long history and a great influence on the course of British politics. The Liberal Unionist party was, at least in its early days, another separate force. Before these parties had disappeared from Westminster the Labour party was on the scene and making itself felt.

As to (b): there has long been a desire on the part of certain people, particularly in the Labour party, to say that the Liberal party "ought" to die out, and even to say that it is dead. But the facts show that Liberalism, for good or ill, persistently declines to die. Even the tre-mendous handicap imposed by the present voting system has not suc-ceeded in killing it, as the big aggregate vote it has secured in election after election shows. In any case it is utterly wrong, for the sake of a theory, to attempt to stifle the views of millions of electors, and force everybody into one or other of two parties. It is only a step from that to the fascist and nazi practice of destroying all but one party.

One other argument in favour of the present system should perhaps be mentioned. This argument is directed to rebut the criticisms of the present system that are made on the ground that a small turnover of votes between one election and the next may produce a big turnover of seats. The argument runs that the small size of the turnover of votes is no measure of its true significance, for the marginal voters who really determine the results of elections under the present system (the "hard core" of each party always voting loyally for that party) are really the most intelligent part of the electorate, and are rightly given what are in effect casting votes.

It would take too long to analyse and rebut this argument in full detail. But it seems to me that it is effectively demolished by two considerations: (a) The marginal voters who change sides between one election and another include not only the intelligent people of independent and critical mind, but also the ignorant and ill-informed, who are the natural prey of the political stunter, the victims of the dishonest "slogan"—and who shall say that these are not more numerous than the others? (b) The marginal voter has no opportunity to make his supposed intelligent casting vote effective in the numerous "safe" seats. Hence, even if there is a grain of truth in the argument, it is a very ineffective one when weighed in the balance against the reasons for getting rid of the present system.

We have now recorded and answered the chief objections that are urged against the single transferable vote and in favour of the present electoral system.* It seems to me, however, that the case for the proposed change is overwhelming if the facts are studied fully and without prejudice. It is not a matter of this or that minor point one way or the other: it is the whole effect of the present system, as set out in detail in Part I of this book and discussed in the later parts, that condemns it. There is a natural reluctance on the part of timid and conservatively minded people of all parties to face up to the need for big reforms: but the need here is great and urgent, and I suggest that the hesitating may be reassured by the indisputable success of the single transferable vote over periods of years in Eire, in Tasmania, and elsewhere.

Finally I commend to the reader these words of Lord Lochee: "I do not believe that the cause of good government is bound up with the maintenance of a distorted representation, or that British statesmanship would be unable to cope with the problems which a better system might bring in its train".†

CHAPTER XXV

SUBSIDIARY REFORMS

THE financial and electoral reforms put forward and discussed in the preceding chapters should go most of the way towards providing the improved parliamentary representation that we desire to see. The

* For further discussions see Ramsay Muir, op. cit., chapter V, sections IV and V; S. R. Daniels, op. cit., chapters 8, 9, and 10; and the publications of the Proportional Representation Society.
† Report of the Royal Commission on Systems of Election (1910), Note by Lord Lochee.

financial proposals should do much to secure a wider choice of candidates and give opportunities for many people now altogether excluded to take their fair share of representation, while the change of electoral system should complete those effects, make better use of the qualities of the electors, and ensure that the House of Commons is better balanced, more suitably equipped, and a more accurate reflection of the state of political feeling and opinion in the country. Nevertheless there are various other matters in which some change seems necessary or desirable, and some minor innovations that might help to secure the results that we desire.

First let us consider a few points in connexion with the personal qualifications of members. It is clear that we cannot by any direct means ensure that every member shall possess the high degree of integrity and intelligence and the particular kind of temperament and education that we have suggested in Chapter XX to be desirable. These are matters in which we must largely rely on indirect measures, and we can hope that the changed conditions and methods, both financial and electoral, that we have suggested would go a long way towards raising the general standard. It would no doubt be a good thing if we could take more positive steps, but we must beware of any temptation to suggest the imposition of restrictions or requirements that might in the long run do more harm than good. Anything in the nature of an examination test, no matter how carefully planned, would almost certainly fall into this category. If it were made of a simple character, success in it would have very little significance, while if it required a comparatively high standard of intellectual ability and knowledge it would almost certainly exclude some potential candidates of sterling character and excellent practical ability. Whatever its superficial attractions might be at first sight, such an expedient could not be regarded as acceptable. We must not deprive the plutocratic class of its present privileges in order to endow with them a new academic governing class.

A more practicable step, and one far less open to adverse criticism, would be to require every candidate to present verified credentials to the electorate he seeks to represent in parliament. He should be obliged to state his age, date of birth, and place of residence; to specify any university degrees, diplomas, professional qualifications, and so on, that he holds; to give the essential facts of his career, including his service on county councils, borough councils, education committees, etc. (if any), and his present occupation if he has one: and he should have to have all these facts verified by some such independent body as the Civil Service Commission, which would be quite impartial and trustworthy.

That should be compulsory: but he should also be given the opportunity of undergoing voluntarily a series of psychological intelligence and aptitude tests, such as those that have been developed by the National Institute of Industrial Psychology for the selection of industrial and other personnel for particular occupations. These tests might be specially devised and prepared for the purpose by the National

Institute, which has the necessary expert staff and experience, but they should be conducted by the Civil Service Commission or some similarly authoritative and impartial body. They should, as I have said, be optional, and there should be no question of passing or failing. But where the tests were taken the results should be officially published, together with the verified particulars of age, career, etc., by the investigating Commission. This would give the electors dependable information about each candidate—now sometimes sadly lacking—and some means of comparing the qualifications, experience, and personal characteristics of those who sought their votes. Candidates who shirked the psychological tests would have to put up with the inferences that the electors might draw as to the reasons for their unwillingness to be tested.

These proposals are, I believe, novel, and I have no doubt that some candidates would find them unwelcome: for example, the rich nonentity who at present is able to "buy" a seat, and the shadier type of candidate with a plausible tongue and, like Chu Chin Chow, "a record strangely clean". But I suggest that anything that can be done to raise the standard of integrity amongst candidates and members is well worth while, and if this verification of credentials helped to exclude doubtful people from parliament it would be doing a real service. The candidate of better type, keen, intelligent, and upright, would have nothing to fear from the process, even if he had the misfortune to be comparatively uneducated in the formal sense. I believe that once the scheme was established and working and its implications realized it could do nothing but good. Selection committees would be driven to paying less attention to wealth and influence and blind party subservience, and more to the qualities of mind and spirit and experience that are desirable and even essential in the potential member of parliament. Electors, with the official records in front of them, would not only have better means than they now have of judging the comparative merits of the candidates who came seeking their votes, but they would also have their interests stirred, first and directly in the candidates and the contest, and second and indirectly in the whole business of politics and public affairs.

Another suggestion for improving the qualifications of candidates has been put forward by Professor Laski. "If members," he says, "were, before their candidature was legal, required to serve three years on a local body, they would gain the 'feel' of institutions so necessary to success. We should then have some evidence of a real wish on their part to grasp the nature of public business; and we should, I think, do not a little to revivify local life by making it the necessary avenue to a career in the national assembly. We should not, thereby, exclude any serious person from a political career, and it would not be difficult to devise alternative qualifications (such as membership of the civil service) for those to whom membership of a local body had been *a priori* impossible."*

* H. J. Laski, *A Grammar of Politics* (1931), page 340.

As a matter of fact, there are already very many members of parliament who have had experience of service on a county, borough, or district council, or on a local education committee. The suggested requirement, however, might do some good, and could not do much harm unless, as might prove to be the case, it presented in particular instances an almost insuperable obstacle. A man or woman cannot obtain the membership of a local body as of right, however meritorious and capable he or she may be, and it would probably be necessary to accept alternative qualifications on a rather wider basis than that suggested by Laski.

It seems probable, by the way, that the greatest benefit from the operation of this regulation would not be found in its effects on parliament, useful though they might be, but in its effects on local councils. These councils are all too often handicapped in their work by the parochial narrowness and ignorance of a considerable proportion of their members. It may be that the application of the regulation would not only directly bring into the ranks of the councils an increased number of men and women of better education and wider outlook, but would also indirectly effect further improvements by tending to raise the general standard required of candidates for election to such bodies.

It is interesting to observe that Laski's proposal would, if adopted, have the effect of raising the lower age-limit for membership of the House of Commons from twenty-one to about twenty-five. This would not make very much difference to the House as a whole, since few members enter before twenty-five now, but it would be a step in the right direction. I should, however, much prefer to see that matter dealt with more directly by requiring all candidates for parliament to have reached the age of thirty at the time of nomination, as suggested in Chapter XX. It is unnecessary here to repeat the arguments there put forward in favour of this change, but I suggest that it is a step which should certainly be taken, and quite as much for its indirect as for its direct effects.

We turn from these questions of the personal qualifications of members of parliament to the question of the franchise. With the lowering of the age at which women were qualified to vote from thirty to twenty-one in 1928 adult suffrage was at last achieved, and the franchise questions that had figured so prominently in programmes of reform for so many years were pretty generally regarded as settled. So they were, no doubt, so far as *extensions* of the franchise were concerned, for practically every adult was now entitled to a vote, and I do not think that it has yet been seriously proposed to give the vote to minors. But the democratic principle of "one elector, one vote" is still contravened by two survivals from the old days of property qualifications and plural voting. These two anomalies are, of course, the university franchise and the occupation franchise. They differ from each other in one important respect: the university voters are organized into special university constituencies and exercise their additional votes only in those constituencies, whereas the occupation voters are not organized into special constituencies, but use their extra votes in ordinary county and borough divisions. This difference, of course, may be regarded as the reflection of the differences in their historical origins. We need not discuss that aspect here, but because of that difference of organization we must consider these two surviving "plural" franchises separately.

The continuance of the university franchise seems to be defended chiefly on two grounds: first, that it gives to educated men and women —who, scattered over the country, are too few in numbers to have much influence locally on elections—a chance to return members to parliament who can represent their particular point of view and make a particular and useful contribution to parliamentary discussions; and, second, that it provides opportunities for a limited number of highly qualified men and women who have attained some eminence in other walks of life but are not party politicians to enter the House of Commons as Independent members. There is, I think, a certain amount of truth in both contentions—we have already noticed that two distinguished Independent members at the present time (Eleanor Rathbone and A. P. Herbert) sit for university divisions—but the history of the university constituencies in general shows that they commonly return members who are indistinguishable in type from the ordinary party members sitting for ordinary county and borough divisions. In these circumstances the case for the continuance of the university franchise and the university seats is not, even under the present system, a particularly strong one. With the adoption of the single transferable vote, and the better opportunities that that system would give to outstanding non-party men and women to secure election, whatever justification it now has would disappear, and we could see it abolished with little or no regret.

But if the case for the retention of the university franchise is not very strong, that for the retention of the occupation franchise appears to be non-existent—except on the old undemocratic assumption that property is of more importance than persons. Even on that assumption, however, the franchise is illogical, indefensible, and ridiculous. If a person is in occupation, for the purpose of business, profession, or trade, of land or other premises situated in a constituency other than that in which he or she resides of a yearly value (defined as the gross estimated rental) of £10 or more, both the person and the wife or husband of the person are entitled to votes in respect of that land or premises in addition to the votes which they get in respect of their residence qualification.* But if a farmer cultivating hundreds of acres, or a business man owning a large store or running a huge cotton mill lives in the same constituency as that in which his business land or premises is situated, neither he nor his wife gets a vote in respect of that business qualification. A small lock-up shop will give two votes if the occupier and his wife live in the next constituency—possibly only a few yards away—but the biggest

* *The Constitutional Year Book, 1933,* page 295.

business in the country will not give one vote if the occupier lives in the same constituency. Could anything be more ludicrous? Whatever case there might be from certain non-democratic points of view for a property qualification for a vote, there is none at all for the present business premises occupation franchise. Clearly it ought to be abolished out of hand.

With these suggestions for the simplification and unification of the parliamentary franchise we may consider our scheme for the co-ordinated and correlated reform of parliamentary representation as a whole to be fairly rounded off. But, though they are of much less general importance, there are certain anomalies in the qualifications for membership of the House of Commons, and in any comprehensive reform legislation these should certainly be rectified. They have already been pointed out near the end of Chapter XIII, and need not be re-capitulated here.

PART IV

THE NEW ERA

CHAPTER XXVI

1945: THE GENERAL ELECTION

WHEN the country went to the polls in July 1945 the occasion marked not only the end of the war that had devastated Europe for six years, and the beginning of a new era in history: it brought to an end also the longest period in modern times without a general election. At the outbreak of the 1914-18 war the House of Commons was 3 years 8 months old, having been elected in December 1910, and it was not until December 1918, just eight years later, that the new House was elected. At the outbreak of the 1939-45 war the House, with remarkable parallelism, was 3 years 10 months old. Like its predecessor in the earlier war, it had its life lengthened to avoid a general election in war-time, and it was not replaced by a new House until July 1945. The interval between pre-war and post-war elections in this case, however, was a year and eight months longer, made up of the two months greater initial age of the House, the seventeen months longer duration of the war (in Europe), and the three weeks concession to decency in the haste to hold the first post-war election.

The interval of 9 years 8 months between the election of November 1935 and that of July 1945 would have been in any circumstances a long period to elapse between elections. As Mark Abrams* has pointed out, nearly five millions of the 1935 electors had died by the time the 1945 election was held, while some seven million new electors had qualified; a big change in the actual electorate. Add to that the colossal political, social, and industrial changes brought about by the war, and we realize that it is no exaggeration to term the 1945 election an epoch-making event in the history of parliament. With the dissolution was brought to an end what we may term for convenience the inter-war era: with the announcement of the election results a new era commenced. The fact that this new era was ushered in by a resounding Labour victory at the polls, whereas the inter-war era was dominated almost continuously by the Conservative party, does not so much constitute the difference between the two eras as serve to emphasize and underline it. Kipling's "For All We Have and Are" might well have been dated 1939 instead of 1914. Now once more we are face to face with the fact that "Our world has passed away": and as the post-war days creep along we realize more and more plainly, for good or ill, that it is a new world upon which we have begun to enter, and not a reconstitution of the old.

* Mark Abrams, *The Labour Vote in the General Election*, Pilot Papers, January 1946.

It is therefore of more than ordinary interest to scrutinize the new House of Commons, to analyse its composition, and to compare it with its predecessors of the dead inter-war era. How long the new House will live, what it will achieve, and what place it will eventually hold in the political annals of the country it is too soon to estimate. But we can at least find out what sort of a House it is and how far it reflects the opinions of the voters, and from a study of these facts we may be able to form some judgement of its quality and make some estimate of its stability. We can also derive further data for use in considering the problems of electoral reform: problems which, in my view, are of more fundamental importance than most politicians are willing to concede. It is not proposed in what follows to discuss these matters at length, however, but rather to provide such an analysis of the new House as, taken in conjunction with the earlier analysis in the preceding Parts I to III, shall help to form a basis for such discussions.*

Since memories are short, it may be useful at this point to give a very brief summary of the events leading up to and immediately arising from the general election. On 8th May 1945 Mr. Churchill announced the victorious end of the war against Germany. Fifteen days later the Coalition Government, formed by Mr. Churchill on 10th May 1940, came to an end. In the intervening fortnight the leaders of the coalition parties exchanged views as to the proper date for the election, which all were agreed must take place within a few months. It appeared that most of the Conservative ministers wanted an immediate dissolution, while the Labour and Liberal ministers considered that the autumn was a more suitable time and that to dissolve at once would be to repeat the "rushed election" tactics of 1918. Finally Mr. Churchill on 18th May told the Labour and Liberal leaders that they must choose between an immediate election and a continuation of the coalition until the end of the Japanese war (which was then expected to go on for another eighteen months or two years), thus ruling out altogether the idea of an autumn election.

The Labour party, in secret session, endorsed Mr. Attlee's refusal to continue the coalition until the end of the Japanese war. So on 23rd May Mr. Churchill resigned and on the same day accepted the King's invitation to form a new government and asked for a dissolution of parliament. Since it had previously been agreed between all parties that at least three weeks' notice of a dissolution should be given, that scanty concession to propriety delayed the date of the dissolution to 15th June, and so fixed the polling day for 5th July. Even so, it was a bare two months from the end of hostilites in Europe to the election; and that election had to be fought on a rather unsatisfactory war-time register, and before demobilization had got under way or the electors had had much time to study the issues at stake.

---

* The author hopes to discuss some of these problems more fully in a separate volume at a later date.

On 25th May Mr. Churchill announced the composition of his new "caretaker" government. This consisted mainly of Conservatives and their close allies the Liberal Nationals, with a few non-party men and a solitary Independent Liberal (Major Lloyd George). None of the other Liberal ministers and none of the Labour ministers were willing to serve. Parliament reassembled four days later, and seventeen days after that it was dissolved. Candidates were nominated on 25th June, and polling should have taken place everywhere on 5th July. It did in most constituencies, but in 23 of them it had to be postponed for a week, or in one case a fortnight, on account of local mass holidays: a reminder of the unsuitability of July for elections. Then followed a strange three weeks in which the country had voted but the results were not known: another very unsatisfactory consequence of rushing the election.

When at last on 26th July the votes were counted and the results announced it was quickly evident that Mr. Churchill and his new government had been badly beaten. Mr. Churchill resigned the same day, and the King sent for Mr. Attlee, who formed a new and purely Labour government. The new parliament assembled on 1st August and just a fortnight later, on the day that Japan surrendered and the world war was at an end, the state opening by the King took place.

Such, in brief, was the course of events.* It seems doubtful whether, had the election been postponed to the autumn as the Labour and Liberal leaders urged, it would have made any really substantial difference to the broad lines of the result; but it would have been fairer to the electors, and especially the service electors, and it would not have left the unpleasant taste in the mouth that a rushed election always does. It is curious to reflect, incidentally, that had Mr. Churchill agreed to an autumn election he would still have been Prime Minister when the Japanese war ended. There, however, we must leave the matter of the election itself, and turn to its effects on the composition and personnel of the House of Commons.

In considering how to present the analysis of the new House, the problem had to be faced whether this could best be done by incorporating the analysis with that for the inter-war elections, or by setting it out separately. At first sight there is something to be said, from the reader's point of view, for the former method. He would then find the statistics for, say, the ages of members, all brought together in the same section of the book. But, apart from the enormous labour, and consequent delay, that would be involved if the whole book, or even Part I of it, had to be re-written completely every time a general election occurred, to say nothing of the expense involved, there seemed to be substantial, and indeed conclusive, arguments against that method.

In the first place the period between the 1914-18 and the 1939-45

* For a fuller account see *The Times House of Commons 1945*, pages 14 to 29; also R. B. McCallum and Alison Readman, *The British General Election of 1945* (1947): this latter was published after this chapter was written.

wars constitutes an era that is in many ways complete in itself. There are, therefore, obvious advantages in leaving the record of that period, and its seven general elections, to stand by itself as a unitary whole. Whatever the post-war period upon which we are entering holds for us, it is certain that it is not a return to the conditions and outlook of the inter-war period: the whole international situation, political and economic, has been radically changed, and so has the domestic situation. The gulf between post-war and pre-war is as wide now as it was in 1918.

This general consideration is reinforced by practical considerations, such as the change in the size of the membership of the House, which would have produced statistical complications in combining the 1945 figures with those for the seven inter-war elections.

Another consideration that tells in the same direction is the inevitable difficulty that would arise in rewriting from a post-war point of view the many passages that, written years before the end of the war, bear the stamp of the then appropriate point of view. It seems to me in every way more fitting to let those passages stand as they are: I find nothing in them to retract, but there would have to be a great deal of recasting if the new edition of the book were to go forth with the implication that the whole of it was written after the 1945 election, and I think that that recasting would involve loss rather than gain.

Finally, since the work has been adopted as a text-book for students of politics and current affairs, and as a book of reference by members of parliament, journalists, and others, it seems likely that inconvenience would be caused if the layout and paging of the first edition were disturbed.

Parts I, II, and III have accordingly been left precisely as they were, and a new Part IV added to cover the 1945 election and other fresh developments. The original three parts stand as the record, in their own field, of a completed era: the new part commences the corresponding record of the new era that is opening out before us.

Advantage has been taken of this arrangement to make some incidental changes that seemed to be called for by the passage of time. In the original work, chiefly as a matter of practical convenience, the field was limited to Great Britain. By excluding the Irish members, whose numbers varied greatly during the period, and of whom the Sinn Fein members never took their seats, a uniform number of 602 members was secured as a sound and convenient basis of comparison between one election and another. Now Great Britain itself has 25 additional members, and the Irish representation seems stabilized: so the opportunity has been taken to present the 1945 statistics on the basis of the whole House of 640 members.

Another change that it has seemed necessary to make is in relation to the "Liberal National" and "National" members. Originally offshoots of the Liberal and Labour parties, they were so treated in the first edition, though towards the end of the inter-war period they were obviously tending to closer and closer association with the Conservative party and becoming more and more remote from their original parties. With the break-up of the coalition after the end of the European war, and the firm decision of the Liberal party to run its own candidates, free from all entanglements with any other party or section, it was evident that the "Liberal Nationals" had sunk into the position of camp-followers of the Conservatives, as the "Liberal Unionists" had done before them, and would almost certainly share the fate of the latter—absorption by the Conservative party—in the end. They and the "Nationals" are accordingly now treated here as Conservatives.* The Ulster Unionists and the two Independent Conservatives are also grouped with the Conservative party, with which they have obviously very close affinity.

Similarly, though for rather different reasons, all definitely Socialist candidates and members have been included in Part IV under the heading of Labour. The Independent Labour party, Common Wealth, the Communists, and the Labour Independent may reject absorption into the official Labour party, or, more usually, be rejected by that party, for what seem good and sufficient reasons on one or both sides, but they, like the official Labour party, are Socialists and will in ninety-nine cases out of a hundred vote with that party. It gives a fairer view, therefore, of the strength of Socialism in the country to group them all together, just as it gives a fairer view of the strength of Conservatism to group the various "Nationals" etc. with the official Conservatives. It will be observed, in any case, that the inclusion of these various "splinter parties" with the two big parties with which they have such close affinity has little numerical effect on the statistics generally, because the "splinter parties" are so tiny in comparison with the big parties. This will be seen at once from Table 40, which gives in detail the figures of party representation in the new House of Commons. To add to the usefulness of this table for general reference purposes, it shows in each case the distribution as between "new" members—those elected for the first time at the July 1945 general election—and the "old" members—those who had sat in the House at any previous time.

To facilitate comparison between the new House and its predecessors, and so to reduce any disadvantage that might be thought to accrue from the giving of the 1945 statistics and analyses in a separate Part, two steps have been taken. The first is to give, under the headings of the tables in Part IV, references to the tables in Part I which give corresponding information about the inter-war period; though it should be noticed that the tables so mentioned do not in all cases give precisely comparable figures. The second is to give within the new tables themselves, wherever appropriate, comparisons with the corresponding average figures for the seven parliaments of the inter-war period. To

---

* That this is just is further evidenced by the fact that, while many "Liberal Nationals" and "Nationals" fought against Liberals in the 1945 election, not one of them fought against a Conservative.

obviate the difficulty of making fair comparison between the inter-war figures based on a membership of 602 and the 1945 figures based on a membership of 640, these comparative figures are, as a rule, given in

TABLE 40.—1945 GENERAL ELECTION: PARTY COMPOSITION OF NEW HOUSE OF COMMONS

Party	Number of Members		
	Old	New	Total
Conservatives:			
Conservative Party	123	65	188
Independent Conservatives ...	2	—	2
Ulster Unionists	6	4	10
Liberal Nationals	8	5	13
Other Nationals	2	—	2
Total	141	74	215
Liberals:			
Liberal Party	7	4	11
Independent Liberal	1	—	1
Total	8	4	12
Labour:			
Labour Party	150	244	394
Labour Independent	1	—	1
Independent Labour Party ...	3	—	3
Common Wealth	1	—	1
Communists	1	1	2
Total	156	245	401
Miscellaneous:			
Irish Nationalists	2	—	2
Independents	9	1	10
Total	11	1	12
Grand Total	316	324	640

the form of percentages, though in a few cases adjustment has been made by other means, which are explained as occasion arises.

It may be added that endeavour has been made, throughout this new part, not merely to give information in relation to the 1945 election corresponding to that given in the earlier parts in relation to the inter-war elections, but also, as opportunity occurs, to provide additional figures and analyses for which there are no counterparts in the first edition. Examples are to be found in Table 40, in the new chapter on Occupations, and in the section on Service on Local Authorities in Chapter XXX. It is hoped that these extensions will add to the useful-ness of the book.

Before passing on to the more specialized chapters, it may be as well here to remind the reader that such tabulations and analyses as are there given involve the handling of large quantities of data which vary considerably in their precision and reliability and in some cases involve an element of evaluation that may introduce the risk of subjective bias. It is desirable to bear this point in mind and not to read into any of these statistics a degree of precision that they cannot possibly possess and that they do not claim. The greatest care has been exercised in collecting the facts, in analysing them, and in presenting the results: but the latter cannot be more precise than the material on which they are founded, and much of this is incapable of exact measurement.

NOTE.—The value of statistics such as those given in the following chapters depends, amongst other things, on the quantitative adequacy of the material used. Hence it may be of interest to give figures show-ing approximately the degree of completeness of the principal data here analysed. This is as follows:

Age	96 per cent of members
Previous Service	100 per cent of members
School Education	89 per cent of members
Occupation	96 per cent of members

Roughly, therefore, 95 per cent of the membership of the present House of Commons is covered by the statistics that follow. This high percentage has been achieved by the use of many sources of informa-tion: see Appendix I(b).

CHAPTER XXVII

1945: AGE AND PREVIOUS SERVICE

1. AGE ON FIRST ELECTION

FOLLOWING the sequence observed in Part I, let us look first at the ages of the *new* members on their election in July 1945. As we have seen, there were 324 such members; but the ages of 15 of them have proved unobtainable. Fortunately these 15 members form less than 5 per cent of the total entry; so, regrettable though their secretiveness is, it cannot much affect the accuracy of our results. Table 41 gives the ages

16

of the other 309, and, for comparison, the corresponding average distribution at the preceding five general elections, 1923 to 1935 inclusive.* It should be noticed that this average distribution is, in a sense, artificial: the actual figures have been taken from Table 1, but they have been multiplied up in the same proportion all round so as to bring the total to the 1945 figure of 309. If this were not done the two sets of figures could not readily be compared by inspection, and the usefulness of the table would be correspondingly reduced. The actual figures, of course, can be found in Table 1 if required.

TABLE 41.—AGE ON FIRST ELECTION: NEW MEMBERS AT
GENERAL ELECTION
[Table 1, page 18]§

5-Year Age-Range†	Number of Members	
	1945	1923-35 Average‡
21-26	3	8
26-31	19	38
31-36	41	40
36-41	67	40
41-46	57	52
46-51	41	53
51-56	28	41
56-61	34	24
61-66	16	10
66-71	3	3
71-76	—	—
Total ...	309	309

§ These references, below the headings of the Tables in Part IV, relate to the Tables in Part I in which more or less closely corresponding information is given.
† Age-range 21-26 includes all ages from 21 years 0 month to 25 years 11 months, and so on.
‡ See explanation in text at top of page.

It will be seen that there are rather curious differences between the age-distribution of the new members in 1945 and that of the new members in the preceding five elections. If we look first at the new members who were under 31 years of age at the time of their election, we find that the 1945 House only included 22, which is less than half of the 1923-35 "average" figure of 46. Similarly the number of 1945 new members who were between the ages of 46 and 56 was only 69, against the previous figure of 94. On the other hand there were in 1945 165 new members between 31 and 46, against 132 in 1923-35, and there were 53 who entered the House at over 56 years of age, against

* The 1918 and 1922 elections are omitted because, owing to the special conditions of the time, the average age of the new members at those elections was abnormally high: see pages 19 and 20.

37 previously. So, proportionately, the new House recruited fewer "young" but more "younger middle-aged" new members, and on the other hand fewer "older middle-aged" but more "elderly" new members than the average pre-war House.

Turning from age distribution to *average age*, the position with regard to new members is given in Table 42. Here again the facts give

TABLE 42.—AVERAGE AGE OF NEW MEMBERS ON FIRST ELECTION
[Table 2, page 20]

1945	1923 to 1935		
	Overall Average	Lowest (1931 and 1935)	Highest (1929)
44y. 6m.	43y. 3½m.	42y. 0½m.	44y. 8½m.

little support to the idea, put about by various writers and speakers, that the new House of Commons is unusually youthful. It will be seen that the average age of its new members is 2 years 5½ months higher than at the two previous elections (1931 and 1935), 14½ months higher than the overall average for the five elections from 1923 to 1935, and only 2½ months lower than the highest of them (1929). It is clear from

TABLE 43.—AVERAGE AGE OF NEW MEMBERS ON FIRST ELECTION
BY PARTIES

Party	1945		Average* 1923 to 1935	
	Years	Months	Years	Months
Conservative	41	4	42	6
Liberal	34	10†	42	9
Labour	45	6½	45	10
Miscellaneous ...	61	10†	43	7½†
All parties ...	44	6	43	3½

* These figures are approximate.
† These figures are of comparatively little significance, owing to the small numbers of members involved.

its average, as it was from its age distribution, that our big influx of new members is not remarkable for its youth.

Let us now, however, look at the average age of the new members according to the parties to which they belong. Table 43 gives the figures, together with approximate figures for the averages at the five general elections 1923 to 1935 for comparison. We see that the Conservative new members show a *reduction* in average age of 14 months, as compared with the 1923-1935 figures, and the Labour new members a reduction of $3\frac{1}{4}$ months, yet the new members of all parties together show an *increase* of $14\frac{1}{2}$ months in average age. This paradoxical result is explained by the fact that there were 245 new Labour members against 74 new Conservatives, and the former, though slightly younger than their Labour predecessors, are older than the Conservative new members, either past or present. (The figures for the Liberal and Miscellaneous new members have little effect on the 1945 all-party average, because of their small numbers.)

It will be noticed that though the average age of the new Labour members has come down by $3\frac{1}{4}$ months that of the Conservative new members has come down by 14 months, so that the gap between the two parties in this respect has widened by $10\frac{1}{4}$ months, from a difference of 3 years 4 months to one of 4 years $2\frac{1}{2}$ months. This is a dis-

TABLE 44.—AVERAGE AGE ON FIRST ELECTION OF ALL MEMBERS
[Table 4, page 24]

Party	1945		All Members 1918 to 1936	
	Years	Months	Years	Months
Conservative ...	40	6	43	$7\frac{1}{2}$
Liberal	37	2*	43	$10\frac{1}{2}$
Labour ...	44	$9\frac{1}{2}$	46	$11\frac{1}{2}$
Miscellaneous ...	50	7*	44	9*
All parties ...	43	4	44	5

* These figures are of comparatively little significance, owing to the small numbers of members involved.

appointing result in view of the statements put about that the parliamentary Labour party is now so much younger than it used to be. There is clearly little foundation for such statements.

Next let us look at the average ages on first election of *all* the members of the new House, old as well as new, and compare them with the corresponding figures for the inter-war period. The figures are given in Table 44, but in studying this it should be borne in mind (a) that the figures for the period 1918 to 1936 include the abnormally elderly members first elected in 1918 and 1922 and also the members elected at by-elections, and (b) that the figures are in all cases those of age on *first* election, not those of age at general elections.

It will be seen that the 1945 figures show a drop of 3 years $1\frac{1}{2}$ months in the case of the Conservatives, one of 2 years 2 months in the case of Labour, and one of 1 year 1 month for all parties together. The average age of first election has come down for Labour members, but it has come down more for Conservatives, so that again the gap between the two has actually increased. Whereas between the wars the average age of new Labour members was 3 years 4 months greater than that of new Conservative members, the average age on first election of all the Labour members of the 1945 House is 4 years 3½ months greater than that of their Conservative fellow-members.

2. AGE AT GENERAL ELECTION

Now let us turn from age on first election to age at general election. Table 45 gives the figures for the new House and compares them with those for the average 1923-35 House. Here, again, the 1923-35 figures

TABLE 45.—AGE AT GENERAL ELECTION
[Table 5, page 27]

5-Year Age-Range*	Number of Members	
	1945	1923-35 Average †
21-26	3	5
26-31	20	29
31-36	49	44
36-41	86	61
41-46	93	85
46-51	83	96
51-56	83	104
56-61	88	88
61-66	64	60
66-71	25	29
71-76	14	11
76-81	7	3
Total ...	615	615

* Age-range 21-26 includes all ages from 21 years 0 month to 25 years 11 months, and so on.
† See explanation in text.

are, in a sense, artificial: that is to say, they give the correct *relative* distribution for the average of those five elections, but the actual figures have been multiplied up to bring the total to 615 for ease of comparison with the 1945 figures. Anyone who wants the actual figures can, of course, get them from Table 5. It will be noticed that the total of 615 is 25 less than the total number of members: this 25 represents the residue of M.Ps. who have an unconquerable aversion from stating their ages. It is a pity that they are so unhelpful; but their peculiar secretiveness has little effect on the final results, since they form less than 4 per cent of the total membership.

The changes shown by Table 45 between the average 1923-35 House and the 1945 House for the ages of all members are very similar in their general effect to those shown by Table 41 for new members. There are only 23 members under 31 years of age in the new House, against 34 in the 1923-35 "average" House—a drop of 33 per cent—and there is similarly a drop of 17 per cent in the age-group between 46 and 56, the numbers falling from 200 to 166. On the other hand the age-group between 31 and 46 has risen from 190 to 228—an increase of 20 per cent—while the age-group between 71 and 81 has risen from 14 to 21 —a 50 per cent increase. Hence, taking the new House as a whole, we find that, as with the new members, there is something of a swing from "young" to "younger middle-aged" and from "older middle-aged" to "elderly".

What is the broad general effect of these changes? We can probably judge of it best by turning again from age-distribution to average age. In Table 46 we have the figures for the new House contrasted with

TABLE 46.—AVERAGE AGE OF HOUSE AT GENERAL ELECTION
[Table 6, page 32]

1945	1923 to 1935		
	Overall Average	Lowest (1931)	Highest (1935)
49y. 10m.	49y. 9½m.	48y. 6m.	51y. 0m.

those for the 1923-35 Houses. Whatever their actual ages, new members collectively are almost of necessity much younger than old members collectively, and there is therefore a strong presumption that a House which contains a high proportion of new members will be considerably younger in its average age than a House which contains only a small proportion. This 1945 House contains much the highest proportion returned at any election within the last thirty years or more. It might therefore be expected to have as a whole a low average age, even though the new members are not particularly young.

The Table shows that the overall average age of the whole House at the five preceding elections was 49 years 9½ months, with a maximum figure of 51 years 0 month in 1935 (when there were only 79 new members) and a minimum figure of 48 years 6 months in 1931 (when there were 206 new members). It is disappointing, therefore, to find that the average age of the 1945 House, with its 324 new members, is 49 years 10 months: 16 months higher than the average age of the 1931 House, and half a month higher than the average for the five preceding elections together.

The accumulated evidence, then, makes it clear that the impression that this is an exceptionally youthful House has no foundation. As a whole it is older than the 1923, 1924, and 1931 Houses; while its new members are older than those of 1923, 1924, 1931, and 1935. Moreover, as we have seen, apart from averages, it does not contain an exceptional number of "young" members.

Before leaving the question of age it may be of interest to set out the average ages in the new House, for old and new members separately and together, by parties. Table 47 gives the figures. These bring out clearly the fact that, as already noted, the average age of new members is always considerably lower than that of old members. The figures should also finally dispose of any idea that this is a youthful House, and particularly of the idea, put forward by some people, that the Labour party in the new House is notable for youth. The average Labour M.P. at the opening of the newly-elected parliament had already nearly thirty years of adult life behind him, and the average

TABLE 47.—AVERAGE AGE AT 1945 GENERAL ELECTION, BY PARTIES

Party	Old Members		New Members		All Members	
	Years	Months	Years	Months	Years	Months
Conservative ...	52	3½	41	4	48	6
Liberal* ...	52	2½	34	10	46	5
Labour	57	7	45	6½	50	2½
Miscellaneous*	59	9	61	10	59	11½
All parties ...	55	2	44	6	49	10

* These figures, given for the sake of completeness, are of little statistical significance, owing to the small numbers involved.

Conservative M.P. was only a year and 8½ months younger. The little band of Liberals averaged a couple of years younger still, but their numbers are too small for this to have much significance. Finally, the average age of the new House as a whole, right at its start, was close on 50 years—some five years or so above the average age of the adult population of the country generally.

3. PREVIOUS SERVICE

In one respect this new House is unique in modern times, in that more than half its members—324 out of 640—when its first session opened had no experience at all of parliamentary life. It might be expected, therefore, that the House as a whole would be the least experienced we have known. When we come to consider average previous service we shall see that—measured in this way—that is not the case. But let us first record the actual amounts of previous service possessed by its members. This is set down in Table 48, together with the inter-war average figures. It should be noticed that the latter have been adjusted to make them total 640 for ease of comparison with the 1945 figures. Those who want the actual inter-war figures will find them on page 36.

It will be seen that 234 members of the new House started with

TABLE 48.—PREVIOUS SERVICE AT GENERAL ELECTIONS

[Table 8, page 36]

Previous Service in Years	Number of Members	
	1945	Inter-War Average*
Nil	324	186
0-5	78	195
5-10	97	114
10-15	59	83
15-20	46	31
20-25	27	15
25-30	6	9
30-35	1	4
35-40	—	2
40-45	2	1
Total ...	640	640

* Adjusted to total 640: see text.

15 years or less of previous experience, as against 392 members of the inter-war average (adjusted) House, while 9 members of the new House had 25 years or more of previous experience against 16 members of the inter-war House. On the other hand the new House included 73 members with from 15 to 25 years of previous experience,

TABLE 49.—AVERAGE PREVIOUS SERVICE AT GENERAL ELECTIONS

[Table 9, page 37]

1945	Inter-War Elections		
	Overall Average	Lowest (1924)	Highest (1935)
5y. 4m.	5y. 11m.	4y. 11m.	8y. 1m.

as against 46 members of the inter-war average House, thus to some extent redressing the balance.

These figures are interesting, but probably their general effect is more easily perceived by looking at the average length of previous service of members, as set out in Table 49. Judged by this criterion the new House is not exceptionally inexperienced, though its average length of previous service is less than the inter-war overall average. On the other hand, of course, it contains the largest proportion on record of completely new members.

CHAPTER XXVIII

1945: EDUCATION

1. SCHOOL EDUCATION

IT may be as well at the outset to remind the reader that, in the classification employed in this book, the "Public Schools" are taken as the schools on the Headmasters' Conference list, "Secondary" is used in its old sense as denoting the education given in grammar schools, high schools, junior technical schools, and schools of similar type (other than Public Schools), and "Elementary" is used to denote the education given in schools carried on until 1945 under the elementary education regulations of the Board of Education and in schools of similar type, including council schools, board schools, "National" schools, "British" schools, etc. It is clearly necessary to ignore the new statutory definition of "secondary" under which all post-primary schools, of whatever calibre, are indiscriminately labelled "secondary"; not only because as yet it is in all too many instances a case of changing the name without in fact changing the reality, but also because even the youngest M.P. completed his school education before the new nomenclature was imposed. For further discussion of the method of classification the reader is referred to pages 41 and 42.

It should also be noted that, as before, only the schools attended in the later part of members' school lives are taken into account. A member who started his education at an infant school, passed thence to an elementary school, and thence to a grammar school is accordingly classified as having had a secondary-school education. Similarly a member who started in a preparatory school and passed in due course to a public school is classified as having had a public-school education.

The basic figures for the school education of the members of the new 1945 House of Commons are given in Table 50; but, useful though these are for reference, they do not bring out all the significant features of the case, nor are they very convenient for comparison with the corresponding figures for the inter-war period. Accordingly we proceed to study various aspects of the subject by means of a further series of tables.

First, however, let us eliminate the "school unknown" figures by distributing the members concerned to the types of school which they have probably attended. As a first approximation we might reasonably assume that this distribution is the same as that of the members *of their own party* whose school education is known. But we can do better than this by taking the new and old members within a party separately before making the distribution. With this refinement it is probable

TABLE 50.—SCHOOL EDUCATION: 1945 HOUSE
[Table 10, page 43]

Party	Number of Members				
	Public School	Secondary School	Elementary School	School Unknown	Total
Conservative	167	27	3	18	215
Liberal ...	3	6	—	3	12
Labour ...	81	86	189	45	401
Miscellaneous	5	4	1	2	12
Total ...	256	123	193	68	640

that the errors made in the distribution will be small, if not negligible, amongst the "school unknown" members themselves; while in the House as a whole, of which they constitute little more than one-tenth, the resultant errors will be of even less importance. Proceeding on these lines, we get the figures set out in Table 51. From these it is at

TABLE 51.—SCHOOL EDUCATION: 1945 HOUSE: ADJUSTED
[Table 14, page 49]

Party	Number of Members			
	Public School	Secondary School	Elementary School	Total
Conservative ...	182	29	4	215
Liberal	4	8	—	12
Labour	92	97	212	401
Miscellaneous ...	6	5	1	12
Total ...	284	139	217	640

once apparent that, even with the very different make-up of the new House, there is still the same marked tendency for the Conservatives to be the public-school party, the Liberals the secondary-school party, and Labour the elementary-school party.

We shall, however, get a clearer view of the educational aspects of the new House if we express these figures as percentages and compare them with the corresponding percentages for the seven inter-war elections. Let us first look at the distribution of members as a whole, irrespective of party, between the three types of school: this is set out in Table 52.

It will be seen that, though the new House contains an appreciably smaller proportion of public-school members than the average inter-war House, this low proportion does not constitute a record, the 1929 House holding that distinction. Similarly, and in complement with the public-school position, though the new House contains an appreciably larger proportion of elementary-school members than the average inter-war House, this high proportion also fails to beat the record

TABLE 52.—SCHOOL EDUCATION
[Table 13, page 46]

Type of School	1945	Inter-War Elections		
		Average	Lowest	Highest
	%	%	%	%
Public	44½	56	43 (1929)	66 (1931)
Secondary ...	21½	21½	18½ (1935)	23½ (1918)
Elementary ...	34	22½	11½ (1931)	35½ (1929)
Total ...	100	100	—	—

established by the 1929 figures. As for the secondary-school membership, fluctuations in this have been comparatively small throughout the period under consideration, and the proportion in the new House, coinciding as it does with the average for the seven inter-war parliaments, calls for no special comment.

Actually the proportionate distribution of members between the three types of school in 1945 is remarkably close to that in 1929, sixteen years earlier. Here are the figures:

	1945	1929
Public schools	44½%	43%
Secondary schools	21½%	21½%
Elementary schools	34%	35½%

These figures do not, of course, tell the whole story, since the party make-up in 1945 is very different from that of 1929: but they serve to dispose of the implication made by some writers* that educationally this is a new type of House of Commons. In education, as in age and

* E.g., Nancy E. Robertson and J. A. Waites, *The Educational Background of the Present House of Commons,* circulated to the press in April 1946.

other matters, the new House makes no radical departure from inter-
war standards, though it does present many features of interest.

Next let us look at the party composition of each of the three groups
of members, derived from the three types of school, as set out in
Table 53. This has its points of interest—for example, the fact that no
fewer than a third of the public-school members, as well as almost the
whole of the elementary-school members, are now to be found on the
Labour benches—but the position it discloses is so much affected by
the drastic change in the party make-up of the House of Commons
resulting from the 1945 election that it is not easy to disentangle the
genuinely educational developments from those due to the fluctuations
of party fortunes. Let us, then, reduce the complications by eliminating
one of the variables—the fluctuations in party strengths—and consider

TABLE 53.—PARTY AFFILIATION OF MEMBERS FROM EACH TYPE
OF SCHOOL

[Table 11, page 44; Table 14, page 49; Table 51, page 250]

| Party | Type of School | | | | | |
| | Public | | Secondary | | Elementary | |
	1945	Inter-War Average	1945	Inter-War Average	1945	Inter-War Average
	%	%	%	%	%	%
Conservative ...	64	82½	21	48	2	6½
Liberal	1½	13	5½	31½	—	7½
Labour	32½	4	69½	17½	97½	85½
Miscellaneous ...	2	½	4	3	½	½
Total ...	100	100	100	100	100	100

the educational distribution within each of the parties. The necessary
figures are set out in Table 54.

Looking first at the figures for the Conservative members of parliament, we see that the differences between the inter-war average percentages and the 1945 percentages are not very marked. They are
interesting, however, and in the direction that previous experience
would lead us to expect. With the Conservatives the safer seats are, in
general, reserved for the more aristocratic and wealthy elements in the
party, and consequently a heavy loss of seats falls harder on the non-
public-school than on the public-school candidates, so that the *proportion* of public-school members in the parliamentary party rises. Had
the party been more successful in the 1945 election it is almost certain
that its composition in the new House would have shown less deviation
from the inter-war average.

When we turn from the Conservative figures to those for the Labour members we find changes that are much more striking. The proportion of public-school members has risen to over $2\frac{1}{2}$ times its inter-war average figure, the proportion of secondary-school members has risen by 60 per cent, and there has been a corresponding drop in the elementary school proportion. Now in the Labour party we find the opposite tendency to that in the Conservative party. With Labour the safer seats are, in general, reserved for the members of trade-union type, who are mostly of elementary-school origin. Hence an increase in the *proportion* of seats held by public-school members, which in the Conservative party is associated with a reduction in the total number of

TABLE 54.—SCHOOL EDUCATION OF MEMBERS OF EACH PARTY
[Table 12, page 45; Table 14, page 49; Table 51, page 250]

Type of School	Party							
	Conservative		Liberal		Labour		Miscellaneous	
	1945	Inter-War Average	1945*	Inter-War Average	1945	Inter-War Average	1945*	Inter-War Average*
	%	%	%	%	%	%	%	%
Public ...	$84\frac{1}{2}$	$79\frac{1}{2}$	33	$46\frac{1}{2}$	23	9	50	$16\frac{1}{2}$
Secondary	$13\frac{1}{2}$	18	67	43	24	15	$41\frac{1}{2}$	67
Elementary	2	$2\frac{1}{2}$	—	$10\frac{1}{2}$	53	76	$8\frac{1}{2}$	$16\frac{1}{2}$
Total ...	100	100	100	100	100	100	100	100

* These figures, given for the sake of completeness, are of little statistical significance, owing to the small numbers involved.

seats held, in the Labour party is associated with an increase in the total number of seats held.

Some part, therefore, of the rise in the public-school and secondary-school percentages within the parliamentary Labour party, and the corresponding fall in the elementary-school percentage, must be attributed to the big increase in the total number of seats held by the party; and should the party suffer substantial losses at a future general election we should expect to see the proportion of public-school and secondary-school members fall and that of elementary-school members rise again.

It seems doubtful, however, whether the whole of the very marked change in the educational make-up of the parliamentary Labour party can be attributed to this cause. It is much more likely that some part of it reflects a genuine expansion of the Labour party within the ranks of the professional and middle classes, who have in general received an ampler school education than the typical manual workers. How far this expansion has gone, and how far it will prove permanent, are perhaps open questions; but of the fact of the expansion there can be little doubt.

In view of these marked changes in the educational composition of the parliamentary party, and the interesting speculations that they stimulate, it may be worth while to pursue the matter a little further and analyse the school origins of the old and new Labour members separately. By "old" members we mean, of course, those who were re-elected in July 1945 after having sat in the House at any previous time: by "new" those who entered it for the first time at that election. As there were 156 of these "old" Labour members and 245 of the "new", the numbers are sufficiently large to make the comparison statistically worth while. The results of an analysis on these lines are interesting. Table 55 gives the figures, and the inter-war percentages

TABLE 55.—SCHOOL EDUCATION OF PARLIAMENTARY LABOUR PARTY

Type of School	Old Members 1945	New Members 1945	Inter-War Average
	%	%	%
Public	17	26½	9
Secondary ...	15½	30	15
Elementary ...	67½	43½	76
Total ...	100	100	100

(for the Labour members as a whole) have been brought in from Table 54 for ease of comparison.

It will be seen that there are pronounced differences between the educational background of the old Labour members re-elected in 1945 and that of the new Labour members who then first entered the House. Proportionately the recruits show a 50 per cent increase in the number of public-school men, a 100 per cent increase in the number of those from secondary schools, and a 35 per cent decrease in those from elementary schools, by comparison with the veterans. But even the latter show a doubling of the public-school element, a slight increase in that from the secondary schools, and an appreciable drop in that from the elementary schools, by comparison with the inter-war distribution for the party. If we go a step further and compare the figures for the recruits with those for the inter-war average of the party, the contrast is even more marked. We find the proportion of public-school members trebled, that of the secondary-school members doubled, and that of the elementary-school members nearly halved.

These are striking changes. They are much too drastic to be attributable to chance: nor can they reasonably be regarded as due solely to the gaining of more seats (*i.e.*, as the mere reverse of the Conservative changes of make-up): in this connexion it should be realized that not all the "safe" seats are held by "old" members, nor all the "doubtful" seats by "new" ones. For the time being, at any rate, there seems little doubt that the Labour party has widened its appeal to the electorate and is less on a "class" footing than it used to be. If this is so, then the changes in the educational and other attributes of the parliamentary party may well be, in part at least, a reflection of similar changes in the party as a whole—or perhaps one should say in the more active elements of the party as a whole. This broadening of the base of the party should, prima facie, give it a more secure position than it would otherwise have: but whether the changes in the type of candidate elected to parliament will commend themselves equally to all the party's supporters—to the trade unions, for example—and whether in the long run they will make for party unity and stability cannot yet be determined.

Now, before leaving the question of school education, let us take just a glance at the position of Eton and Harrow in the 1945 House of Commons. Between the wars roughly one-fourth of all the Conservative members of parliament had been educated at Eton, and one-third at either Eton or Harrow. In the 1945 House at least 57 of the 215 Conservative members, that is, $26\frac{1}{2}$ per cent, come from Eton, and at least 71, or 33 per cent, from either Eton or Harrow. So there seems to be no diminution as yet in the hold that these two schools have so long had on the party.

In the average inter-war House as a whole, Eton accounted for about $17\frac{1}{2}$ per cent of the membership and Harrow for another 7 per cent. In the new House Eton can claim at least 64 members (10 per cent of the total membership) and Harrow can claim at least 16 ($2\frac{1}{2}$ per cent). So even in this largely Socialist House of Commons one member in every ten is an old Etonian, and one in every eight is either an old Etonian or an old Harrovian. We may remind ourselves in this connexion that, on a population basis, the proportionate representation of Eton would be about one-fifth of a member and that of Harrow about one-tenth of a member.*

2. University Education

The numbers of members of the 1945 House of Commons who are known to have attended a university (or universities) are set out in Table 56. It is probable that some of these figures may be to a small extent understatements, because of the lack of information about the minority of members who are unwilling to disclose anything about themselves. It is unlikely, however, that such deviations from com-

* See pages 51 and 52.

pleteness are anything more than trifling, since university men are not usually so secretive about themselves. It should be noted that by no

TABLE 56.—UNIVERSITY EDUCATION: 1945 HOUSE

[Table 15, page 53]

Party	Number of Members					
	Oxford	Cambridge	London	Other British	Overseas	Total*
Conservative ...	62	44	4	16	5	124
Liberal	3	4	1	3	—	8
Labour	38	21	30	44	12	129
Miscellaneous ...	4	1	1	1	1	7
Total ...	107	70	36	64	18	268

* Apparent discrepancies in these totals are due to the fact that some members have attended more than one university.

means all the members included in the table are graduates: many of them left the university without taking a degree.

Table 56 gives the essential facts and is useful for reference, but we

TABLE 57.—UNIVERSITY EDUCATION

[Table 18, page 57]

University	1945	Inter-War Elections		
		Average	Lowest	Highest
	%	%	%	%
Oxford	17	17½	13½ (1929)	22½ (1931)
Cambridge ...	11	13½	11 (1923)	17 (1931)
London	5½ ⎫	4 ⎫		
Other British ...	9½ ⎬ 16½	9½ ⎬ 13½	12 (1935)	15 (1931)
Overseas ...	3 ⎭	2 ⎭		
Total* ...	42	42	37 (1923)	51 (1931)

* Apparent discrepancies in these totals are due to the fact that some members have attended more than one university.

shall get a clearer view of the position if, using percentages, we compare the 1945 figures with those for the inter-war period. This comparison, for the House as a whole, is set out in Table 57.

It will be seen that one member of the new House in every six has been at Oxford, one in every nine has been at Cambridge, and one in six has been at some other university. The Oxford proportion is a little below the inter-war average, but well above the minimum (1929) figure. Curiously enough—for it disagrees superficially with previous trends*—the Cambridge proportion is down to the minimum inter-war figure of 11 per cent reached in 1923. On the other hand London, though still poorly represented, has done better than before; while the universities other than Oxford and Cambridge have collectively reached a higher percentage than at any of the inter-war elections.

Taking the university-educated members as a whole, the proportion in the new House—42 per cent—is just the same as that in the average

TABLE 58.—PARTY AFFILIATION OF UNIVERSITY-EDUCATED MEMBERS
[Table 16, page 54]

Party	University					
	Oxford		Cambridge		Other	
	1945	Inter-War Average	1945	Inter-War Average	1945	Inter-War Average
	%	%	%	%	%	%
Conservative ...	58	84	63	76½	20½	50
Liberal	3	11	5½	16	3	28½
Labour	35½	4	30	7	74½	19½
Miscellaneous ...	3½	1	1½	½	2	2
Total ...	100	100	100	100	100	100

inter-war House, and also that in the 1924 House. The make-up, however, in 1924 was rather different from that in 1945: here are the figures:

	1945	1924
Oxford	17%	17½%
Cambridge	11%	14%
Others	16½%	13½%

Nevertheless, considering that the 1924 House included 400 Conservatives and only 151 Labour members, whereas the 1945 House includes 401 Labour members and only 215 Conservatives, the differences between them in respect of university education are remarkably small.

Now let us see how the product of the universities divides itself among the parties, comparing the new House in this respect also with the average inter-war House. Table 58 gives the appropriate percent-

* See page 56.

ages.* It will be seen that though the proportion of Labour men in the Oxford total has risen considerably, the Oxford product is still predominantly Conservative; and the same is true of the Cambridge product. In the case of the other universities, however, the reverse is true: here Labour predominates. But all the figures in this table are much affected by the respective party strengths, and the fluctuations in these make it difficult to discern the more strictly educational trends in the party make-ups. Let us, therefore, turn to the distribution of university education within the parties separately, as set out in Table 59. It should be noticed that the percentages in this table show merely the *proportionate* distribution between the different universities: that is, the figures have been adjusted to allow for the fact that a number of

TABLE 59.—UNIVERSITY EDUCATION OF MEMBERS OF EACH PARTY
[Table 17, page 56]

University	Party							
	Conservative		Liberal		Labour		Miscellaneous	
	1945	Inter-War Average	1945*	Inter-War Average	1945	Inter-War Average	1945*	Inter-War Average*
	%	%	%	%	%	%	%	%
Oxford ...	46½	46	30	24	26	17	57	28
Cambridge	33	33	40	28	14½	23	14½	11
Other ...	20½	21	30	48	59½	60	28½	61
Total ...	100	100	100	100	100	100	100	100

* These figures, given for the sake of completeness, are of little statistical significance, owing to the small numbers involved.

members have attended more than one university. This point may be illustrated by referring back to Table 56, from which it will be seen that just half the university-educated Conservatives have been at Oxford; but a number of these have also attended other universities, and the percentage figures have had to be adjusted accordingly.

Looking first at the Conservative percentages, we see that there is very little difference between the figures for 1945 and those for the average inter-war House. Such difference as there is, however, shows a trend towards Oxford and away from the newer universities. This is in accordance with the tendency we observed in discussing school education: it reflects the diminution of the party's representation in the

* In comparing these figures with those in Table 16 it should be noticed that the latter relate to all inter-war members, not to the average House.

House, the safer seats in general being held by the members educated at the older universities.

When we turn to the Labour percentages we find a much bigger rise in the Oxford figures, accompanied by a fairly heavy and rather unaccountable fall in those for Cambridge, and a drop, though much smaller, in those for the newer universities. As with the Conservatives, there is a slight trend towards the older universities; but, as with other similar dual trends already noticed, it is probably due in the two parties to precisely opposite reasons—in the Conservative party to the loss of seats—in the Labour party to their gain.

As we have seen, Table 59 shows merely the *proportionate* distribution, as between one university and another, of those members of each

TABLE 60.—UNIVERSITY EDUCATION OF MEMBERS OF EACH PARTY

University	Party							
	Conservative		Liberal		Labour		Miscellaneous	
	1945	Inter-War Average	1945*	Inter-War Average	1945	Inter-War Average	1945*	Inter-War Average*
	%	%	%	%	%	%	%	%
Oxford ...	27	24	20	12	8½	2½	33½	12
Cambridge	19	17½	26½	13½	4½	3½	8½	5
Other ...	12	11	20	23½	19	9	16½	26½
Non-University	42	47½	33½	51	68	85	41½	56½
Total ...	100	100	100	100	100	100	100	100

* These figures, given for the sake of completeness, are of little statistical significance, owing to the small numbers involved.

party who have had some sort of university education. But these proportions do not provide the only criterion of comparison. Let us now take a wider view and include non-university as well as university-educated members. Then we get the percentages set out in Table 60. Here again it should be noticed that, because of the fact that a certain number of members have been at more than one university, there is unavoidably a slight ambiguity about the figures.

In each of the two big parties, it will be seen, taken separately, there is a marked increase in the number of members with a university education, amounting in the case of Labour to a doubling of its percentage. Now, no doubt, some part of each of these increases is due to the cause we have already noticed—loss of seats by the Conservatives and gain of seats by Labour—but the increases seem too heavy to be accounted for by that alone. I suggest that in both parties they reflect also the expansion of university education that is taking place in the community generally, while in the Labour party there is in addition a third cause: the wider appeal that, as we have already observed, the party is making amongst professional and middle-class people. An indication, though of course not a proof, of this last factor is to be found in the fact that whereas a bare 24 per cent of the "old" (i.e., re-elected) 1945 Labour members are university men or women, some $37\frac{1}{2}$ per cent of the "new" ones fall into that category. Finally we may note the paradoxical result that, although each of the two big parliamentary parties includes in its ranks a markedly greater proportion of university-educated members than before, the proportion of such members in the House as a whole shows no increase over the inter-war average of 42 per cent. The explanation is, of course, as before: the growth in each party is relative and is balanced by the big change in the party strengths in the House.

CHAPTER XXIX

1945: OCCUPATION

BEFORE turning to the facts and figures about the occupations followed by members of parliament, it may be as well to draw attention again to the special difficulties with which this particular question confronts the investigator. There is no need to repeat what has been said on this point in Chapter VII, but it is necessary to ask the reader to bear it in mind. It should be realized that in classifying the occupations of members the investigator has in many matters to rely on his own judgement to a much greater extent than he would wish. It is not merely that the data themselves are at many points obscure or capable of more than one interpretation: even if all the obscurities were cleared up, and if the proper interpretation of the facts in each individual case were settled there would still be problems as to the best way of presenting the material so amassed. For example, to specify precisely the very varied occupations of all members, even if it could be done, would result in a presentation so complicated that it would serve little useful purpose: yet as soon as one attempts to simplify by grouping together closely related occupations one is up against the fact that there are many alternative methods by which this might be done, and it has to be realized that there is no one solution that meets all the difficulties.

Hence different investigators, working separately, would be almost certain to produce results which showed some discrepancies, however honest and however painstaking they might be; and the statistics that follow, though prepared with the greatest care, must not be assumed to possess a precision that they do not claim and indeed could not possibly be given.

Careful consideration of the general problem of presentation suggests that in dealing, as we now are, with the results of a single general election, there is much to be said in favour of a method rather different from that employed in Part I, where we were concerned with the whole inter-war era, including no less than seven elections. It has been decided, accordingly, instead of following the XXXII Census Groups as was there done, to adopt a more realistic procedure, allot to each member what appears to be his most appropriate occupational label, and then tabulate the occupations of members in the order of frequency with which these "labels" occur. This has the advantage of showing more clearly at a glance the distribution of occupations, and it is, indeed, more accurate, because it avoids the serious blunders* into which the Census grouping falls.

The practical difficulty, as already indicated, is to know how many labels to use and what to put on them. If one uses too many, in the endeavour to be precise, the result is so elaborate as to be tedious and unenlightening. If, on the other hand, one uses too few, the labels may become almost meaningless and the result, though simple, of little value.

Table 61, which gives the occupations of all parties together in the new House, represents the best compromise between these contending considerations that it has been found possible to achieve. It has been planned with great care, and it is hoped that it will be found both useful and interesting. The centre column contains the "labels": the occupations, or groups of closely-related occupations, that they cover are placed in the order of their frequency of occurrence in the 1945 House, this order being stated in the first column, on the left of the table. In the second column will be found the number of members of that House to whom the given "label" appears to be appropriate. On the other (right-hand) side of the centre column are given comparative figures for the average inter-war House, the fourth column containing the number of members and the last column the order of frequency. Since Part I did not give this information in this form, these last two columns will, it is hoped, prove a useful supplement to that part, giving a fresh view of the average inter-war House in its occupational aspect.

Since the new House, with its 640 members, is larger than the inter-war House, the numbers in this fourth column have been proportionately adjusted, so as to give a fair comparison with the numbers in the second column.

A few further points should perhaps be made before we consider the actual figures in the table. "Barristers" includes only those who, so far as can be ascertained, have actually used their qualifications in legal practice, at the bar, on the bench, etc. (For particulars of the total numbers of members qualified as barristers, whether practising or not, reference should be made to Table 68.) "Regular Officers" includes Navy, Army, and Air Force: it does *not* include officers serving on

* See pages 58 and 59.

purely war-time or Territorial commissions. "Civil Servants" includes diplomats, but does not include either clerks or manual workers. "Railwaymen" includes only distinctively railway workers, such as station officials, enginemen, guards, and signalmen: it does not include such people as clerks and craftsmen merely because they are employed

TABLE 61.—OCCUPATIONS: ALL PARTIES

1945		Occupation	Inter-War Average	
Order	Number		Number*	Order
1	67	Barristers	83	1
2	56	Teachers and Lecturers ...	23	8
3	51	Regular Officers ...	64	2
4	45	Miners	42	4
5	41	Journalists and Authors ...	26	5
6	36	Clerks and Secretaries ...	19	9
7	29	Manufacturers	51	3
8	18	Metal Workers	14	10
9	17	Civil Servants	12	12
10-11	{ 16 ⟨ 16	Solicitors ... ... Farmers	25 10	6 14-15
12-13	{ 14 ⟨ 14	Physicians and Surgeons ... Railwaymen	11 5	13 21-25
14	11	Professional Engineers ...	13	11
15-16	{ 10 ⟨ 10	Merchants ... ... Accountants	24 5	7 21-25
17	9	Wood Workers	7	17-18
18	8	Political Organizers	5	21-25
19-21	{ 7 ⟨ 7 ⟨ 7	Stockbrokers ... ... Insurance and Underwriters... Retailers	8 6 4	16 19-20 26-28
22	6	Printing Operatives	3	29-31
23-25	{ 5 ⟨ 5 ⟨ 5	Textile Operatives ... Ministers of Religion ... Building, etc., Operatives ...	6 4 } 4 }	19-20 26-28
26-28	{ 4 ⟨ 4 ⟨ 4	Seamen and Boatmen ... Land Agents ... ... Boot and Shoe Operatives ...	5 2 1	21-25 — —
29-33	{ 3 ⟨ 3 ⟨ 3 ⟨ 3 ⟨ 3	Shipowners ... ... Bankers and Bank Officials ... Postal Workers ... ... Estate Agents ... ... Advertising Agents ...	10 7 2 2 —	14-15 17-18 — — —
—	—	Builders, etc.	5	21-25
—	2	Agents and Travellers ...	3 }	29-31
—	1	Theatre, etc., Managers ...	3 }	

* The figures in this column have been slightly adjusted in order to give a fair comparison with the corresponding figures for 1945: see text.

on a railway. "Building Operatives" includes bricklayers, housepainters, etc., but not carpenters and joiners, who are classified as "Wood Workers".

Further, because of the extreme difficulty of distinguishing between those who are Company Directors or Trade Union Officials as their main jobs in life and those to whom such descriptions are incidental to the following of some other occupation, no figures are given in this table for either category. Information about both categories will be found in Table 68. Somewhat similar remarks apply to "Unoccupied" members: for these, however, reference should be made to Table 67.

Finally, Table 61 has been limited in length by the exclusion of occupations to which, in neither the 1945 House nor the average inter-war House, as many as three members are known to belong. It will be seen that the table, prepared on these lines, includes 540 members of the new House: the 100 not included (a) belong to occupations that can claim less than three members each, or (b) are company-directors or trade-union officials not otherwise classifiable, or (c) have ambiguous occupational descriptions (e.g., "In business"), or (d) have declined to give any information about their occupations.

As usual Barristers head the list of parliamentary occupations, with 67 members of the new House of Commons, excluding those who have never practised. But though they retain pride of place they are not quite so predominant as in the average inter-war House. Next, on this occasion, come Teachers and Lecturers with 56 members, displacing Regular Officers of the fighting forces from second to third place. This big rise in the number of Teachers—from 23 (inter-war adjusted average) to 56—is one of the outstanding features of the new House from the occupational point of view. They have jumped from 8th place in the list to 2nd. The drop in the number of Regular Officers (who are nearly all Conservatives) from 64 to 51 is remarkably small, considering the sweeping changes in the political complexion of the House. The number of Miners is noticeably constant: they mostly sit for safe seats in mining areas, which are little disturbed by political changes, up or down.

Journalists and Authors show a substantial increase in numbers: not, perhaps, very surprising in the circumstances. Clerks and Secretaries show a number nearly double their inter-war average, while Manufacturers drop to little more than half their inter-war average strength, and Merchants do even worse. So we could go on down the table: but the reader can make further comparisons for himself, aided by Table 62, which gives the percentage changes in a number of leading occupations.

Contemplation of these two tables not only reminds us of the peculiarly uneven and unsatisfactory representation of occupations in the House of Commons,* but also suggests doubts of the merits of an electoral system which transfers large slices of political power from, say, merchants and manufacturers to teachers, clerks, and journalists, or vice-versa. The balance of occupations in the country does not change at a general election, and there is something wrong with a system that produces such drastic occupational changes in parliament. It must, of course, be borne in mind that most of the changes are due, in part at least, to the changes in the party composition of the House,

* See, for example, pages 162 to 166.

since many occupations—Regular Officers, Stockbrokers, Miners, and Metal Workers, for example—are strongly associated wtih a particular party. But that fact, while it explains some of the changes, does not in itself justify them. It is a striking indication, moreover, of the class character of both the Conservative and Labour parties: so long as they differ as they do, in education, occupation, and other characteristics, neither party can be considered truly national.

If now we wish to gain a clearer idea of the changes that have taken place in the occupational make-up of parliament, other than those directly due to the change from a predominantly Conservative to a predominantly Labour House, we must look at the figures for each of the two big parties separately. (The Liberal parliamentary party and

TABLE 62.—CHANGES IN PROPORTIONS OF HOUSE DRAWN FROM
LEADING OCCUPATIONS
(1945 compared with inter-war average)

ALL PARTIES

Occupation	Change
Teachers and Lecturers	150% increase
Clerks and Secretaries	90% ,,
Journalists and Authors	55% ,,
Farmers	55% ,,
Civil Servants	45% ,,
Metal Workers	30% ,,
Physicians and Surgeons ...	25% ,,
Miners	5% ,,
Professional Engineers	20% decrease
Regular Officers	20% ,,
Barristers	20% ,,
Solicitors	35% ,,
Manufacturers	45% ,,
Merchants	60% ,,

the Miscellaneous group of members are each, of course, too small to make a similar analysis of their occupations worth while.)

Looking first at the Conservatives, we have in Table 63 a comparison of their leading occupations in the 1945 House with those in the inter-war average House, on the same lines as that given in Table 61 for all parties together. The inter-war figures have been slightly adjusted, as in Table 61, to allow for the difference in size of the two Houses (but not, of course, for the difference in size of the party representation). It will be seen that, amongst Conservatives in the new House, Regular Officers of the fighting services are well ahead of all other occupations, whereas in the inter-war average House they shared first place with the Barristers. This change is not due to any falling-off in the proportionate number of Barristers—that number, in fact, has slightly increased— but to a substantial rise in the proportionate number of Officers. Manu-

facturers come third in both cases, but they have lost ground all the
same. Solicitors have dropped from fourth place to seventh-eleventh,
and Merchants from fifth place to twelfth-fifteenth. On the other hand
Civil Servants, Farmers, and Stockbrokers have gained ground in the
new House, both in actual numbers and relatively.

It will, of course, be realized that the number of Conservative
members in the new House (215) is considerably less than that in the
average inter-war House (347), and this fact needs to be borne in mind
in studying Table 63. To facilitate comparison, Table 64 shows the
proportionate rise and fall in the leading occupations on the Conservative side of the new House by comparison with the inter-war average

TABLE 63.—OCCUPATIONS: CONSERVATIVES

1945		Occupation	Inter-War Average	
Order	Number		Number*	Order
1	46	Regular Officers	59 ⎱	1-2
2	37	Barristers	59 ⎰	
3	17	Manufacturers	35	3
4-5	⎰ 11	Civil Servants	8	9
	⎱ 11	Farmers	7	10-12
6	7	Stockbrokers	6	13
	⎛ 5	Solicitors	16	4
	⎜ 5	Professional Engineers ...	11 ⎱	6-7
7-11	⎨ 5	Clerks and Secretaries ...	11 ⎰	
	⎜ 5	Journalists and Authors ...	9	8
	⎝ 5	Teachers and Lecturers ...	7	10-12
	⎛ 4	Merchants	14	5
12-15	⎨ 4	Insurance and Underwriters...	5	14-16
	⎜ 4	Accountants	4	17-18
	⎝ 4	Land Agents	2	—
	⎛ 3	Shipowners	7	10-12
16-18	⎨ 3	Physicians and Surgeons ...	5 ⎱	14-16
	⎝ 3	Bankers and Bank Officials ...	5 ⎰	
—	—	Builders, etc.	4	17-18

* See footnote to Table 61.

House, making allowance for the increase in the total number of
members of parliament. It should not be forgotten that in most of these
occupations the numbers are, from a statistical point of view, very
small, and that therefore it would be unwise to attach any great importance to the exact figures of this or that particular change. Increases of 160 per cent in the proportion of Farmers and 130 per cent
in the proportion of Civil Servants, for example, may be a little
startling at first sight; but the actual numbers involved are so small
that a good portion of them may well be due as much to chance as to
anything else.

Probably the most significant changes are those relating to Regular
Officers and Merchants, and these are likely to be due largely to the

loss of seats by the party and the type of candidate put up for the safer seats, on which we have already remarked. There seems nothing in the results, taken as a whole, to suggest that there is any long-term significant change, occupationally, in the make-up of the Conservative parliamentary party. Certainly there is nothing to suggest that the sources from which the party draws its members of parliament have been extended: for example, by the inclusion of the "working-men Conservatives" about whom we hear from time to time. For such changes as there are, the ordinary effects of chance, combined with those due to the party's substantial loss of seats, seem to account pretty completely.

Let us now turn to the Labour party. A survey of the occupations of its members in the new House, and comparison with those of its members in the inter-war average House, disclose some interesting facts. Here, too, chance has no doubt played a considerable part, and

TABLE 64.—CHANGES IN PROPORTIONS OF CONSERVATIVE PARTY DRAWN FROM LEADING OCCUPATIONS

(1945 compared with inter-war average)

Occupation	Change
Farmers	160% increase
Civil Servants	130% ,,
Stockbrokers	90% ,,
Regular Officers	35% ,,
Teachers and Lecturers	15% ,,
Barristers	5% ,,
Journalists and Authors	5% decrease
Manufacturers	15% ,,
Clerks and Secretaries	20% ,,
Professional Engineers	25% ,,
Solicitors	45% ,,
Merchants	50% ,,

so no doubt has the heavy gain of seats. But the occupational changes in the parliamentary Labour party, unlike those in the Conservative party, do seem to indicate a widening of the catchment-area from which its membership is recruited. Table 65 sets out the essential facts for Labour on the same lines as Table 61 set them out for the whole House and Table 63 for the Conservatives. On the left are the figures for 1945—numbers of members in the leading occupations and order of magnitude—and on the right are the corresponding figures for the inter-war average House.

Most noticeable, and probably most significant, are the changes in the position of the Miners and the Metal Workers. In the inter-war average House Miners were easily at the top of the occupational table with 41 seats, the next place—a long way behind—being taken by Metal Workers with 13 seats. The most numerous group of professional workers—the Teachers and Lecturers—only achieved third place, with

11 members: little more than a quarter of the number of Miners. In the new House the Teachers have shot up from third place to the top of the table, ahead of the Miners and a long way ahead of the Metal Workers, who drop back from second place to sixth.

There is, indeed, a very noticeable swing-over in the parliamentary Labour party from the manual workers who for so long formed its backbone, indeed almost its whole body, to the professional and so-called "black-coated" workers. Not only Teachers and Lecturers but Journalists and Authors, Clerks and Secretaries, and, even more

TABLE 65.—OCCUPATIONS: LABOUR

1945		Occupation	Inter-War Average	
Order	Number		Number*	Order
1	49	Teachers and Lecturers ...	11	3
2	45	Miners	41	1
3	31	Journalists and Authors ...	10	4
4	30	Clerks and Secretaries ...	7	5-6
5	27	Barristers	4	8-12
6	18	Metal Workers	13	2
7	14	Railwaymen	4	8-12
8-9	{ 11	Manufacturers	4	8-12
	{ 11	Solicitors	1	—
10	10	Physicians and Surgeons ...	4	8-12
11	9	Wood workers	7	5-6
12-16	{ 6	Printing Operatives	3	13-15
	{ 6	Political Organizers	3	13-15
	{ 6	Merchants	1	—
	{ 6	Retailers	1	—
	{ 6	Accountants	—	—
17-20	{ 5	Textile Operatives	6	7
	{ 5	Building, etc., Operatives ...	4	8-12
	{ 5	Regular Officers	1	—
	{ 5	Professional Engineers ...	—	—
21-23	{ 4	Seamen and Boatmen ...	3	13-15
	{ 4	Ministers of Religion ...	2	—
	{ 4	Boot and Shoe Operatives ...	1	—
24-26	{ 3	Postal Workers	2	—
	{ 3	Civil Servants	2	—
	{ 3	Insurance and Underwriters...	1	—

* See footnote to Table 61.

markedly, Barristers and Solicitors have come in like a tidal wave. We must not, of course, lose sight of the fact that the strength of the parliamentary party has risen from its inter-war average of 154 members to its 1945 figure of 401 members; in order to allow for this, Table 66 sets out the percentage changes in the *proportions* of the party drawn from leading occupations in the new House by comparison with the inter-war average proportions. It will be seen at once how heavily the professional occupations have gained, and correspondingly how heavily the leading manual occupations have lost. Lawyers, Teachers, Journalists, Physicians—all have secured a much bigger share of the party seats. Miners, Metal Workers, Wood Workers, Textile Operatives—all have had to be content with a much smaller share than formerly. So far as the Miners are concerned, of course, their actual numerical representation fluctuates but little. It averaged 41 between the wars, and is 45 in the new House. As already pointed out, the Miner M.Ps. mostly sit for safe seats in the mining areas, and the fluctuations in party fortunes, up or down, affect them relatively little.

It may be advisable here to point out again that, especially in the smaller occupational groups, chance plays a considerable part in determining parliamentary numbers, and the significance of the figures in Table 66 could easily be exaggerated—particularly, for example, in such a case as that of Solicitors. But, making every allowance for this, there is clear evidence in the figures for the parliamentary Labour party of fundamental changes in its sources of supply; whereas in the

TABLE 66.—CHANGES IN PROPORTIONS OF LABOUR PARTY DRAWN
FROM LEADING OCCUPATIONS
(1945 compared with inter-war average)

Occupation	Change
Solicitors	400% increase
Barristers	175% ,,
Teachers and Lecturers	90% ,,
Clerks and Secretaries	75% ,,
Railwaymen	45% ,,
Journalists and Authors	20% ,,
Manufacturers	20% ,,
Physicians and Surgeons	15% ,,
Metal Workers	45% decrease
Wood Workers	45% ,,
Miners	55% ,,
Textile Operatives	65% ,,

parliamentary Conservative party there is no such evidence. How far these changes are likely to be permanent, how durable they would prove if the Labour party met defeat at a later election, it is impossible to say. In the not altogether unlikely event of the rebirth of a vigorous and effective Liberal party, there might be considerable desertions from Labour, especially amongst the non-manual workers; for, however regrettable we may think it, the political world seems never to lack people whose principles are closely akin to those of the Vicar of Bray, and who can always find some reason, satisfactory to themselves if to no one else, for deserting to the winning side. Apart from this, moreover, there is still some uncertainty how far the "proletarian" and "intelligentsia" elements in the party can live permanently in concord. Nevertheless, after noting these considerations, we may still think it unlikely that the broadening of the basis of the party, reflected in these new occupational figures, will disappear entirely within any foreseeable time, even if there should be some contraction.

Let us now turn from the consideration of individual occupations to the question of occupational status. The method of classification adopted has been explained on pages 73 to 75 and need not be repeated here. The results for 1945 are set out in Table 67, which also gives for comparison the corresponding results from the inter-war average House.

It will be seen that, while Professional Workers occupy an outstanding position in each of the two big parties separately and in the new House as a whole, there is a marked contrast between Conservatives and Labour in relation to the first two categories in the table. Roughly, Employers and Managers occupy in the Conservative party the posi-

TABLE 67.—OCCUPATIONAL STATUS

[Table 23, page 74]

Occupational Status	1945			Inter-War Average, All Parties
	Conservatives	Labour	All Parties	
	%	%	%	%
Employers and Managers ...	32½	9½	17½	25
Rank-and-file Workers ...	3	41	27	21
Professional Workers ...	61	48½	53½	45
Unpaid Domestic Workers ...	½	1	1	—
Unoccupied	3	—	1	9
Total	100	100	100	100

tion that in the Labour party is taken by Rank-and-File Workers; though there is, as we have already observed, a considerable swing-over in the latter party from manual to professional workers. Taking the new House as a whole, there are substantial increases in the proportions of both Rank-and-File and Professional Workers in comparison with the inter-war average House, with corresponding drops in the proportions of Employers and Managers and the Unoccupied. As usual, Unpaid Domestic Workers (housewives, etc.), who form a very big section of the general population, have little direct representation in the House: the rise to power of the Labour party has had little effect in that respect.

Probably the most significant feature of this table is the rise it discloses in the proportion, already high, of professional workers. The rise in the proportion of rank-and-file workers was only to be expected in view of the great increase in the strength of Labour in parliament, and it may be correspondingly discounted. But the rise in the numbers of professional workers cannot be explained like that; for it will be seen that not only in the House as a whole but also in the Conservative and Labour parties separately the proportion is higher than in the inter-war average House. It would be interesting if we could compare these results with similar figures for the state of affairs fifty and a hundred years ago. The distribution then would almost certainly prove very different from that obtaining to-day; and the differences would by no means be due entirely to the absence then and the presence now of a Labour party in the House.

Let us close this chapter by taking a look at those rather ambiguous categories the lawyers, the company directors, and the trade-union officials. We have seen in earlier chapters* why these categories are ambiguous, but it may be as well briefly to reiterate the main points.

Unlike such occupations as journalism, the legal profession provides definite qualifications, and a man or woman either is or is not a barrister or solicitor, as the case may be. On the other hand, while a barrister or solicitor may be in full practice as a lawyer, he may alternatively be employed as a civil servant or as a municipal official (for example), or again he may not use his legal status in any occupation but merely treat it as an academic qualification, like a university degree.

Company directors, again, vary from the man who is primarily a merchant or a manufacturer, an engineer or a publisher, and is a director merely because his business is run as a limited-liability company, to the man who makes his living as a director of a dozen or more companies and has no other occupation.

Similarly, the trade-union official may be a man whose life-work is essentially that of a miner or a cotton-weaver, a clerk or a cabinet-maker, and whose appointment as a trade-union official is, so to speak, merely incidental to that work. On the other hand he may be one who at an early stage in his career has taken up trade-union organization and made of that his life-work.

Hence to label a man as a lawyer or a company director or a trade-union official does not tell us whether we may legitimately regard the label as indicative of his major occupation, or indeed of any occupation at all. In the statistics given earlier in this chapter we have only recorded lawyers as such where it appeared that the members concerned were actually following legal occupations, while in the case of company directors and trade-union officials we have, wherever it could reasonably be done, assigned them to such other occupations—for example, as manufacturers or miners—and omitted for the time being those who could not properly be so allocated. It will be clear, however, to anyone who considers the matter, that it is by no means easy to determine the proper course to follow in the fairly numerous borderline cases, including cases in which the known facts lack precision.

* Reference may be made, for example, to pages 76 and 161.

Let us, therefore, now take *all* the members who can be identified as bearing these labels, whether they do or do not indicate a full-time occupation, see what proportions they claim in the membership of the new House, and compare the figures with the corresponding figures for the inter-war average House. Table 68 sets out these facts, giving the figures for the Conservative and Labour parties separately, as well as for the House as a whole.

It will be seen that the proportion of lawyers has gone down a little in the parliamentary Conservative party, nearly doubled in the Labour party, and fallen considerably in the House as a whole, though it is still very high—some may think still unduly high. It may be noted in passing that apparently about 3 out of every 14 members who hold legal qualifications do not practise, and have not practised, as lawyers.

TABLE 68.—PREDOMINANT OCCUPATIONS
[Table 25, page 77]

Occupation	Party					
	Conservatives		Labour		All Parties	
	1945	Inter-War Average	1945	Inter-War Average	1945	Inter-War Average
	%	%	%	%	%	%
Lawyers	24½	26½	12	7	16½	23
Company Directors ...	39	31½	9	3	20	23
Trade-Union Officials ...	—	—	32	49½	20½	13
Total*	56½	52½	50	58½	52½	54½

* Apparent discrepancies in these totals are due to the fact that some members belong to more than one of these categories.

Not all of the other 11, moreover, have been or are in full and continuous practice.

From the table it appears that the proportion of company directors has increased in both the Conservative and Labour parliamentary parties, taken separately. This may occasion some surprise, but it must be remembered that this is a category of which it is not at all easy to pin down precisely every member. The figures for 1945, however, may be taken as pretty accurate, the information having been supplied in large part by the members concerned themselves. The figures for the inter-war average House, on the other hand, may be a little on the low side, so that the apparent increases may not really be quite so high. Even so, it must be perfectly clear that there is little if any *diminution* in the proportion of members in either party who hold directorships.

This conclusion is in no way contradicted by the fact that in the House as a whole there is some decline in the percentage of members who are company directors, for we have the effects of the big swing-over in party representation to take into account. Though the Labour party now includes a far higher proportion of directors than ever before, it is still not so permeated by them as is the Conservative party: consequently the marked change in the political complexion of the House produces in this, as in so many matters, the paradoxical result of an increase in both parties accompanied by a decrease in the House as a whole.

Finally, the proportion of trade-union officials has gone down by a third in the Labour party, where they all belong, but has gone up by half in the House as a whole: yet another paradoxical result of the sweeping Labour victory.

CHAPTER XXX

1945: OTHER ASPECTS

1. HEREDITARY TITLES

USING the term "aristocratic" in the sense defined in Chapter IX, we find, as we should expect, that the 1945 House of Commons is considerably less aristocratic than its predecessors. The facts, as far as they can be ascertained, are set out in Table 69. It is probable that the true figures are somewhat higher than those given, but it is unlikely

TABLE 69.—HEREDITARY TITLES: 1945
[Table 26, page 78]

Classification	Number of Members				
	Cons.	Lib.	Lab.	Misc.	Total
I. By Descent	44	1	3	—	48
II. By Creation or Marriage ...	20	—	2	—	22
Total	64	1	5	—	70

that those for Category I are much out. As for Category II, this is necessarily rather ill-defined, and the reader's attention is drawn to the remarks about it on page 79.

The change-over from the Conservative preponderance of the average inter-war House to the Labour preponderance of the 1945 House would in itself have sufficed to reduce the strength of the aristocratic element, since this is always found mainly on the Conservative benches. For comparative purposes the percentage which this element forms and has formed of the strength of each party is given in Table 70. For the reasons stated on pages 79 and 80, the figures for "First Category Only" are more reliable and more significant than those for "Both Categories" taken together.

Looking, then, at the former, we see that there is little change in the Conservative parliamentary party in this respect: the drop from 22 per cent to 21 per cent is too small to have much significance. Indeed, since the 1945 figures are probably less complete than the inter-war figures, it may be that the true percentage has even risen a little, as we should expect from the party's loss of seats, arguing on the lines set out near the top of page 81.

TABLE 70.—HEREDITARY TITLES: PERCENTAGES
[Tables 27 and 28, pages 80 and 81]

Party	Both Categories		First Category Only	
	1945	Inter-War Average	1945	Inter-War Average
	%	%	%	%
Conservative ...	30	42	21	22
Liberal	8*	22	8*	11
Labour	1	4	1	3
Miscellaneous ...	—	—	—	—
All parties ...	11	28	8	15

* These figures are of little statistical significance, because of the small numbers involved.

The drop in the percentage for the parliamentary Labour party (from 3 per cent to 1 per cent) is, perhaps, a little surprising, in view of the broadening base of that party, to which reference has already been made. But three observations may be made on this. In the first place, that broadening has been made into the ranks of the professional and middle classes rather than into those of the titled families. In the second place, as already noticed, the 1945 figures are probably less complete than those for the inter-war period. Finally, the total numbers involved are so small that chance must necessarily play a greater part than it would with large numbers.

The figures for the "Miscellaneous" group, and the 1945 figures for the Liberal members, are clearly of little significance, because of the small numbers involved. But the inter-war Liberal figures have some value for comparative purposes.

18

To sum up: there is no evidence of any diminution in the aristocratic character of the Conservative parliamentary party, and no evidence of its growth in the other parties. The smaller part taken by it in the House as a whole appears to be due almost entirely to the swing-over in its composition from Conservatism to Labour.

2. SERVICE ON LOCAL AUTHORITIES

It was stated at the top of page 232 that "there are already very many members of parliament who have had experience of service on a county, borough, or district council, or on a local education committee," but no figures were there given. It may be of interest to have such figures for the 1945 House, and they are accordingly set out in Table 71, which gives the actual numbers of members who are known

TABLE 71.—SERVICE ON LOCAL AUTHORITIES

Party	Number of Members				
	County Council	Town or City Council	District Council	Other Local Authorities	Total*
Conservative	28	17	12	5	54
Liberal ...	—	1	2	—	3
Labour ...	73	133	43	26	223
Miscellaneous	1	2	—	1	3
Total ...	102	153	57	32	283

* The totals in this column are not in general the exact sums of the figures in the preceding columns, because in a good many cases members have served on more than one type of local authority; for example, on a county council and on a district council.

to have served on a local authority, and Table 72, which gives the percentages that such members form of their respective party strengths. Under the heading "Other Local Authorities" are included local education committees (co-opted members), parish councils, boards of guardians, etc. As in other matters, it is probable that all these figures are a little on the low side, because of those members (fortunately a minority, and not a large one) who prefer to conceal the facts about themselves. It is unlikely that the true figures would differ greatly from those given, but such differences as there were would be by way of increase not decrease.

While Table 71 gives the greater amount of detail, Table 72 is perhaps the more immediately instructive, for it shows that four out of every nine members of the new House of Commons as a whole have had service on local authorities of one type or another. In the Labour parliamentary party the proportion is as high as five out of every nine—well over half its total membership—while among the non-Labour members only one in four has had such service: a marked contrast. Even so, the figures show that the House as a whole should be in no danger of losing sight of the fact that many questions have a rather different aspect, when seen from a local council chamber, from that seen from Whitehall.

It will be noticed that, in the parties separately, the proportion of new members (that is, those elected for the first time at the 1945 general election) who have local authority experience is smaller than the corresponding proportion of old members. This is only to be expected, since the new members in general are so much younger and less experienced altogether than the old members. In the House as a

TABLE 72.—SERVICE ON LOCAL AUTHORITIES: 1945

Party	Percentage of Party Strength		
	Old Members	New Members	All Members.
	%	%	%
Conservative	28	19	25
Liberal*	25	25	25
Labour	60	53	56
Miscellaneous*	27	—	25
All parties	44	44	44

* These figures are of little statistical significance, because of the small numbers involved.

whole the influx of new members is balanced in this respect by the much higher proportion of Labour members, so that in the grand totals the proportion is the same in both cases.

It may be worth recording that the county, city, borough, district, and other councils on which members of the present House of Commons have served are scattered over the length and breadth of the land and include both rural and industrial areas. Naturally the London County Council takes pride of place amongst them, with 34 of its members or ex-members in the House: 10 Conservative and 24 Labour.

It may also be of interest to note that in the 1945 House of Commons there are at least 44 past or present mayors and lord mayors, making 1 in 14 of the total membership; while at least 64 members, or 1 in 10 of the total number, are or have been aldermen.

CHAPTER XXXI

1945: PARTY

Tables 29 to 35, in Part I, summarized for each of the seven inter-war general elections the numbers of candidates nominated, the effective votes they obtained, the numbers of members elected by the principal parties, the "ideal" numbers that would have been elected if seats had corresponded with votes, and the excess or deficit of seats obtained by comparing the actual with the "ideal" numbers. In Table 73 we continue the series by giving similar data for the 1945 election.

Though the information given in Table 73 is strictly comparable in form with that given in Tables 29 to 35, it may be as well to point out some slight differences. In the first place, the earlier tables refer to Great Britain alone, whereas the new table includes the 13 seats in the "six counties" of Northern Ireland. Secondly, the number of seats in Great Britain, which was 602 for each of the inter-war elections,

TABLE 73.—Votes and Members: 1945 Election
[Tables 29 to 35, pages 89 to 93]

Party	Candidates	Effective Votes	Number of Members		Excess or Deficit
			Elected	"Ideal"	
Conservative ...	630	10,081,000	215	258	— 43
Liberal	307	2,240,000	12	57	— 45
Labour	656	12,316,000	401	314	+87
Miscellaneous ...	90	409,000	12	11	+ 1
Total ...	1,683	25,046,000	640	640	——

was increased to 627 for the 1945 election. Thirdly, political parties are never completely stable and unchanging entities, and the slow turning of the political kaleidoscope has made it necessary to reconsider the position of the Liberal Nationals. Not to repeat all that has been said on the point in Chapter XXVI,* it has clearly become necessary now to regard them as Conservatives. Finally, the heading "Miscellaneous" has been substituted for "Independents", as being a more accurate description for a grouping which includes not only the true Independents but also the Scottish, Welsh, and Irish Nationalists. For the explanation of the heading "Effective Votes" see pages 88 and 89.

Even apart from the outstanding fact that this is the first general

* See page 242.

election in which the Labour party has secured a clear majority of seats, there are a number of points of interest in the table to which attention may be drawn. In the first place there is the large number of candidates. This is not a record, for there were 24 more in 1929, but it easily beats the figures for all the other inter-war elections, as will be seen from Table 74. Of more significance than the actual numbers, however (since there were more seats in 1945 than at any other of the elections), is the average number of candidates for each seat. Here also 1929 holds the record, with an average of 2·84 candidates per seat, but 1945 is not far behind, with 2·63 candidates per seat. These figures are of interest in connexion with the question of voting method, for they afford an indication of the comparative rarity of the "straight fight" between two candidates on which the present method of voting was based when it was introduced in 1884.

TABLE 74.—CANDIDATES AT GENERAL ELECTIONS

General Election	Number of Candidates	Average Candidates per Seat
1918	1,411	2·32
1922	1,428	2·37
1923	1,423	2·36
1924	1,404	2·33
1929	1,707	2·84
1931	1,276	2·12
1935	1,333	2·19
1945	1,683	2·63
Inter-War Average ...	1,426	2·37
Overall Average ...	1,458	2·40

Reverting to Table 73, the figures in the "Effective Votes" column show clearly that the Labour party—even including with it, as we have done, the I.L.P., Common Wealth, Communist, and Labour Independent candidates—did not obtain a majority of the votes cast. The total vote for Socialists of *all* kinds was 12,316,000, but the total vote for non-Socialists was nearly half a million greater at 12,730,000. Moreover the official Labour party, from which alone the present government is drawn, only secured 12,032,000 votes: it was therefore in a *minority* of nearly a million (982,000) votes at the general election. Clearly the claims made by Labour party spokesmen that the government has a "mandate from the people" for drastic changes, such as wholesale "nationalization" of our economy, are entirely without foundation. To say this is not, of course, to express any opinion on the merits or demerits of the Labour party programme: it is simply to point out the plain fact that only a minority of the electors voted for that programme.

The next column of Table 73 shows the numbers of members elected. The official Labour party won 394 seats and obtained therefore a clear majority of 148 over *all* other parties. But 7 other Socialist candidates won seats, and the total Socialist majority over non-Socialists is therefore 162. The nation's votes, however, had they all carried equal weight, would have given a majority of 12 against Socialism and of 26 against the official Labour party. Such is the way our present electoral system works!

Another illustration of this working is to be found by comparing the electoral fortunes of the Liberals with those of the Miscellaneous group. The 307 Liberal candidates received two and a quarter million votes: the 90 Miscellaneous candidates received less than half a million: yet there were as many of the latter elected as of the former.

There used to be a popular cry "one vote, one value!" Here is the number of votes (to the nearest thousand) that each party received for each seat it obtained:

Labour	...	...	...	...	31,000
Miscellaneous	...	...	...	34,000
Conservatives	...	...	...	47,000
Liberals	...	...	...	...	187,000

Had the Liberals won seats as cheaply as Labour did, they would now hold 73. Had Labour had to pay as dearly for its seats as the Liberals did, they would now hold only 66. Such a turning of the tables would therefore have given the Liberals a majority of 7 seats over Labour.

Another point of interest that Table 73 brings out is the fact that, for the first time for many years, the Conservative party secured fewer seats than its voting strength should have given it. If the reader will refer back to Table 36, on page 96, he will see that at every one of the seven inter-war elections that party obtained more than its proper number of seats, varying from 17 too many in 1923 to 122 too many in 1924, with an average of no fewer than $82\frac{1}{2}$ too many for the whole series of seven elections. Moreover, if allowance is made for the varying durations of the seven parliaments, the average excess representation enjoyed by the Conservatives comes out at about 95 for the whole inter-war and war period, 1918 to 1945. One can imagine the stupefaction of the Conservative party managers on finding that this long-standing privilege, which they had accepted with so much complacency for so many years, had disappeared overnight, and that their party had now to suffer by the operation of the unjust electoral system that they had themselves insisted on retaining. To drop from an average of 95 seats too many to 43 seats too few!—no wonder it took some time for the party to recover its breath after the election results appeared.

Yet such a result could have been foreseen and, in fact, was foreseen—though not by the Conservative leaders and organizers. If the reader will turn to the foot of page 114 he will read these words: "The Conservative party has, since the last war,* profited extremely by the electoral gamble, but there is no guarantee that this will continue: there are signs that before long it may be the turn of the Labour party to have a similar, and equally undeserved, run of luck. Its voting strength steadily increases, and in 1935 it secured the highest percentage of the total vote it has yet had. Soon our capricious 'system' may give it an overwhelming majority in the House while it is still only a minority in the country."† The 1945 election has brought about exactly the position the present writer foretold when he wrote those words in 1942. Moreover, this result could have been averted by the Conservatives had they been wise in time; for, at the Speaker's Conference held in the spring and summer of 1944 definite proposals were submitted for electoral reform by the adoption of either the single transferable vote or the alternative vote. In the membership of that conference the Conservative party held an absolute majority of places: and, moreover, the reform proposals were backed by the votes of a group of non-Conservative members of the conference, so that, given the will, the Conservatives could easily have carried either proposal.‡ But no! Luck had favoured their party so long: the gambler would still gamble—and this time he lost, and badly.

Another interesting point in connexion with Table 73 is that of the Labour vote. As we have seen, this did not amount to a majority of the grand total of votes given, but it did achieve a new high record for the party. It has been said, since the election, that "The achievement of a firm clear majority, after forty-five years of campaigning, was all the more surprising and satisfactory since it came, not as the result of a steady growth, but after two disasters and a long period of depression."§ But this is to mistake the achievement in *seats*, which is the erratic and almost unpredictable result of our gambling method of voting, for a measure of the growth of electoral support for the party. Actually the success of the Labour party at the polls in 1945, grossly exaggerated by our irrational voting system though it was, did come "as the result of a steady growth"—the steady growth of the proportion of the votes of the electorate given to Labour. This is demonstrated by the figures given in Table 75. It will be seen that, with the single exception of 1931 when Ramsay MacDonald so disastrously split his own party, the Labour vote has risen every time, and risen, all things considered, with remarkable steadiness.

Correspondents have suggested to me, in all seriousness, that if in this election, instead of the single-member relative-majority system, we

---

* *I.e.,* that of 1914-1918.
† See also the penultimate paragraph of page 100.
‡ See also Chapter XXXII and Appendix IV.
§ Margaret Cole, *The General Election 1945 and After* (Fabian Research Pamphlet No. 102, October 1945), page 15.

had had the single transferable vote, (*a*) it would have brought about the election of fewer Conservative and more Labour members and the extinction of the Liberal party, and (*b*) that it would have won the election for the Conservatives. Since such wildly divergent views are apparently held by reasonably intelligent people, it may be worth while to give a little consideration to the problem and see, as near as may be, where the truth of the matter lies.

Whatever system of voting has been employed in an election, it is clearly impossible to determine precisely from the actual results what would have been the results had a different system been employed. This is so not merely because of the arithmetical complications involved, but also because if you change fundamentally the method of voting you change with it the bases of the whole election, affecting the result in many ways, indirect as well as direct. Nevertheless, it is improbable that such a change would substantially alter the political views of the electorate—the lifelong Conservative would remain a Con-

TABLE 75.—GROWTH OF THE LABOUR VOTE

General Election	Labour Vote as Percentage of Total Vote
1918	25·8%
1922	29·5%
1923	29·8%
1924	33·9%
1929	37·8%
1931	31·3%
1935	40·5%
1945	49·1%

servative and the ardent Socialist would remain a Socialist under any free system of voting—and taking this as a reasonable assumption we can make a fairly good estimate of the sort of result such a change of method would produce.

As a first approximation to that result we may take the figures in the column headed "Ideal" in Table 73. It is sometimes assumed that, had a system of proportional representation been employed, this would in fact have been almost exactly the result of the election. This assumption, however, is unsound, for it ignores some important factors in the case.

In the first place there were 10 divisions with no Conservative candidate, 333 divisions with no Liberal candidate, and 16 divisions with no Labour candidate.* Now, as was pointed out in Chapter XXIII and elsewhere, there is no division in the country in which the elector-

* The 656 Labour candidates shown in the second column of Table 73 include I.L.P. and other Socialist candidates as well as those put forward by the Labour party.

ate is wholly one-party or even wholly two-party; and therefore in the divisions just mentioned many electors had no candidate of their own party for whom to vote. With the single transferable vote, and constituencies returning from 3 to 7 members each, this would be most unlikely to happen. As a first step, therefore, we have to estimate how the electors faced with this quandary did in fact use the votes they could not give to candidates of their own parties. It is clearly impossible to determine this at all closely, but for our present purpose we shall probably not be far out, taking one constituency with another, if we assume that of the Conservative electors who had no Conservative candidate for whom to vote half would vote Liberal and half would abstain from voting. Similarly we may assume that where there was no Liberal candidate a third of the Liberal electors would vote Conservative, another third Labour, and the remaining third would abstain. Labour voters with no Labour candidate to support would probably be similarly divided, half voting Liberal and half abstaining.

Our next step, therefore, is to transfer, to the best of our ability, these cross-voters and abstainers back to their own parties. Table 73 shows that, to the nearest hundred, the average number of votes received by each *candidate* was as follows:

Conservatives	...	...	...	16,000
Liberals	...	...	...	7,300
Labour	...	...	...	18,800
Miscellaneous	...	...	...	4,500

Since these averages (except that for the Miscellaneous candidates, who need not concern us in this connexion) are based in each case on hundreds of candidatures, in divisions large and small, borough and county, all over the country from John o' Groat's to Land's End, it seems fairly reasonable to conclude that they may be taken to represent tolerably well also the average numbers of electors, in other divisions, who *would* have voted for their respective parties if those parties had given them the chance. It may be contended against this that the seats uncontested by each party were those in which it had the least chance of success, and that therefore the average numbers in the uncontested divisions would be lower. This is probably true, so far as the seats uncontested by the Conservative and Labour parties are concerned, and to that extent it may conceivably give those parties some undeserved advantage. But the number of seats in each case is small, and the resulting errors will be correspondingly trivial for our present purpose: moreover, as between those two parties, the errors will more or less cancel out.

The case of the Liberal party is different and needs separate consideration. This party had planned to run some 500 candidates had the election been held in the autumn, as was hoped and expected. The July election found it unprepared, and lack of organization as well as lack of funds compelled it to leave 333 divisions—more than half the total number—uncontested. There is no reason to suppose that the average number of Liberal electors in these 333 divisions was appreciably lower than the average in the 307 that were in fact contested. But, even if such a supposition were justifiable, its effects would be offset by another factor.

The Conservative and Labour parties each ran over 600 candidates and were aiming—and were universally recognized as aiming—at winning the election and forming the Government. The Liberal party, on the other hand, by leaving uncontested more than half the seats, was clearly out of the running altogether. It was not merely unlikely to gain power: it was totally impossible for it to do so. In these circumstances, it seems pretty clear, many Liberal voters, even where they had the chance, did not vote for the Liberal candidate, taking the view (whether rightly or wrongly is beside the point) that it was wiser to vote for the party that they thought would prove the less obnoxious of the two who were actively competing for power. In other words, it seems certain that many Liberals, thinking it useless to vote for their own candidate, voted for the Conservative in order to "keep the Socialists out" or voted Labour to "keep the Tories out".

Hence the average number of votes actually given to Liberal candidates must be appreciably less than the average number of Liberal electors in the same 307 divisions. It follows that in taking 7,300 as the average number of Liberal voters we are understating the real strength of the party, and correspondingly overstating the real strength of the Conservative and Labour parties. If, therefore, we base our calculations on the average party votes actually recorded, we are almost certainly biasing the results in favour of Conservatism and Labour and against Liberalism. However, it would be unsafe to attempt even to estimate to what this bias amounts, measured in votes, and we acordingly accept the figures given as sufficiently near the truth for our purpose.

Returning, then, to the constituencies uncontested by one or more of the three parties, we find that, on the assumptions already made, the transfers of votes that are necessary to get a measure of the voting with all seats contested by each of the three parties, come out as follows:

The Conservatives would gain some 160,000 votes and lose some 810,000: a net loss of 650,000.

The Liberals would gain about 2,430,000 votes and lose about 230,000: a net gain of 2,200,000.

Labour would gain roughly 300,000 votes and lose roughly 810,000: a net loss of 510,000.

It will be seen that these figures show a net gain for the Liberals exceeding the sum of the net losses of the other two parties: this is because of the substantial reduction to be expected in the number of electors abstaining from voting.

These changes would bring the total votes for the parties to the following figures (to the nearest 10,000 votes):

Conservatives	...	...	...	9,430,000
Liberals ...	...	...	...	4,440,000
Labour ...	...	...	...	11,810,000
Miscellaneous	...	...	...	410,000
Total	...	..	...	26,090,000

This probably represents as close an estimate as it is possible to make of the way the nation's votes would have been given had all the three major parties run candidates for all the 640 seats. It may be taken, therefore, as a rough estimate of the true alignment of political opinion in this country at the time of the 1945 election. From that point of view it may be convenient to restate the figures on a percentage basis: we then have:

Conservative voters	...	...	say 36%
Liberal voters	...	...	say 17%
Labour voters	...	...	say 45%
Miscellaneous voters	...	...	say 2%
			100%

Although this is not, and cannot be, anything more than a rough estimate, it is improbable that it contains any serious error. I should expect, for example, that the true figure for the Liberal voters, if it could be determined, would not be less than 16 per cent nor more than 18 per cent, and that the true figure for the Labour voters would not be less than 43 per cent nor more than 46 per cent. But that is about as far as we can go.

Accepting, then, these figures as a rough but reasonably correct estimate of true voting strengths, what a reflection it is on our voting methods—and on our sense of political values—that 45 per cent of the electorate should have secured $62\frac{1}{2}$ per cent of the seats in the House of Commons, and should be imposing its minority views on the nation wholesale and at high speed! Is this haste, perhaps, a reflection of the party's awareness of its lack of moral authority? These comments, of course, do not touch on the merits of the policy in question: they relate merely to the fact that it is a minority policy.

From these figures we can readily calculate the numbers of seats that would have been won by the various parties if their successes had been in proportion to their (estimated) true voting strengths. They are as follows:

Conservatives	...	...	...	231
Liberals ...	...	...	...	109
Labour ...	...	..	...	290
Miscellaneous	...	...	...	10
Total	...	...	...	640

We are now one stage nearer to the answer to our question. The figures just given are the nearest estimate we can make of the allocation of seats that would correspond to the state of public opinion at the time of the 1945 election. They do not, however, represent, even as an estimate, the actual results we should expect from the adoption of the single transferable vote (or, for that matter, of any practicable form of proportional representation).

The reason is this. Under the present system of voting the more popular party or parties get more—often far more—than their due share of seats, while the less popular party or parties get correspondingly less than their share. With the single transferable vote this exaggeration of success would be very greatly reduced and would be deprived of its dangerously violent and erratic qualities, but it would not be altogether eliminated; unless, perhaps, we were to adopt the original Hare scheme of one enormous constituency for the whole country. Nobody in their senses would now dream of doing that: we must have constituencies of manageable size, and a constituency returning seven members is now generally regarded as the largest that should be created.* But, as has been pointed out more than once,† the smaller the constituency the less closely can it be relied upon for the distribution of seats in strict proportionality to votes. Consequently, with any practicable system of proportional representation, there will still be some tendency for the results to favour the more popular parties.

How far this tendency will go depends, then, apart from the incalculable factors we call chance, on the size of the constituencies; but it will certainly not produce anything like the present wild departures from proportionality. Making what we might term a reasonable guess, however, we might expect Labour in the present case to have gained another score or so of seats through it, giving the party about 7 per cent more seats than it ought to have. These gains, of course, would have been at the expense of the other parties, and proportionally more at the expense of the Liberals than of the Conservatives. Let us guess, then, that the Conservatives might have lost 11 seats from this cause (a 5 per cent loss) and the Liberals 9 (an 8 per cent loss). The final result would then be:

Conservatives	...	...	...	...	220
Liberals ..	...	...	...	...	100
Labour ...	...	...	...	...	310
Miscellaneous	...	...	...	...	10
Total	...	...	...	...	640

These figures, it will be noticed, are all round numbers (multiples of ten), and that serves to remind us that these are estimates and subject to a fairly wide margin of error. Nevertheless, there is good reason to believe that they give a pretty close idea of the sort of House of Commons that the election of July 1945 would have given us if we had employed the single transferable vote. Comparing the figures with those of the actual results, it will be seen that they give the Con-

* Personally I should fix five as the maximum number, but a discussion of this point would be out of place here.
† See, for example, James Hogan, *Election and Representation* (1946).

servatives 5 more seats than they actually won, and the Liberals 88 more, while Labour loses 91 of its actual gains and the Miscellaneous group loses a couple of seats.

Another point worth noticing is that these final figures differ considerably from those shown in the penultimate column of Table 73. That column records the numbers of seats proportionate to the numbers of votes actually recorded for the various parties: the figures given here show the probable results of the election had it been conducted with a different and more accurate and reliable method of voting. Of the political effects of such changes we must leave the reader to judge for himself: but the House of Commons so constituted would have reflected the views of the electorate far more closely than the present House does.

CHAPTER XXXII

ELECTORAL REFORM 1944-1946

ELECTORAL reform has been discussed fairly fully in Parts II and III of this book, but it may be useful to add to the survey there given a brief outline of some of the more important happenings in connexion with the subject since the first edition of the book was published in 1943.

On 1st and 2nd February 1944 the House of Commons held a full-dress debate on Electoral Reform and at the end resolved: "That this House welcomes the proposal of His Majesty's Government to set up a Conference on Electoral Reform and Redistribution of Seats and to invite Mr. Speaker to preside." The debate, as reported in Hansard, makes interesting reading, but it is not easy to summarize. A few points which may be worth noting are (a) the general agreement amongst speakers of all parties that, in the words of Mr. Edmund Harvey, "the obstacles standing in the way of any candidate who is at present hindered by lack of means from serving in the House, should no longer be there," and in particular that the cost to candidates of contesting elections should be substantially reduced; (b) the marked disagreement —not strictly on party lines—on the subject of voting methods; and (c) the cynical speech of Mr. Arthur Greenwood.

Six days after the debate the Prime Minister, Mr. Churchill, wrote to Mr. Speaker formally inviting him to preside over the conference, and setting out the terms of reference, which were as follows:

"To examine, and, if possible, submit agreed resolutions on the following matters:

(a) Redistribution of seats.

(b) Reform of franchise (both parliamentary and local government).

(c) Conduct and costs of parliamentary elections, and expenses falling on candidates and members of parliament.

(d) Methods of election."

With regard to (c) the Prime Minister explained "that, to meet the widely expressed desire that the conference should consider expenses falling on candidates and members of parliament, such as charitable contributions, the scope of category '(c)' has been somewhat extended." He also expressed the Government's desire that the conference should "submit early reports on redistribution and the question of assimilating the parliamentary and local government franchises."

Subsequently Mr. Speaker wrote to the Prime Minister saying: "As soon as I received your letter I issued invitations to a number of peers and members of parliament. These invitations were issued roughly in proportion to party strength in the House of Commons and were also intended to secure, as far as possible, representation of various shades of opinion, different types of constituency, and all parts of the country."

The actual party composition of the conference, as so set up, was as follows:

	Peers	M.P.'s	Total
Conservatives	1	16	17
Liberals	1	1	2
Labour	1	8	9
Others*	—	4	4
Total	3	29	32

* These consisted of one Liberal National, one Labour Independent, one I.L.P., and one Independent member.

This distribution corresponded as closely as could have been expected with the state of parties in the House of Commons at the time of the conference. It will be seen that the Conservatives had an absolute majority in the conference by 17 members to 15.

The distribution of the members of parliament by types of constituency and parts of the country was as follows:

	Borough	County	University	Total
England	10	8	2	20
Wales	1	2	—	3
Scotland	3	2	—	5
Northern Ireland	—	1	—	1
Total	14	13	2	29

This distribution, also, corresponded as closely as could be expected with the then existing state of affairs in the House of Commons.

The conference met for the first time on 16th February 1944, and had held fourteen meetings when, on 24th May, Mr. Speaker sent his first report* to the Prime Minister. This dealt with items (a), (b), and

* Cmd. 6534, May 1944. See Appendix IV.

(*d*) of the terms of reference. Subsequently the conference held a further six meetings, of which the last was on 19th July. Next day Mr. Speaker sent his second and final report* to the Prime Minister, giving the conclusions of the conference on item (*c*). In all, therefore, the conference held twenty meetings, spread over a period of a little more than five months.

Such, in outline, was the course of events leading up to the recommendations made by the Speaker's Conference of 1944. We must now consider briefly those recommendations and the steps taken in parliament to give effect to them.

REDISTRIBUTION OF SEATS

Most of the decisions of the conference on the subject of the redistribution of seats appear to have been unanimous, or at least *nemine contradicente*. The only recorded exception is that relating to the representation of the City of London.

As a temporary measure, the conference recommended the immediate subdivision of constituencies which, under the 1939 register, were "abnormally large", subject to the proviso that the total temporary increase in the number of seats should not exceed twenty-five.

It also expressed itself as "in favour of a general redistribution of seats as soon as practicable", and laid down the conditions which it considered should apply to such a general redistribution. The more important of these conditions may be summarized as follows:

(*a*) Four separate permanent Boundary Commissions to be constituted (one each for England, for Scotland, for Wales and Monmouthshire, and for Northern Ireland) with Mr. Speaker as *ex-officio* Chairman of each Commission, and with in each case a Deputy-Chairman who would for certain purposes act as Chairman.

(*b*) A full redistribution scheme to be prepared immediately after the completion of the temporary scheme of subdivision of abnormally large constituencies.

(*c*) Periodic reviews to be subsequently undertaken by each Commission at intervals of not less than three and not more than seven years.

(*d*) The total number of non-university members of parliament for Great Britain to remain "substantially" at the old figure of 591, with no reduction in the numbers for Scotland or Wales, and with no change in the number (12) for Northern Ireland.

(*e*) Redistribution to be effected "on the basis of qualified electorate", with a quota ascertained by dividing the total electorate in Great Britain by the total number of non-university seats existing "at the time the Boundary Commissioners report".

(*f*) Double-member constituencies to be abolished, except where after local enquiry it is found in any particular case "that abolition is

* Cmd. 6543, July 1944. See Appendix VI.

undesirable". (No definition or explanation is given to show what is meant by "undesirable" in this context.)

(g) The City of London to continue to return two members.

So far as machinery is concerned, these recommendations are substantially in agreement with those of the Departmental Committee on Electoral Machinery, which reported in November 1942,* and they call for no special comment. The substitution of *electorate* for *population* as the basis of redistribution, and the abolition (if not found "undesirable"!) of double-member constituencies, represent improvements in principle, though the changes involved would be unlikely to have any very marked effect on the results of general elections as a whole.

The ban on any reduction in the numbers of members for Scotland and Wales, combined with the limitation of the total number for Great Britain to the old figure of 591, is a more serious matter. It involves a further discrimination against the English electorate, whose votes will count for less than those of the Scottish and Welsh electorates to an even greater extent than they do now. Here are the correct distribution of seats in accordance with the 1945 electorate figures and, in contrast, the old distribution that the conference proposes to retain:

					Correct	Proposed
England	...	...	...	...	497	485
Wales ...	...	...	...	...	33	35
Scotland	...	...	...	...	61	71
Total	...	...	...	...	591	591

It will be seen that the English electorate is to be deprived of no less than twelve seats, two of which are to be given to the Welsh electorate and ten to the Scottish electorate. The conference's contempt for the principle of "one vote, one value" is further shown by its recommendation that the City of London, which on voting strength is barely entitled to one-fifth of a member, shall continue to return two members; though this resolution, carried by 15 votes to 13, was evidently forced through by the Conservative majority.

The recommendation as to the "quota" contains two curious blunders: first, it takes "the total electorate" instead of the total *non-university* electorate; second, it takes the number of seats existing "at the time the Boundary Commissioners report", which will presumably be 616 (*i.e.*, 591 + 25), whereas obviously it should be 591.

On the broader general question of redistribution, the adoption of a makeshift temporary scheme for the subdivision of abnormally large constituencies, with a rather more thorough (though far from perfect) scheme for subsequent periodical redistributions, probably represents about the best arrangement that could be reached for the time being, in view of the very substantial changes in population distribution resulting from the war, and the great uncertainty as to the post-war dis-

* Cmd. 6408, December 1942.

tribution.* But it is difficult to understand why the temporary increase of the number of members from 615 to 640 should not be allowed to remain, more or less exactly, after the permanent redistribution; it would be helpful. After all, the present figure of 640 is below the normal size of the House of Commons in modern times: here are the figures for the membership from 1801 to the present time:

1801 to 1885 (84 years)	...	...	...	658†
1885 to 1918 (33 years)	...	...	...	670
1918 to 1922 (4 years) ...	...	...	...	707
1922 to 1945 (23 years)	...	...	...	615
1945 to present time	...	...	...	640

It will be seen that for the 121 years from 1801 to 1922 the membership of the House was considerably greater than its present size of 640. During the whole of that long period, moreover, the population of the country was smaller than it now is, and the electorate was only a fraction of its present size.

The "House of Commons (Redistribution of Seats) Bill" was introduced in the House on 3rd August 1944 and received the Royal Assent on 26th October. The Act follows pretty closely the recommendations of the conference, but the following points may be noted:

(a) The "abnormally large" constituencies to be subdivided are specified by name in the Second Schedule to the Act. They are all in England, and the determination of the boundaries for the new constituencies so created is made the first duty of the Boundary Commission for England.

(b) The permanent redistribution scheme for each of the four parts of the United Kingdom is to be based on the electorate figures at the "enumeration date", which means broadly on the then current figures.

(c) The City of London is excepted from the operations of the Boundary Commission for England and it is to continue as a separate constituency. A curious rule in the Third Schedule provides that the City "shall return either two members or a single member as may be determined by the future Act giving effect to" the permanent redistribution scheme finally approved by parliament.

(d) The blunders about the quota in the conference report are rectified.

REFORM OF FRANCHISE

The substance of the chief recommendations of the conference may be stated as follows:

(a) The local government franchise to be assimilated to the parlia-

* For a discussion of these population problems see the Report of the Committee on Electoral Machinery.

† The disfranchisement of certain constituencies reduced the effective number of members to 652 for part of this period.

For details of the distribution of seats during these periods reference may be made to *Debrett's House of Commons*.

19

mentary franchise, and both sets of elections to be held on the same register.

(b) The business premises franchise to be retained, but the spouse qualification to be abolished.

(c) Every university graduate to be registered automatically and without fee for the university franchise.

(d) Registration to be limited to not more than one place of residence and not more than one place of business "provided that such an arrangement is administratively practicable".

Resolutions were put forward in the conference for the abolition of plural voting and for the reduction of the qualifying age from 21 to 18, but both were rejected by large majorities.

The first recommendation, (a), made by the conference proposes a notable and long-overdue step forward, simplifying registration and making the local government franchise as democratic as that for parliament.

The recommendations on the business premises franchise obviously represent a compromise between the "left" view that this franchise should be abolished and the "right" view that it should be retained in its existing form.

The university franchise recommendation sponsors a very desirable reform. So long as university seats are retained, the electorate should certainly include all graduates, while registration should be automatic and free of cost to the elector.

The proposed limitation of registration to not more than one place of residence and not more than one place of business, though unlikely to have far-reaching effects (since the number of persons affected is relatively small) is nevertheless to be welcomed as an improvement on the position in which a person, if qualified, may be registered for any number of constituencies (though not allowed to use more than two votes at a *general* election).

The Representation of the People Act, 1945, introduced as a Bill on 13th December 1944, received the Royal Assent on 15th February 1945. This lengthy and complicated Act is very largely concerned with temporary provisions arising out of the war: but it deals with some of the matters of franchise reform on which recommendations were made by the Speaker's Conference. In particular it provides for the extension of the local government franchise to all electors entitled to the parliamentary franchise (though making provision for a "ratepayers register" of local government electors not entitled to the parliamentary franchise), and abolishes the spouse qualification for the business premises vote. Further, it enacts that a person shall not be entitled to be registered in the business premises register or in the ratepayers register unless he makes an application, in the proper form, to be so registered. No provision is made with regard to the changes recommended by the

Speaker's Conference in relation to the registration of university graduates for the university franchise.

METHODS OF ELECTION

A comprehensive resolution, reaffirming the principle of "one vote, one value", drawing attention to the defects of the present method of voting, accepting the principle of proportional representation with the single transferable vote, and recommending its application to all constituencies save those affected by special geographical considerations, was rejected by 25 votes to 4. A second resolution, recommending that some measure of proportional representation should be applied to the election of the next House of Commons by way of experiment was rejected by 24 to 5. A third resolution, in favour of the use of the alternative vote in single-member constituencies where there are more than two candidates was rejected by 20 to 5. Thus decisively did the conference, itself constituted to give proportional representation to the parties in the House of Commons, decline to give such representation to the electors who had sent them there! The conference seems to have been blissfully unconscious of the irony of its behaviour in this respect.

On this matter of methods of election, evidence was submitted to the conference from several sources (including a memorandum on certain special aspects, submited by me*), but it seems very doubtful whether this evidence had any appreciable effect on the decisions reached. To say this is, of course, not to imply the slightest knowledge of what took place inside the conference, whose meetings were strictly private, and as to which the only available information is that contained in Mr. Speaker's two reports to the Prime Minister. But anyone who will read through the Hansard report of the House of Commons debate on Electoral Reform, of 1st and 2nd February 1944, and then read through the reports of the conference, can hardly avoid the conclusion that the summary rejection of proportional representation was only to be anticipated.

ELECTION EXPENSES

On this subject, as already noted, the debate of February 1944 had disclosed general agreement. Members of the House, of all parties, vied with one another in declaring that the costs of elections should be very much reduced. Sir Herbert Williams, Sir Douglas Hacking, Mr. Edmund Harvey, Mr. Glenvil Hall, Major Lloyd, Flight-Lieutenant Raikes, Mr. Gallacher, and Colonel Arthur Evans were amongst those who spoke to that effect. No opposition was expressed to the idea that, as Mr. Glenvil Hall put it, "If we are to help younger people into the House, we must realize that it should be our object to make the fighting of elections as cheap as possible." Most members, however, seemed

* See Appendix V.

to be under the illusion that the desired result would be achieved simply by a reduction in the legal limits of expenditure. But Flight-Lieutenant Raikes put his finger on the fallacy of this argument, and went on boldly to suggest a state contribution (half the cost) towards election expenses.

Having made a special study of election expenses, I submitted to the conference a memorandum on the subject,* in which, after an analysis of the actual facts, I suggested the dropping of the separate allowances for agents' fees and for personal expenses; the reduction of the legal limits of expenditure; the introduction of a new basis for those limits, including in each case a lump sum plus a smaller per-elector allowance; and the payment of a state grant towards election expenses on the lines already set out in Chapter XXII of this book.

The main recommendations of the conference may be summarized as follows:

(a) The legal maximum of candidates' expenses to consist partly of a basic figure (lump sum) and partly of a per-elector allowance.

(b) The separate allowance for agents' fees to be dropped.

(c) No change to be made in the existing provision with regard to the personal expenses of candidates.

(d) Poll cards to be issued to electors at public cost by the Returning Officer, and no other poll cards to be issued.

(e) The payment of speakers' expenses to be permitted.

The conference "agreed not to accept a proposal that the state should afford direct financial assistance to candidates".

There is no space here to compare in detail the recommendations made by the conference with the suggestions put forward in my memorandum; but those readers who are interested in the subject will find both documents reproduced in full in Appendices VI and VII respectively.†

It might have been expected that the conference recommendations on election expenses, which presumably were unanimous, and which followed on such widespread and apparently heartfelt protestations from all parts of the House of Commons, would have been given the force of law, in common with the recommendations on redistribution and franchise reform; but no such action was taken by the Coalition Government, nor has its successor, the present Labour Government, thought fit to remedy this failure. It would be interesting to learn the reasons for this inaction. In any event, the result has been that the 1945 election took place with the old regulations as to election expenses still in full force; so that the chorus of pre-election sympathy for the younger and less well-off candidates expressed so eloquently in the House of Commons has produced just exactly nothing in the way

---

* See Appendix VII.
† I hope to publish a further study of the subject elsewhere at a later date.

of practical help. Another case of "sound and fury signifying nothing"?

OTHER MATTERS

The second report of the Speaker's Conference, in addition to dealing with election expenses, makes recommendations on a number of other matters, including subscriptions to charities, contributions to party funds, forfeiture of deposit, polling facilities, use of conveyances, broadcasting, etc. For all these, reference should be made to Appendix VI. Some of them are of considerable interest, but considerations of space forbid any detailed discussion here.

THE SPEAKER'S CONFERENCE: A FOOTNOTE

Meditation on the constitution, procedure, and results of the three Speaker's Conferences which have now been held* leads me to wonder whether this is the proper method for dealing with the types of problem involved. There is clearly an implication in the way these conferences have been constituted, perhaps also in their terms of reference, and certainly in their procedure, that the questions they have been invited to consider are the concern solely of members of parliament (including peers) and the political parties to which they belong. It does not seem to have occurred to the authorities that the matters under consideration are the concern of the electors as well as the elected. The secrecy of the proceedings, the absence of published evidence, the failure to give any argument for or against the decisions reached: all these point in the same direction and suggest a fundamental misapprehension of the situation. There is much that could be said on these points, but it must be deferred to another time and place. Meanwhile, of course, nothing in these comments should be taken as reflecting in the slightest degree on the zeal or integrity of the members of these conferences or their distinguished chairmen: it is not personalities but principles that are in question.

MEMBERS' EXPENSES

Though this is not strictly a matter of electoral reform, the subject of members' expenses and remuneration is one that is closely related thereto, and, in view of the discussion of the question in Chapters XV and XXII of this book, it may be worth while just to record the setting-up on 15th November 1945 by the House of Commons, on the motion of the Chancellor of the Exchequer, of a Select Committee of the House "to consider the expenses incurred in connection with their parliamentary and official duties by members of this House, including ministers whose salary is less than £5,000 per annum; their remuneration; and their conditions of work".

The committee held 13 meetings, and reported to the House on

* Viz., in 1916, in 1929, and in 1944.

6th March 1946. The report has been printed and published* and makes interesting and instructive reading, though fuller comment on it must be deferred. The major, though by no means the only, recommendation of the committee was for an increase of the remuneration of members of parliament from £600 a year to £1,000 a year: † this recommendation has since been accepted and put into force.

* By H.M. Stationery Office, in March 1946.
† See, in this connexion, page 208 above.

APPENDICES

APPENDIX I

(a) LIST OF PRINCIPAL AUTHORITIES CONSULTED IN THE PREPARATION OF PART I

> Whitaker's Almanack.
> Constitutional Year Book.
> Debrett's House of Commons.
> Dod's Parliamentary Companion.
> The Times House of Commons 1935.
> Who's Who.
> Who Was Who.
> Who's Who in Engineering.
> Universities Year Book.
> Board of Education Annual Report.
> Census of England and Wales.
> Census of Scotland.

University Calendars, Professional Lists, Peerages, etc., were also consulted.

(b) PRINCIPAL AUTHORITIES CONSULTED IN THE PREPARATION OF PART IV

These include those listed in (a) above, so far as requisite and so far as available, together with

> The Times House of Commons 1945.
> Who's Who in Parliament.

Much further information was obtained by means of a questionnaire sent to all members of the new House of Commons. Grateful acknowledgement is made of the helpful replies that were received from a large proportion of the members in question.

APPENDIX II

CENSUS OCCUPATION-GROUPS

    I. Fishermen.

   II. Agricultural Occupations.

  III. Mining and Quarrying Occupations.

 IV. Workers in the Treatment of Non-Metallic Mine and Quarry Products.

   V. Makers of Bricks, Pottery, and Glass.

 VI. Workers in Chemical Processes: Makers of Paints, Oils, etc.

VII. Metal Workers (not Electro-Plate or Precious Metals).

VIII. Workers in Precious Metals and Electro-Plate.

 IX. Electrical Apparatus Makers and Fitters (not elsewhere enumerated) and Electricians.

  X. Makers of Watches, Clocks, and Scientific Instruments.

 XI. Workers in Skins and Leather and Makers of Leather and Leather Substitute Goods (not Boots or Shoes).

XII. Textile Workers.

XIII. Makers of Textile Goods and Articles of Dress.

XIV. Makers of Food, Drinks, and Tobacco.

XV. Workers in Wood and Furniture.

XVI. Makers of and Workers in Paper and Cardboard: Bookbinders, etc.

XVII. Printers and Photographers.

XVIII. Builders, Bricklayers, Stone and Slate Workers: Contractors.

XIX. Painters and Decorators.

XX. Workers in Other Materials.

XXI. Workers in Mixed or Undefined Materials (not elsewhere enumerated).

XXII. Persons employed in Transport and Communications.

XXIII. Commercial, Finance, and Insurance Occupations (excluding Clerks).

XXIV. Persons employed in Public Administration and Defence (excluding Professional Men, Clerical Staff, and Typists).

XXV. Professional Occupations (excluding Clerical Staff).

XXVI. Persons Professionally engaged in Entertainments and Sport.

XXVII. Persons engaged in Personal Service (including Institutions, Clubs, Hotels, etc.).

XXVIII. Clerks and Draughtsmen: Typists.

XXIX. Warehousemen, Storekeepers, and Packers.

XXX. Stationary Engine Drivers, Dynamo and Motor Attendants.

XXXI. Other and Undefined Workers.

XXXII. Retired or Not Gainfully Occupied.

APPENDIX III

EXTRACTS FROM A MEMORANDUM BY MR. IAN HARVEY

A Plutocratic System

*Facts regarding the selection and adoption of
Candidates for Parliament in the Conservative Interest.*

1. *The Method of Selecting a Candidate.*

Anyone desiring to become a Candidate for Parliament in the Conservative interest must first of all be approved by the Executive Committee of the Party. This is altogether right and proper. Next, his name is placed upon the Central Office list and whenever vacancies occur it is forwarded to the local selection committees concerned for their consideration. It is here that the trouble starts. There are roughly three categories of candidates:

Class 'A': those who are willing to pay all their election expenses (anything between £400 and £1,200) and to subscribe between £500 and £1,000 a year to the local Association.

Class 'B': those who are willing to pay at least half their election expenses and to subscribe between £250 and £400 a year to the local Association.

Class 'C': those who are unable to pay anything towards their election expenses and only able to subscribe £100 or less to the local Association.

According to present standards, 'A' class have always an excellent chance of being adopted, 'B' class a reasonable one, and 'C' class hardly any chance at all. These standards are set up not, as is usually alleged, by Central Office, but by the local Associations themselves.

2. *Relative Positions of Conservative Central Office and the Local Associations.*

It is generally assumed that the selection of candidates is dictated by Conservative Central Office. In actual fact, the final decision rests almost entirely with the local Associations. Naturally, Central Office is prepared to make recommendations and to give advice, but the ultimate selection rests with the Selection Committee and with the General Meeting of the local Association. In nearly every case the question of finance is of primary importance because it is an undeniable fact that nearly all the Conservative Associations in the country rely at the present time on the subscription of their member to keep them going. This state of affairs is completely wrong, as the whole point of an association is to aid the member in his work and not to obstruct him by placing a heavy financial toll upon his own resources. For this reason, the personal qualifications and abilities of the candidate have to take second place. Thus it often happens that Mr. C., whose father left him

297

an enormous fortune but omitted to leave him a similar heritage of intelligence and ability, gains preference over Mr. A., who has proved himself time and time again to be the very kind of man the Party needs in Parliament, but has not sufficient resources to meet the demands of the local Association.

3. *The Problem of Poor Constituencies.*

Immediately the proposition to reduce the financial demands made on candidates is put forward, the problem of the poor constituencies is raised. Money is needed to pay the agent's salary. Money is needed to keep up the local headquarters, and money is needed to finance local Conservative activities. The Conservative supporters cannot afford to make big subscriptions. Central Office has not sufficient funds, neither has the area Council. Here is, indeed, a real problem which must be carefully and sympathetically approached, and for which a solution may be hard to find. The most obvious solution is to form a central fund, of larger proportions than any fund formed so far, into which contributions may be paid from the richer constituencies and those where a member is unopposed. Here there is a difficulty and a danger. The difficulty is that even in the rich constituencies it is hard enough to get local people to subscribe to local enterprise, and to demand a subscription towards keeping up a constituency elsewhere might not be very appealing. The danger is that when an organization knows that it can draw on a central fund for its running costs, there is less enthusiasm for canvassing and the vitality of the organization decreases. It should, nevertheless, be an accepted practice that good candidates should be adopted by poor constituencies even if it means a reduction of local activities and the closing of headquarters rather than bad candidates who are rich enough to pay for an organization but who are unfit to represent the interests of our Party.

4. *The Real Abuse.*

The real abuse is that of the rich constituencies who persist in demanding exorbitant sums from their members when, if a real organization were in action, they could pay for them two or three times over. Their name is legion. Hendon is an example. Here are strongholds of the Conservative Party where it ought to be possible to put men of paramount ability without fear of their ever being removed from the parliamentary service of the Party at a critical time, even though a landslide were to occur. Here, in actual fact, the only real test of a candidate is his pocket.

*   *   *   *   *

5. *The Opposition.*

At this point it is relevant to consider the state of affairs in the Socialist Party. Finances come largely from the co-operative movement and the trade unions. Although there are disadvantages in this, all the criticisms that can be made of such a system do not apply from a Socialist point of view. From a purely party standpoint, therefore, they are not criticisms. What is important, however, is that for only £25 or less a man can become M.P. in the Socialist interest. Moreover, it is not untrue or unfair to estimate that there is hardly a Socialist Member of Parliament to-day who does not receive £1,000 a year.

6. *Principle Involved.*

The most serious aspect of this situation is not the actual incompetence or the impoverishment of talent in the Conservative Party, but the very grave threat to the whole principle and structure of democracy which results out of this perverted system. The people choose one of their number to legislate on their behalf. In a good democracy that one is worthy to represent the many. He is a man fit for public service and a man of ability. Conservatives never cease to boast that their Party is the only one which can put true democracy into effect, and yet it is they who restrict the representatives of the people by pernicious financial demands. Thus electors can choose only that man submitted by the Conservative Party, selected in most cases for his wealth, or they must turn to some other party—and this they will undoubtedly do.

*   *   *   *   *

1st January 1939.   IAN HARVEY.

(NOTE.—The asterisks denote omitted passages: these passages are, in the main, concerned with matters of domestic interest to the Conservative party.)

APPENDIX IV

CONFERENCE ON ELECTORAL REFORM AND REDISTRIBUTION OF SEATS

LETTER FROM MR. SPEAKER TO THE PRIME MINISTER

Presented to Parliament by Command of His Majesty
May 1944

Cmd. 6534

(NOTE.—This report is Crown copyright and is here reproduced by permission of the Controller of H.M. Stationery Office.)

SPEAKER'S HOUSE, S.W.1.
24th May, 1944.

MY DEAR PRIME MINISTER,

On 2nd February, the House of Commons, after a two days' debate, agreed to a resolution welcoming "the proposal of His Majesty's Government to set up a Conference on Electoral Reform and Redistribution of Seats and to invite Mr. Speaker to preside".

Following the adoption of this resolution, you wrote to me on 8th February formally inviting me to preside over the proposed Conference and setting out the terms of reference. It would, I think, be convenient to record in full the relevant parts of your letter:

> "10, *Downing Street*.
> *8th February*, 1944.

"MY DEAR MR. SPEAKER,

As you know, the Government propose that a Conference of Members of Parliament should be set up to consider electoral reform and redistribution of seats, and, in accordance with the wishes of the House, I write now formally to invite you to preside over the Conference. I am reluctant to ask you to add to your already heavy burdens by undertaking this task, but it is most important that the issues before the Conference, directly affecting as they do the interests of all the political parties, should be considered in as impartial a spirit as possible, and the Government are sure that the best method of realizing this object is by following the precedent of 1916 and asking you to preside.

The following will be the terms of reference of the Conference:

'To examine, and, if possible, submit agreed resolutions, on the following matters:

(a) Redistribution of seats.

(b) Reform of franchise (both Parliamentary and local government).

(c) Conduct and costs of Parliamentary elections, and expenses falling on candidates and Members of Parliament.

(d) Methods of election.'

You will see that, to meet the widely expressed desire that the Conference should consider expenses falling on candidates and Members of Parliament, such as charitable contributions, the scope of category '(c)' has been somewhat extended. I trust that you will concur in the amendment.

As was explained to the House by the Home Secretary, we should like the Conference to submit early reports on redistribution and the question of assimilating the Parliamentary and local government franchises.

The Government have, as you know, announced their intention of legislating on redistribution and their readiness to adopt the recommendations of the Departmental Committee on Electoral Machinery on the machinery which should be established, but it will be necessary to incorporate in the Bill a statement of the principles by which the Boundary Commissioners are to be guided, and legislation must await the report of the Conference on this matter. Before legislating, the Government will also wish to consider any views the Conference may express about the machinery.

The urgency as regards the local government franchise lies in its bearing on the question of resuming local elections. It is generally agreed that they should be resumed as soon as practicable, but they cannot be resumed until a register of local electors is brought into existence. Before legislation can be introduced to set in motion the preparation of such a register, it is necessary to decide whether the local government franchise is to be assimilated to the Parliamentary franchise, with the consequence that use would be made for local elections of the continuous registration system introduced for Parliamentary elections by the Parliament (Elections and Meeting) Act, 1943. The Local Elections and Register of Electors (Temporary Provisions) Act will come up for consideration again in the autumn, and it is desirable that this point should have been settled in time for any legislative action which may be necessary to be taken then. . . .

Yours very sincerely,

(Signed) WINSTON S. CHURCHILL."

As soon as I received your letter, I issued invitations to a number of Peers and Members of Parliament. These invitations were issued roughly in proportion to Party strength in the House of Commons and were also intended to secure, as far as possible, representation of various shades of opinion, different types of constituency, and all parts of the country.

The following Peers and Members of Parliament—thirty-two in number—agreed to serve on the Conference: Viscount Margesson, Lord Rea, Lord Ammon, Mrs. Adamson, Mr. Buchan-Hepburn, Mr. Erskine-Hill, Colonel Arthur Evans, Mr. Foster, Miss Lloyd George, Mr. Walter Green, Mr. James Griffiths, Sir Douglas Hacking, Mr. Glenvil Hall, Mr. Harvey, Sir Austin Hudson, Mr. Hutchinson, Mr. Kerr, Sir Joseph Lamb, Major McCallum, Mr. Magnay, Mr. Maxton, Sir Joseph Nall, Sir Hugh O'Neill, Mr. Parker, Mr. Petherick, Mr. Pethick-Lawrence, Mr. Pickthorn, Mr. Pritt, Mr. Scott, Mr. Turton, Sir Herbert Williams, and Mr. Woodburn.

Mr. Philip Allen of the Offices of the War Cabinet and Mr. A. C. Marples of the House of Commons Offices were appointed as Joint Secretaries to the Conference.

The Conference met for the first time on 16th February and have. up to the present, held fourteen meetings.

You asked for early reports on (a) the redistribution of seats and (b) the assimilation of the Parliamentary and local government franchises. The Conference felt, however, that it was not possible to reach firm conclusions on the question of redistribution of seats until they had decided whether or not to recommend any change in methods of election. In particular, the adoption of any measure of Proportional Representation would have directly affected their proposals with regard to redistribution. They also felt that both the questions on which you asked for early reports would be affected by their decisions on the business premises qualification and on University representation.

The Conference accordingly decided to complete their consideration of the various questions arising under items (*b*) and (*d*) of their terms of reference before submitting an interim report, and I am now in a position to report the decisions of the Conference on all except their third term of reference (namely, conduct and costs of Parliamentary elections and expenses falling on candidates and Members of Parliament).

The Conference are proposing to resume their sittings after Whitsuntide and I will submit a further report on the matters covered by the third term of reference as soon as possible.

The conclusions so far reached by the Conference are set out in the following series of Resolutions. Where Resolutions are shown as having been passed by a majority, particulars of the voting are given. Most of the other Resolutions were adopted unanimously; in the remaining cases there was a large majority in favour, and the minority accepted the conclusion and did not desire their disagreement to be recorded.

I give in an Appendix to this letter the terms of Resolutions rejected by the Conference, together with particulars of the voting.

I. REDISTRIBUTION OF SEATS

GENERAL

1. The Conference are in favour of a general redistribution of seats as soon as practicable.

TEMPORARY RULES

Sub-division of "abnormally large" constituencies.

2. For the purpose of an election held before general redistribution has taken effect, a constituency which under the 1939 Register has an electorate that is deemed to be abnormally large shall be sub-divided.

Definition of "abnormally large".

3. For this purpose, an electorate which, under the 1939 Register, was not less than approximately 190 per cent of the quota for Great Britain (which was 53,110) shall be deemed to have been abnormally large and the constituency shall, therefore, be sub-divided into two constituencies; and, similarly, if the electorate was not less than approximately 290 per cent or 390 per cent of the quota, the constituency shall be sub-divided into three or four constituencies respectively.

Limitation on temporary increase in size of House of Commons.

Provided that the total temporary increase in the number of Members of Parliament thereby added to the House of Commons shall not exceed twenty-five.

Contiguous Constituencies covered by the rules may be treated as one area.

4. Where the Boundary Commissioners have decided, within their Instructions, that two or more contiguous constituencies had abnormally large electorates, they shall be at liberty to regard the said contiguous constituencies as one area for the purpose of sub-division.

DATE OF FIRST COMPLETE REDISTRIBUTION

5. The Boundary Commissioners shall begin to prepare a full redistribution scheme immediately after the completion of the temporary scheme of sub-division of abnormally large constituencies.

PERMANENT RULES

Total number of Members of Parliament.

6. The total number of Members of the House of Commons for Great Britain shall remain substantially as at present (*i.e.,* 591, excluding University seats).

Special provision for Scotland and Wales.

7. There shall be no reduction in the present number of Members of the House of Commons for Scotland or for Wales and Monmouthshire.

Redistribution to be based on electorate.

8. Redistribution shall be effected on the basis of qualified electorate.

Quota for each seat.

9. The standard unit of electorate for each Member of the House of Commons for Great Britain shall be a quota ascertained by dividing the total electorate in Great Britain by the total number of seats in Great Britain (other than University seats) existing at the time the Boundary Commissioners report.

Limits of toleration.

10. The Boundary Commissioners shall not be required to modify an existing constituency if its electorate falls short of or exceeds the quota by not more than approximately 25 per cent.

Double-Member constituencies.

11. Constituencies at present returning two Members shall be abolished, except where after local enquiry by the Boundary Commissioners it is found in any particular case that abolition is undesirable,

Provided that no county or borough shall continue to return two Members if the electorate falls short of double the quota by more than approximately 15 per cent.

Boundaries to coincide, where convenient, with local government boundaries.

12. The boundaries of Parliamentary constituencies shall, where convenient, coincide with the boundaries of local government administrative areas.

City of London.

13. The City of London shall continue, as at present, to return two Members. (This Resolution was passed by a majority—Ayes 15; Noes 13.)

Northern Ireland.

14. It shall be an Instruction to the Boundary Commissioners for Northern Ireland, in applying the foregoing rules, that there shall be no change in the present number of Members of the House of Commons for Northern Ireland, and that the quota for Northern Ireland shall be ascertained by dividing the total electorate by twelve (that is, the number of Northern Ireland seats, other than the University seat).

Discretionary powers of Boundary Commissioners.

15. The Boundary Commissioners may depart from the strict application of these rules if special geographical considerations (including the area, shape, and accessibility of a constituency) appear to them to render such a course desirable.

University constituencies.

16. Nothing in the foregoing rules shall apply to University constituencies.

The terms of a Resolution, rejected by the Conference, recommending that the representation of the City of London should be reduced to one Member, together with particulars of the voting, are given in the Appendix, paragraph 1.

I was asked by the Conference to draw attention to the fact that the practical application of their recommendations relating to redistribution of seats may somewhat reduce the existing representation of the administrative County of London on the London County Council and thus increase the proportionate strength of the representation of the City of London on that body.

MACHINERY OF REDISTRIBUTION

In your letter you explained that the Government had announced their readiness to adopt the recommendations of the Departmental

Committee on Electoral Machinery as to the permanent machinery which should be established for the redistribution of seats, but that, before legislating, the Government would wish to consider any views the Conference might express about these proposed machinery provisions.

The Conference wish to submit the following comments:

Four separate Commissions.

17. There should be four separate Boundary Commissions—one for England; one for Scotland; one for Wales and Monmouthshire; and one for Northern Ireland.

Mr. Speaker to be ex-officio Chairman.

18. The Speaker should be ex-officio Chairman of all four Commissions.

Mr. Speaker to nominate Deputy-Chairman.

19. The Speaker should nominate one of the members of each Commission as Deputy-Chairman of the Commission.

Representations from Party organizations.

20. Each separate Boundary Commission should sit (its Deputy-Chairman presiding) to hear any representation from the Chief or National Officers of the Party organizations with respect to the Commission's provisional proposals for redistribution.

Periodic reviews by Boundary Commissions.

21. Each Boundary Commission should be required to undertake, at intervals of not less than three years and not more than seven years, a general review of the representation in the House of Commons of that part of the United Kingdom with which it is concerned.

Power to submit special reports.

22. The Boundary Commissions should, in addition, have authority to submit special reports at any time recommending changes in respect of any particular constituency or group of constituencies.

Action to be taken on reports of Boundary Commissions.

23. The reports of the Boundary Commissions should be submitted to the Secretary of State concerned, and the Secretary of State should be required to lay every such report before Parliament, together with a draft Order in Council giving effect to any recommendations (with or without modification) for redistribution, and providing for any consequential or incidental matters. Any such draft Order should be subject to affirmative resolutions.

There should, however, be a special provision that when the Boundary Commissions have made their first general reports

20

with respect to the whole of the United Kingdom, effect should be given to this first comprehensive scheme by Bill, and not by Order in Council.

II. REFORM OF FRANCHISE (BOTH PARLIAMENTARY AND LOCAL GOVERNMENT)

Assimilation of the Parliamentary and Local Government franchises.

24. The local government franchise shall be assimilated to the Parliamentary franchise and Parliamentary and local government elections shall be held on the same Register,

  Provided that Peers shall not lose their right to vote in local government elections.

Business premises qualification.

25. The business premises qualification shall be retained,

  Provided that no person shall be entitled to be registered as an elector by reason of the fact that he or she is the husband or wife of a person having a business premises qualification.

University representation.

26. The existing University representation and methods of election shall be retained,

  Provided that every person who has received or receives a degree (or its equivalent) shall be automatically registered and that no fees shall be charged for registration expenses.

Registration of electors.

27. A person shall be entitled to be registered for not more than one residence qualification and for not more than one business qualification, provided that such an arrangement is administratively practicable. (This Resolution was passed by a majority—Ayes 21; Noes 8.)

The terms of a Resolution, rejected by the Conference, recommending that no person at any election should vote more than once, together with particulars of the voting, are given in the Appendix, paragraph 2.

The terms of a Resolution, rejected by the Conference, recommending a reduction in the qualifying age for the franchise, together with particulars of the voting, are given in the Appendix, paragraph 3.

III. METHODS OF ELECTION

Proportional Representation.

28. The system of election known as Proportional Representation shall not be adopted in respect of any constituencies where it does not apply at present. (This Resolution was passed by a majority—Ayes 24; Noes 5.)

The term of Resolutions, rejected by the Conference, advocating the adoption of Proportional Representation, either generally or as a partial, experimental measure, together with particulars of the voting, are given in the Appendix, paragraphs 4 and 5.

The Conference also rejected a Resolution recommending the adoption of the method of voting known as the Alternative Vote. The terms of this Resolution, together with details of the voting, are given in the Appendix, paragraph 6.

As will be seen from Resolution 26 above, the Conference decided that the existing methods of election at University elections should be retained.

Representations were addressed to the Conference with regard to methods of voting in local government elections, but the Conference agreed that this was a matter falling outside their terms of reference.

The Resolutions I have set out above discharge the major portion of our task. The problem that remains is not so much the adjustment of conflicting principles as that of finding practical methods for dealing with detailed questions arising out of the conduct and costs of parliamentary elections and related subjects.

The conclusions set out in this report, and the amount of general agreement that we have achieved, undoubtedly represent for all a subordination of personal opinions sincerely held which would not have been possible unless all members of the Conference had been determined, from the first, to tackle without bias the thorny problems which confronted us.

I should like as Chairman to render my personal thanks to every member of the Conference for the great help given me during our sittings, and to bear witness to the admirable temper and conciliatory disposition which have been shown by all and have enabled us to reach what, I trust, will be regarded as a substantial measure of general agreement.

I cannot conclude without expressing on behalf of all members of the Conference our warm appreciation of the great assistance given to us by our Secretaries, Mr. Philip Allen and Mr. A. C. Marples. Their unfailing courtesy and their care in the preparation of our material and agenda have eased our task enormously.

Yours very sincerely,
(Signed) D. CLIFTON BROWN.

The Rt. Hon. W. S. Churchill, C.H., M.P.,
  10, Downing Street, S.W.1.

APPENDIX

1. The following Resolution was rejected by the Conference:

"That the Conference recommend that the representation of the City of London be reduced to one Member."

Ayes—13.   Noes—15.

2. The following Resolution was rejected by the Conference:

"That the Conference recommend that no person at any election should vote more than once."

Ayes—6.   Noes—25.

3. The following Resolution, with regard to the qualifying age for the franchise, was rejected by the Conference:

"That the Conference recommend that the franchise be extended to all who have reached the age of eighteen."

Ayes—3.   Noes—16.

4. The following comprehensive Resolution on the subject of Proportional Representation was rejected by the Conference:

"(i) That the Conference, reaffirming the resolution of the Speaker's Conference of 1917, accepts as governing any scheme of redistribution the principle that each vote recorded shall, as far as possible, command an equal share of representation in the House of Commons.

(ii) That the Conference considers that this principle should apply to methods of elections equally with schemes of redistribution.

(iii) That the present method of election fails to produce results fully and truly representative of the views of the voters.

(iv) That the principal reason for this failure is the distribution of the country into single-member constituencies (or double-member constituencies in which each elector has two votes), under which it may be observed—

(a) there can be and has in fact been in the years 1922-3, 1924-9, and 1935 to date a majority in the House of Commons of one party based on a minority of votes for that party in the country;

(b) coalition government has prevailed during the years 1918-22 and 1931 to date, and government by a single party, having no majority in the House of Commons, during the years 1923-4 and 1929-31;

(c) there has not been at any time since the Speaker's Conference of 1917 a Government formed by any one party supported by a majority of the voters.

(v) That the best remedy for the shortcomings of the present method of election is the adoption of some system of Proportional Representation whereunder each elector has a single transferable vote and constituencies return several members, a method which in the words of the present Prime Minister 'is incomparably the fairest, the most scientific, and on the whole the best in the public interest'.

(vi) That the Conference accepts the principle of Proportional Representation with the single transferable vote and recommends that it be applied to all constituencies save those affected by special geographical considerations."

Ayes—4.   Noes—25.

5. The following further Resolution on the subject of Proportional Representation was rejected by the Conference:

"That the Conference recommend that some measure of Proportional Representation should be applied to the election of the next House of Commons by way of experiment."

Ayes—5.   Noes—24.

6. The following Resolution on the subject of the Alternative Vote was rejected by the Conference:

"That the Conference recommend that at any election in a single-member constituency where there are more than two candidates (other than University constituencies) the election be held on the method of voting known as the Alternative Vote."

Ayes—5.   Noes—20.

MEMORANDUM SUBMITTED TO THE CONFERENCE BY DR. J. F. S. ROSS
ON METHODS OF ELECTION

1. In considering methods of voting at parliamentary elections much attention has been paid to the effects of alternative methods on party representation and on the formation of governments, and relatively little to the effects on the electorate and on the calibre of members. This memorandum accordingly is devoted to the latter aspects.

2. The events of the last thirty years, culminating in the present war, have laid great stress on the importance of forms of government, and this country in consequence has reaffirmed in no uncertain manner its belief that, for us at least, the democratic way is the best, if not the only one. All the major parties (and most others) are agreed on this, and it is the basis of all the arguments that follow.

3. Democracy, then, being our chosen way of government, it is essential to see that our methods of election (amongst other things) are such as to make the fullest use of the resources of democracy. This involves (again amongst other things), (a) that we should draw from the common man, the ordinary woman, the utmost contribution that they are capable of giving, and (b) that we should obtain as members of parliament the men and women best fitted to carry out the onerous tasks that fall on the House of Commons.

4. Lincoln's famous epigrammatic definition of democracy, "Government of the people, by the people, for the people," is clearly open to criticism on the score that government *by* the people is impossible in a modern community, if only because of the huge number of people concerned. In a small city-state, such as those of ancient Greece, every citizen might have some direct share in the work of government: in the modern state, with millions of citizens, that is clearly impossible. Can the common man, then, ruled out from any direct share in government, usefully take any part in it at all?

5. Since we now have universal adult suffrage, there is superficially a case for saying that we have done all that is possible in that direction. But the nominal possession of a vote is not in itself sufficient: we have to see that the elector can make full and effective use of it, and it is here that the present system breaks down. Under this system the elector can seldom use his vote in a way that is consistent with his dignity as a thinking human being or with his rights as a citizen. This is an injustice to the individual man and woman, but it also results in our failing to extract from the electors anything like their maximum potential contribution to the good government of the country.

6. We have to recognize the political limitations of the great majority of ordinary men and women; but if we really believe in democratic government we ought to see that they are given every opportunity and encouragement to take that share in it of which they *are* capable. This

is not merely a question of individual rights; it is a matter of political wisdom. Having chosen the democratic way of life, it is ordinary common sense to see that it is made to work efficiently. We ought to do all we can to develop an alert, interested, and competent electorate, and to utilize to the full its valuable qualities.

7. I suggest that in the choice of the best possible method of voting we have a very valuable means towards this end. Such a method could provide a way of educating the ordinary man and woman, of awakening and developing in the general run of voters an interest in and an understanding of public affairs and political problems. If our method of voting is a stupid one, giving the elector no real voice—or even no voice at all—in the choice of his representatives, it will teach him nothing, it will deaden his interest in public affairs, and render him apathetic to political issues. If, on the other hand, it gives him the opportunity to use his wits, to exercise his judgement, and to feel that he counts for something in the scheme of things, he will be influenced to develop his powers, to use his vote wisely, and to understand the significance of the issues he is helping to decide. If we wish to get from adult suffrage all it is capable of giving us, we must treat the voters *as* adults and not as ciphers.

8. Judged by these standards the present method of voting fails lamentably. It offers little incentive to the elector to interest himself in either political problems or in the personnel of parliament. In many constituencies he has no chance to use his vote at all, there being no contest, and even where there is a contest his choice is so circumscribed and the effect of his vote so doubtful that he cannot feel that he is really participating in the choice of someone to represent *him*.

9. In this connexion it is important to realize that the number of people in any constituency who are *actively* members of a political party is relatively very small. There is, I think, real danger that members of parliament, candidates, party organizers, committee members, and ardent workers may not appreciate how very different their knowledge of affairs (and consequently their attitude) is from that of the great majority of electors who do not fall into any of these categories and are normally mute and passive. It seems desirable to make a special effort, therefore, to see elections from the point of view of the ordinary electors, who lack inside information and are very differently placed from the politically active.

10. The ordinary elector takes no part in the choice of the candidates who seek his vote, and he has very little idea how they have been chosen. There they are, and all he can do is to exercise such choice as the names on the voting paper give him; and that, under the present system, is extremely limited. From this point of view elections under the present system fall normally into one of three categories: (*a*) those in which there is no contest, (*b*) those in which there is a choice between two candidates, and (*c*) those in which there is a choice between three candidates.

11. In the first case the elector cannot exercise his vote at all; he is completely excluded from any share in the election. The member is chosen not by the electorate but by the inner circle of the predominant party. In this connexion it may be recalled that at the 1918 election there were no fewer than eighty unopposed returns, so that over 13 per cent of the electorate were, in effect, disfranchised.

12. In the second case the elector can go to the polling station and record his vote; but if one party is much in the majority he knows—whether he belongs to the majority or to the minority—that his vote has little real effect: the result is a foregone conclusion. When the parties are more equally matched he is a little better placed, but neither of the candidates may be of the same party as he himself favours, in which event he must either vote for someone with whose political views he is in disagreement or else abstain from voting. He cannot use his vote in any way that is satisfactory to himself.

13. In the third case he is more likely to find a candidate of his own political views for whom to vote; but there is a strong probability that, with three candidates for one seat, the successful candidate may represent only a minority of the voters. In the 1929 election 315 members—well over half the House of Commons—were elected by a minority of the votes actually given in their constituencies.

14. Moreover, under the present system, the elector has in practice no opportunity of expressing his views on the personal suitability of the candidates. Elections as a whole must turn largely on the bigger political issues of the moment; that is right and proper. But the elector should have some voice in the choice of personnel as well as party. Given that he must be content with a member whose views are only broadly those that he himself holds, that in voting he must associate himself with one or other of the major parties, he should yet have some small share in securing the best man to represent that party. The present system denies him any such share; it reduces him from a thinking human being to a mere party unit; and in so doing it deprives the community of a valuable contribution that it might receive towards good government.

15. This is a point to which little attention has been paid, but it is, I suggest, of prime importance. With all due respect I venture to submit that though there are in the House of Commons men and women of first-class calibre admirably fitted to serve there, yet the *average* level of integrity and ability in the House is far from being as high as it could and should be. If this view is correct, then it is of the utmost importance to take every possible step to improve the position; and one such step, I suggest, is to make better use of the qualities of the ordinary voter. At present the ordinary elector has little or no scope for the exercise of his faculties of judgement and idealism in relation either to political issues in any true sense or to the personality of the candidates put before him. He must in effect vote on mechanical party lines or not at all. But give him a choice between two or more

candidates whose views and proposals do not constitute an outrage on all he has been brought up to believe in, give him a choice of candidates where party prejudice is at a discount, and he will, I suggest, choose well. He will choose well because, ignorant though he is in so many directions, he has, when it comes to weighing up one man against another, a native shrewdness, an insight, that is worth much. Hence if the electors were given a wider choice of candidates, and especially a choice between more than one candidate of their own party, there would be a marked improvement in the average quality of the successful candidates.

16. Quite apart, therefore, from the unsatisfactory results of the present method of voting on the representation of political opinion in the country as a whole, that system displays serious deficiencies both from the point of view of getting from the electors their maximum contribution to the common good, and from the point of view of getting the best possible members of parliament. In the grave times ahead it is of more than ordinary importance to secure stability in political matters and to have an enlightened and reasonably contented electorate. The present method of voting promotes apathy in the exercise of the franchise and contempt for political institutions. The ordinary elector has no share whatever in the selection of the candidates that are put before him; and he has little or no effective choice between them. If he could be made to feel that his vote really counted, that he had an effective, as distinguished from a purely nominal share in choosing a member to represent him, he would at once be more contented politically and more ready to take that interest in public affairs that is so desirable.

17. Further, in many parts of the country the voters of all but one party are to all intents and purposes permanently disfranchised. Quite apart from its effects on representation as a whole, this is an injustice to the electors of the parties so disfranchised. The Conservative voter in a predominantly mining district, the Liberal or Labour voter in the "Home Counties"—to give but two examples—feel a sense of injustice because, as things are, they never can and never do have a member to represent them. It is no doubt true, as was pointed out in the recent debate in the House of Commons, that once a member is elected he tries to serve all his constituents, of whatever party, so far as personal troubles or grievances are concerned. But that work, valuable though it is and arduous though it may be, only represents a relatively minor part of a member's task, and on all *political* issues he can only speak and act and vote as the representative of the party that sent him to the House, and the other parties in his constituency must remain unrepresented. It is cold comfort, moreover, for the elector to be told that his views can be put forward by members of his own party elected for constituencies at the other end of the country. That may satisfy outsiders, but it does not at all meet *his* views of what he wants and needs.

18. It may be admitted that most of this discontent remains without public expression, that much of it is not consciously realized in definite

form by the people who feel it. But the fact that they are inarticulate is not a sufficient reason for doing nothing about it. Discontent of this kind leads to apathy in the exercise of the franchise on the one hand, and to contempt for politics and politicians on the other; and that is not a healthy state of affairs.

19. It is desirable to notice that the present method of voting does not merely suffer from local and temporary deficiencies; it is fundamentally and intrinsically unsuited to the proper representation of political opinion, even on the broadest lines. There is no constituency in the country where all the electors are of one mind politically; yet the system is such that in each constituency only one party can secure any representation at all. It is all or nothing; one party gets all the representation—the others get none. It is a basic requirement for proper political representation, therefore, that every constituency should return at least three members; for only so is there the opportunity for even the main streams of political thought to receive representation. This is no question of small and peculiar minorities; they cannot normally expect to have separate representation. But the present system does not even allow of the two or three major parties being represented within the constituency. That is why such devices as the second ballot and the alternative vote are unsatisfactory. They cannot make a one-party member the proper representative of a three-party electorate, or even of a two-party electorate.

20. All these considerations, then, point to the necessity for a complete change of voting method; and the only system that meets the case is, I suggest, the single transferable vote. If that system were adopted, and when it had time to make its effects felt, we should, I suggest, find a great awakening and revitalizing of political thought and interest amongst the common people, the ordinary electors of both sexes and of every class, who form the great bulk of the electorate. Elections would become a real and vital concern of the community, apathy would largely disappear, we should have an electorate better informed, more alert, and less likely to be stampeded by dishonest scares and stunts; and not least we should encourage the best possible selection of candidates and so obtain a higher general standard of membership in the House of Commons.

21. For all these reasons (and for many others), and because I believe profoundly in the importance of the matters herein discussed, I urge that the change to the single transferable vote should be made; if not in all constituencies at once, at least in a sufficient number to give the system a chance to prove its merits as a means towards more truly democratic government.

J. F. S. ROSS.

15th March, 1944.

FOOTNOTE.—I desire to make it clear that this memorandum does not purport to state the whole case for the single transferable vote. I have

purposely confined myself to certain aspects, in the belief that this might best suit the convenience of the Conference. But I should be quite ready to deal with other aspects, either in writing or orally, should it be desired, and also to answer objections that might be put forward.
—J. F. S. R.

APPENDIX VI

CONFERENCE ON ELECTORAL REFORM AND REDISTRIBUTION OF SEATS

LETTER DATED 20TH JULY 1944 FROM MR. SPEAKER TO THE PRIME MINISTER

Presented to Parliament by Command of His Majesty
July 1944

Cmd. 6543

(NOTE.—This report is Crown copyright and is here reproduced by permission of the Controller of H.M. Stationery Office.)

SPEAKER'S HOUSE, S.W.1.
20th July 1944.

MY DEAR PRIME MINISTER,

I wrote to you on 24th May last reporting the conclusions of the Conference on Electoral Reform and Redistribution of Seats on three of their four terms of reference. I am glad to be able to inform you that my colleagues and I have completed our task, and that I am now in a position to let you know our conclusions on our remaining term of reference—namely, conduct and costs of Parliamentary elections, and expenses falling on candidates and Members of Parliament. You will remember that, following the debate in the House of Commons on 1st and 2nd February, you decided to extend somewhat the scope of this particular term of reference to meet the widely expressed desire that the Conference should consider expenses falling on candidates and Members of Parliament, such as charitable contributions.

Since I wrote to you on 24th May the Conference have held six meetings, of which the last was on 19th July.

In the course of our enquiries, we had put to us a number of suggestions for detailed and technical amendments of the present electoral law. Certain of our recommendations, if accepted, will involve amendments of the Ballot Act, 1872, and the Corrupt and Illegal Practices Prevention Act, 1883; but the Conference asked me to suggest that, in addition, it would be desirable if these Acts could be examined departmentally by the Home Office and the Scottish Office, possibly with the help of the Party Agents, with a view to the repeal or amendment of those provisions which are no longer appropriate to modern conditions. If you agree, I will send direct to the Home Secretary and the Secretary of State for Scotland a note of various detailed points brought to our notice which we think might be included among those which would be suitable for review by a departmental enquiry of this kind. The Conference appreciated that such an enquiry could not be completed for some time and assumed that it would not be possible for the findings to be included in any early legislation which may be introduced to implement the various recommendations which they have made for the amendment of the electoral law. I should add that the Conference considered that it would be desirable to consolidate the various Acts relating to Parliamentary elections, but realized that there was little prospect of this at present.

The resolutions adopted by the Conference were in nearly all cases unanimous. Two resolutions—namely, those dealing with substantial contributions to local charities and to party funds—were passed with the full knowledge that legislation could not deal effectively with these abuses; but all members agreed that the resolutions of a Speaker's Conference on these subjects should be a definite help to candidates and to Members of Parliament exposed to unreasonable demands, and should also act as a deterrent to those party organizations inclined to put the financial contributions of a candidate or Member before considerations of merit and ability.

As in my earlier letter, I give in an Appendix the terms of resolutions rejected by the Conference, together with particulars of the voting where there was a division.

CONDUCT AND COSTS OF PARLIAMENTARY ELECTIONS AND EXPENSES FALLING ON CANDIDATES AND MEMBERS OF PARLIAMENT

ELECTION EXPENSES

Reduction in legal maximum scale of candidates' expenses.

1. The legal maximum scale of candidates' expenses in Great Britain should consist partly of a basic figure and partly of an allowance in respect of each elector. In the case of borough constituencies, the basic figure should be £450 and the allowance should be at the rate of 1d. in respect of each elector; and, in the case of county constituencies, the basic figure should be £450 and the allowance should be at the rate of 1½d. in respect of each elector.

No alteration in the scale of candidates' expenses in Northern Ireland is recommended, in view of the reduction made by the Government of Northern Ireland Act, 1920.

As regards double-member constituencies, if any be retained, the existing provision should remain whereby, when there are two or more joint candidates at an election, the maximum amount of expenses for each of the joint candidates is the amount produced by multiplying a single candidate's maximum by one and a half and dividing the result by the number of joint candidates.

The Conference agreed not to accept a proposal that the State should afford direct financial assistance to candidates.

Agents' fees and candidates' personal expenses.

2. The whole of the fees paid to Agents should be included in the legal permitted maximum of election expenses.

The Conference agreed not to recommend any change in the existing provision with regard to the personal expenses of candidates.

Expenses incurred by party organizations or by individuals other than the candidate.

3. Section 34 of the Representation of the People Act, 1918, should be amended so as to cover any expenses incurred by a political or other organization or by an individual for the purpose of promoting or procuring the election of a candidate or candidates; and particulars of all expenses so incurred by an organization or individual should be returned to an office of the Crown with a verifying declaration.

Issue of poll cards by the Returning Officer.

4. Poll cards should be issued to electors by the Returning Officer at public cost, in adequate time before an election, and no other poll cards should be issued, provided that no restrictions should be placed on candidates communicating the information given in poll cards otherwise than in the actual form of a poll card.

The Conference agreed that, apart from the issue of poll cards, no postal and printing facilities should be afforded to candidates by the State in addition to those already provided.

Speakers' Expenses.

5. The payment of speakers' expenses should be permitted. Such expenses should be included in the candidate's return of expenses.

Relief in respect of venial errors.

6. Provision should be made to enable relief in respect of inadvertent or venial errors in returns of expenses to be sought through a county court, corresponding provision being made as regards Scotland.

Use of Schools and Halls for election meetings.

7. All schools and halls maintained in whole or in part out of State or local funds should be made available to candidates for elec-

tion meetings, and maximum charges should be regulated in respect of such schools and halls to take account only of expenses of lighting, cleaning, and heating.

Premises exempted from the payment of rates should not lose entitlement to such exemption merely by reason of their being used for election meetings.

SUBSCRIPTIONS TO CHARITIES AND CONTRIBUTIONS TO PARTY ORGANIZATIONS

Subscriptions to charitable, social, or sporting organizations.

8. The Conference agreed to place on record their view that it was to be deprecated that a prospective or adopted Parliamentary candidate or a Member of Parliament should give any substantial donation or contribution to any charitable, social, or sporting organization in the constituency or to any charitable fund specifically benefiting the constituents.

Contributions to Party Funds.

9. The Conference agreed to place on record the fact that they regarded with disapproval the direct or indirect payment or promise of payment of substantial contributions or annual subscriptions to party organizations (including local party organizations), designed to influence the action of such organizations in selecting any particular individual as a Parliamentary candidate.

CANDIDATE'S DEPOSIT

Forfeiture of Deposit.

10. Where there are two or three candidates (or, in the case of a double-member constituency, not more than six candidates) the deposit should be returned, as at present, if a candidate polls one-eighth of the total votes cast; and where there are more than three candidates (or, in the case of a double-member constituency, more than six candidates) the deposit should be returned if a candidate polls one-tenth of the total votes cast.

11. Adjustments should be made in the provisions with regard to the forfeiture of the deposit in the case of University constituencies returning two or more members to take account of the fact that in such constituencies each elector has only one vote.

Acceptance of Deposit by Returning Officer.

12. It should be made lawful for the deposit to be received by the Returning Officer at any time between the issue of the writ and nomination day; and, further, the deposit should in future be payable either by cash or by banker's draft drawn by a reputable bank.

Included in the Appendix are particulars of resolutions rejected by the Conference that the deposit should be abolished; that the deposit should be reduced to £100; and that the deposit should in all cases be returned if a candidate polls one-tenth of the total votes cast.

ACCEPTANCE OF NOMINATION PAPERS BY RETURNING OFFICER

13. It should be made lawful for nomination papers to be lodged with the Returning Officer at any time between the issue of the writ and nomination day.

POLLING FACILITIES

Increase in polling facilities.

14. Increased polling facilities should be provided, particularly in rural areas. If necessary, these polling stations should be of a temporary character.

Hours of polling.

15. The hours of polling should be the same throughout the United Kingdom and should not be subject to local variation.
16. The fixed hours of polling should be 7 a.m. to 9 p.m.

The Conference agreed that there were overwhelming objections to the provision of travelling polling booths.

USE OF CONVEYANCES

Particulars of a resolution rejected by the Conference with regard to regulating the number of conveyances plying with voters to the polling booths are given in the Appendix.

The Conference agreed not to recommend the removal of the present restrictions on the hiring of conveyances.

ABSENT VOTING BY PERSONS PHYSICALLY INCAPACITATED

17. The categories of persons entitled to be placed in the Absent Voters' List should be enlarged to cover persons who are physically incapacitated; and Registration Officers should be authorized to place an elector on the Absent Voters' List on being satisfied that on grounds of physical incapacity the elector is unlikely to be able to vote in person at a forthcoming election.

BROADCASTING

18. It should be an offence for any British subject to promote or to aid in promoting any broadcast affecting Parliamentary elections from wireless stations outside the United Kingdom.

The Conference felt that, having regard to the impossibility of forecasting future developments, it would be out of place for them to make any recommendations with regard to the regulation of broadcasting within the United Kingdom for election purposes.

SERVICE VOTERS

19. The Conference attached great importance to the exercise of the franchise by members of the Services and merchant seamen, and asked the Government to keep the whole matter under constant review (including the possibility of arranging for postal votes by Service voters overseas or for elections in the field).

20. Whilst aware that this was a matter outside their terms of reference, the Conference wished to place on record their opinion that the present method of registering Service voters should be improved by the introduction of automatic registration.

I should like to say again how grateful I am to all the members of the Conference for their generous help throughout our sittings; and to put on record our unanimous appreciation of the work of our Joint Secretaries, Mr. Philip Allen and Mr. A. C. Marples, who have been of the greatest assistance to all members of the Conference.

Yours very sincerely,

(*Signed*) D. CLIFTON BROWN.

The Rt. Hon. W. S. Churchill, C.H., M.P.,
    10, Downing Street, S.W.1.

APPENDIX

1. The following resolution was rejected:

    "That the Conference recommend that the deposit by candidates at Parliamentary elections should be abolished."

2. The following resolution was rejected on a division:

    " That the Conference recommend that the deposit by candidates at Parliamentary elections should be reduced to £100."

Ayes—4.   Noes—18.

3. The following resolution was rejected:

    "That the Conference recommend that the deposit should in future be returned if a candidate polls one-tenth of the total votes cast."

4. The following resolution was rejected on a division:

    "That the Conference recommend that some additional limitation and regulation be imposed on the number of conveyances plying with voters to the polling booth."

Ayes—14.   Noes—15.

APPENDIX VII

SPEAKER'S CONFERENCE ON ELECTORAL REFORM, 1944

MEMORANDUM SUBMITTED TO THE CONFERENCE BY DR. J. F. S. ROSS ON CONDUCT AND COSTS OF ELECTION

CONTENTS

I. INTRODUCTION

1. In order to be able to deal satisfactorily with the question of election expenses it is essential first to be quite clear about the existing position. The official "Return of Election Expenses" for the last general election (1935) supplies the necessary data, but does not give them in a form suitable for the present purpose. The basic and by far the most significant case that has to be considered is that of the contested election in a single-member constituency, borough or county. In the "Return", however, the position is obscured by the mixing-up of double-member with single-member constituencies and of uncontested with contested elections. Moreover, the figures given in the "Return" for each candidate's "legal maximum" expenditure only cover that part of it which is based on the allowance of 6d. per elector in a county division and 5d. per elector in a borough division, whereas the figures given for his "total expenses" include also his agent's fee and his personal expenses, which are the subject of separate additional allowances: hence the two sets of figures afford no direct basis of comparison. Indeed, in a number of cases, the "total expenses" recorded exceeds the "legal maximum" stated for the respective candidates.

2. Clearly a considerable amount of abstraction, adjustment, and rearrangement has to be made, involving much exact calculation,

before the essential facts can be set out in useful and readily comprehensible form. I have done this work, and details of the calculations are available if required; but for the purposes of the present memorandum it seems sufficient to give only those final results which are necessary for the argument.

3. The cases of double-member constituencies and of uncontested elections will be referred to later. Setting them on one side for the time being, I give first the essential facts relating to the contested single-member constituencies, since they form the backbone of the problem, covering nearly 90 per cent (538 out of 602) of the seats in Great Britain. (Northern Ireland is excluded throughout.)

II. "PER-ELECTOR" EXPENSES

4. The average *number of electors per candidate* (which is not precisely the same thing as the average number of electors per constituency) is as follows:

Borough candidates	50,408
County candidates	53,653

5. Correspondingly, the average *legal maximum* for the "per-elector" part of a candidate's expenses (*i.e.*, excluding the special allowances for agents' fees and personal expenses) is as follows:

	£
Borough candidates (at 5d. per elector) ...	1,050
County candidates (at 6d. per elector) ...	1,341

6. The average amount of the corresponding *actual "per-elector" expenditure* (*i.e.*, excluding personal expenses and such part of agents' fees as can be charged as an extra) is as follows:

	£
Borough candidates	452
County candidates	507

7. This is equivalent to an average *actual expenditure per elector* as follows:

	Per Elector
Borough candidates	2·15d.
County candidates	2·27d.

8. The *ratio of the actual to the permissible "per-elector" expenditure* is therefore as follows:

	Per Cent.
Borough candidates	43·0
County candidates	37·8

9. Hence the average candidate, borough and county alike, spends well below half of what he is allowed by law to spend. There is, therefore, a *prima-facie* case for considering that the present limits of "per-elector" expenditure are quite unnecessarily high.

10. The county candidate is allowed by law to spend 20 per cent more, per elector, than the borough candidate (*i.e.*, 6d. as against 5d.). Actually, however, as shown in paragraph 7 above, he only spends, on an average, a little over 5 per cent more. There is, therefore, a *prima-facie* case for considering that the present extra expenditure "per elector" allowed to a county candidate by comparison with a borough candidate is quite unnecessarily high.

11. Comparison of the actual expenditure in small constituencies with that in large constituencies shows that actual expenditure is by no means proportionate to the size of the electorate. For example, the six largest single-member borough constituencies show the following results:

	Six Largest Single-Member Boroughs	All Single-Member Boroughs
Average number of electors per candidate	95,839	50,408
Average legal maximum "per-elector" expenditure	£1,997	£1,050
Average actual "per-elector" expenditure	£619	£452

It will be seen that in these six constituencies the average number of electors per candidate (and consequently the average "legal maximum") is 90 per cent higher than in the single-member boroughs as a whole, yet the average expenditure is only 37 per cent higher. It is clear that the principle of fixing maximum expenditure chiefly on the basis of so much per elector is unfair as between large and small constituencies. The actual figures given in the "Return" show that the cost of contesting an election does not increase in direct proportion to an increase in the size of the electorate. Hence a limit "per elector" which, in the case of a very big constituency, gives a total "legal maximum" far beyond the needs of even an extravagant candidate, in the case of a very small constituency, gives a "legal maximum" which will not be much above what an economical candidate will spend.

12. We have, then, three definite results from the analysis of this part of the data provided by the official "Return":

(*a*) The present limits of "per-elector" expenditure are quite unnecessarily high.

(*b*) The present extra expenditure "per elector" allowed to a county candidate by comparison with a borough candidate is quite unnecessarily high.

(*c*) The "per-elector" basis of permitted expenditure is in itself unfair as between constituencies of markedly different size, since costs as a whole do not vary directly as the size of the electorate.

(All these results, it will be noted, are independent of any question of reducing the actual costs of elections.)

III. Agents' Fees and Personal Expenses

13. In borough constituencies (contested single-member) the amount spent on agents' fees varies greatly, ranging from nothing at all in a considerable number of cases up to £150, with an average for the whole country of nearly £44. Up to £50 the expenditure of each candidate under this head may be charged as an extra; anything beyond £50 must be included with the general expenditure charged against the allowance of 5d. per elector.

14. In county constituencies the amount spent on agents' fees varies even more widely, ranging from nothing at all in a number of cases up to £398, with an average for the whole country of just over £84. Up to £75 the expenditure of each candidate under this head is allowed as an extra; anything beyond £75 must be charged against the permitted 6d. per elector. Large numbers of candidates considerably exceed the £75, but on the other hand many do not nearly reach it.

15. In these circumstances the figures of £50 and £75 seem to have little practical significance, and it is accordingly suggested that the special allowance for agents' fees should be dropped altogether.

16. The personal expenses of a candidate may be charged as an extra up to any amount (provided, of course, that they are legitimate in character and *bona fide*). The average amount spent under this head by borough candidates (in contested single-member constituencies) is a little over £29, while that spent by county candidates is nearly £33. The amount spent does not seem to be appreciably affected by the distance from London, for the candidates for Scottish constituencies spent on an average appreciably less than those for English constituencies and a great deal less than those for Welsh constituencies.

17. In these circumstances, and in view of the small proportion which personal expenses form of a candidate's total expenses (a little over $5\frac{1}{2}$ per cent on the average), there seems no sufficient reason for treating them as an extra, and I therefore suggest that they should be treated on the same lines as any other expenditure and included within the limits of the general legal maximum.

IV. Total Expenditure

18. Assuming that special allowances for agents' fees and personal expenses are to be dropped, it becomes necessary to consider the figures for actual total expenditure. The average amounts of this are as follows:

	£
Borough candidates	516
County candidates	593

19. This is equivalent to an average actual expenditure per elector (for all purposes) as follows:

				Per Elector
Borough candidates	...	...	...	... 2·46d.
County candidates	...	...	...	... 2·65d.

20. The ratio of the actual *total* expenditure to the permissible "*per-elector*" expenditure is therefore as follows:

				Per Cent.
Borough candidates	...	...	...	... 49·1
County candidates	...	...	...	... 44·2

21. Hence the *total* expenditure for the average candidate absorbs barely half of the permitted "*per-elector*" expenditure in boroughs and appreciably less than half in counties.

22. The actual *total* expenditure of the average county candidate per elector is only 8 per cent more than that of the average borough candidate, though his "per-elector" allowance is, as already noted, 20 per cent higher and his "agents' fees" allowance is 50 per cent higher. This emphasizes the fact that, as already pointed out, the extra expenditure allowed to county candidates is excessive.

V. THE CASE FOR REFORM

23. There is clearly a case, then, on general grounds for effecting changes in the present limits of permissible expenditure in three respects, viz.:

    (*a*) Reducing the total amounts that may be spent by candidates.
    (*b*) Decreasing the difference between county and borough limits of expenditure.
    (*c*) Altering the basis on which maximum permissible expenditure is calculated.

Such changes can obviously be justified by the actual facts revealed by analysis of the figures given in the "Return", irrespective of any desire to effect a general reduction in the level of expenditure.

24. But, on top of this, it is, I suggest, desirable that there *should* be a general reduction in the cost of contesting an election, and, judging by the debate in the House of Commons in February last, there is at least a considerable amount of agreement on this point amongst members of all parties, and particularly on the ground that it is desirable to encourage the candidature of younger and less-well-off men and women, on whom the present level of costs is widely agreed to bear hardly. I shall suggest later that this latter result cannot be effected merely by altering the legal limits of expenditure, but nevertheless such alterations seem eminently desirable, and I proceed to suggest how they might be made.

VI. New Bases for Limits of Expenditure

25. I put forward two alternative methods by one or other of which I suggest that in future legal limits of expenditure should be calculated, and for convenience of reference I term these Scheme A and Scheme B. Both of them possess the great merit of simplicity, and either of them would, I believe, be a great improvement on the present scheme. But Scheme B seems to me to be definitely sounder in principle than Scheme A, and even simpler to apply in practice.

26. *Scheme A.* If, by a comprehensive measure for the redistribution of seats, all constituencies were given an approximately equal number of electors, and if means were provided by which further measures of redistribution at fairly frequent intervals would keep them more or less equal, then something might be said for fixing the limits of election expenditure on the simple basis of so much per elector, without any extra allowances.

27. Assuming that this were agreed upon, and assuming also that it is desired to keep down the cost of elections, there would be a *prima-facie* case for limiting total expenditure to figures approximately equal to the present average rates of actual expenditure—viz., 2·46d. per elector in boroughs and 2·65d. per elector in counties.

28. There are, however, three factors which, taken together, suggest that such rates might prove unduly low. These factors are as follows: (*a*) Under present conditions many candidates, through lack of means, are unable to spend even a moderately adequate sum on their election expenses, and these cases, of course, bring down the average for the country, though perhaps not to any very marked extent; (*b*) some constituencies are undoubtedly more expensive to work than others, and too severe a limitation of permissible costs might cause hardship in difficult cases; (*c*) costs (for example, those of printing, stationery, and postage) have risen considerably above the 1935 level.

29. Taking these factors into account, I suggest that if the limits of expenditure are to be purely on a "per-elector" basis, the rates should be as follows:

SCHEME A

	Per Elector
Borough candidates	3½d.
County candidates	3¾d.

These rates would permit an average total expenditure of £735 in boroughs and £834 in counties, which is in each case approximately 40 per cent above the present average level of actual total expenditure; this 40 per cent takes account of the three factors mentioned in the preceding paragraph. The rates would also give a ratio for county expenditure to borough expenditure which corresponds closely with that shown by experience to be necessary.

30. *Scheme B.* I put this forward as preferable to Scheme A in any

case, and as highly preferable to it if constituencies are to remain decidedly unequal in the size of their electorates, or are likely soon to revert to inequality, as they have always done in recent times. Under this scheme the maximum permissible expenditure on election costs would consist of a lump sum plus a per-elector allowance.

31. The figures I suggest are as follows:

SCHEME B

Borough candidates	...	£300 + 2d. per elector
County candidates ...	...	£380 + 2d. per elector

These rates would, in *average* constituencies, allow amounts of maximum expenditure (£720 in boroughs and £825 in counties) which are approximately equal to those suggested in paragraph 29 above (Scheme A); but they would be very much fairer between large and small constituencies.

32. I believe this scheme (B) to be thoroughly sound in principle and extremely simple and convenient in practice. and I strongly recommend it for adoption.

33. The effect of these two schemes may be illustrated and compared by giving the appropriate figures for the largest and smallest constituencies, borough and county, at the last general election (1935). These are as follows:

Largest Borough (Ilford)—

Legal maximum now ...	...	£2,278 + personal expenses
Legal maximum, Scheme A	...	£1,560
Legal maximum, Scheme B	...	£1,191
Average actual expenditure	...	£619

Smallest Borough (South-West Bethnal Green)—

Legal maximum now ...	...	£623 + personal expenses
Legal maximum, Scheme A	...	£401
Legal maximum, Scheme B	...	£529
Average actual expenditure	...	£317

Largest County Division (Romford, Essex)—

Legal maximum now ...	...	£4,273 + personal expenses
Legal maximum, Scheme A	...	£2,624
Legal maximum, Scheme B	...	£1,779
Average actual expenditure	...	£1,032

Smallest County Division (Barnard Castle, Durham)—

Legal maximum now ...	...	£758 + personal expenses
Legal maximum, Scheme A	...	£427
Legal maximum, Scheme B	...	£608
Average actual expenditure	...	£360

It will be seen that in each case Scheme B gives the figures that bear the most reasonable relation to the average actual expenditure, while allowing a sufficient margin to cover increased costs since 1935 and the other factors already specified.

VII. THE BURDEN OF ELECTION EXPENSES

34. It will be seen that the arrangements I propose (Scheme B) would effect substantial reductions in the legal limits of election expenditure (from £1,100 + personal expenses to £720 in the average borough, and from £1,416 + personal expenses to £825 in the average county). I suggest that, having regard to all the factors involved, no further substantial reduction is practicable or advisable. Within these new limits, however, the burden of election costs would still be considerable; this is a reflection of the fact that the contesting of an election, if it is to be done effectively, must inevitably involve in normal circumstances an expenditure of several hundred pounds. Hence, even with these fairly drastic reductions in the legal limits, election expenses would remain a heavy burden on the younger and less-well-off candidates that members of all parties desire to encourage.

35. I suggest accordingly that the needs of the younger and poorer candidates cannot be adequately met by a mere reduction in the legal limits of expenditure (desirable though such a reduction undoubtedly is), and that more positive steps are necessary if the object in mind is to be achieved. To this end I put forward the proposal that a more or less substantial part of a candidate's legitimate election expenses be met by the State. Moreover, quite apart from any question of individual hardships, it is in the interest of the community that we should secure the best possible members of parliament and therefore that candidates otherwise eminently suitable should not be shut out by reason of their inability to face the expense of an election. Expenditure necessary to secure this result is therefore a legitimate charge on public funds. It may be noted, too, that the principle has already been conceded, since free postage is provided for candidates' election addresses. If it is right for the State to meet this expense, it cannot be wrong for it to meet others. The proposed grant therefore involves no new departure from established principle, and the extent to which it should be made is simply a matter of expediency.

36. Suggestions have been made elsewhere from time to time for providing assistance of this kind (a) by the State paying the whole of a candidate's election expenses, (b) by the State paying some definite fraction, say half, of his expenses, or (c) by the State contributing a flat rate lump sum towards his expenses. I submit that all these methods are open to serious objections, the gravest of which is that they would tend to encourage frivolous and irresponsible candidatures.

37. Instead of these proposals I desire to urge that (as first suggested in my book *Parliamentary Representation*) a State grant should be made towards each candidate's election expenses based on the number of valid votes which he receives in the election. On this footing

the amount of grant a candidate received would depend on the extent to which his candidature was endorsed by the votes of the electors. Irresponsible and "freak" candidates would get correspondingly little encouragement.

38. Since the object of this proposal is not to encourage a general increase in the amounts spent on elections but to decrease the strain on candidates' resources, substantial reductions in the legal limits of expenditure, such as I have suggested above, would be all the more desirable, if not indeed essential. Otherwise the result of making the grant might be to increase outlay all round, while still leaving the poorer candidates and parties at an unfair disadvantage.

39. The rate at which this grant should be calculated would, of course, depend on the view which was taken as to the amount of help it would be desirable to give. In the case of Scheme A above, I suggest that a suitable rate would be double the legal maximum per-elector allowance: that is, 7d. per valid vote received in a borough constituency and 7½d. in a county constituency. In considering this suggestion it is important to bear in mind that, whereas the legal maximum allowance is per elector on the register, the grant would be per vote recorded for the candidate in question. It should hardly be necessary to add that the grant would only be payable on the actual expenses incurred, and that these would continue to be subject to the usual restrictions and safeguards.

40. If, as I have recommended, Scheme B were adopted for the limits of expenditure, then the strictly logical thing might seem to be to make the grant, also, consist of a lump sum plus so much (say 4d.) per vote. But it would be difficult to determine what the lump sum should be, and any such payment, moreover, would give just that encouragement to irresponsible and frivolous candidates that it is sought to avoid. I therefore suggest that with either Scheme A or Scheme B the rate of grant should be 7d. per vote received in boroughs and 7½d. in counties.

41. It may be advisable to reiterate that the case for the reforms suggested above (reduction in the legal limits of expenditure, plus a State grant towards expenses) does not depend solely on the hardships caused under the existing system to individual candidates who find the cost of contesting an election a heavy burden. Any arrangement which tends to exclude suitable candidates from standing for election just because they cannot find the necessary money, must obviously tend to restrict the field from which candidates can be drawn to those who either possess fairly substantial private means or have the backing of a trade union or other body which is prepared to give financial assistance. This clearly (a) encourages what has been termed the "selling of seats", where a candidate's wealth is regarded as of more importance than his character and ability; (b) reduces the proper independence of members who have secured their seats by means of subsidies and so will be expected to serve as representatives of those bodies rather than as representatives of the community; and (c) altogether excludes people

who may be eminently suited for service in the House of Commons but neither possess the necessary financial resources themselves nor have the backing of a trade union or similar body. If we are to secure the best possible choice for membership of the House it is essential to change the present state of affairs, which in actual fact excludes many suitable candidates on purely financial grounds.

42. It is, moreover, generally agreed that the *average* age of first entry to the House (44 years 5 months, as shown in my book) is much too high, and that the consequent average age of members is also much too high. This latter average, of course, fluctuates, but its mean value is nearly 9 years higher than the average age of the *adult* population of the country as a whole, and about 20 years higher than the average age of the *whole* population. Clearly a major factor in producing these undesirably high average ages of first election and of membership is to be found in the financial burdens of candidature and membership, and an important part of that burden is the cost of contesting elections.

43. Moreover the fear of having to face that cost may have indirect but undesirable effects on the votes of members when faced with some issue on which may hinge the prospects of an early general election. I do not suggest that members will consciously vote against their consciences in order to avert the threat of such an election, but I suggest that it is eminently undesirable that they should be placed in such a position that their votes may land them not only in the chances and inconveniences of an election but may involve them in an expenditure on election costs that they can ill afford.

44. On all these grounds, therefore, I urge that not only should the legal limits of expenditure be remodelled and reduced as I have suggested, but also that such a grant as I have proposed should be made to all candidates.

VIII. DOUBLE-MEMBER CONSTITUENCIES

45. I personally hope that double-member constituencies, as they exist at present, may be abolished; for their continuance is an anomaly which appears to have nothing to commend it. But in order to round-off this memorandum and to provide for dealing with their costs of election should they be continued, I give the data and suggestions which follow. As with the single-member constituencies, the data have been calculated in relation to contested elections only.

46. (*a*) The average *number of electors per candidate or pair of candidates* is 97,502.

(*b*) The average *legal maximum* for the "per-elector" part of a candidate's or pair of candidates' expenses is as follows:

Dual candidatures (at 7½d. per elector): £3,137 per pair (=£1,569 per candidate).

Single candidatures (at 5d. per elector): £1,987 per candidate.

(c) The average amount of the corresponding *actual "per-elector" expenditure* is as follows:

> Dual candidatures: £1,002 per pair (=£501 per candidate).
> Single candidatures: £607 per candidate.

(d) These are equivalent to average *actual expenditures per elector* as follows:

					Per Elector
Dual candidatures	...	...	...	...	2·41d.
Single candidatures	...	...	...	...	1·68d.

(e) The *ratios of the actual to the permissible "per-elector" expenditure* are therefore as follows:

					Per Cent.
Dual candidatures	...	...	...	...	32·2
Single candidatures	...	...	...	...	33·6

Hence the average candidate in a two-member contested election spends barely one-third of what he is allowed to spend (per elector).

(f) The average *total expenditure* (including agents' fees and personal expenses) is as follows:

> Dual candidatures: £1,126 per pair (=£563 per candidate).
> Single candidatures: £673 per candidate.

(g) This is equivalent to an average *actual expenditure per elector* (for all purposes) as follows:

					Per Elector
Dual candidatures	...	...	...	...	2·71d.
Single candidatures	...	...	...	...	1·86d.

(h) The ratio of the actual *total* expenditure to the permissible *"per-elector"* expenditure is therefore as follows:

					Per Cent.
Dual candidatures	...	...	...	...	36·1
Single candidatures	...	...	...	...	37·2

Hence the actual *total* expenditure of the average candidate, for all purposes, absorbs only about four-elevenths of the permitted *"per-elector"* expenditure.

(i) The ratio of the average total expenditure per elector on a dual candidature to that on a single candidature is 1·46—*i.e.*, on an average a double candidature costs 46 per cent more than a single candidature.

47. On the position disclosed by these figures, I recommend that, if double-member constituencies are continued, the permitted limits of expenditure (including agents' fees and personal expenses) be as follows:

SCHEME A

					Per Elector
Dual candidatures ...	...	...	...	...	4d.
Single candidatures	...	...	...	...	2¾d.

or alternatively:

SCHEME B

				Per Elector
Dual candidatures	...	...	...	£700 + 2¼d.
Single candidatures	...	...	...	£500 + 1½d.

In the *average* double-member constituency these limits would give maximum total expenditures as follows:

Dual candidatures	{ £1,625 under Scheme A { £1,614 under Scheme B
Single candidatures	{ £1,116 under Scheme A { £1,109 under Scheme B

As before, I strongly recommend Scheme B in preference to Scheme A.

48. As before, also, I recommend that the State grant payable towards election expenses should be double the legal maximum allowed in Scheme A—*i.e.*, 8d. per vote received by a pair of candidates, and 5½d. per vote received by a single candidate (irrespective of whether Scheme A or Scheme B is adopted).

IX. UNCONTESTED ELECTIONS

49. The average actual expenditure in uncontested elections is much below that in contested elections. But I see no reason to suggest that the present practice, by which the limits of expenditure are the same whether the election is contested or not, should be changed. There is little temptation to extravagant expenditure in an uncontested election; and, moreover, under the proposals I have put forward, no State grant would be payable in an uncontested election, since no votes would be recorded.

X. PROPORTIONAL REPRESENTATION

50. Should the single transferable vote be adopted in all or any constituencies, the rules for legal maximum expenditure and for State grant would have to be adjusted accordingly. Only experience could show definitely what are the most appropriate figures, but present experience with single and double constituencies, and with single and dual candidatures in the latter, gives a fairly clear indication of the lines on which they should be settled.

51. At this stage, however, it does not seem profitable to work out all the limits that would be required, and it will probably suffice to give as an indication of their probable trend the following table of suggested legal maximum expenditures per elector for all purposes under what I have termed Scheme A.

Constituency	*Candidature*				
	Single	*Dual*	*Treble*	*Quadruple*	*Quintuple*
3-member ...	2¼d.	3¼d.	4¼d.	—	—
4-member ...	1¾d.	2¾d.	3½d.	4½d.	—
5-member ...	1½d.	2¼d.	3d.	3¾d.	4½d.
6-member ...	1¼d.	2d.	2½d.	3d.	3½d.
7-member ...	1¼d.	1¾d.	2d.	2½d.	2¾d.

At first sight this may look complicated, but it would be perfectly simple to use in practice. Should Scheme B be adopted a corresponding table could be worked out, but this would best be done when more information was available as to the size and nature of the constituencies.

52. State grant should be, as before, *per vote received*, at double the legal maximum *per elector* under Scheme A, as set out in the preceding paragraph.

XI. Election Deposits

53. At the present time every candidate for parliament must deposit with the Returning Officer at the time of nomination the sum of £150. This deposit is repayable to each candidate who receives not less than one-eighth of the valid votes recorded in the election, but is forfeited by each candidate who fails to receive that number of votes. This rule was instituted with the object of discouraging irresponsible and "freak" candidatures. Experience, however, suggests that it is of doubtful value for this purpose, while on the other hand it bears hardly on many candidates who could by no means be described as irresponsible or "freak". At the last general election 81 candidates forfeited their deposits, and of these the great majority (80 per cent) were candidates put forward in the normal way by well-recognized parties. Moreover, the rule does not succeed in preventing occasional "freak" candidates from standing, and there are notorious cases of candidates of this type who have stood over and over again. The plain fact is, of course, that the suitability of a candidate cannot be measured by merely financial standards: a wealthy nonentity or eccentric can forfeit his deposit repeatedly without turning a hair, while a candidate of first-rate quality, in every way suitable to enter parliament, may be hard put to it to face the expense involved, including the risk of forfeiting his deposit.

54. For all these reasons I strongly urge the abolition of the rule requiring this deposit. If its abrogation should lead to the candidature of a few additional irresponsible candidates no great harm would be done, while on the other hand a step forward will have been taken in the process of helping those younger and less-well-off candidates whom (as already noted) members of all parties have expressed the desire to encourage.

55. Should it be considered that the abolition of the deposit is too drastic a step to be taken at once, I desire to urge that the amount of the deposit should at least be reduced, preferably to £50, but certainly to not more than £100.

56. I submit, also, that the rule as to the limit for repayment (one-eighth of the votes recorded) needs reconsideration. This rule at present applies indiscriminately to both single- and double-member constituencies, and irrespective of the number of candidates standing. This is illogical: for clearly the greater the number of candidates standing, the smaller will be the proportion of the total votes that each is likely to secure. If, in a single-member constituency, only two candidates stand, it is most unlikely that one of them will forfeit his deposit, since, for that to happen, his opponent must secure more than seven times as many votes as he does. On the other hand, if four candidates stand, one of them may forfeit his deposit, although his successful opponent receives little more than twice as many votes.

57. I accordingly suggest that the rule should be amended so that the deposit is forfeited only by candidates who fail to secure one-quarter as many votes as the average number received by all the candidates in that constituency. This amended rule would mean that where only two candidates stand for a single-member constituency the fraction of the total votes necessary to avoid forfeiture of deposit would be one-eighth, as at present, but where three candidates stand it would be one-twelfth, with four candidates one-sixteenth, and so on. Consideration will show that this amendment would produce much more equitable results than the present rule, as between one constituency and another. It should be borne in mind that, on the average, the successful candidate receives rather more than half the votes where two candidates stand, rather more than one-third where three candidates stand, rather more than one-fourth where four candidates stand (including two-member constituencies), and so on. Clearly, where the fraction of the total vote necessary for success varies so widely, the fraction necessary to avoid forfeiture should have some corresponding variation.

XII. Subscriptions and Donations

58. A further financial reform of a different character that seems urgently required is an extension of the Corrupt and Illegal Practices Act so as to prohibit the payment of large sums of money by a candidate or prospective candidate to the local party organization. At the present time "It is bribery to give, lend, or promise money or money's worth in order to induce an elector to vote or to abstain from voting for a particular candidate. The consequences are the same whether the payment is made directly or indirectly, and whether before, during, or after an election" (*Constitutional Year Book*). Contributions to party funds made as an inducement to secure the adoption of the contributor as candidate, though presumably not a contravention of the letter of

the law, are clearly contrary to its spirit, and I submit that they should be treated accordingly. I suggest that contributions by candidates or members of parliament to party funds should be limited by law to a maximum of, say, £5 or £10 a year, and that any payment in excess of this should be a corrupt practice and punishable accordingly. Moreover, any such excess payment within the previous five years should render the payer ineligible to stand for election. The present practice of paying or promising large sums of money in order to secure adoption is in essence the wholesale purchase of votes: and wholesale bribery is at least as objectionable as bribery of individuals.

59. A similar reform seems to be called for in connexion with subscriptions and donations to clubs, societies, charities, bazaars, etc., within the constituency. Some difficulty might arise, of course, in the case of a candidate or member who had long been resident in, or closely connected with, the division in question and had contributed over many years to some charity or similar organization that was dear to his heart irrespective altogether of any question of his candidature for or membership of parliament. It should not, however, be impossible to devise some form of words in the regulations which would allow him to continue contributions to some one or two specified charities where he could show that he had first given them a number of years ago and had made them regularly ever since.

60. Both these proposed reforms would need very careful consideration in respect of the terms in which they were expressed, and it may be that neither could, in practice, be made absolutely watertight. But I submit that any difficulties encountered, either in wording or in enforcement, would be of a relatively minor character, and that the results achieved would be well worth while, both from the point of view of eliminating what are in effect corrupt practices, and from the point of view of reducing the financial burden on candidates and members.

XIII. Summary of Suggestions

61. (i) That the separate allowances for agents' fees and for personal expenses be dropped.   (Section III.)

(ii) That the legal maximum for all election expenses, including agents' fees and personal expenses, be calculated on one or other of the two following alternative bases:

Single-member constituencies—   (Section VI.)

SCHEME A

	Per Elector
Borough candidates	3½d.
County candidates	3¾d.

SCHEME B

Borough candidates	£300 + 2d. per elector
County candidates	£380 + 2d. per elector

Double-member constituencies— (Section VIII.)

SCHEME A

	Per Elector
Dual candidatures	4d.
Single candidatures	2¾d.

SCHEME B

Dual candidatures	£700 + 2¼d. per elector
Single candidatures ...	£500 + 1½d. per elector

(iii) That in each case Scheme B be adopted in preference to Scheme A.

(iv) That every candidate be given a State grant towards the cost of his election expenses, calculated as follows:

Single-member constituencies— (Section VII.)

	Per Valid Vote Received
Borough candidates	7d.
County candidates	7½d.

Double-member constituencies— (Section VIII.)

	Per Valid Vote Received
Dual candidatures	8d.
Single candidatures	5½d.

(v) That should the single transferable vote be adopted the legal limits of expenditure be as set out in paragraph 51 above. (Section X.)

(vi) That the rule requiring each candidate to deposit £150 with the Returning Officer be abolished. (Section XI.)

(vii) That, in default of its abolition, the amount of the deposit be reduced from £150 to £50 or at most £100. (Section XI.)

(viii) That, if the deposit is not abolished, the rules for its forfeiture be amended by the substitution of "one-quarter of the average number of votes received by the candidates in the constituency" in place of "one-eighth of the total votes recorded". (Section XI.)

(ix) That contributions by candidates or members to party funds, in excess of say £5 or £10 a year, should be made a corrupt practice and punishable accordingly. (Section XII.)

(x) That any such excess payment within the previous five years should render the payer ineligible to stand for election. (Section XII.)

(xi) That a similar rule should be enforced, with or without specified exceptions, in the case of contributions to clubs, societies, charities, etc. (Section XII.)

XIV. CONCLUSION

62. I desire to state that all the figures I have given relating to the present cost of elections, etc., have been worked out by me with the most scrupulous care and to a high degree of accuracy. I think they can be

relied upon. I also desire to say that the figures I put forward in my suggestions for new legal limits of expenditure are in no sense haphazard guesses: they are the result of most careful calculation and consideration.

63. I believe the arguments I have submitted to be thoroughly sound and the suggestions I have made to be completely practicable. If there is any point about them that I have failed to make clear I shall be very ready to explain it, while if there is any further information that I could give and that would be of service to the Conference I should be very glad of an opportunity to supply it.

J. F. S. ROSS.

8th May 1944.

INDEX

References are to pages